Also by Peter Gizzi

SOME VALUES OF LANDSCAPE AND WEATHER

ARTIFICIAL HEART

PERIPLUM

The Outernationale

Wesleyan University Press Middletown, Connecticut

Peter Gizzi

THE OUTERNATIONALE

WESLEYAN POETRY

Published by Wesleyan University Press
Middletown, CT 06459
www.wesleyan.edu/wespress

Design and composition by Quemadura
Printed on acid-free, recycled paper
in the United States of America

5   4   3   2   1

Library of Congress Cataloging-in-Publication Data

Gizzi, Peter.

The outernationale / Peter Gizzi.

p. cm. — (Wesleyan poetry)

ISBN-13: 978-0-8195-6736-9 (acid-free paper)

ISBN-10: 0-8195-6736-1 (acid-free paper)

I. Title.

PS3557.I9409O8 2007

811'.54—dc22

2006033935

Contents

A PANIC THAT CAN STILL COME UPON ME   1

THE QUEST   12

STUNG   13

SCRATCH TICKET   17

I WANTED THE SCREEN DOOR OF SUMMER   19

THE OUTERNATIONALE   20

UNTITLED AMHERST SPECTER   23

A TELESCOPE PROTECTS ITS VIEW   24

AUBADE AND BEYOND   26

HUMAN MEMORY IS ORGANIC   27

*

BEACON   31

FROM A CINEMATOGRAPHER'S LETTER   38

THAT'S LIFE   40

NOCTURNE   43

LINES DEPICTING SIMPLE HAPPINESS   45

PHANTASCOPE (1895)   46

VINCENT, HOMESICK FOR THE LAND OF PICTURES   47

BIPOLAROID   54

LAST CENTURY THOUGHTS IN SNOW TONIGHT   55

WINTRY MIX   56

CHEAP IMITATION   58

SATURDAY AND ITS FESTOONED POTENTIAL   59

*

HOMER'S ANGER   63

LUMIÈRE   72

A PAPER WIND   74

THE MOONLIGHT DEFENSE   78

BOLSHEVESCENT   79

DEAD AIR   80

FRETLESS   81

ON WHAT BECAME OF MATHEW BRADY'S
    BATTLE PHOTOGRAPHS   86

PROTEST SONG   88

A WESTERN GARDEN   89

THE OUTERNATIONALE   92

*

FROM HERE LAUGHTER SOUNDS LIKE CRYING   105

Acknowledgments   109

*I think there is no light in the world
but the world*

And I think there is light

—GEORGE OPPEN

The Outernationale

A PANIC THAT CAN STILL COME UPON ME

If today and today I am calling aloud

If I break into pieces of glitter on asphalt
bits of sun, the din

if tires whine on wet pavement
everything humming

If we find we are still in motion
and have arrived in Zeno's thought, like

if sunshine hits marble and the sea lights up
we might know we were loved, are loved
if flames and harvest, the enchanted plain

If our wishes are met with dirt
and thyme, thistle, oil,
heirloom, and basil

or the end result is worry, chaos
and if "I should know better"

If our loves are anointed with missiles
Apache fire, Tomahawks
did we follow the tablets the pilgrims suggested

If we ask that every song touch its origin
just once and the years engulfed

If problems of identity confound sages,
derelict philosophers, administrators
who can say I am found

if this time you, all of it, this time now

If nothing save Saturdays at the metro and
if rain falls sidelong in the platz
doorways, onto mansard roofs

If enumerations of the fall
and if falling, cities rocked
with gas fires at dawn

Can you rescind the ghost's double nakedness
hungry and waning

if children, soldiers, children
taken down in schools

if burning fuel

Who can't say they have seen this
and can we sing this

if in the auroras' reflecting the sea,
gauze touching the breast

Too bad for you, beautiful singer
unadorned by laurel
child of thunder and scapegoat alike

If the crowd in the mind becoming
crowded in streets and villages, and trains
run next to the freeway

If exit is merely a sign

2.

It isn't alright to want just anything
all the time, be specific sky

I can read the narrow line above the hills

The day unbraids its pretty light
and I am here to see it

This must be all there is
right now in the world

There are things larger than understanding

things we know cannot
be held in the mind

If the sun throbs like a drum
every five minutes

what can we do with this

the 100,000 years it takes a photon
to reach the surface of the sun

eight minutes to hit our eyes

If every afternoon gravity and fire
it's like that here

undressed, unwound

3.

If today and today I am speaking to you, or
if you/I whisper, touch, explain

If they/you hate those phrases
if we struggle to get to the thing
the body and the other noises

If a W stumbles here even in private
there was this man we said
everywhere between us

if speech can free us

If summer fall winter spring
the broadcast day spins round my head
its grin stuck out there

when I am a tiger inside the DMZ
or if I am a tiger man
if no one believes what I see

If behind the grail and new elm
the pink light saying welcome earthling

my biography as an atom
picture of my smile

is this what my body said

If I forget my notebook
if these gaps I feel are also the gaps
I am built inside, thinking it's all good

If the sun sharp and hot and still
but deep and clarifying, walking its boulevards

if bound by the most ignoble cords
if squatting in time

If every day a struggle, the blue copse speaking
sky arching over nothing—uh-huh

If every struggle ice-cream truck tinkle
interrupting the cosmological

if everyday strife, everyday *sprecenze*
if everyday uh

is this what my body says
my buddy said

and if I die
and begin to lose consciousness
and the flag

There was this man we said
this W here even in private

I said in my letter
if I see you again

4.

A branch and the scent of pine in summer
the bridge and the water in the creek
the stones and the sound of water
the creek and my body
when hair and water flowed over me

If I am a bridge I am standing on, thinking,
saying goodbye to myself
when I stood by the water in life
thinking of my life, pine boughs
the hill next to water

The sun in the creek on the bridge
on my hair and pine boughs
in wind mixed with water,
one crow skating by, the life
of water, life of thinking
and moving, a crow passes by
this place in the mind, on my eyes

5.

So the vocalise day imprinted a sound

I'm not stupid
I too unwind in the most circuitous fashion
I undress water directly

Who hasn't seen unnumbered sparrows
enter the silhouette of a tree

why shouldn't I come in from the cold

Sure, there is the monument
the grass and the plate it grows on

If the answer becomes sun
then sun inside, normal things, okay

the ribbon above our heads is not a banner

Scaling this leafy architecture
we say wind / night sky / moon / clouds / stars
if silver stands for syncopation

indeed, symphonic dailiness is felt order

I have felt it at the back of me,
light on the table, the book open

If we struggle for a name
if colors change

if mood is connected to naming, to color

If say a ship's in deep water
and a piece of sky empties the mind

or when I was frigate-tossed

if I wanted to go all over a word
and live inside its name, so be it

There is my body and the idea of my body
the surf breaking and the picture of a wave

THE QUEST

It's true, the horizon empties into
a throat, a vibrato escaping its orbit
in the form of a string

Pianissimo, I want you
muted in the overall chromo

Begin again small wonder
building notes to touch the ground,
all is opening, diurnal, andante

All to tell you this thing
The world, also, could not be found

STUNG

A child I became a question
sitting on the grass.
To be told how lucky I am.
An open field.
This corporeal expanse
was a body too
in silver magnetism.
If I became this light
it wasn't luck. It was easy.
Bells falling away
along the divide of night.
Along the divide of night
an old face. A sorry dormer
leaning in askew
below the incoming thunder.
This was true and even if ever
I ran away. I ran
away. Above everything
I held one true thing.
This scene moved through me,
a seesaw. A picture
inside a question inside

the coming night.
These trees rang
round my head, shored
up the sky. I went on
and on like a trial balloon
over the houses. Over
the roofs. Over my head.

•

To remember correctly
the color of pale grass in March,
its salt hay blonde flourish.
To see it as it was,
faded cloth, mute trumpet,
the seam inside a day
the sun climbs.
Simple the life of the mind
standing outside in the grass
in March. Outside memory.
Spring interrupts
one cardinal monody
transmuted by a signal red
developed against
a draining blue horizon.
To want to go there
and to have been there
and to be there now.

This walking right now
by a river, simple and not so clear
when transcribing this
unstable multiplying narrative spring.
It can't be called anything.
We too are sprung and wound
with evolution, I want to say.
That's it: love. Not spring.
I have felt it also
in quilted drowning snow
under the sheets
in a clanking house.
Clank, I love you.
Clank. Not spring.
Glossy grass wigging
in a brightening sky.
The thrill of hair
standing on my limbs.

•

To be and not to understand.
To understand nothing
and be content
to watch light against
leaf-shadowed ground.
To accept the ground.
To go to it as a question.

To open up the day inside the day,
a bubble holding air
bending the vista to it.
To be inside this thing,
outside in the grass place,
out in the day
inside another thing.

SCRATCH TICKET

Confetti in April
Confetti in May

This was the last party
the animal sun asleep

O stymie dewy surprising thing
Leaf, you have arrived again

The web is on the vine
and the cricket clicks

If the blue toned arc
inside the vender's luck

If time itself doubled back
and unwound the string

How is it this afternoon
being wide be also crystal—

the total vista bright
Let this and that begin

O wind remember the tune
Bird, enough of your trill

I WANTED THE SCREEN
DOOR OF SUMMER

Opening sounds of blackbirds everywhere
everywhere in the day lost in sun

opening the screen doors of summer
a blackbird glitter in afternoon haze

all day long riding a fiddlehead
in Mahler excess calling thither

The TV screen afterlife reflects trees outside
jets overhead in the yard

I am powerless in the air
after the stock report before jeopardy

the table laid out our hopes laid out
I wanted the screen door of summer

a dew drop gazing ball
utopia bent and snapping

THE OUTERNATIONALE

The sun deploys its shadows
and things grow in dark too.
Leaves arch over everything
they are so democratic
to us our viewer in a world of secrets
in a world of navigable
foreshortening emotional registers.
In the park, breeze-shaken
wrappers drift outward.
The sand here seems coliseum-like
it is so contesting
just plain old.
Who can we turn toward
walking the hills' unbridled shoulders
breathless far from the story?
The day blooms in its self-knowledge.
It's that simple when we ask about faith.
How can I answer
not to inhibit
any single point in this ray?
Out of this house and out into the day
things come to focus

silver-tipped antennae tweak the blue
and sheets of rainwater
at the foot of the statehouse.
Something is something
when the administration
of money flows backward.
In this word time seems a trip,
come back, little sheen of products
in rows behind glass.
We went to the store and why not
we go to the moon
jeweled box on a shelf.
In summer we open and opening
we wander and
before we were happy
we were unhappy.
Such is the dialectical
awakening everyone
is hankering to embrace.
When the TV's on
the faces in the stands echo
and bounce far into the field.
The hopes and suspense
so often submarine
made plain as a runner rounding 2nd.
There is reason to watch
unlike the blinking reflection

in a darkened window glass.
We find purpose
in the game and together,
this crucial passage given flight
when detail disappears into a crowd
that too quickly invested
and then discarded power.
It's getting dark
indigo setting on the glass
just sitting there. Reminding us
days gallop into grass rushing wind
into miles of cable.
When the pistons call,
when I was a wedge of sun
over steel mills,
when I asked what happened
I meant what happened to us?

UNTITLED AMHERST SPECTER

a sound of open ground having been taken

now a silver wisp winking on the roof

silver imp waving from a long shaft ago

I am a leaf storm night

I have seen the long file of mule trains and metal

the cavalry

these sounds we live within speaking to you now

sir, I was a soldier in these woods

A TELESCOPE PROTECTS ITS VIEW

I like to read the dead.

Part of a whole lost era campaign.

The bridge is up.

A portrait of you from what you aren't saying.

On my sleeve. The verb to be.

I'm plucky but thankful.

Death and the imagination equals life itself.

Letters from an old bottle,
junk in space.

A book or a boat?

The black ribbons of a spring day
might sound mawkish

but I like to read under a pale blue sky
animated and deepening.

I like to read the dead.

There's so and so going by
everyone, outside

everyone

the words scroll onto air.

Synecdoche: act of receiving from another.

Metonymy: change of name.

Who hasn't found themselves
praying in an awkward room.

She said but what of their sad work
by the river's edge

sad way of working the moth paper light

trellis of dented garbage cans
and debris at dawn.

AUBADE AND BEYOND

Are there not words to visit the body?
The hips, nipples, the ass. Sounds to repair
the bent fender, flat tire?
O, the sun opens the material ache
and the bed is again on fire.
Labor calls and calls forth the hammer
the pen, the scythe, the laundry line
folds in the curtain
alive in morning wind and light.
Let the word speak for itself.
Let blue say its piece or a green ray alive
in a bottle inside the head, alive.
This small piece of metonymy
can speak for itself, piece of everyday sight.
All things partake of a signal green.
Is this what we mean when we say it's spring
and is this our ambition to stay true to the sky
to one another in early sun?
Everything seems to be falling in sheets today.
Sheets of glare and sheets of wind, paper
sheets and more, more sun, glint
near the monument. Such sheets in stone.

HUMAN MEMORY IS ORGANIC

We know time is a wave.

You can see it in gneiss, migmatic
or otherwise, everything crumbles.

Don't despair.

That's the message frozen in old stone.

I am just a visitor to this world
an interloper really headed deep into glass.

I, moving across a vast expanse of water

though it is not water maybe salt
or consciousness itself

enacted as empathy. Enacted as seeing.

To see with a purpose has its bloom
and falls to seed and returns

to be a story like any other.
To be a story open and vulnerable

a measure of time, a day, this day one might say
an angle of light for instance.

Let us examine green. Let us go together

to see it all unstable and becoming
violent and testing gravity

so natural in its hunger.

The organic existence of gravity.
The organic nature of history.

The natural history of tears.

BEACON

You can always keep giving away
every shiny thing
gliding through daydream hedges
and fields
in the heat of the classroom
stuck in a corner
looking at the H I J K L banner.
Or you can start laughing
it kinda works as a relief from other things
labor, sleep, stories with a setting.
But standing up on dry land
isn't as easy as it once was, is it?
We forget to laugh
I was going to say
but that's no good
that isn't even a start
trying to record a reason
face to face
and make it all better.
Better than what?
A really symphonic thought
to finally embrace the noise,

the afternoon light too,
the dog's swagger and the kite
sailing beyond.

•

If it touches you
will you carry that unloosening
into a beautiful talk
of tomorrow, how satisfied you are
with your choices? Not the ones
you can choose among
but the ones you're made of—
the flowers that came into your lines
wanting to say the accident of flight.
Faces too are a book,
like reading the stained glass—
à la to wit, we spent the day
reading glass in Rouen
I was going to say
remembering you
once you are gone
but that isn't it. How I loved
so much more than that.
The whole dizzying horizon
blooming around you.
Tears electrical and stinging
in every tiny cell

hiding from winter
and the long gaps
of wanting and actual being here
with you like this
listening to my voice
as if it were enough
just this once
to rescue doubt into loving
the fact we are here
and that you too
are here taking in the air.

●

It won't help to call out
intermittently: I am free!
Even if we didn't go west
who wouldn't have missed
the cornflower and poppies
on our goofy way to market.
The goofy present ribboning
highway to promise. What is it
dictating my hand
on its way to contact?
Can one ever expose the charge
beneath a surface?
Are you still with me, dear face?
Can you hear the cuckoo

as the doplered sirens squeeze past
flipping the pages of a blank book.
A reflection that gave up the ghost—
wan and translucent, paling
like an unopened letter
momentous on the breakfront in sun.
We fade, come in and out
of summer in and out of sound.
I see it glittering in the sun.
I see the sun. The promenade alive
with radio air and streamers,
the crush of citizens—
to think I've known
about the sky all my life.
Or light on the floor through a window
from the streetlamp. Night.
That part of expectation.

•

This begins as all stories begin
with a small boat and a body of water
like an icy winter star,
fuzzy hills blue beyond
your neck and shoulder.
You are inside my projector
turning overhead and me
coming in and out of focus

when your light won't reach me.
I know you're there
even when I need
to stand in the dark
to find out why
I'm standing in the dark.
If everything were different
then this might be the same
in a rusty town when the sun
strokes the windows
and the dust of industry
across the soot and debris
of last season or into a tiny frame
looking at a flag
from my father's car window
delivered even for an instant
to the right place and time.

•

The no, not, never,
not even, nothing of the day.
The nothing, nada, no thing,
not now of morning.
When the big arc zooms
into an acute angle,
and all your pictures still please
after the years and habit

lived among them.
I cannot greatly say
I am a rich landscape
or he who works the world
by observation alone is accurate.
The most distant sound
might be the truest
when nerves resemble
summer rain at 2 A.M.,
the noise in back of things,
its deep seeding.

•

But if you were hoping
to think a way
between moonlight
and the dictionary
between summer
and the constitution
steering your craft
into safe haven,
it isn't as far as today's
relentless polished horizon
awash with tinsel.
I lost my way.
Can I say that
and still be trusted?

Can you ever trust

the rugged outline

of tree-lined boulevards in August.

The heavy narcotic

of the changing season.

What is it anyway

to navigate the gorgeous

swath of leaves

turning twilight wind,

birds pick up,

little things

awaiting the sun's grand exit.

All things reach

when called. That's the law.

I heard my name

one day from the road.

It startled me, that alias

bringing me inside.

FROM A
CINEMATOGRAPHER'S LETTER

Dear Saturday, thank you for the hidden circuitry

these stunning visuals
in sympathetic weather backlit
about the shoulders.

Our talk, malachite flecks vamping the periphery
of everything you were wearing.

Crinoline felt closer to Kino.

Even the highway seemed conspiratorial
in garrulous rain, bleating, sidelong.

One moment a blunt contrast and then
accidentally, out the jeweled windshield

a face of waving poppies.
It's not enough though, accident.

To remember why I came here

and the revolutions of a face
caught outside its frame.

THAT'S LIFE

It couldn't be closer than Mars
these days. First you're off on a tangent,
then glittering beyond the call
in the backyard to no good effect.
Later when you shrugged you were blue,
I mistook it for "that's life" not "help me."
I mistake many things in dusk
like seeing liberty everywhere today,
smallish unacknowledged moments
of door holding, tossing coins
into a worn paper cup, smiling.
To rediscover our neighborhood
one wrapper and bum at a time.
Where am I going with this?
Down to the riverbank to watch the light
dazzle and showcase trees
in all their prehistoric movement.
Two more animals blinking in the breeze.
The guest-host relationship is
bigger than a house, older
than cold planets in space.
One of the earliest manuals

is about the guest-host thing.
Sit down, breathe deeply and
welcome yourselves. If you listen
you can faintly recall the song.
The sweet height of it all
breaking free from a canopy of leaves.
Remember the day
you first took in the night sky?
I mean really let it enter
and unfold along the interior
when the architecture of the body
resembles a cauldron for a dying star,
twinkle twinkle inside, and inside that
a simple hole. So now you know
what it is to be sucking air,
to be walking upright, to love.
Why not enjoy the day,
this moment to moment thing,
and the furnace above sending
you messages: breathe, dummy.
Birds do it and the rest of the ark
all following the great blank of what's next.
What's next is courage.
To take it all in and feel it for keeps,
that persons you meet
have a hole too and a twinkle.

Embrace them and have a meal.
Look straight into their impermanent flash,
the nervous-system tic of their talk.
Welcome their knowing
not knowing their coming and going.

NOCTURNE

To know is an extreme condition
like doubt, and will not rest.

Even the dailies unravel in the end.
The aperture shut tight.

Is it so difficult to admit light
in its unconditional noise

its electric blur, its red
cherry red, red of the advertisements

or yellow, cool as yellow gold
flat as mustard yellow.

And bright-bright Gatorade green
green dusky as gray forest-shade green.

All, under blue, a prison shirt blue
that torch song blue of the crooner's eyes

or the blue between tenements
between trees, kids, air.

The throaty blue
in a doorway after a party.

LINES DEPICTING
SIMPLE HAPPINESS

The shine on her buckle took precedence in sun
Her shine, I should say, could take me anywhere
It feels right to be up this close in tight wind
It feels right to notice all the shiny things about you
About you there is nothing I wouldn't want to know
With you nothing is simple yet nothing is simpler
About you many good things come into relation
I think of proofs and grammar, vowel sounds, like
A is for knee socks, E for panties
I is for buttondown, O the blouse you wear
U is for hair clip, and Y your tight skirt
The music picks up again, I am the man I hope to be
The bright air hangs freely near your newly cut hair
It is so easy now to see gravity at work in your face
Easy to understand time, that dark process
To accept it as a beautiful process, your face

PHANTASCOPE (1895)

Is there a map to Wakefield?
A potion for nepenthe?
A sound emitting

from the eves inside thought?
I have twirled, dropped crumbs,
spent days in archives.

I have captured fireflies on the equinox,
rescued the mountain gentian,
torn my garments in the square at noon.

The summer haze brings music
and vexed feelings before sleep.
An antique airship, spider webs, a flute.

VINCENT, HOMESICK FOR THE LAND OF PICTURES

Is this what you intended, Vincent
that we take our rest at the end of the grove
nestled into our portion beneath the bird's migration
saying, who and how am I made better through struggle.
Or why am I I inside this empty arboretum
this inward spiral of whoop ass and vision
the leafy vine twisting and choking the tree.
O, dear heaven, if you are indeed that
or if you can indeed hear what I might say
heal me and grant me laughter's bounty
of eyes and smiles, of eyes and affection.

To not be naive and think of silly answers only
nor to imagine answers would be the only destination
nor is questioning color even useful now
now that the white ray in the distant tree beacons.
That the sun can do this to us, every one of us
that the sun can do this to everything inside
the broken light refracted through leaves.
What the ancients called peace, no clearer example

what our fathers called the good, what better celebration.
Leaves shine in the body and in the head alike
the sun touches deeper than thought.

O to be useful, of use, to the actual seen thing
to be in some way related by one's actions in the world.
There might be nothing greater than this
nothing truer to the good feelings that vibrate within
like in the middle of the flower I call your name.
To correspond, to be in equanimity with organic stuff
to toil and to reflect and to home and to paint
father, and further, the migration of things.
The homing action of geese and wood mice.
The ample evidence of the sun inside all life
inside all life seen and felt and all the atomic pieces too.

But felt things exist in shadow, let us reflect.
The darkness bears a shine as yet unpunished by clarity
but perhaps a depth that outshines clarity and is true.
The dark is close to doubt and therefore close to the sun
at least what the old books called science or bowed down to.
The dark is not evil for it has indigo and cobalt inside
and let us never forget indigo and the warmth of that
the warmth of the mind reflected in a dark time
in the time of pictures and refracted light.
Ah, the sun is here too in the polar region of night
the animal proximity of another and of nigh.

To step into it as into a large surf in late August
to go out underneath it all above and sparkling.
To wonder and to dream and to look up at it
wondrous and strange companion to all our days
and the toil and worry and animal fear always with us.
The night sky, the deep sense of space, actual bodies of light
the gemstone brushstrokes in rays and shimmers
to be held tight, wound tighter in the act of seeing.
The sheer vertical act of feeling caught up in it
the sky, the moon, the many heavenly forms
these starry nights alone and connected alive at the edge.

Now to think of the silver and the almost blue in pewter.
To feel these hues down deep, feel color wax and wane
and yellow, yellows are the tonality of work and bread.
The deep abiding sun touching down and making its impression
making so much more of itself here than where it signals
the great burning orb installed at the center of each and
    every thing.
Isn't it comforting this notion of each and every thing
though nothing might be the final and actual expression of it
that nothing at the center of something alive and burning
green then mint, blue then shale, gray and gray into violet
into luminous dusk into dust then scattered now gone.

But what is the use now of this narrow ray, this door ajar
the narrow path canopied in dense wood calling

what of the striated purposelessness in lapidary shading and line.
To move on, to push forward, to take the next step, to die.
The circles grow large and ripple in the hatch-marked forever
the circle on the horizon rolling over and over into paint
into the not near, the now far, the distant long-off line of daylight.
That light was my enemy and one great source of agony
one great solace in paint and brotherhood the sky and grass.
The fragrant hills spoke in flowering tones I could hear
the gnarled cut stumps tearing the sky, eating the sun.

The gnarled cut stumps tearing the sky, eating the sun
the fragrant hills spoke in flowering tones I could hear
one great solace in paint and brotherhood the sky and grass.
That light was my enemy and one great source of agony
into the not near, the now far, the distant long-off line of daylight
the circle on the horizon rolling over and over into paint.
The circles grow large and ripple in the hatch-marked forever.
To move on, to push forward, to take the next step, to die.
What of the striated purposelessness in lapidary shading and line
the narrow path canopied in dense wood calling
but what is the use now of this narrow ray, this door ajar.

Into luminous dusk into dust then scattered now gone
green then mint, blue then shale, gray and gray into violet
that nothing at the center of something alive and burning
though nothing might be the final and actual expression of it.
Isn't it comforting this notion of each and every thing

the great burning orb installed at the center of each and
   every thing
making so much more of itself here than where it signals.
The deep abiding sun touching down and making its impression
and yellow, yellows are the tonality of work and bread.
To feel these hues down deep, feel color wax and wane
now to think of the silver and the almost blue in pewter.

These starry nights alone and connected alive at the edge
the sky, the moon, the many heavenly forms
the sheer vertical act of feeling caught up in it.
To be held tight, wound tighter in the act of seeing
the gemstone brushstrokes in rays and shimmers.
The night sky, the deep sense of space, actual bodies of light
and the toil and worry and animal fear always with us
wondrous and strange companion to all our days.
To wonder and to dream and to look up at it
to go out underneath it all above and sparkling
to step into it as into a large surf in late August.

The animal proximity of another and of nigh.
Ah, the sun is here too in the polar region of night
in the time of pictures and refracted light
the warmth of the mind reflected in a dark time
and let us never forget indigo and the warmth of that.
The dark is not evil for it has indigo and cobalt inside

at least what the old books called science or bowed down to.
The dark is close to doubt and therefore close to the sun
but perhaps a depth that outshines clarity and is true.
The darkness bears a shine as yet unpunished by clarity
but felt things exist in shadow, let us reflect.

Inside all life seen and felt and all the atomic pieces too
the ample evidence of the sun inside all life
the homing action of geese and wood mice
father, and further, the migration of things.
To toil and to reflect and to home and to paint
to correspond, to be in equanimity with organic stuff
like in the middle of the flower I call your name.
Nothing truer to the good feelings that vibrate within
there might be nothing greater than this
to be in some way related by one's actions in the world.
O to be useful, of use, to the actual seen thing.

The sun touches deeper than thought
leaves shine in the body and in the head alike
what our fathers called the good, what better celebration.
What the ancients called peace, no clearer example
the broken light refracted through leaves.
That the sun can do this to everything inside
that the sun can do this to us, every one of us
now that the white ray in the distant tree beacons.

Nor is questioning color even useful now
nor to imagine answers would be the only destination
to not be naive and think of silly answers only.

Of eyes and smiles, of eyes and affection
heal me and grant me laughter's bounty.
Or if you can indeed hear what I might say
O, dear heaven, if you are indeed that
the leafy vine twisting and choking the tree
this inward spiral of whoop ass and vision.
Or why am I I inside this empty arboretum
saying, who and how am I made better through struggle
nestled into our portion beneath the bird's migration
that we take our rest at the end of the grove
is this what you intended, Vincent.

BIPOLAROID

If you find the body a slow fuse
and aren't content to smolder
in the tenebrosity of shadow
in starlessness. The intense pitch.

You want to say "It's not fair"
but beginning there is useless.
Tho uselessness is a good thing
when imagining the body, right?

It just wants to sleep, move about
freely, nuzzle, eat, shit and not
always in that order. And not always
everything either all the time. Time?

That too is a piece of the body
its continuities, gaps, empty places
along with vast boredom and thirst
given to overcast, and the darkling.

I meant to say sparkling, studded,
stroboscopic, bioluminescent
you know, rainbow like, all lit up
and flashing, totally photogenic.

LAST CENTURY THOUGHTS IN SNOW TONIGHT

This is winter where light flits at the tips of things.
Sometimes I flit back and glitter.

Too much spectacle conquers the I.
This is winter where I walk out underneath it all.

What could I take from it? Astonishment?
I wore an extra blanket.

This is winter where childhood lanterns skate in the distance
where what we take is what we are given.

Some call it self-reliance. *Ça va?*
To understand our portion, our bright portion.

This is winter and this the winter portion
of self-reliance and last century thoughts in snow.

WINTRY MIX

The 6 A.M. January
encaustic clouds
are built
in a waxy gray putty
whizzing by with spots
of luminous silvery
crack-o'-the-world light
coming through, an eerie
end-o'-the-world feeling
yet reassuring
like an old movie.
Do I really have to go out there?
Now a hint of muted
salmon tones breaking
a warmish band
of welcoming pinkish light.
Is it like this every morning?
My head still in the dark.
Worry, eck! But the brightening
russet tipped cloud ballet
reminds me of something
in Pliny, yea, Pliny.

Can't imagine opening
the door today in a toga.
Work and more,
yes, work
sends us into the draft.

CHEAP IMITATION

Through a single pane
a distant hemlock signals
in northern light
a distant light weirds the field
pole star notes on cold
stone, on blue light
a dirty birch light
a fathomless muzzle-gray
pussywillow stone light
the day Socrates died
into evergreen light, cold
cold light of mind.

SATURDAY AND ITS
FESTOONED POTENTIAL

Faces unlike weather
never return
no matter how closely
they resemble rain

In this theater, time
isn't cruel, just different

Does that help?

When the overgrown skyway
becomes calm
humans get quiet

When the notion of myth
or collective anything
is undone by wind chimes
by a gentle tink tink

When the mind is opened forth
by a gentle tink tink

or light speckled
and whooping in the periphery

When light whooping
and speckled is most pleasing
to a body at rest

When thought, open
attaches itself to repose
to the forehead

When twigs swaying
just outside
the library's large glass
signal, scratch, and join
to an idea of history

When twigs scratching
join to an idea of time
to a picture of being

Like to be beside and becoming
to be another and oneself
to be complete inside the poem

To be oneself becoming a poem

HOMER'S ANGER

Real things inside me he said.
You've gotten it all wrong.

I see you and hear you
and that is the beginning of a poem.

Not a circle but a ray
not a definition but a journey

flowering in scenes.
This composition is still all the time

coming into view.
The depth we might say.

I am seeing through you
like transistor songs

from a postcard beach town,
two loves caught in cinemascope.

A movement inside movement
unlike the stars and flag.

ii.

I was going to tell you how it is
and then leaves out the window

ask me to respond.
Not just color and shine

but a total relinquishing
of the headlines.

If today is ash then
we have come from a great fire

and the heat is beginning
to consume the present.

To say rhythm is dangerous
is to miss the day entirely

to push the body on
in ungainly order

and the fate of fire
is to consume fuel from any source.

iii.

Should we discuss the news?
The meteorological epiphenomena

day in day out. It's unforecastable,
not going to stop.

Here we are, caught
by a luminous blue fuzz

touching everything out our windows.
It's not what you thought.

The smell of earth and hot sun.
Reassuring to lilacs too.

Loneliness is structural after all,
you have to really come with us

across the page, and if we are
indeed, alone together,

mighty are the numbers
drifting out there.

iv.

That's it then, everything opening,
memory fuzzing, dandelion projection—

a falling upward at last. If you can
move like those motes

casting random shadow casting
liberty, the low progress in air.

To Carthage I came, to shadow
the lovely outside pouring upon the desk.

The lowing flickering branch
making a picture to show you.

I searched, traveled in stacks
all day and now I've found you.

Empty light forming a dais
on the page. A valuable blank.

This craving for notes, momentum,
that I came to love the struggle,

inner engine spitting years,
splintered, what are years?

v.

I am listening to a life
unlived any other way.

Think of it. The notes remain
even as the song-sparrows change

from dirt to egg. Spring
to spring. Maybe that's it.

The molecular world
falling and rising

within a single melody.
So why not liberty?

Today we'll be talking
about the government.

It's important to remember.
All those scattered dispatches

on the back page. Human damage.
Working people and the right

to life, their pursuits,
not happiness,

not victories—
an endless series of victory.

vi.

One eye is more green than another
one more gray, a golden band

circles both pupils, dilates
as the creature breathes.

One eye is best looking for police,
they circle the block.

One for waves and motion
undulating from trees.

The eye is an instrument of emotion
like memory lives in the mouth.

Do you know what I mean
when I say anger is not emotion?

When everyone is stolen
I will begin in rain.

Not to be wrong
but uncertain, to want

more than this sentence.
If I say darkness is still

when it falls, understand
I am moving toward you.

LUMIÈRE

2 shots fired off screen

3 peace officers in the field

a body of a young woman

some moviola music

the ticking of a clock

den with worried housewife

the image fades its borders

image pulsing with the clock

cut to bed of lilies

arbor and vine, swing, nymphs

black screen

smoke, the sound of beating wings

fire dissolves the frame white

it's spring

A PAPER WIND

Across the colonnade
small kids with cones

making bug eyes in the square.
Laughter near the king's house.

7 kids oscillating in late sun, whir,
humming along

beneath the statue of the general.
Though nothing was free, not even rest

nothing was the better part of it
breaking, night fell in a reef

over the place. The incoming wedge
indomitable across the plaza

crushed flowers on cobbles
in primary yellows and red.

Men closed storefronts.
The day sank into violet.

Big marquees took the night,
blackened the sky, it was dark.

When the moon appeared on cue
it seemed meaningful, and others too

would concur the glittering
face throbbed,

the pale signal
sank into memory

and deeper than memory,
want and expectation.

As the disc rose over the park
women gathered their shawls.

How bizarre, how common.
Our little plot of time

had begun to grow stale
and even feckless.

But rising now, in this wind,
we find ourselves. How?

Just what is it that ferried us
over into laughter

settling into tea-light glittering tightness
and glances, fathomless happiness?

Each metaphorically sinking
alone, to the bottom

of a reflecting pool, a tiny ribbon
unfurling in the dark.

Even if we can't live there
inside this buoyed reverie

strange and inflected as it is,
we belong, or one can say, at least,

at last I belong, and in that
singularity an uncommon obligation.

Call it a nation, or a language.
Call it ourselves standing

in the dark in the wind
with a friend, it was night

and the book was closing,
the city was almost asleep.

We gestured toward home,
we were home.

THE MOONLIGHT DEFENSE

Why shouldn't it begin at midnight
when the doorman is asleep in his loge
and the spinning chrysalis in perfect equanimity
with earth, slippers under the chair,
toothbrush back on its thingy.
If tomorrow were promise, then tonight is real.
Let us pray before the bearded poplar
morphing in up-late celestial wonder.
Celestial wonder inscribed on sleeping lids.
I wander through doors and cascade in noise.
Libraries tower in their occult light.
Yes, solar wind, now windows bloom,
the body waves beyond itself.
Not all speech unuttered equals silence
nor a dropped curtain signals an end.
There are sudden days every animal secure
in one virtue. The bedrock vision,
and the road unraveling, gentle traveler,
the great thing is about to begin.

BOLSHEVESCENT

You stand far from the crowd, adjacent to power.
You consider the edge as well as the frame.
You consider beauty, depth of field, lighting
to understand the field, the crowd.
Late into the day, the atmosphere explodes
and revolution, well, revolution is everything.
You begin to see for the first time
everything is just like the last thing
only its opposite and only for a moment.
When a revolution completes its orbit
the objects return only different
for having stayed the same throughout.
To continue is not what you imagined.
But what you imagined was to change
and so you have and so has the crowd.

DEAD AIR

They got mobocratic on me
in parking lots, shopping malls

in cineramas across the lanes, across
interstates, turnpikes, parkways.

What could I do but run
until I was hidden in plain sight.

I am to you like a nation
at its knees, I am to you

a vast majority of red scarves
waving in an evergreen sea.

Such depth to this land.
Such long unexpected vistas.

Show me your days in the sun.
Show me everything.

Don't you leave me out here
don't you leave me out.

FRETLESS

We're off the grid, mother
sweep aside the lightning.
Then every gigantomachia
the day was:
a blue blue event
and still one wants to know.
Wants to be free of it
to be touched
and held again' it.
To regard oneself in the glass.
To regard oneself.
To be on the ground
always at the base of it
to say there I am.

Everything gets to him
from the edges
of the thing.
The dense lilacs
coming in
on the page.
But I wanted this

to be a narrative.
I still do
want a holiday in reality.
The air alive with style
want style
a hundred percent fiction
a hundred percent fact.
Its blurred registration.
To be on the ground
in my lanes
lifting off.
Did I say flight?

It's shitty to reckon
the end-of-day
shapelessness.
A rabbit in moonlight.
A dirty patch of snow.
Twig diorama
lit from afar.
Such emanations
made vast
like all goodnight stories.
The bear slept in the porridge
and we skated off
into a bed of honeysuckle
and away we are

when in your room
we say belonging
to a name
if belonging
to anything.

It's late, mother.
The house is a noise in my head.
The house is not empty alpha
late omega.
How much longer?
How much more radiator clank?
I have come to regard
the winter fly.
To regard electricity
its purpose and charge.
Regard life
no matter the voltage.
A voice comes to one.
A voice becomes *un-*
when spoken.
Unspoken
maybe the sun
controls these walks, waves, talk.

The body teaches, mother
its slow arc

attraction to a good
every good.
Call it cellular
this stereoscopic depth.
Remarkable things went on
in each place.
No time to remember
unless it be words
before him
in open air
at ease with company
with all things green.
The day before him
shadows, mid-earth
time and its weather.
To imagine
air spanked clean.
To think of everything.

To say my age, blown
as vapor on the glass
evaporating, reflected.
To read the lace curtains
and figures in cut glass
a deep focus
invariable as weather.
These choices

swallow you.
The snow unspoken.
A little cardinal
through the air
at the edge
of night.
Then the edge
of everything.

ON WHAT BECAME OF MATHEW BRADY'S BATTLE PHOTOGRAPHS

Sunlight and plant light
glass and stain
the campaign the conflict
the dead frozen in air
the sun and the sweat
the swell of fetid flesh
the tears the ache
the empty gut the ache
the heat of loss
the nerves burn
and the shock
of never returning burns
in the belly
and the brain alike
these images lifting off
into air, dissolving
into heat and light

defy gravity
lifting off
they are going now
Mother, they are gone

PROTEST SONG

This is not a declaration of love or song of war
not a tractate, autonym, or apologia

This won't help when the children are dying
no answer on the way to dust

Neither anthem to rally nor flag flutter
will bring back the dead, their ashes flying

This is not a bandage or hospital tent
not relief or the rest after

Not a wreath, lilac, or laurel sprig
not a garden of earthly delights

A WESTERN GARDEN

The fog dictates lost sailors
tumbling in the waves.
We're almost home
the sine and cosine sing,
the clear single azure dome
and shiny air all say.

•

The wood grain is deeper
than a forest
deeper than the sea.
The solid indication
of space in time
these whorls testify
this pattern inside.

•

Whoa, Saturday.
Whoa, morning.
The wind chimes
empty the air,
sculpt the empty blue.

•

To be here in this light.
In this table lamp light.
In the overhead table lamp light.
To find oneself
on a quiet street
in a written speech.

•

So often we measure
by what is false.
We should measure
by what is barely legible
barely in our dailiness.
It is the invisible that doesn't lie
the invisible through which
we see ourselves finally
on a back street in the world.

•

The dark falls fast these afternoons.
The edge of sky moves in.
The sea and night are the same.
The fog and the night are the same.
The night is dark by the sea.
Can you hear the night?
Can you hear the chimes
the sea and the sky?

•

In a western garden
there are broken tiles
like the broken history
like the objects broke under
the rims of the conqueror's wheels.
In a western garden
it gets darker faster.
It is home this dark
this flag invisible in wind.

•

Standing at nth and twilight,
at twilight and liberty
ordinary as molecules.
The sun moves along the horizon.
Pedestrians float
across the esplanade.

•

The form of fire is air.
The form of water is air.
The form of air, earth.
Moving. Breathing. Burning.

THE OUTERNATIONALE

One has emotions for the strangest things.
　　—W. C. WILLIAMS, *Kora in Hell*

So the bird's in the hand
and now what?
The penny shiny
in the dark belly of mr. piggy.
The day dawns and dawns
and may be in trouble
of actually going anywhere.
Trees migrate secretly up-
ward. They might be saying
all we need to be here
if we would only stop
talking and listen up.
I love you, said the wood.
One sonic color into
the egregious public air.
Start from nothing and be-
long to it. I guess
the rosy and bluish streaks
move counter to the feelings

exposed beneath them.
The signal and its noise
-itsy, -ancy, -oid.
So many strangers
alive in a larynx.
So much depends on x
so much more
on the book in your hand.
Start from nothing
and let the sound reach you.

There is that field
in the window once again
and to write of this field
again is certainly a failure
of any inward rigor
or life. To live certainly
on the surface -ing, -ed, or
things pinging off
the metal empty core
scrolling for a perfect tune
to cue the mood
outraged or bittersweet,
vintage etc. and emptier
than the supra-empty
of the mood stabilizer
flat line -less, -let

-like, -ly. The cold parts
of the car body.
Why can't I just admit
I'm dead, have been dead
since I met me, -metry, -ality
unseen and undone
by the no time
I was raised into
out of the incubator
-obic, -etic, -istic
the stain of the world
got on me.
You see it on TV.
Everyday weather
and the everyday weatherman.
The car racing
into a slow fade.
Rain opening the next shot,
falling everywhere
around the boy falling digitally
just now as you read this.
It is always raining
in pictures, inside
this feeling of mercy
-ency, -esse
or this writing along the edge
which is of course

writing about hope
if we could only open
our hardware
to rewrite the software
down deep, the body
coming to, inside
this wooden structure
-archy, -ology, -ocracy.

Skylark, do you
have anything
to say to me?

Have you come
as a flower on the hill?

I am beside you
alive in the folds
of your parka.

Have you a single
new idea? Yes,
I carry the oldest ones.

Who will live
inside the song?

Is it only sand?
The voice of sand
-mandias, -icious, -rex.

The box is spitting electro-
magnetic lies into the room
again. I get sick and weak
just gawking to find
myself already full
of onions and laughter
-illiant, -ismus, arrogance.
I don't want to go there.
Don't want the lockdown
the bray, the cobbled headgear.
Can't it be clear? Can't it?
So often the inklings
the starter round
the jerk and huh of morning.
But the instants, the lake walks
and for a *blip* open sky
unshackling a bad history.
Nothing more personal
than headlines.
But what of the colors
in the new season sky?
It is only where
spring and death meet

-sic, -cide, -ulation.
Who says we are lacking
in courage?

The most forgotten history
is often the best. Best?
Ruined tar paper
against brick factory lots,
brick, brick,
smokestack, sky.
Even the light fades badly.
These old windows
bend the world.
I could never find
my way there and now
we are only here.
That's something
more than spectacular sunsets,
fading shafts on water.
With each one dies a world.
Or an empty casement
letting light in
bricolaged, alive for a moment
and then obfuscation
of late afternoon.
If only I knew then
what I know to be

outside my head
rain-washed and open.
Can't one stumble beyond
the cheap effects
of planet light, planet tilt
and all that gaggle?

Once the sweet laughter
of indestructibility
cackled from my mouth.
No hiding the pain
my body was in space
and the empathy borne
of earthly gravity
earthly sentience
weighted to the bed,
the floor, the street,
the planet, -mania,
-polis, -ment.
Such cruelty comes
from lack of everything
or so I imagined,
having failed
to save anyone
from anything
in this empty house.
From this empty empty house

in first dull winter light
staring hard into spackle.
How could I save anyone
from the truly gnarly
unnecessary -osis
of a steel wind off a boulevard
rich with dog shit and perfume
carbon monoxide and subway grates
the confusion of sex and death
of childhood and decay
of sideway glances and
dinnish noises
of all things dented
and almost destroyed
amidst the once of beauty
and ankle bracelets.
The whole wide whorl
of economics charted
on a dart board
in bed sheets, -th,
-onomy, -illion, -ation.

The time to breathe
is now, there will be no time
to think but perhaps
you have no doubt.
I would like

to expose doubt itself
to open up
the mechanics of want
-ivorous, -etic, -esque, so
someone can feel it.
So someone can feel it
and break it down
inside themselves.
To rip out the gears
and belts, to empty
once and for all expectation,
the guitar sound
of young adult life
-ectric, -philia, -phyte.
The radio backdrop
speckled and moving.
The car window specked
and the sky moving.
The neighborhood
coming into view.
So the new poverty is just
like the old poverty.
The system has been upgraded
but the light, dishwater,
is mucking up the mood.
Whoever said
absolute powerlessness

corrupts absolutely?
Does it get any better?
Jeweled spots, translucent
over the windshield,
now pierced in white stinging
-hood, -holic, -hedron.
The cellular body
fuzzed out in sun,
oversaturated in Polaroid
reddish brown.
Where are we going
in the mechanical seconds
of this handheld movie,
this color that touches down?

If we could say
the world has changed,
it has changed. If we say
the world is the same
then so it is. But nothing
changes everything
and we know this.
We earn this the hard way.
Even the beloved
evolves into nothing
-unction, -iction
for all its iron and science.

A bridge expands over foliage.
The river dappled
with wind and speed
and the sensation of night.
Throw back your head
to the milky tears.
All types and shapes
of silent light.
Here the crab, the bear,
the dipper, the wheel
and the little tightnesses
that keep us wanting.
The wanting that keeps us
looking hard into the dark.
The dark we hope to unpack
and move into
that one day
we might find ourselves lit up.

FROM HERE LAUGHTER SOUNDS LIKE CRYING

When time becomes
we become
when day becomes
we begin to break

Take it, all of it,
in consecutive units

What of the plough
the mental field
the bedrock pediment
in time and in
the ancient street
so feeling of Lincoln

I'm nobody
for a change
I take the form
of everyone waiting

No day no bird
taking off

The wood pigeon is no bird
a sound pouring
into itself

We call this
broken and boarded

It is not a dream
not gated

Inside the groundlessness
comes to rest
a largesse of ought

Melville has bled
into the local runoff

So much
so much more translation
in the yard
as if insisting
against falling

I want my house
to burn
and build from
nowhere
just there

Let us be
appendages to evolution
mysteries
in the face of violence
even with the shades

Acknowledgments

Grateful acknowledgment is made to the editors of journals where some of these poems have appeared: *American Poet*, *Bomb*, *Brooklyn Rail*, *Boston Review*, *The Call*, *The Canary*, *Chicago Review*, *Conjunctions*, *Crowd*, *Denver Quarterly*, *Five Fingers Review*, *Fulcrum*, *Grimm*, *The Hat*, *Jubilat*, *Meena*, *The Modern Review*, *N+1*, *1913*, *No: A Journal of the Arts*, *Poetry Review*, *A Public Space*, *Shuffle Boil*, *The Tiny*, *Tin House*, *Viz.*, and *Yawp*.

Many thanks to the editors who selected poems to be included in their anthologies: *American Poets in the 21st Century: The New Poetics*; *The Gertrude Stein Awards in Innovative Poetry 2006*; *Poetry Calendar 2006: 365 Classic and Contemporary Poems* and *Poetry Calendar 2007*; *Structure and Surprise*; and *Under the Rock Umbrella: Modern American Poets from 1951–1976*.

•

Many thanks to Anna Moschovakis, Genya Turovskaya, and Matvei Yankelevich for publishing "A Panic That Can Still Come Upon Me" as a limited-edition chapbook (Brooklyn: Ugly Duckling Presse, 2006). This poem takes its title from a "salvage" work by Jess; the phrase comes from Robert Duncan's essay "The Truth and Life of Myth."

"The Quest" was also published as a broadside and included in *For Tom and Val*, collected by Miles Champion, William Corbett, and Lyn Hejinian (New York: Granary Books, 2004).

"A telescope protects its view" is a phrase from John Ashbery's poem "Clepsydra."

Thanks to Thomas Evans for publishing an earlier version of "From a Cinematographer's Letter" as a limited-edition folio with original artwork by Tom Raworth (London: Tolling Elves, 2004).

Phantascope is the name of an early moving picture device.

The phrase "homesick for the land of pictures" is from Vincent Van Gogh's letters to his brother Theo.

"Cheap Imitation" is the title of John Cage's composition after Eric Satie's "Socrate."

"Lumière" takes its title from the early pioneers of film and was inspired by David Lynch's one-minute film using their original camera.

The word "bolshevescent" comes from Osip Mandelstam's poem "Stanzas."

"On What Became of Mathew Brady's Battle Photographs": after the war, Brady's glass negatives were sold wholesale to farmers to build greenhouses.

"Protest Song" was written for the composer Michael Fiday, for a song commissioned by the musical ensemble Sequitur.

•

For their generous support during various stages of this book I would like to thank the John Simon Guggenheim Memorial Foundation for a fellowship and The MacDowell Colony for an artist's residency.

Peter Gizzi

is the author of four books of poetry, including *Some Values of Landscape and Weather* (Wesleyan, 2003), and the editor of *The House That Jack Built: The Collected Lectures of Jack Spicer* (Wesleyan, 1998). His honors include the Lavan Younger Poet Award from the Academy of American Poets (1994) and a fellowship in poetry from the John Simon Guggenheim Memorial Foundation (2005). He teaches at the University of Massachusetts, Amherst.

5/3/07

AFRICAN ART & LEADERSHIP

THE UNIVERSITY OF WISCONSIN PRESS

Madison, Milwaukee, and London

African
Art &
Leadership

Edited by

DOUGLAS FRASER *and*

HERBERT M. COLE

Published 1972
The University of Wisconsin Press
Box 1379, Madison, Wisconsin 53701

The University of Wisconsin Press, Ltd.
70 Great Russell Street, London WC1B 3BY

First printing

Printed in the United States of America
NAPCO, Inc., Milwaukee, Wisconsin

ISBN 0-299-05820-4; LC 72-157391

In Memoriam

ROBERT ELWYN BRADBURY

1929–1969

Contents

Illustrations   ix

Maps   xiii

Preface   xv

Contributors   xvii

Introduction   3

1   The *Kindi* Aristocrats and Their Art among the Lega
        DANIEL BIEBUYCK   7

2   Chokwe: Political Art in a Plebian Society
        DANIEL J. CROWLEY   21

3   *Ndop:* Royal Statues among the Kuba   JAN VANSINA   41

4   *Gon:* A Mask Used in Competition for Leadership
     among the BaKwele   LEON SIROTO   57

5   Ibo Art and Authority   HERBERT M. COLE   79

6   Humorous Masks and Serious Politics among Afikpo
    Ibo   SIMON OTTENBERG   99

7   Royal Sculpture in the Cameroons Grasslands
                                     SUZANNE RUDY   123

8   The Symbols of Ashanti Kingship   DOUGLAS FRASER   137

9   The Diffusion of Ashanti Political Art
                                     RENÉ A. BRAVMANN   153

10 Kwahu Terracottas, Oral Traditions, and Ghanaian
    History   ROY SIEBER   173

11 Gold-Plated Objects of Baule Notables
                                     HANS HIMMELHEBER   185

12 Ife, The Art of an Ancient Nigerian Aristocracy
                                     FRANK WILLETT   209

13 The Sign of the Divine King: Yoruba Bead-
    Embroidered Crowns with Veil and Bird
    Decorations   ROBERT F. THOMPSON   227

14 The Fish-Legged Figure in Benin and Yoruba Art
                                     DOUGLAS FRASER   261

    Art and Leadership: An Overview
            DOUGLAS FRASER AND HERBERT M. COLE   295

    Index   329

Illustrations

1.1	Lega. *Mwami* of the Highest Level in the *Kindi* Grade	12
1.2	Lega. Large Ivory Statue *Nina*	13
1.3	Lega. Ivory Statue Representing Kuboko Kumozi	14
1.4	Lega. Ivory Statue Representing Kakinga	14
1.5	Lega. Display of Ivory Statues at the *Kinsamba* Rite	16
2.1	Chokwe. Dance Masks Chihongo and Katoyo	25
2.2	Chokwe. Bark-Cloth Mask Chikusa	26
2.3	Chokwe. Bark-Cloth Mask Kalelwa	27
2.4	Chokwe. Wooden Mask Mwana Pwo	28
2.5	Luena. Dance Mask Linya Pwa	29
2.6	Chokwe. Throne	33
2.7	Chokwe. Detail of Throne	34
3.1	Kuba. *Nyim* Mbop aMabiinc in State Regalia	42
3.2	Kuba. *Ndop* of Shyaam aMbul aNgoong	43
3.3	Kuba. *Ndop* of Mbomboosh	43
3.4	Kuba. *Ndop* of Mishaa Pelyeeng aNce	46
3.5	Kuba. *Ndop* of Mbo Pelyeeng aNce	46
3.6	Kuba. *Ndop* of Kot aMbul	47
3.7	Kuba. *Ndop* of Miko miMbul	49
3.8	Kuba. *Ndop* of Mbop Kyeen	49
4.1	BaKwele. *Gon*-Masker	64

4.2	Skull of Adult Male Gorilla	66
4.3	BaKwele. *Gon* Mask	67
4.4	BaKwele. *Ndyaadal* Mask	71
4.5	BaKwele. *Gon* Mask	72
4.6	BaKwele. *Gon* Mask	73
4.7	BaKwele. *Gon* Mask	74
4.8	BaKwele. *Gon* Mask	75
4.9	BaKwele. *Gon*-Related Mask	76
5.1	Ibo. Ozo Title-Society Member	86
5.2	Ibo. Stool Associated with Ozo Title-Society	87
5.3	Ibo. Stool Associated with Highest Grades of Ozo Title-Society	87
5.4	Ibo. Titled Man's Elephant Tusk Horn	88
5.5	Ibo. Carved Wooden Compound Entrance Door and Panels	89
5.6	Ibo. Ikorodo Mask	93
6.1	Ibo, Afikpo. Dancer Wearing the *Nne Mgbo* Mask	102
6.2	Ibo, Afikpo. Another *Nne Mgbo* Mask	103
6.3	Ibo, Afikpo. Group of Okumkpa Players	104
6.4	Ibo, Afikpo. Scene from Play Ridiculing Moslems	104
6.5	Ibo, Afikpo. Actors Playing Out a Skit	106
6.6	Ibo, Afikpo. Two Men Dancing About between Skits	106
6.7	Ibo, Afikpo. Mask of Senior of Two Play Leaders	108
7.1	Bamileke Group, Bakowen Chiefdom. Seated Chief Holding Pipe and Calabash	127
7.2	Bangwa Subgroup (West Cameroon). *Fosia*(?)	129
7.3	Tikar Group, Bafut Chiefdom. Chief Seated on Stool	130
7.4	Tikar Group, Banso (Nsaw) Chiefdom. Large Seated Figure Holding Bowl	131
7.5	Bamileke Group, Bangangte Chiefdom. Seated Female with Child	132
7.6	Bangwa Subgroup (West Cameroon). *Aini*	134
8.1	Ashanti. Golden Stool	140
8.2	Ashanti. Asantehene and Golden Stool in State	141
8.3	Ashanti. Man's Ceremonial Stool	143
8.4	Ashanti. Detail of an Engraving of a Yam Festival	146
8.5	Twifo State. Akokobatan Ne Ne Mma	148
8.6	Ashanti. Treasure Container	150
8.7	Ashanti. Detail of Figure 8.6	151
9.1	Nafana. Kwaku Sorma	161

9.2	Nafana. Eight State Swords	165
9.3	Nafana. Mma Gwa Stool	167
9.4	Nafana. Chief and Linguist	168
9.5	Nafana. *Akonkromfi* Chair	169
10.1	Kwahu. Funerary Terracotta	174
10.2	Kwahu. Terracotta Heads from a Shrine	176
10.3	Kwahu. Terracotta of Woman and Child	177
10.4a	Kwahu. Grave of a Priest with Terracotta	178
10.4b	Kwahu. Close-Up of Head in Figure 10.4a	179
10.5	Kwahu. Fragmentary Head	180
10.6	Kwahu. Terracotta Representing First Queen Mother of Asakraka	181
11.1	Baule, Subtribe Atutu. Carver Tanu	187
11.2	Baule, Subtribe Uarebo. Figures on Fly-Whisk Handles	188
11.3	Baule, Subtribe Uarebo. King Anoubli and Followers	189
11.4	Baule. *Laule*	190
11.5	Baule, Subtribe Atutu. Artisan Hammering Out the Gold Leaf	192
11.6	Baule, Subtribe Atutu. Artisan Pressing Gold Leaf into Grooves of Ornaments	193
11.7–12	Baule. Designs Used in Gold-Plating	195
11.13–23	Baule. Designs Used in Gold-Plating	196
11.24–29	Baule. Designs Used in Gold-Plating	198
11.30–32	Baule. Designs Used in Gold-Plating	199
11.33	Baule. Relief of Crocodile on Sword Handle	199
11.34	Baule. Fly-Whisk Handle	201
11.35	Baule. Gilded Fly-Whisk Handle	202
11.36	Baule. Gilded Fly-Whisk Handle	203
11.37	Baule. Head of Linguist's Staff	204
11.38	Baule. Fly-Whisk Handles	205
12.1	Yoruba. King's Beaded Crown	211
12.2	Yoruba. Chief Obakire	214
12.3	Yoruba. Badge of Chief Obakire	215
12.4	Ife. Brass Head No. 4	216
12.5	Ife. Brass Figure of an Oni of Ife	217
12.6	Ife. Upper Part of Chest of Terracotta of Queen	218
12.7	Ife. Stylized Heads in Terracotta	222
12.8	Ife. Three Conical Heads	222
12.9	Ife. Group of Terracotta Sculptures	223

13.1   Ijebu Yoruba. Beaded Crown with Veil of Ruler   231
13.2   Tada. Middle Niger River, Nupe. Standing Bronze
            Figure of a Traditional Ruler   234
13.3   Tada. Detail of Figure 13.2   235
13.4   Benin. Bronze Head Surmounted by Four Metal
            Birds   237
13.5   Iperu. Remo Yoruba. Brass Ceremonial Crown   239
13.6   Ijebu Yoruba. Brass Ceremonial Crown   240
13.7   Benin. Medicine Staff   250
14.1   Benin. Detail of Brass Plaque   264
14.2   Benin. Brass Bell with Snake   265
14.3   Benin. Motifs Appearing on Various Brass Bells   266
14.4   Benin. Oba Figure   268
14.5   Yoruba. Ijebu. Oshugbo (Ogboni) Society Drum   271
14.6   Yoruba. Owo. Detail of Ivory Armband   274
14.7   Yoruba. Ijebu. Detail of Ivory Armband   274
14.8   Yoruba. Owo. Detail of Ivory Armband   275
14.9   Yoruba. Owo. Ivory Armband   276
14.10   Sierra Leone. Sherbro. Detail of Afro-Portuguese
            Ivory Vessel   277
14.11   Switzerland. Geneva. Romanesque Figure   279
14.12   Italy. Parma. Romanesque Relief   280
14.13   France. Poitiers. Romanesque Figure   280
14.14   Switzerland. Gothic Relief   281
14.15   Italy. Hellenistic-Etruscan. Triton   283
14.16   Iran. Luristan. Bronze Figure   284
14.17   India. Mathura. Figure   284
14.18   Afghanistan. Begram. Triton. Ivory.   285
14.19   India. Mathura. Figure   285
14.20   Afghanistan. Begram. Triton. Ivory.   286
14.21   Yoruba. Owo. Detail from Ivory Beaker   286
15.1   Benin. Decorated Ceremonial Sword *Ada*   298
15.2   Kalabari Ijaw. Ancestral Screen *Duen Fobara*   301
15.3   Cameroons Grasslands. Bamileke Group. Lintel
            Woodcarving   316
15.4   Benin. Brass Plaque   317

Maps

1   Congo Area   8
2   Distribution of the BaKwele and Culturally Related
        Peoples around 1900   59
3   Southern Nigeria   80
4   Central Cameroons   124
5   Central Guinea Coast   138
6   Banda Area   154

Preface

This volume had its genesis in a symposium entitled "The Aristocratic Traditions in African Art," which was held at Columbia University in May 1965. The conference was organized by Douglas Fraser. Professor (now Emeritus) Paul S. Wingert of the Columbia Department of Art History and Archaeology chaired the two sessions at which six papers were read and discussed. Daniel Biebuyck, Herbert Cole, Douglas Fraser, Suzanne Rudy, Roy Sieber, and Robert Thompson were the speakers.

The Columbia symposium raised more questions than it answered and at the same time indicated the value of this type of comparative approach to the study of African art. The sessions also dramatized the need for additional information on the subject and suggested that Africanists in various disciplines would find value in a further investigation of the interactions between African leaders and art forms. For these reasons the editors decided to publish the six original essays in book form, together with eight additional contributions solicited from other scholars who had not been able to attend the meeting. It is hoped that this beginning will encourage others to pursue and develop this line of inquiry.

In compiling this book, many debts have been incurred that need to be acknowledged. Each of the contributors has, of course, helped in numerous ways, but special thanks are due Leon Siroto for his critical reading of the introduction and overview. The late R. E. Bradbury,

William Fagg, Paul Gebauer, Richard Harris, G. I. Jones, Peter Morton-Williams, Kenneth Murray, and others have contributed their skills to the intellectual sharpening of the volume. Among those who have also helped develop the ideas expressed here are Robert P. Armstrong, Mino Badner, Allen Bassing, Marvin Cohodas, Philip Dark, Paul Engo, Tonye V. Erekosima, Mrs. Tove Hall, A. A. Y. Kyerematen, Albert Maesen, Daniel McCall, Mrs. Sarah Gill Merwyn, David Okwudili, Peter Pipim, George Preston, and many more. For their kindnesses in facilitating research and publication, our thanks go also to Monni Adams, Hans Becher, Admiral Brian Egerton, H. van Geluwe, F. Hayford, Eleanor Howard, Aldona Jonaitis, Phillip Lewis, John Picton, Mrs. Frieda Rosenthal, Irene Winter, and others. Our thanks go also to Eliot Elisofon for permission to use his photograph of the Kuba king Mbop aMabiinc on the dust jacket of the book. In many ways, this picture epitomizes to us the concept of African art and leadership.

DOUGLAS FRASER
New York, New York

HERBERT M. COLE
Santa Barbara, California

June 1971

Contributors

DANIEL BIEBUYCK
Professor of Anthropology, University of Delaware

RENÉ A. BRAVMANN
Assistant Professor of Art, University of Washington

HERBERT M. COLE
Assistant Professor of Art, University of California, Santa Barbara

DANIEL CROWLEY
Professor of Anthropology and Art, University of California, Davis

DOUGLAS FRASER
Professor of Art History and Archaeology, Columbia University

HANS HIMMELHEBER
Heidelberg, Germany

SIMON OTTENBERG
Professor of Anthropology, University of Washington

SUZANNE RUDY
Princeton, New Jersey

ROY SIEBER
Professor of Fine Arts, Indiana University

LEON SIROTO
Associate Professor of Anthropology, University of Delaware

ROBERT FARRIS THOMPSON
Associate Professor of the History of Art, Yale University

JAN VANSINA
Professor of History, University of Wisconsin

FRANK WILLETT
Professor of African Art and Archeology, Northwestern University

AFRICAN ART & LEADERSHIP

Introduction

The widely held opinion that art is a luxury and serves no vital purpose is, at least as far as Africa is concerned, a myth. For, apart from having well-known social and religious functions, much of Africa's art also plays a prominent part in the sphere of political leadership, that is, in the governing of the people. This book deals primarily with such art forms—figures, masks, carved seats, terracottas, etc.—and with various items of regalia ranging from crowns and staffs to ornamental swords, all of which are intimately involved in the exercise of leadership in Africa.

The study of African art has, until recently, been characterized by two distinct approaches. The first consists of the general visual survey, usually a cataloging of art forms geographically by tribe clustered into areas such as "Guinea Coast" which are cited as though they were consistent style regions. The description of formal properties and the differentiation of styles are major concerns. Some attention is given to the function of individual pieces, but there is no attempt, as a rule, to synthesize this information above the tribal level. The second approach involves the examination of a single art style or ceremony in detail, and is usually more concerned with function than with aesthetic matters, indeed often going to the opposite extreme of treating art objects *solely in terms of their cultural context* as if they were so many pieces of firewood. Both types of publication have served useful purposes in the study of African art; but the time has come when a fusion of

3

these methods, together with a comparative approach, can bring new and necessary light to this vast field.

In this volume, an attempt is made to bridge the intellectual gap between the functionalist and formalist approaches. In addition, we hope to reveal more clearly how and why *art* is used to promulgate a culture's fundamental values, a matter hardly ever discussed in any publication. We will not be concerned here with analyzing the peculiarities of form that make a piece either Ibo or Ibibio; rather we are interested in finding cross-cultural regularities of appearance and use, many more of which exist than have heretofore been recognized.

Our subject will be treated in two different ways and in two separate sections. The first part is an anthology of fourteen essays on aspects of art and leadership in a dozen or so specific areas. The second section—an overview—is an interpretative essay which attempts to discover the ways in which art and leadership relate to one another in African cultures. In both sections, political activity is defined broadly and includes certain social, economic, and religious functions that are so intimately bound up with the exercise of leadership in traditional Africa.

Many things are *not* attempted here. None of our contributors would claim to have dealt exhaustively with his subject, nor are all the many types of African political systems represented. Emphasis, not surprisingly, has tended to fall on the relatively centralized societies that put heavy stress on the visual arts, such as the Kuba, Ashanti, and Yoruba. Nevertheless, we believe that the *principles* advanced here are reasonably valid for countless other African societies.

Recognizing, as we do, that nearly *all* the arts discussed here function in essentially theatrical contexts, we regret that music, the dance, praise songs, and other aspects of the performing arts do not play a larger role in this volume. Unfortunately, these facets of African life are if anything even less well recorded (and understood) than are the plastic arts. We hope, though, by the frequent use of field photographs, to convey something of the dramatic staging that so often attends the public functioning of art in Africa.

There is, of course, no such thing as "the correct way" to study African art. Besides differences in training and life experiences, each investigator has his own particular interests which are, to some extent, a function of the culture he is studying. Thus, in the essays that follow, certain authors stress technical, functional, or contextual analysis, while others concern themselves with history, iconography, or content. Such an array of interests underscores the enormous diversity inherent in each African art style.

The sequence of the fourteen essays is to some extent arbitrary. The first three studies discuss the art of certain Congolese societies in order of increasing socio-political centralization. The first essay, by Daniel Biebuyck, concerns masks and figures used by members of the Lega *bwami* society, a graded organization having widespread political influence among this acephalous people. Next, Daniel Crowley discusses masquerades and chief-related paraphernalia in the light of the history of the Chokwe, a people having recognized leaders but no stress in recent times on kingship or elaborate administrative hierarchies. The well-known commemorative "portraits" of Kuba kings are then analyzed by Jan Vansina in terms of their stylistic, symbolic, and historical meaning. Equatorial Africa is represented by Leon Siroto's chapter on a BaKwele masking cult which centers around men who are in competition for positions of leadership. The focus then shifts northward to the Ibo peoples of southeastern Nigeria, whose art is described by Herbert Cole and Simon Ottenberg. Cole's chapter is an introduction to Ibo title-society paraphernalia and to masks used by several politically powerful secret societies. Ottenberg elucidates a single type of masquerade, performed in the Afikpo area, that employs dramatic performances to influence social and political leadership. The next essay, written by Suzanne Rudy, analyzes the structural and symbolic character of monumental court-associated statuary found in the several Cameroons Grasslands kingdoms.

The four following chapters address themselves to the art of certain Akan and related peoples of Ghana (Ashanti, Kwahu, and Nafana) and the Ivory Coast (Baule). First, Douglas Fraser surveys the intrinsic meaning and symbolic significance of various items of Ashanti regalia, including the famous Golden Stool. In the next chapter, René Bravmann documents the presence of (and changes effected in) certain Akan objects acquired from various south Ghanaian leaders (including the Ashanti king) by the non-Akan peoples of northwestern Ghana. The little-publicized terracotta heads and figures of the Kwahu and other Akan peoples are then discussed by Roy Sieber, both from a stylistic and a historical point of view. Hans Himmelheber's essay analyzes items of Baule regalia with special reference to gold-plating techniques, ornamentation, history, and parallels with other Akan groups.

The final three chapters return to Nigeria for a consideration of the arts of the highly centralized Yoruba and Benin peoples. Frank Willett discusses the artistic and archaeological evidence of kingship in ancient Ife, the sacred Yoruba city, illustrating various aspects of this widely admired, aristocratic tradition. Robert F. Thompson then examines the iconography and values associated with the Yoruba kings' beaded crowns, employing evidence from many sources, including Yoruba groups living in the New World. A distinctive motif—the fish-legged figure—which is found in both Benin and Yoruba art is then discussed by Douglas Fraser, who offers a wide-ranging historical and iconographical analysis of this enigmatic emblem of divine kingship.

In the concluding essay—the overview—an effort is made to build upon the preceding essays and to articulate general principles that govern the relationship between art and leaders in Africa.

CHAPTER 1

The *Kindi* Aristocrats and Their Art among the Lega

Daniel Biebuyck

In order to gain a full understanding of the background of meanings and functions associated with Lega wood and ivory carvings, a precise knowledge about certain key aspects of the culture of the Lega is necessary A discussion of the details of various significant features of their social institutions cannot be undertaken here. I shall, therefore, restrict myself to a succinct examination of some of their basic characteristics. The Lega have developed a large number of functional groups of carvings, all of which are connected with different stages of initiation into the *bwami* association. I shall concentrate only on those ivory figurines that are made for, used, owned, and transmitted by the members of the uppermost initiatory level of the highest grade of the association.

BASIC CHARACTERISTICS OF THE LEGA

The Lega people number about 250,000 and live in the eastern part of the Republic of the Congo, Kinshasa, some five hundred kilometers south of Kisangani (Stanleyville), in an abundant forest environment. They are a culturally and linguistically homogeneous people, who are strongly aware—as is evidenced in their ethnohistorical traditions—of their common origins, common experiences, and common culture. There

Note: Field work among the Lega of the territories of Mwenga, Shabunda, and Pangi was done in 1952–1953 under the auspices of l'Institut pour la Recherche Scientifique en Afrique Centrale. The author has revisited the Lega on various occasions since 1954.

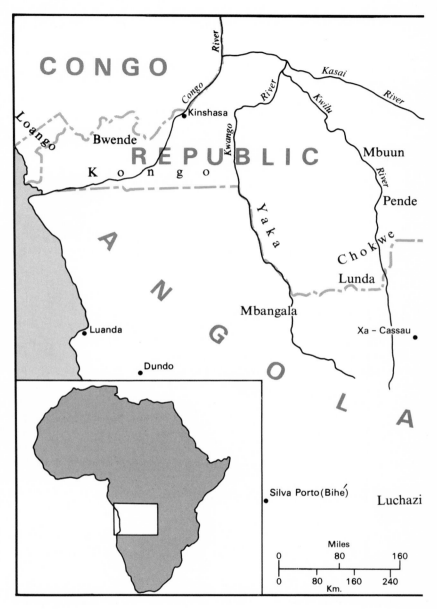

MAP 1. Congo Area.

8

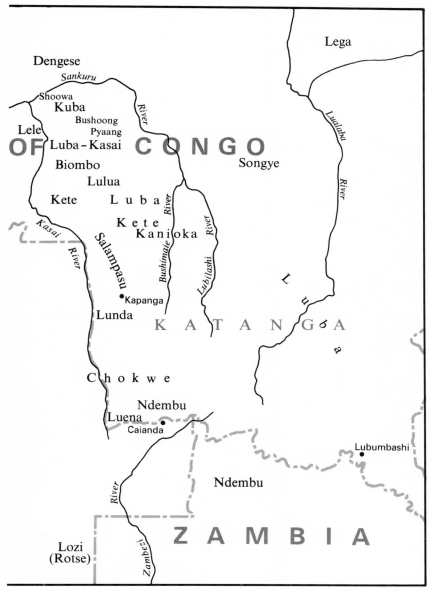

Map by University of Wisconsin Cartographic Laboratory.

are, of course, striking regional differences within the group which are the outcome of various contacts with other cultural entities, of local experience, and so on; these differences, however, manifest themselves more in form and amplitude than in structure or function. This is evidenced, for example, in the styles and the quantity of art objects produced in the various Lega areas. The subsistence economy is centered around the growing of plantain bananas, hunting and trapping (game is still found in very large numbers), the gathering of natural produce, and, to a lesser extent, fishing. Game and plantains are prominent in the diet and in technology, exchanges, initiations, symbolism, and the value system. The meanings conveyed by many of the initiatory items, including carvings, are intimately connected with these central activities and the values placed on them.

The Lega are organized into corporate, localized patriclans. These clans are segmented into a number of lineages of different span and depth, which perform diverse but complementary functions. Relations traced through the nonconnecting parent (mother), and the nonconnecting grand- and great-grandparents, with their respective patrilineages, are particularly strong and provide individuals and family groups with a broad framework of social interaction outside their own lineage and clan. Many features of initiation and correlated acquisition of emblems, including carvings, must be interpreted in the light of these kinship connections. Transfer of carvings, and individual or group control over them, can only be understood through this perspective.

The Lega are not organized into states; they have a segmentary lineage organization. Political relationships are thus rooted in the localized clans and their component lineages. The *bwami* association, which is universal among the Lega, cuts across the existing kinship and territorial subdivisions. It thus provides a framework for many forms of solidarity and cooperation that transcend immediate kinship relationships.

THE *BWAMI* ASSOCIATION

All Lega plastic art is connected with this association, whose members use it for a variety of purposes in well-defined contexts. *Bwami* is a hierarchically constituted body of initiates. Basically, it comprises five grades for men and three complementary grades for women. The men's grades are subdivided into a vast number of initiatory cycles which, in the case of the two highest grades, are grouped into levels and subgrades. The women's grades are more simply structured in a limited number of initiatory cycles. All male Lega have potential access to *bwami* after circumcision. All aspire to it and all endeavor to reach the first grade and to work themselves up from there. It is fair to say that 95 percent of Lega males achieve rank in the lowest grade of the association, but the bulk of them never get further than the three lower grades. Only when a woman is married to an initiate can she be initiated herself, and even then she can never achieve a grade that would be higher than her husband's. Initiation into any of the grades is not merely a question of individual enterprise; rather, it is conditioned by a wide variety of factors, including support from kinsmen and initiates even from other lineages and clans, sponsorship by prominent members of *bwami,* and the availability of large numbers of diverse (but specific) goods to be used as fees and gifts. In addition, admission is affected by the internal structure of the kinship groups and by that of the broader ritual communities within which initiations are organized, as well as by the moral qualities of the candidate, and so on.

Every cycle of initiations (with increasing complexity and amplitude as a man moves higher and higher in the hierarchy of grades and subgrades) is characterized by appropriate rituals, dances, songs and teachings (all in proverbial form), initiatory objects, paraphernalia, and emblems. Many of the objects used are derived from the natural environment: chimpanzee skulls, hornbill beaks, turtle carapaces, pangolin claws and scales, giant snail shells, and hundreds of similar objects. Others are man-made artifacts done primarily in wood, ivory, and bone, but occasionally also in soapstone or resin. In this classification would be included not only the well-known human and animal figurines and masks and masquettes, but also strictly ceremonial objects, such as hornbill knives, daggers, hammers, axes, pins, and spoons, as well as miniature wooden doors, shields, and chairs.

Figurines and masks represent only one of the many categories of objects used by the *bwami,* and they convey but one set of teachings and meanings within the total framework. From the Lega point of view, the top part of a pangolin tail is just as significant, just as charged with symbolism and meaning, as any of the beautiful statues.

THE *KINDI* ARISTOCRATS

In most areas of Lega country the highest *bwami* grade is called *kindi* (see fig. 1.1). It is subdivided into three or four subgrades, each with its own set of initiatory cycles. The various initiations that lead from the lower grades to *kindi* are time- and energy-consuming. Few individuals get as far as *kindi,* and no one makes it before the age of 50. Attainment of this highest grade, however, is not restricted to members in certain privileged lineages or clans, nor is it related to a man's structural

FIGURE 1.1. Lega. *Mwami* of the high-est level in the *kindi* grade, wearing paraphernalia of his rank: hat with ele-phant tail, belt from bongo antelope skin, skirt of wild-cat skin. Kivu Prov-ince. (Photograph: author, 1952.)

position in these groups. Males in almost all known clans in both junior and senior lineage groupings have been initiated into *kindi*. Most clans at any given time will have more than one member who has reached *kindi* grade.

The completion of all cycles of the highest subgrade of *kindi* is considered by the Lega to be the greatest possible ritual and social achievement. Persons who have reached this grade have shown them-selves to be masters of social relationships (since they needed much cooperation from many people to reach it). They are looked upon as outstanding examples of virtue and morality. They have successfully passed through all initiatory experiences, assimilating the teachings and values connected with them, and for that reason they are also consid-ered the very wisest. We would be inclined to call them aristocrats, although the simple Greek concept *aristoi* (very best) would be a better designation for them. Lega have many comments to make about the *kindi*. Among other things, the *kindi* are said to be unifiers, men of love (*malebo*), men of peace (*kinkutu*). They are men with a heart; com-pared to them, all others are like "shoulderbags with a mouth but with no heart." They are sharers and distributors, generous and responsible (*mukota wa kabilundu*). They are strong men, "strong as the stam-

FIGURE 1.2. Lega. Large ivory statue considered to be *nina* (mother) of all smaller statues held by the *kindi* of a single ritual community. A symbol of social cohesion and ritual autonomy, the statue was called Wankenge (the Beautiful Youth). Musée Royal de l'Afrique Centrale, Tervuren (55.3.145). Ht. 7.4" (18.7 cm). (Photograph: Museum.)

peding of elephants." It is noteworthy that these virtues are represented iconically in ivory statues (see figs. 1.2–1.4).

Kindi members of highest achievement, in principle, all have equal status; membership in specific kinship groups certainly does not influence their position. Nonetheless, there are distinctions based on seniority in the grade and on prestige and fame connected with generosity, equity, and skill as a preceptor. To be a complete *kindi,* a man must have at least one of his wives initiated into the highest female grade (*bunyamwa*), which establishes an indissoluble marriage bond between the spouses.

FIGURE 1.3. Lega. Ivory statue individually held by a *kindi*. It represents Kuboko Kumozi (One Arm), the quarrelsome man who became disfigured as a result of his aggressiveness. Author's collection. Ht. 5.4″ (13.7 cm). (Photograph: author.)

FIGURE 1.4. Lega. Ivory statue individually held by a *kindi*. It represents Kakinga, the little woman who indulged in adultery and disturbed the social and ritual balance of the group into which she married. This is an example of the frequent absence of form-meaning equivalence in Lega art. Musée Royal de l'Afrique Centrale, Tervuren (55.3.24). Ht. 4.4″ (10.9 cm). (Photograph: Museum.)

MEANING AND FUNCTION OF *KINDI* ART

Practically speaking, all wooden, ivory, and bone animal and human statues are made for, owned, and used by members of the two highest *bwami* grades (*yananio* and *kindi*). There are marked differences in the usage of these objects and in the conditions of their ownership and transfer. In some areas, members of various subgrades within the two highest grades are entitled to particular categories of masks and statues; in other areas, only members of the highest subgrade in each of the two highest grades may own and use them. Regardless of geographical origin, ownership of ivory objects is the privilege of members of the highest grade; wooden objects are shared by members of the two highest grades, but are most numerous among those of *yananio*. Members of the three lower grades are not entitled to possess or manipulate these objects; this, however, does not prevent their occasional use and interpretation in the context of lower initiations (in which members of the highest grades invariably participate). The question now is: what do these carvings do in these initiations and what do they mean to their owners? I will focus my attention on the ivory and bone human figurines used by the highest *kindi* (see figs. 1.2–1.5).

The major display of these statues usually occurs in one of the very last initiatory rites of *kindi*. This rite is known both as *kinsamba* (a word which refers to a multitude of very white and highly coveted mushrooms) and as *bele muno* ("those who are among us"). In contrast to most others, this rite is always extremely simple. The group of *kindi* initiates sits in a circle, either in the initiation hut (*lubungu*) or in the middle of the village (from which noninitiates and all initiates who have not gotten as far as this stage in the rite have been cleared). The new initiate is led in by his tutors. A proverb, "His one, his one, the great one of the *kabilundu* tree," is sung by one of the preceptors; this is a sign. The initiates who are present take off their hats, place them on the ground in front of them, and from their shoulderbags take one or more statues, which they rest against their hats. One of the initiates then places a large ivory statue (see fig. 1.5) in the middle of the circle of hats and smaller statues. There is none of the drumming, dancing, or singing which occur in almost all other rites. The situation is unique in that some of the statues are explained by means of proverbs. A considerable distribution of goods takes place, and following this exchange the initiate receives one or more statues from his *mukomi*-tutor. This statue (or these statues) may have been left by a dead *kindi* of the new initiate's kinship group whom he now replaces. There may not be any such statues available, in which case the new initiate receives in temporary trust the above-mentioned large statue until his own smaller statue

FIGURE 1.5. Lega. Display of ivory statues in the middle of the *kindi* hats at the *kinsamba* rite. The larger ivory figurine is the "mother" of the others. The hats have a raffia framework on which buttons or beads (formerly cowries or small nutshells) are sewn; they are surmounted by an elephant tail. The number of hats and statues displayed is generally much greater than that seen in this photograph, depending upon the number of participating *kindi*. Kivu Province. Ht. ranges from 4″ (10 cm) to 8.5″ (21.5 cm). (Photograph: author, 1952.)

has been carved. At the end of the rite, the order to "pluck the *kinsamba* mushrooms" is given by one of the preceptors, and all *kindi* put their statues back in their shoulderbags. The entire rite is impressive both because of the magnificent display and because of the unusual parsimony of words, gestures, and rhythms.

Some of the meanings of the ivory statues can readily be derived from this context.

a. They are badges or emblems of rank, like many other objects which the same *kindi* possess. Only persons of the right initiatory experience can hold and manipulate these objects. None of the *kindi* are permitted to participate in the *kinsamba* rite if they fail to produce their statue(s).

b. They are prestige symbols. Few individuals get to the initiatory level where they are allowed to possess these ivory carvings. Once they have achieved this level, however, they become involved in an effort to acquire many statues, either permanently or temporarily in trust. When, for example, a *kindi* dies, a colleague known for his wisdom and virtue is chosen to act as *mukondi we idumba,* guardian of the grave. After the mourning period is over, that person receives in temporary trust statues and masks which were in the dead *kindi's* possession. It is understood that these sculptures are to be transferred ultimately to the new initiate who will replace the dead *kindi,* but several years may elapse before such a successor is found. Nobody is thought to be a perfect *kindi* until he has fulfilled the guardianship function at least once in his lifetime. When an individual at the *kinsamba* rite displays several statues, it is an immediate indication of his virtue and perfection, a source of his prestige and reputation.

c. All statues are associated with proverbs, one or more for every piece. The proverbs contain valuable teachings for the initiates. They express the ethical code of *bwami,* either positively (fig. 1.2) or in a contrasting negative way (figs. 1.3, 1.4). The values which the statues convey are not fundamentally different from those expressed through the medium of much simpler objects at other stages of the *bwami* initiations. But these teachings, when iconically represented in *kindi* art forms, reach a dramatic climax of intensity and directness. Yet nothing is more deceptive than to try to read meanings into the forms of Lega ivory statues. Only the Lega know those meanings and their associations with specific forms or contexts. The forms of Lega statues only occasionally exhibit a visible connection with the meanings associated with them. For the large majority of carvings, equivalences between form and meaning are totally absent or, at least for us, not directly understandable.

Let us take a few examples. Many Lega statues have more than one head or face; some have two heads, some others have from two to six faces. Regardless of the number, these carvings invariably represent "The man with many big heads who has seen an elephant on the other side of the large river." In one set of interpretations they illustrate one group of qualities expected from a *kindi:* equity, wisdom, discernment, and the gift of looking in various directions. In another set of interpretations they represent the idea of continuity: one *kindi* dies, another *kindi* will be initiated; a father dies, his son succeeds him. In this case one can certainly find some link between form and the meaning conveyed by it. There are also statues with one arm which symbolize the aggressive and quarrelsome individual (what a *kindi* never should be!) who lost an arm as a result of hot temper (fig. 1.3). There are still others with huge raised hands which represent the *kindi* as peacemakers and arbiters and express the threat of *kitampo* (the destructive effect originating from the nonobservance of the *bwami*'s decisions). In most cases, however, these fairly easy form-meaning equations cannot be found. This holds particularly for the many statues that represent the Trouble-Maker, the Old Man, the Beautiful Youth, the Young Maiden (fig. 1.4), the Ill-Tempered One, and so on.

Basically, all Lega ivory statues fall into one of two categories of meanings: those that stand for *bunene* (good, good luck, perfection, greatness, achievement, success, and reputation) and those that illustrate *bwanya* (evil, bad luck, lack of moderation, and any other behavior patterns which a real *kindi* should not exemplify). Finally, more than one meaning may be conveyed by a single statue, and two or more statues may have complementary meanings and be used jointly.

We have already mentioned the larger ivory statue that is placed in the middle of a circle of hats and smaller figurines during the *kinsamba* rite (fig. 1.5). These larger pieces are not possessed individually. Members of a localized clan or, in some cases, a number of ritually linked maximal lineages, eventually of different clan origin, share but one such carving. These statues are kept in trust for the whole community either by the most ancient *kindi* of that group or by that lineage, one of whose members is said to have reached the *kindi* grade in the remote past. Such statues are not classified by the Lega under a special generic term; they are called *iginga* like all the others. But in their interpretations the *kindi* tend to conceive of them as *nina* (the mother), as female progenitors from whom all the other individually held ivory figurines originated. Whatever the case may be, these pieces are symbols of social cohesion and of ritual autonomy. The final *kindi* rites within a given community (a localized clan or linked maximal lineages) cannot be held without the presence of such a statue. Mock resistance on the part of its guardian must be overcome by gift-giving and dialogue. On the other hand, any community which has acquired such a statue can autonomously organize its highest *kindi* rites.

It is noteworthy that one of the names of the rites in which the main display of statues occurs is *kinsamba*. This term, as mentioned before, refers to a particular species of very white mushrooms which grow gregariously. As does the name for the bongo antelope, the word *kinsamba* stands for everything very beautiful and good. In this ceremony the *kindi* implicitly emphasize the great beauty and goodness of both their statues and themselves. These two concepts, expressed as *busoga,* arise over and over again within the context of all *bwami* initiations. The great *kindi* is beautiful and good. Utmost care, in this respect, is given to the ivory statues, which are oiled with castor oil and perfumed in the same manner as the *kindi* oil and perfume their own bodies.

Some other meanings and usages of the ivory statues are not fully illustrated within the framework of the *kinsamba* rite. It is clear that none of them serves as a medium through which worship for ancestors or spirits is channeled. Yet connections with basic religious ideas are apparent from the following usages. A dead *kindi* is buried in the house of his first *kanyamwa,* the wife with whom he passed through the *itutu* (roof-top) rite. His ivory statues, ivory mask, and some other paraphernalia are displayed on the tomb until after the end of the mourning period, at which time these objects are taken into temporary trusteeship by the guardian of the grave. Rather than asserting that the spirit or the soul of the dead *kindi* enters the statue, the Lega, on the contrary, repeatedly stress the fact that the dead are *kiligeza,* that they disappear altogether and never come back. What continues to exist, the people affirm, is the *bwami* association in which the dead *kindi* represent a vital chain, together with the objects that were associated with them and are destined to pass on to the succeeding *kindi*. One could say then that these statues, among other things, are the external symbols of this never-ending chain of initiations and thus of the perenniality of *bwami* itself. Any ivory statue which has passed through several hands over a number of generations symbolizes a chain of linked dead *kindi*.

The supreme rite in which the ivory statues are used en masse is also called typically *bele muno* ("those who are among us here"). The inference that might be drawn from this is that the *kindi* ranks are composed of two entities: the living *kindi* and the statues, which represent a known chain of successive generations of *kindi* linked through common kinship and ritual substitution for one another. It is not strange, then, that for the Lega, these ivory statues contain and present *magala* (force). In cases of distress or illness, the *kindi* sandpapers the back of his statue with leaves until he creates some dust, which he then mixes with water and drinks as a potent protective.

The story of Lega sculpture within the context of the *bwami* association is an intricate and multifaceted one. In the total system of initiations, the human figurines in ivory and bone represent only a minor fraction of the entire set of devices used dramatically to underline the ethics and ideas for which the association stands. The analysis presented here has established the multivalence of meanings and functions attached to a single category of carved objects. Simple stereotypes cannot account for this multivalence. Lega sculpture is deeply embedded in a system of ideas and social relationships which are typical, though

by no means unique, for the Lega. Their art cannot be arbitrarily iso-
lated from this system without gross distortion, nor can it be readily
reduced to our current functional interpretations. The ivory statues are
the iconic abstracts of these ideas and values. They do not depict these
things, but rather they *are* the values. They—the statues, the values—
sustain the *bwami* association and the Lega society at large and sym-
bolize the cohesion and endurance of both institutions. Perhaps coinci-
dentally, the generic term *iginga,* which is used to refer to all the human
figurines, is paralleled by the Lega with the verb *kuginga,* "to sustain, to
protect from falling or collapsing." The *bwami* association itself acts as
an integrator of Lega society, preserving among potentially conflicting
kinship groups an ethical code built on goodness, virtue, and peace.

CHAPTER 2

Chokwe: POLITICAL ART IN A PLEBIAN SOCIETY

Daniel J. Crowley

The chief significance of Chokwe art in the present context stems from the fact that though the Chokwe are a poor plebian people with little claim to aristocracy, they nevertheless produce magnificent objects expressive of status distinctions. The lowly social position of the Chokwe results primarily from their mixed origins, but it has been intensified by the poverty of their homeland, by their immigrant status in neighboring countries, and, recently, by their excessive willingness to conform to European ways. Chokwe legendary history helps explain these peculiar relationships with surrounding peoples.

In the early sixteenth century, a tribe then called Bungu is said to have migrated from the northeast and settled in the region between the Bushimaie and Lubilashi rivers in what is now the southwestern Congo (Kinshasa). This people's present name, Lunda (from their word for "friendship"), reflects the good relations which existed among various subgroups, who recognized an elder chief as final authority. Since they were matrilineal, one would expect that the ruler would be succeeded by his sister's son, but evidently the Lunda paramount chief customarily chose his own son as his successor. Several centuries ago, one of these supreme chiefs, named Yala Mwaku, or Konde, had two sons, Chinguli and Chiniama, and a daughter, Lueji. Because of a family quarrel he

Note: The field research on which this chapter is based was carried out between January and August 1960 from headquarters at Dilolo Gare, Katanga. The author wishes to thank the Ford Foundation Foreign Area Training Program for the support which made this research possible.

by-passed the two brothers and chose Lueji as chieftainess, an unusual alternative but still well within the range of possibility in matrilineal societies. Lueji, a remarkable woman who reigned at the end of the sixteenth century, married an aristocratic Luba hunter named Chibunda Ilunga. Soon after, while she was segregated in the menstrual hut, her husband stole the symbol of Lunda authority, the *lukano,* a magical bracelet made from male genitalia. Henceforth he ruled the Lunda and changed their kinship system to one based on patrilineal descent to ensure that his sons would succeed him.

In disgust at his father's disregard for tradition, Chinguli and his followers then left the court and founded a new ethnic group, the Mbangala, in northwestern Angola. The second brother, Chiniama, with other disaffected nobles, journeyed southward to the Zambezi basin, intermarried with the aboriginal Ganguella-Mbwela peoples, and established the Luena or Luvale people. Subsequent migrations produced the Chokwe, Luchazi, and other groups; indeed, the name Chokwe is thought to derive from Lueji's dictum to the dissident nobles, "Akioko a ku Kinguri" ("Go then to Chinguli"). The successors of Lueji established the powerful, centralized Lunda empire, whose ruler is called the Mwata Yamvo (Mwatsiavua in Chichokwe) and to this day rules from Musumba near Kapanga in the southwestern Congo. The Chokwe grudgingly recognize Lunda suzerainty over them by paying tribute, but at least three times in the last half of the nineteenth century they invaded Lunda territory and captured or killed the reigning Mwata Yamvo. Relations between the two peoples have evidently always been ambivalent; frequent affirmations that they are "sons of the same mother," extensive intermarriage, and peaceful interpenetration and settlement of each other's territory are balanced against murderous riots and raids. Actually the two cultures are now fairly distinct in language, kinship, and political organization within the framework of the Central Bantu culture province. Understandably the Chokwe resent the grand manner, casual language, and condescension of the Lunda, who in turn disdain the Chokwe as greedy upstarts.[1]

Unfortunately, the Chokwe have an even more powerful antagonist in the Portuguese, who have controlled their homeland for the last century. Uchokwe is an area of desolate scrub land divided by swampy valleys with rivers that flow northward to empty into the Congo tribu-

1. The Lunda and Chokwe legendary history synthesized here has been reported in many conflicting sources; for the most useful compendium, see McCulloch 1951, pp. 9–14, 32–35. For a brilliant synthesis of the Lunda point of view, see Vansina 1966, pp. 155–179.

taries. Before the Portuguese domination of northeastern Angola, the Chokwe lived as hunters and desultory agriculturalists in this forbidding land. As their numbers grew and the game decreased, they took over the role of slavers, raiding their neighbors and selling the slaves to the Portuguese factors at Bihé (now Silva Porto). Indubitably a number of Chokwe were also enslaved in this process, since political enemies, criminals, and captives from intertribal conflicts were also sold into slavery. As the Portuguese extended their hegemony, the Chokwe political leaders fought them at every opportunity, and with each successive defeat more and more Chokwe migrated eastward into the Congo (Kinshasa) and northwestern Zambia, where they settled, more or less peacefully, in the lands of the Lunda and the Lozi (Rotse). Even today Chokwe continue to leave Angola to escape Portuguese forced labor in lieu of paying taxes.

Any such migration is inevitably selective, with those who are younger and more active migrating while the older and more complacent remain at home. This selectivity explains to a certain extent the reputation for aggressiveness the Chokwe have earned among the Belgians and British, and for that matter among the other Africans whose territory they have infiltrated. Ironically enough, colonialists all too often seem to admire the conservative local groups that resist acculturation and hold to their traditional ways, and to despise the groups that seek advancement in the colonial hierarchy through conformity and conversion. Cases in point are the Lulua, consistently favored by the Belgians over the more Europeanized Luba-Kasai, or the Lozi, whose centralized kingdom was singled out by the British for status superior to that of all other ethnic groups in Zambia. In fairness it must be added that the Europeans were following local African precedents in both cases, because these conservative groups, like the Lunda, are considered to possess the *droit du premier occupant* (Griaule 1938, p. 55). In effect this much-debated legal position means not that these ethnic groups are actually the aboriginal inhabitants of their territory, but merely that they were in possession of it at the time of the European takeover less than a century ago. Inevitably, with the exploitation of natural resources and the development of cities, there have been vast movements of population, not the least of which was the diaspora of the Chokwe. Their colonies can now be found in Kinshasa, Lubumbashi, Luanda, Livingstone, and even in far-off Johannesburg; and Chokwe agriculturalists appear in large numbers in southern former Léopoldville Province, in western former Katanga Province of the Congo (Kinshasa), in the Balovale and Barotseland areas of Zambia, and throughout Angola south and west of Uchokwe.

Thus the Chokwe, who now number almost one million, live in at least five countries, have experienced three colonial regimes, and are everywhere subject to alien political power, whether that of the Portuguese at home, the Lunda in all the lands around Uchokwe, or the various governments of the Congo, Zambia, Rhodesia, and South Africa. The Chokwe, moreover, long ago developed their own social structure with distinct levels of aristocracy in the families of Grand Chefs and chiefs of *chefferies* and villages. As in other aspects of Chokwe culture, regional variation is the rule, so much so that there is no "paramount" chief known to and accepted by all of the Chokwe, and no traditional concept of centralized rule. Even within Angola, the Congo, and Zambia, opinions differ widely as to which chief is superior to which other chief, a matter that depends largely on lineage loyalties, and is more or less independent of the chiefs' official position in the central government hierarchy. Furthermore, traditional status has been modified through long contact with the Lunda overlords, by the colonial pre-emption of traditional governmental structures, and by the imposition by the former colonial powers of quasitraditional officers such as the Congolese *Chef du Secteur,* roles largely continued by the now independent African governments. The result is predictably chaotic, with chiefs of questionable credentials given governmental recognition and support while other authentic traditional chiefs who command the loyalty of thousands remain unrecognized and unsupported by government, sometimes as much through the chief's own choice as through the ignorance or ill will of government officials. Because of the constant struggle for place among the lineages and their various representatives, revocation of official chiefly status, assassinations, and extended legal battles are all commonplace in modern Chokwe political life.

Suffice it to say that for all the low status assigned the Chokwe by others, they themselves understandably ascribe the highest status to their own Grand Chefs, whom they consider to be at least on a par with those of the Lunda. The effects of this double standard of status on Chokwe art forms, an analysis of the functions of the art objects in manifesting and supporting Chokwe political authority, and a comparison of Chokwe-Lunda artistic relations will be the subject of the remainder of this chapter.

THE FORMS OF CHOKWE ART

The Chokwe distinguish between only two types of artists, the *songi* or woodcarver, and the *fuli* or blacksmith; but they also consider as aesthetic certain objects produced in such media as clay, leather, bark

ꜰɪɢᴜʀᴇ 2.1. Chokwe. Dance masks. Chihongo (left) and Katoyo (right). Mwa Tshisenge's lage, Lualaba (Katanga). Ht. 10″ (25.4 cm). (Photograph: Frank O. Biedka.)

cloth, fiber, and a number of grasses, reeds, and roots used in basketry. A great deal of nonsense has been written about the supposed indissoluble relationship between African traditional religion and art; as far as the Chokwe are concerned, religious art is limited to a folk expression practiced by most men when they are called upon to make shrine figures *(mahamba)* and miniature charms *(jinga)* for use in private hunting, love, and fertility magic. In fact, each Chokwe male who has been through the ritual circumcision and initiation "school" *(mukanda)* has received at least a modicum of training in dancing, musicianship, and carving, and considers himself a potential expert. Famous carvers and blacksmiths are considered fully professional, even though they usually supplement their income by growing their own staple foods. In the larger villages, professional male potters and tailors, and both male and female matmakers and basketmakers, ply their trades, selling from door to door and in the weekly markets. There is also considerable

FIGURE 2.2. Chokwe. Bark-cloth mask. Chikusa, master of the *mukanda* lodge. Museum of Cultural History, University of California, Los Angeles (X67-2125). Ht. 56" (142.2 cm). (Photograph: Museum.)

exchange of art objects and craft products through an elaborate system of gift exchanges, particularly among women.

The masked dancers who conduct the *mukanda* ceremonies are the prime subjects of Chokwe art. It is estimated that there are about thirty stock characters (singular, *mukishi*; plural, *mikishi*) represented by masked dancers throughout Uchokwe, but it is uncertain—in the minds of most contemporary Congolese Chokwe at least—whether they represent guardian spirits or deified ancestors. In any case, only four of these masked personages are essential in today's *mukanda*, although eight or ten commonly appear. The four, listed below, are so common

FIGURE 2.3. Chokwe. Bark-cloth mask. Kalelwa. Musée Royal de l'Afrique Centrale, Tervuren (33781 4/1). Ht. 30" (76.2 cm). (Photograph: Museum.)

they will be recognized immediately by anyone who has examined even a few pieces:

a. Chihongo (Chirongo in Angola) (fig. 2.1, left), a stern old chief represented by a bark-cloth or wooden mask with jutting horizontal beard and large, swooping, "off-the-face" headdress (often mistakenly called a coiffure). He is perhaps the commonest representation in Chokwe art.

b. Chikuza (fig. 2.2), the "master of the *mukanda* lodge," another stern-faced bark-cloth mask with a horizontal beard and tall conical headdress surmounted by a dangling tassel.

c. Kalelwa (fig. 2.3), a third male mask of bark cloth, surmounted by a large sombrero-like headdress with wide, curved brim and high, elaborated crown.

d. Mwana Pwo (fig. 2.4), a wooden mask representing "Young Girl," but always danced by a man in a skin-tight knitted fiber costume with false breasts and a bustle-like appendage decorated with fringe or tassels.

Other masks that appear frequently include Chizaluke, a smaller bark-cloth mask with a headdress of three raised knobs and a semi-circular, "existentialist" beard; Chiheu, "Impotent Man," a small bark-cloth mask with protruding teeth and knobs at the temples (the Chiheu dancer sometimes employs a large wooden phallus); Ngondo, a bark-cloth mask with large concave eyes and a high crest from nose to back

FIGURE 2.4. Chokwe. Wooden mask. Mwana Pwo (Young Girl). Musée Royal de l'Afrique Centrale, Tervuren (32510). Ht. 8.8" (22.5 cm). (Photograph: Museum.)

of head; and Linya Pwa (fig. 2.5), a bark-cloth or wooden mask with bulging cheeks and a high, rounded crest which runs from ear to ear across the top of the head. Most of the other *mukanda* masks are variants of these and cannot readily be differentiated by any but Chokwe elders. Women are taught to believe that the masked dancers are actual spirits, but of course they recognize their husbands, brothers, and sons. Two non-*mukanda* masks also occur frequently in Chokwe art: Ngulu,

FIGURE 2.5. Luena. Dance mask.
Linya Pwa (Beautiful Woman).
Katende Chipoye village, Lualaba
(Katanga). Ht. 24″ (61 cm).
(Photograph: Frank O. Biedka.)

a realistic wooden mask of a pig; and Katoyo (fig. 2.1, right), a bark-cloth mask with a strip of contrasting color across the eyes, indicating illness or insanity. Both masks are clowns and are used in village dances, political rallies, and sometimes in conjunction with *mukanda* masks when they appear at secular festivals.[2]

It would be deceptively simple to describe the *mikishi* as the deities of the Chokwe, but actually the Creator god, Nzambi or Kalunga, is aloof from the affairs of men and never appears in iconography. In the contemporary Congo, where half the Chokwe are Christian, the religious aspect of the *mikishi* might be compared to that of Santa Claus in an American·city—figures of ancient piety now reduced to generalized symbols of festivity. It is in this way also that the *mikishi* are used on most of the art objects made for leaders—that is to say, as suitably ethnic decorations with only vague reference to religious belief. This attitude was observed among the Katanga Chokwe at least, but may not be the case to the northwest in the Kwango and Kwilu, nor in deepest Angola, although I observed secular use of *mukanda* masks near Dundo and Xa-Cassau, Angola, in May 1960.

The Chokwe aristocratic tradition is most clearly objectified in obviously secular objects, particularly in the furnishings and decorations of a chief's house. The variety, number, and high quality of these objects are surprising, and indeed their surface decoration has been the subject of a two-volume monograph (Bastin 1961). In fact, the contrast between the spectacular coloristic qualities of *mukanda* and the somber surface richness of secular objects gives Chokwe art a range of styles lacking elsewhere in Africa; only the Yoruba and perhaps the Kuba appear to produce a comparable variety of objects in contrasting styles.

THE ART OF CHOKWE CHIEFS

No matter how lowly the origins of the initiates, the *mukanda* is always organized and supported by at least one village chief, and more often by a chief of a *chefferie*. In this context, the *mukanda* can be seen to be an institution wherein Chokwe religion, art, and social organization are transmitted to the next generation in a secret, dramatic manner which excludes women and uncircumcised boys. But if *mukanda* does not

2. Bark-cloth masks are formed over a framework of bent sticks and are then decorated with black tree-resin and red and white clay. Brown paper, commercial paints, and red trade cloth sometimes replace the more traditional materials. José Redinha (1956, p. 16) thinks these masks represent a type more ancient than the wooden masks, even those depicting such *mukanda* subjects as Chihongo, Mwana Pwo, and Linya Pwa.

make the initiates any more than fully enculturated Chokwe men, it does serve to impress them with the rightness of the traditional political status quo and of the quasihistorical bases of class distinctions. As a result, for all the turmoil brought on by independence, the Chokwe, along with other more politically sophisticated African peoples, have tended to put their political trust in their chiefs and have not yet seriously questioned their right to privilege. Such continuity is not accidental, since Chokwe chiefs have consistently played their traditionally assigned roles to the fullest and used every available device to impress their followers with their power, magnificence, and right to rule.

The chief of a Katangese Chokwe *chefferie* lives in a carefully laid-out village built around an open space called a *place* (after the French word). Most houses are whitewashed, often with a high pink or earth-red wainscotting, and have small, wooden-shuttered windows and crudely adzed doors. In some villages women and boys paint stick figures, outlines of *mukanda* personages, and abstract designs (Redinha 1953) on the whitewashed exterior walls of their houses; in other villages which have access to commercial paints the houses are decorated à la Gauguin in six or eight deep contrasting colors. The chief's house and related outbuildings usually fill one side of the square, and other sides may have an open structure used for the proceedings of the local judiciary, the homes of wives or male relatives of the chief, a storage house for drums, *mukanda* costumes and masks, and other dancing paraphernalia, a traveler's resthouse (often in an advanced state of disrepair), and invariably in the square itself a flagpole and a small circular *chota,* or men's hut. The *places* are mostly bare of grass, but it is there the *muyombo* or ancestor tree is planted.

The central square is the setting for all communal activities of the village—secular dancing, the opening and closing ceremonies of *mukanda,* political activities, and official functions of the chief's court. Every chief worthy of his title maintains a staff of artist-courtiers, most of whom are semiprofessionals who supplement what they earn in cash or in kind from the chief with the produce of their own agricultural labors. When the occasion arises, as at the surprise visit of a political dignitary, a very presentable dance can be arranged in the matter of a half hour, with boys running to bring out the drums and *chikuvu* (slit gong) and others making small fires to tense the drumheads. The lead drummer warms up on any handy surface, while the dancers don their masks and are sewn into their knitted fiber costumes. If a visitor is sufficiently important, the chief will change his khaki trousers and shirt for a pleated kilt of "African print" trade cloth, a waiter's white jacket, a traditional crown of brightly colored trade beads threaded on wire, long Argyle stockings, heavy polished brogues, silver medals presented by Belgian sovereigns, and, as a final flourish, a small leopard skin thrown across his lap or under his feet. He will carry a ceremonial hatchet of local metalwork, elaborate in form and richly incised, with a carved wooden handle, and may wear a fine locally made sword in a tooled leather scabbard. A large wooden hair comb may be tucked into his belt; and, if he plans to dance, he may carry a fly whisk made of a gnu or antelope tail, with a carved wood or bone handle sometimes decorated with nailheads or trade beads.

The chief occupies the place of honor on the raised verandah in front of his home, usually under the central catenary arch reminiscent of Belgian domestic architecture. His chair is either an imported ply-wood model or an overstuffed lounge chair, unless he still owns a carved Chokwe chair, more correctly called a throne (fig. 2.6). These truly fantastic creations are among the largest objects ever made by African artists, and almost certainly derive from Renaissance models, possessing as they do such telltale characteristics as splat backs, runners, leather seats, and a plenitude of imported brass nailheads. One throne now in the collection of the Museu do Dundo in Angola (Companhia de Diamantes de Angola 1959, pl. 9; Bastin 1961, 2, pl. 192) is well over six feet tall, and every splat and runner is covered with genre sub-jects and *mukanda* personages. Other superb examples in diverse styles can be found in Dundo, Lisbon, Berlin, Tervuren, and numerous pri-vate collections, which explains in part why chiefs nowadays tend to sit on plywood.

With their deeply carved backs and arms and sagging leather seats, these thrones are spectacularly uncomfortable to sit upon; but in the past the Chokwe, accustomed to stools but not to chairs, undoubtedly rested their weight only on the front edge of the seat and did not lean back to be impaled on the carved splats. Small thrones resembling chil-dren's chairs and approximately the height of stools are often carried around for the occasional use of a chief when walking through a village or visiting a market. Although some very old thrones exist in the collec-tion of the Sociedade de Geografia in Lisbon, no documentation has yet been uncovered to prove that these were originally commissioned by Portuguese. On the contrary, the arrangement and content of the scenes do not seem to follow an overall plan such as a European might request, the illustration of a folktale or the progressive stages in a ritual (fig. 2.7). Instead, genre subjects (such as women pounding in a mortar) are mixed with scenes of *mukanda* circumcision, Europeans in pith helmets being carried in tipoys, rows of dancers in grass skirts, soldiers with rifles, Chihongo and Mwana Pwo, abstract animals carved in the simplified style of *mahamba* (shrine figures), and, most curious of all,

FIGURE 2.6. Chokwe. Throne, gift of Mwa Tshisenge. Musée Royal de l'Afrique Centrale, Tervuren (53.67.10). Ht. 40″ (101.6 cm). (Photograph: Museum.)

erotic subjects. The contemporary Chokwe are rather repressed and puritanical, painfully modest, strict in prohibiting women from working or visiting outside the home, and not given to ribaldry or humorous badinage. Since these activities are left to masked dancers, particularly the phallic Chiheu, the eroticism on the thrones may simply be representative or compensatory, but the "French postcard" effects were undoubtedly popular with European soldiers and administrators as trophies of their African adventures.

Although the thrones are the most spectacular examples of all Chokwe aristocratic paraphernalia, many other subjects elaborated far beyond the requirements of function are made in support of chiefly

FIGURE 2.7. Chokwe. Throne, detail. Musée Royal de l'Afrique Centrale, Tervuren (48.40.48). Ht. (overall) 29.5″ (75 cm). (Photograph: Museum.)

power. Stools of several types are used as portable seats. Caryatid stools were evidently made in northeastern Angola; these are cylindrical in form with a kneeling female caryatid, not unlike the stools of the neighboring Kanioka and Luba. Four-legged stools with leather seats are still common, some being decorated with *tuponya* (singular, *kaponya*), small doll-like figures of masked dancers or animals colored with *ngula* (red clay) and fastened to the runners with pegs. Like the thrones, these *tuponya* stools tell no story but are simply an assemblage of traditional carving subjects. Beautifully crafted four-legged stools and, occasionally, chairs are made in the Alto Zambeze Province of east central Angola, probably near Caianda; they can be recognized by the thinness of the legs and splats, the flat, incised crosshatching, and the delicate low relief carvings of abstract human figures and snakes. These stools also have leather seats and are sometimes polychromed in dull gray and earth tan. Their rareness and the specific provenience so often given in otherwise casual documentation suggest that they are the products of a single small regional "school" of carvers. Other fine four-legged stools have each leg carved as a *kaponya* or figure, usually of *mukanda* origin (Bastin 1961, 2, pl. 180), and may even have free-standing *tuponya* in place of a back.

Other kinds of chairs made by the Chokwe include a heavy, squarish version of an upholstered parlor chair done in wicker basketry over a wooden frame and a folding deck-chair which has genre carvings on the frame and a sling made of fine matting (Bastin 1961, 2, pl. 201), which is too slippery, however, to allow the sitter's body to stay in place. These objects, although offensive to the antiquarian, are no more neologistic than the thrones and serve just as well to display the worldly connections of the chief and, by extension, those of his carvers.

The front verandah of the chief's house has already been described as the stage on which he performs many of his professional functions. In the mild climate of Katanga it also serves as his reception and waiting room and is suitably furnished with a melange of imported and traditional objects. Among the latter are fine fiber mats on the floor, and large *tuponya* figures, often three feet or more in height, carved from a single tree trunk. These figures, used exclusively by chiefs, stand or lean against the verandah wall and have no function beyond the decorative. Their style is abstract and simplified, the undercutting being somewhat carelessly executed; the features and cicatrizations are crudely indicated by pyroengraving, and the whole figure is then washed over in red clay. Subjects are minimally described *mukanda* personages such as Chikuza, who is shown with his characteristic conical hat but is otherwise undifferentiated from any other figure. Although biologically complete, these figures almost always wear a skirt or kilt of trade cloth nailed or tied around the torso.

Equally frequent articles of interior decoration are the carved wooden snakes and birds which are found in almost every house, chiefly or not, that has any pretensions toward elegance. These carvings are executed in light wood and are either painted with commercial colors or, more commonly, blackened with lampblack or by means of pyroengraving and are then incised in intricate two-tone designs. Both birds and snakes are varied enough to be identified by their local taxonomic names and are often the subject of admiring comments as they grace table tops and verandah railings. Trusted informants were asked about possible religious or symbolic significance; they consistently denied any, and one retorted, "This is what we like. What do you want us to make for your house?" Understandably, the European custom of decorating walls with masks and other ceremonial paraphernalia is hardly suitable in a society where these objects are forbidden to women. Albert Maesen (1964 personal communication) reports finding similar snakes and birds among

Kwango Chokwe with some indication that they once had fertility significance.

Another symbol of wealth, also not limited to the homes of chiefs, is the *mulondo* (plural, *milondo*) or pottery water pitcher, a large, nearly spherical teapot-like ewer with an integral pottery handle and spout, often surmounted by a sculptured top or lid in the form of a human head, an animal, or a bird. One old example, said to derive from Angola, shows a full-length female figure seated atop the *mulondo*. Most of the subjects are generalized human beings, but *mukanda* personages, *kanga* birds, and turtles are also common. The pots are nearly always blackened, with a pocked, shiny surface which is neither polished nor glazed, but a few examples from the Luena *chefferie* of Katende Jean are a biscuit white. These ewers are almost certainly of European inspiration, but no potter could be found who did not consider them to be entirely traditional Chokwe ware.

A chief's house also contains fine baskets made by his wives, sisters, and retainers, but similarly fine baskets can be found in many other homes as a result of the widespread basketmaking skill of Chokwe and Luena women. One particular type of basket, the *kafuku*, a cylinder of delicately patterned grass matting on a larger plaited base with a domed, plaited lid, is considered an appropriate gift for a chief to bestow on anyone in his favor. Theoretically, such baskets are supposed to function as portable containers for manioc paste, which is the Katangese staff of life; in practice the Chokwe rarely carry food during field work or go on picnics; in any case, these baskets with their matting sides and single-strand handles are much too fragile for any use beyond display. This is a clear case of the aristocratic bestowal of a virtually functionless art object that forever after symbolizes the approval its possessor once held in the eyes of the reigning power.

CHOKWE-LUNDA ARTISTIC RELATIONS

There are those who feel that Chokwe art represents a decadent tradition either borrowed wholesale from the genuinely aristocratic Lunda and allowed to degenerate, or worse, crudely copied from the Europeans in hopes of equalling the envied Lunda. In this regard, Henri Lavachery (1954, pp. 120–121; translations mine) has pointed out that ". . . the art of the Batshioko [Chokwe], which cannot be distinguished from that of conquered or repelled Balunda, is an important manifestation of the African aesthetic . . . the fact that these images [of fierce, realistically sculpted ancestor figures] were found at the end of the nineteenth century at the moment when the Lunda kingdom collapsed, could suggest that it is a question of a Balunda court art which disappeared with that dispossessed court." Of less realistic, less detailed Chokwe figures he asks, "Archaic art of hunters? Decadent art, like many popular arts? In any case, different in spirit and in form from that represented by the beautiful fierce figures."

Since the historical record described above refers to three Chokwe invasions of the Mwata Yamvo's court, none of them terminal to Lunda power or prestige, one is forced to look elsewhere for an explanation of these two supposedly distinct art styles. Frans Olbrechts (1959, p. 81), however, agrees that it is not easy to distinguish the production of the Chokwe from that of the Lunda and describes Lunda style as similar to that of the Chokwe in all such major details as eyes, genre subjects, and animal motifs, except that the Lunda forms are rounder; even then he postulates a third hybrid style between these two. The only characteristics he assigns exclusively to the Lunda are the "mitre-shaped hairdresses" and the "incised furrow the length of the dorsal spine." These "mitre-shaped hairdresses" are in actuality wigs of fiber dipped in liquid clay, which were worn in past times also by Chokwe notables, particularly women, and are still to be seen on many of the finest Mwana Pwo masks collected in Angola. The incised furrow down the back is also found on many Chokwe pieces, including recent ones made in Katanga.

In point of fact, Chokwe artists, both *songi* and *fuli,* have long been recognized as the masters they are, and the prestige of their skills is so great that chiefs aspire to it (Jaspert and Jaspert 1930, p. 18). The title of John T. Tucker's book, *Angola, the Land of a Blacksmith Prince* (1933), is not without foundation. If a chief lacks such skills, he will be all the more eager to encourage these craftsmen to settle in his capital, become his courtiers, and supply sculpture and fine metalwork to his court and *chefferie.* For example, an important Chokwe chief, the late Mwa Tshisenge of the Lualaba area of southwestern Katanga, employed an Angolan refugee, one Ululi Kombania (that is, "Companhia," so named because he had been born in the enclave of the Companhia de Diamantes de Angola) as court carver; and the young Luena chief Katende Tshilemo paid an old *fuli* handsomely to work in his village. Considering also the high quality of very old pieces in the Lisbon, Tervuren, and Dundo collections, which are always specifically credited to the Chokwe, there seems little reason to accept the contentions of Denise Paulme (1962, p. 130) that "It is difficult to distinguish their [Chokwe] art from that of the earlier masters of the country, but the quality of their modern work is vastly inferior; hence the postulate of a court art of the Lunda disappearing with the collapse of their empire."

Katanga Chokwe like to point out that the Lunda are *not* carvers and use no masks except rudimentary pieces of goatskin with crudely cut-out eyes. They believe that all art objects attributed to the Lunda were actually made by Chokwe, many of whom have served the Mwata Yamvo as courtiers and helped build up his reputedly incomparable collection. If this be so, it helps explain why such dispersed Lunda groups as the Ndembu of northwestern Zambia and the Kazembe Lunda of the Luapula Valley also do not carve, use masks, or make any but the most ordinary crafts.

The simplest explanation in accord with the known facts is that Chokwe art styles vary radically in space and time. The realistic "ancestor figures" so admired by Lavachery (usually representing Chihongo with a European rifle) belong to a northeastern Angolan style which also includes some of the most famous of the Mwana Pwo masks and thrones. This style is distinguished by realistic detail but exaggerated proportions, and polychromy is sacrificed in favor of dark, smooth, highly polished surfaces covered with shallow, blocky bas-relief with little incising. Objects in this style were being produced by Chokwe in Angola as recently as 1954, and there is no evidence to connect them with the imperial Lunda court of the Mwata Yamvo over a hundred miles westward in the Congo. Many other strikingly different styles have been collected from Chokwe carvers, some of them huge and crudely spectacular, and others small and carefully crafted. Considering the theatrical functions of much of Chokwe art, one suspects that the preference of Lavachery and others for small, carefully finished pieces in hard wood merely reflects the European bias toward "good craftsmanship" and against rapidly executed flamboyance, a bias unfortunately equally apparent in European and American ethnographic museum displays.

If my hypothesis is correct, the Chokwe, now surrounded on three sides by peoples without sculptural traditions, have preserved their carving skills because of their functional necessity in the *mukanda*. The patronage (and occasional participation) of their own and other chiefs has encouraged the development of many luxury products—elaborated beyond necessity and often derived from European models and materials—which give plastic expression to recognized class distinctions. Thus a lowly and isolated people have found means of ordering their environment, while gaining respect and income from their neighbors, and a measure of recognition in the annals of art.

REFERENCES

BASTIN, MARIE-LOUISE
    1961   *Art décoratif tschokwe*. Subsídios para a história, arqueologia e etnografia dos povos da Lunda, Companhia de Diamantes de Angola (DIAMANG), Publicaçoes culturais, no. 55. 2 vols. Lisbon.

COMPANHIA DE DIAMANTES DE ANGOLA (DIAMANG)
    1959   *Breve noticia sobre o Museu do Dundo*. 3d ed. Lisbon.

GRIAULE, MARCEL
    1938   *Masques dogons*. Travaux et mémoires de l'Institut d'Ethnologie. Vol. 33. Paris.

JASPERT, FRITZ AND WILLEM
    1930   *Die Völkerstämme Mittel-Angolas*. Frankfurt a/M.

LAVACHERY, HENRI
    1954   *Statuaire de l'Afrique noire*. Brussels.

McCULLOCH, MERRAN
    1951   *The Southern Lunda and Related Peoples*. Ethnographic Survey of Africa, West Central Africa, pt. 1. London.

OLBRECHTS, FRANS
    1959   *Les arts plastiques du Congo belge*. Brussels. Translation of *Plastiek van Kongo*. Brussels, 1946.

PAULME, DENISE
    1962   *African Sculpture*. New York. Translation of *Les sculptures de l'Afrique noire*. Paris, 1956.

REDINHA, JOSÉ
    1953   *Paredes pintadas da Lunda*. Subsídios para a história, arqueologia e etnografia dos povos da Lunda, Museu do Dondo, Publicaçoes culturais, no. 18. Lisbon.
    1956   *Mascaras de madeira da Lunda e Alto Zambeze*. Subsídios para a história, arqueologia e etnografia dos povos da Lunda, Museu do Dondo, Publicaçoes culturais, no. 31. Lisbon.

TUCKER, JOHN T.
    1933   *Angola, the Land of a Blacksmith Prince*. London.

VANSINA, JAN
    1966   *Kingdoms of the Savanna*. Madison.

CHAPTER 3

Ndop: ROYAL STATUES AMONG THE KUBA

Jan Vansina

Among the celebrated artistic achievements of the Kuba of the central Congo, the most famous are undoubtedly their commemorative statues (*ndop*) representing different kings (*nyim*) (figs. 3.1, 3.2). These sculptures have been portrayed countless times and have given rise to much lively discussion. Frans Olbrechts, the pioneering Belgian anthropologist and student of African art, for example, concluded that Kuba sculpture should be divided into two styles: the first, a "court style" comprising the *ndop* and various other objects, and the second, a "popular style." For Olbrechts, this was the only instance in the Congo basin where a distinctive courtly art could be recognized on the basis of style.[1] Since more is now known about the background and function of the *ndop,* a reexamination of his view is in order. After a few remarks on Kuba political organization, I will describe the socio-political roles of these carved figures and discuss their style, concluding with some remarks about the *ndop* in time perspective, a subject mentioned but briefly by previous authors.

Note: The Kuba live between the Kasai and Sankuru rivers in the Republic of Congo, Kinshasa. Fieldwork was undertaken there from 1953 to 1956 under the auspices of the Institut pour la Recherche Scientifique en Afrique Centrale (IRSAC).

1. Olbrechts 1959, pp. 53–59, pls. 1 and 50–67, reproduces all examples of the "court style" known in 1939.

FIGURE 3.1. Kuba. *Nyim* (king) Mbop aMabiinc in state regalia. (Photograph: Musée Royal de l'Afrique Centrale, Tervuren.)

THE *NDOP* IN KUBA SOCIETY

Ndop statues represent a human figure sitting cross-legged on a throne with a carved wooden object in front which is attached to the throne (see appendix A to this chapter). The figures wear personal emblems, such as hats, arm-rings, belts, swords, and ceremonial pieces of cloth on their backs, but no other common clothing. These items are attributes of Kuba kingship. In the eyes of the people, each statue is a monument to a particular Kuba king. Ostensibly they know which king is represented because the *ndop* is his portrait; actually the king is identified by the personal symbol of his reign, his *ibol,* which is repre-

FIGURE 3.2. Kuba. *Ndop* of Shyaam aMbul aNgoong (Shamba Bolongongo), c. 1650. British Museum, London (1909. 12-10.1). Ht. 21.5" (54.6 cm). (Photograph: Museum.)

FIGURE 3.3. Kuba. *Ndop* of Mbomboosh (Bom Bosh), seventeenth century. Brooklyn Museum (61.33). Ht. 19.4" (49.4 cm). (Photograph: Museum.)

sented in front of him.[2] Since it was forbidden to depict any deformity the king might have, Kuba royal portraits could not be too realistic. Indeed these statues are really quite stylized; in only one case—the figure of Mbomboosh (fig. 3.3)—is a personal characteristic shown, obesity

2. The idea of portraiture is not altogether foreign to the Kuba, however, for in 1956 I collected an image of a sculptor's daughter who had died in childbirth. Made "so her father would remember her," it was a generalized representation rather than a precise portrait.

being indicated by the three lines on his neck and by a somewhat stout torso. But the Kuba still insist that these statues are real portraits and even claim that if the kings had not been present, the statues could not have been carved. This belief may be due, however, to the role the *ndop* played in the installation of the monarch.

The ceremonies for the enthronement of a Kuba king were long and complex. During the first of these ceremonies, the king-designate announced his official praise-name, indicated a geometric pattern of decoration which would become his sign and would be carved on his drum of office (*pel ambish*), and selected his emblem or *ibol*. After the various rites of investiture were completed and he had been crowned in his new capital, the king ordered a sculptor to carve his *ndop* and his drum of office. Only one *ndop* could be made for a king. In theory, therefore, there should be as many *ndop* as there have been kings, since the time of Shyaam aMbul aNgoong, who introduced the practice about A.D. 1650 (Vansina 1963, pp. 113–116, 253–286). *Ndop* statues were made of the heaviest hardwood and were frequently anointed with red camwood and palm oil so that they were protected from the usual tropical hazards of rain and white ants. If a figure did become decayed, it was permissible to carve as exact a replica of it as possible. When the king died, according to certain accounts, the sculptor was buried alive head-first as a sacrifice.

The *ndop* itself performed various functions during the king's lifetime and after his death. If anything happened to the person of the king, it was felt that it would be reflected in the *ndop*. Informants report that when King Mboong aLeeng was mortally wounded by a sword stroke, a similar cut appeared suddenly on his *ndop* and is still there. Whether, conversely, damage to the *ndop* would reflect itself on the king's body is not clear; the Kuba simply do not recall any case where this has happened. During the king's life, the figure also was supposed to house his double, the counterpart of his soul. This explains why the Kuba insist that these statues are portraits and why they claim that the king had to be present when his statue was carved.

While the king was still alive, his statue was kept in his women's quarters. Some of the general powers of fertility clustered in Kuba kingship were believed to adhere to the image itself; for when a woman of the harem was about to give birth, the statue was placed near her to insure a safe delivery. It was also a substitute for the king himself to his womenfolk, who would anoint, stroke, and fondle it in their husband's absence.

After death, Kuba kings were believed to become nature spirits (*ngesh*), ancestor worship being unknown among the Kuba. Then the *ndop* became a commemorative object and was removed along with the royal drum to a storage room, sometimes near the grave of the deceased (as in 1900; see Drion in van der Linden 1910, p. 234). But even these *ndop* were exhibited on certain important occasions. In 1892, William H. Sheppard, the first European to visit the Kuba capital, saw four of the statues elevated on an earth platform in "the king's council chamber" (Taylor-Wharton 1952, pp. 37–38; Kellersberger 1947, p. 55).

But the central function of the *ndop* was something quite different. Albert Maesen was told that when the king died, his *ndop* was put close to the death bed to catch the life force of the deceased monarch. After the successor to the king was selected, he spent a certain period in isolation, during which time he would lie beside and sleep next to the *ndop* of his predecessor, thus allowing the life force of kingship to be incubated in him (Maesen 1960, pl. 19). This concept is somewhat analogous to the rites of the Oyo Yoruba in which the new ruler had to eat the heart of his predecessor in order to be endowed with the royal life force. Although my own inquiries have not yet corroborated Maesen's findings, his data seem to fit very well with the basic attitudes of the Kuba toward the *ndop*.

Which leaders, then, were entitled to own and use such carvings? The Bushoong, the ruling group among the Kuba, maintain that *ndop* were made only for kings. Despite this claim, the eastern Pyaang tribes insist that they too carved *ndop* figures for their chiefs. But these Pyaang statues are completely different in style and in genre from the Kuba king figures, since they do not represent persons wearing royal regalia but, rather, show them dressed in the skirts and hats worn by commoners. As with the Bushoong, though, these Pyaang *ndop* were used by the wives of the chiefs when they gave birth, as well as in their husband's absence. At the other end of the Kuba kingdom, the Shoowa of the northwest carve feminine figures (*mwaan kum*) adorned with the emblems of female chiefs. These images were placed on a throne (*bulell*) when a woman of the village died or whenever there was dancing. Such figures were obviously not *ndop* even though they were connected with political authority. We may conclude, then, that with the exception of the eastern Pyaang, whose statues were completely different, no other Kuba group besides the Bushoong had *ndop*.

THE COURT STYLE

Five *ndop* (those of Shyaam, Mbomboosh, Mishaa Pelyeeng, Mbo Pelyeeng, and Kot aMbul; see figs. 3.2–3.6 and appendix A) have been described by Olbrechts as forming an "archaic style." These are all the

FIGURE 3.4. Kuba. *Ndop* of Mishaa Pelyeeng aNce (Misha Pelenge Che), eighteenth century. British Museum, London (1909.5-13.2). Ht. 20.8″ (52.8 cm). (Photograph: Museum.)

FIGURE 3.5. Kuba. *Ndop* of Mbo Pelyeeng aNce (Bope Pelenge), eighteenth century. British Museum, London (1909.5-13.1). Ht. 21.1″ (53.7 cm). (Photograph: Museum.)

statues of the earlier kings that survive except the one of Mboong aLeeng, which I have not been able to see. The differences among the individual statues, though real (cf. hairlines, mouths), are so slight that Maesen expresses doubts, shared by others, that these images could have been carved while the models were alive (Maesen 1960, pl. 19). Yet granting they are not portraits from life and not the work of one

FIGURE 3.6. Kuba. *Ndop* of Kot aMbul (Kota Mbula), eighteenth century. Musée Royal de l'Afrique Centrale, Tervuren (15256). Ht. 20.1" (51 cm). (Photograph: Museum.)

hand, they are so homogeneous that the question arises whether such close similarity could have been maintained through at least a century (Olbrechts 1959, pp. 54–57). Since the statues were collected at various times and under differing circumstances, this visual unity is a real one—not the result of systematic collecting bias by, say, the Torday expedition. In other words, either the five Kuba statues were copied by several hands at about the same time (which would satisfy those who claim that such unity cannot be maintained over time) or the sculptures do in fact represent an archaic style.

That other objects besides *ndop* exist in this style is important to observe. Figurines called *noon,* which represent the torso of a man ending in a spike, closely resemble the *ndop,* as Olbrechts has observed

(1959, p. 58, pl. 65). I collected one of these among the Pyaang Mbaanc at Nnem;[3] it was said to come from the northernmost Lulua who border on the Pyaang. Apparently either the Pyaang carved the *noon* images as ancestor figurines, or else they made them for export to the Lulua. The Ntul aNshedy statue (Olbrechts 1959, pl. 55), although something of a freak, is certainly also an example of the archaic style. The archaic *ndop* are closer, then, in style to the canons of the southern and southeastern Bushoong and Pyaang than are the other *ndop*. Their facial forms are rounded almost to a smooth oval like those of the best dolls from the southeastern area. The absence of sharp angles in the treatment of elbows, knees, and other parts of the body, which are shown as smooth swellings rather than as distinctly carved features, is additional evidence of a connection. This style of *ndop* carvings is, I feel, indeed archaic. *Ndop* carvers, as I see it, would have followed the model of earlier *ndop* as closely as possible, their skill being sufficient to achieve a close approximation of the earlier models time after time. After all, in a land of sculptors the royal carver must invariably have been one of the best.

The other *ndop* form several distinct stylistic clusters. The images of Miko miMbul and Mbop Kyeen (figs. 3.7, 3.8, and appendix A) clearly constitute a pair. The treatment of the upper jawbone and the angle of the lower jaw, the tendency toward squareness in the face, the typical stylization of the mouth (which is quite unlike that of the archaic group), the characteristic hairline (more baroque than in the older images), and the presence of scarification marks on the temples (which are lacking in the archaic statues) all support this contention.[4] Unfortunately Miko miMbul and Mbop Kyeen reigned at opposite ends of a long period lasting over a century, for which no other statues are available. We might perhaps call the style of these images that of the nineteenth century. Of course if the first statue is a copy, the nineteenth-century style really stems only from the beginnings of the twentieth.

The *ndop* of Kot aPe, if genuine, stands alone. Made in 1904, it shows some of the characteristics of the previous group (hairline and mouth) while other aspects (the ears and the absence of an *ibol*, which is replaced by an object held in the hand) link it with the next set. Its general slenderness, though, gives it a character all its own.

Three of the remaining *ndop*, all with parrot *ibol*, form another group which is characterized by the tight treatment of the mouth and ears and

3. Our collections (1956) were kept in the IRSAC museum at Lwiro and were lost, together with the detailed records, after the independence of Congo, Kinshasa.

4. In the earlier statues there is perhaps a hint of these features in the rectangle just under the hairline on the temple of the statue of Kot aMbul.

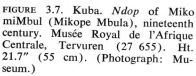

FIGURE 3.7. Kuba. *Ndop* of Miko miMbul (Mikope Mbula), nineteenth century. Musée Royal de l'Afrique Centrale, Tervuren (27 655). Ht. 21.7″ (55 cm). (Photograph: Museum.)

FIGURE 3.8. Kuba. *Ndop* of Mbop Kyeen (Bope Kena), twentieth century. Musée Royal de l'Afrique Centrale, Tervuren (50.24.1). Ht. 21.7″ (55 cm). (Photograph: Museum.)

the high, almost cubical throne. These figures belong with the larger of the two statues attributed to Kot aMabiinc. In my view, all such works are modern and were made for sale in the 1920s. One notes immediately the lack of proper proportions and the inferior finish compared with earlier statues. The same is true of the remaining three statues, which seem to be even more recent copies, dating perhaps from the 1930s. Unfortunately they are not sufficiently well reproduced in Olbrechts' book to make a close analysis possible. By the 1940s and

1950s the carving of *ndop* had become a major source of cash income for some sculptors at the Kuba capital and even elsewhere.

We must now try to decide whether or not in Kuba art there really is a court style. We have indicated the connection between the archaic *ndop* and the *noon* figures. Olbrechts (1959, p. 59, pl. 66) also compared the former with a type of charm representing seated figures, which he dubbed "Renaissance court style." In the course of field work I have encountered many of these charms and some of them are undoubtedly old; but like the *noon,* these charms are popular objects, not made at the capital. In fact, what makes a *ndop* a real *ndop* is not its style characteristics or even the typical seated posture, but the presence of regalia. *Ndop* are an obligatory theme, not really a style per se. To speak of a court style obliterates the major stylistic distinctions observable in Kuba art: those between the various geographical areas and, even more important, that separating masks and other ritual objects such as initiation statues and cult statues (*ishak ndweem*) from purely secular work. Similarly, over and beyond regional differences, two clusters of motifs in decorative art may be distinguished. One set is used for female scarification, some types of textile ornaments, and certain funeral objects (*mboong i tool*); the other is used in pottery and wood decoration and on the remaining types of textiles. This division is not, as one might think, between secular and religious ornament, but it is no less real. Nowhere in either the religious-secular contrast or in the decorative groups is a stylistic division apparent between the art of the court and that of the Kuba people.

THE *NDOP* IN TIME PERSPECTIVE

That individual *ndop* are connected with certain kings and that these images divide into a sequence of at least two styles has been established. Can anything now be said about the age of *ndop?* In dating African carvings several sorts of information may be of help. The best documented Central African examples are the Lower Congo *mintadi,* which, being of soapstone, are far less perishable than the hardwood *ndop.* We know that *mintadi* existed in the seventeenth century because four of them, now at the Pigorini Museum in Rome, were brought to Europe before A.D. 1700 (Leuzinger 1960, p. 160; Verly 1955, passim). The date of their transfer is established by written documents. Oral tradition, on the other hand, suggests that the custom of carving *ndop* was introduced into Kuba culture around 1650 by King Shyaam. The difference between these records is mainly one of type of historical documentation;

oral traditions have proved to be far more reliable than was formerly believed.

No one really knows how long hardwood, covered with a patina of palm oil mixed with camwood and carefully tended, can survive. I believe such objects may last for several centuries, and there are enough cracks and eroded areas in most of the early *ndop* to suggest that they are of some antiquity. But even if they are not and the original monuments are merely copies, their value remains much the same, since in the case of the *ndop* it may be assumed they are faithful to the originals. Moreover, if copies had been necessary, probably only two or three of the oldest statues would have had to be duplicated (that of Shyaam for instance) and since presumably only one copy would be required, alteration through successive copying may be regarded as negligible. In other words, the statues represent substantially the style and the details of the genre as it arose under Shyaam, and they can be used as accurate evidence of the past. Hypercritical attitudes here would seem to me to be just as uncalled for as uncritical ones and for the same reason: both simply mess up the evidence.

We have evidence, then, in *ndop* not only of a Kuba style and genre going back to the second half of the seventeenth century but also of such things as royal dress and attributes. From this we can infer that the early kings wore arm-rings, probably of brass, a plaited belt (*mwaandaan*) identifying them with the members of the coronation council and the highest court, a ceremonial woven cloth (*iyeet*) across their buttocks, one or two discoid ornaments over the shoulders (made of decorated cloth stretched on cane hoops or hippopotamus tusks), armrings of woven cloth stitched with cowries (*mabiim*), and a belt of the same material. They used the war sword (*iloon*), which already had the emblem of the sun on its handle. Their hats were different from the royal hats worn nowadays, although the early type is still found in the southern parts of the kingdom as a sign of chieftainship. These hats consisted of cloth with woven or stitched decoration, more likely the former. We recognize the throne (*bulell*) and also the drum known as *pel ambish,* as well as the type of drum which is now more common in the northwestern part of the Kuba area, though its decorations are very similar to those on the statue of Mbomboosh (appendix A, note b).

Examination of the *ndop* also yields considerable art-historical evidence. For example, a string of beads is worn by the *ndop* of Mbo Pelyeeng aNce; in all the earlier statues, such decoration is limited to cowries. Prior to the reign of Kot aNce, when beads are first mentioned (Vansina 1963, p. 316), the oral traditions also refer only to cowries.

Mbo Pelyeeng aNce, in whose *ndop* the innovation first occurs, reigned directly after Mishaa Pelyeeng aNce, who succeeded Kot aNce. That the idea of representing beads was not maintained in later statues indicates that the artists generally returned to the model of the genre showing only the archaic features of royalty depicted in the earliest statues. Kuba art differs in this respect from Benin style, where the addition of later emblems of kingship resulted in major changes in genre. But the very stability of the *ndop* imagery further reinforces the authenticity of what is actually illustrated. One change, however, has been maintained consistently: the indication of Bushoong cicatrice markings. These may not have been included in the early statues because the first *ndop* represented King Shyaam, who was not a Bushoong. Only beginning with Kot aMbul's *ndop* is some indication of these marks given.

In broader perspective it would be interesting to discover whether anything like the *ndop* occurs in the Kwango area, since Shyaam is said to have come from the west, more specifically from the Mbuun, whence he also brought the plans for his capital. The Mbuun no longer have paramount chiefs, but regional chiefs or leaders in the surrounding areas might have the functional equivalent of *ndop*. If these do occur and are at all close to the *ndop*, both genres would appear unquestionably to date from the seventeenth century. Important, too, is the cross-legged pose which is common to the *ndop* and Kongo *mintadi*, though this pose is almost unknown outside of the Kuba and Kongo areas. This fact has led many scholars to the conclusion that the ultimate model for *ndop* sculpture must have been the *mintadi* of the Kongo region.

REFERENCES

BOONE, OLGA
    1951   "Les tambours du Congo belge et du Ruanda-Urundi." *Annales du Musée du Congo Belge. Nouvelle série in-4° Sciences de l'homme: Ethnographie*, 1. 2 vols. Tervuren.

ELISOFON, ELIOT, AND FAGG, WILLIAM B.
    1958   *The Sculpture of Africa*. London.

KELLERSBERGER, JULIA
    1947   *A Life for the Congo: The Story of Althea Brown Edmiston*. New York.

LEUZINGER, ELSY
    1960   *Africa: The Art of the Negro Peoples*. New York.

LINDEN, FRITZ VAN DER
    1910   *Les Congo, les noirs et nous*. 2d ed. Paris.

MAESEN, ALBERT
1960   *Umbangu; art du Congo au Musée Royal du Congo Belge.*
             Brussels.
OLBRECHTS, FRANS
1959   *Les arts plastiques du Congo belge.* Brussels. Translation of
             Plastiek van Kongo. Brussels, 1946.
TAYLOR-WHARTON, ETHEL
1952   *Led in Triumph.* London.
TORDAY, ÉMIL, AND JOYCE, THOMAS A.
1910   "Notes ethnographiques sur les peuples communément
             appelés Bakuba ainsi que les peuplades apparentées: les
             Bushongo." *Annales du Musée du Congo Belge. Ethnogra-
             phie, anthropologie, Série 3. Documents ethnographiques
             concernant les populations du Congo belge.* Vol. 2, part 1.
             Brussels.
VANSINA, JAN
1963   "Geschiedenis van de Kuba van ongever 1500 tot 1904."
             *Annalen van het Koninklijk Museum voor Midden-Afrika.
             Reeks in-8°. Wetenschappen van de mens.* No. 44.
             Tervuren.
1964   "Le royaume kuba." *Annales du Musée Royal de l'Afrique
             Centrale. Série in-8°. Sciences humaines.* No. 49. Tervuren.
VERLY, ROBERT
1955   "La statuaire de pierre du Bas-Congo (Bamboma-Mus-
             surongo)." *Zaïre* 9, no. 5: 451–528. Louvain.

APPENDIX A. Kuba Kings and Their *Ndop*

Date of reign	Name of king	Number of *ndop*	Olbrechts illustration number	*Ibol* (emblem)
c. 1650	Shyaam aMbul aNgoong	1[a]	51	*mankala* or *lela* game
17th century	Mboong aLeeng	1	—	unknown
	Mbomboosh	1	50	drum type II[b]
	Mbakam	—	—	—
18th century	Kot aMbweeky I	—	—	—
	Mishe mi Shaang II	—	—	—
	Kot aNce	—	—	—
	Mishaa Pelyeeng aNce	1	52	drum type I
	Mbo Pelyeeng aNce	1	53	anvil
	Kot aMbul	1	1	drum type I
c. 1800–c. 1835	Miko miMbul	1	56[c]	woman[d]
c. 1835–c. 1885	Mbop Mabiinc MaMbul	??[e]	—	parrot
	Miko Mabiinc	—	—	—
ruled in 1892	Kot aMbweeky II	—[f]	—	—
died 1900/1901	Mishaape II	—	—	—
	Mbop Kyeen	1	54	drum type II
	Miko miKyeen	—	—	—
1904–1916	Kot aPe	1	60–62	none, but basket and hammer[g]
1916–1919	Kot aMbweeky III	—	—	—
1919–1940	Kot aMabiinc	2[h]	63	parrot
1940–1969	Mbop aMabiinc	?	—	—
	uncertain	7[i]	57, 59, 63	—

a. Another image said to represent Shyaam (Olbrechts 1959, pl. 58) is not an original *ndop* but a miniature copy of one. Its style is actually that of the Kuba drinking cups, and Olbrechts regarded it as a modern work.

b. When no specific *ibol* is included, a drum with the king's special geometric design on it is carved in front of him. These drums are identical to actual Kuba drums as classified by Olga Boone (1951). The *pel ambish* drum seen in front of Kot aMbul (fig. 3.6) is her Type I and is illustrated in Boone (1951, 1, p. 50, ill. 27); Type II is wider and smaller, and the body rests on four or six curved legs which join it to the base (Torday and Joyce 1910, pl. XIV 1).

c. Olbrechts would attribute a second *ndop* to Miko miMbul's reign from the pair of figures that have drums instead of *ibol*. Since there is an *ibol* here and the identity of the king is well established, it seems unwise to accept either of the other images as *ndop* of this individual. In addition, the other statues were collected only after 1945!

d. Usually believed to be a slave woman, since the king was the first to allow free men to marry slave girls (Olbrechts 1959, p. 57; Torday and Joyce 1910, p. 31; Vansina 1964, p. 319). But one of the *ibol* (in the national basket [*ncyaam*], where the *ibol* were deposited after the death of the king) is a head said to represent a particular king's power over life and death; this could be the real meaning of the carved figure, especially since the *ndop* were carved at the beginning of the reign, presumably before the new ruling on marriage was made.

e. His *ibol* was a parrot. No *ndop* is ascribed to him, but there are four with parrots which are not attributed to any particular king. One of these might be his. However, Kot aMabiinc also used a parrot as *ibol*.

f. William H. Sheppard saw four statues in 1892, presumably four of the seven listed above. Why no more than four statues were exhibited remains unexplained.

g. There is no *ibol* on the throne, but the king's arm rests on the basket of a high official (*nkweemi*). Kot aPe also holds a hammer. The basket may have something to do with the belief that the king lifted a curse put on Kot aMbweeky II which was hidden in a basket.

h. One of these two *ndop* has no *ibol* at all, the other has a drum; neither has a parrot as would be expected from the known *ibol* of the king. Probably neither image is authentic, since the king was still ruling when they were collected and thus the statues could not perform the functions of *ndop* as outlined above.

i. Seven *ndop* are not attributed; four of them have parrot *ibol*, two have drum symbols, and the last is a small statue ascribed to a certain Ntul aNshedy, who was not a king. If the first four represent Kot aNce, as I think they do, they cannot on stylistic grounds be considered authentic old *ndop*. The fifth and sixth images, collected in the 1920s and 1930s, may prove to be real *ndop* or one of them may, although personally I doubt it. The last one, which is a genuine old work, is not really a *ndop*. It resembles the appearance of a *ndop* because of the regalia portrayed; but it is too small, probably being a sculptor's copy of a real *ndop*. Imitations of carved objects are very common among the Kuba, some of whom take great delight in this game.

CHAPTER 4

Gon: A MASK USED
IN COMPETITION FOR LEADERSHIP
AMONG THE BAKWELE

Leon Siroto

INTRODUCTION

I will here present an account of an art form used in the competition for leadership in one African group and will discuss briefly the theoretical significance of this form from the viewpoint of this book. An awareness of the part played by art forms in helping individuals to attain as well as maintain leadership will add depth to our understanding of these objects. Even today salvage anthropology sometimes makes it possible to discern aspects of leadership art in societies that may be called less differentiated or acephalous.

My data concern the traditional uses of a mask (*gon*,[1] plural, *egon*) by the BaKwele,[2] a Bantu-speaking people who live in the Dja and

Note: This discussion centers upon the eastern group of the BaKwele, since the greater part of my field work was conducted among them. I spent less time among the western BaKwele, whose very close contact and admixture with the Ngwyes have made them quite different in a number of significant ways. My field work was supported by the Ford Foundation Foreign Area Training Program, although that institution bears no responsibility for the statements made in this article.

1. Here and in similar BaKwele words, the final "n" is pronounced like "ng" in the English word "sing."

2. The term "BaKwele" needs some explanation. Essentially a colonial administrative convention that has been accepted by the people themselves, the word began as a by-name for one subgroup. "BaKwele" is the Lingala version of the self-term "BeKwyel." Its use does not conform to what we would expect in a Bantu prefix system: the root is always employed in what we would take to be

Ivindo river basins of western equatorial Africa. According to oral traditions of the BaKwele, they began using this mask about one hundred and fifty years ago, when they first settled in the region they now occupy, and discontinued its use after the establishment of European colonial power.

BAKWELE CULTURE

At the beginning of the nineteenth century the BaKwele lived around the headwaters of the Ivindo, to the north and west of their present location. At that time guns were beginning to come in from the trading centers on the Atlantic coast. The geographical position of the BaKwele put them at the mercy of their neighbors to the west. Raids by groups who had acquired guns decimated the BaKwele and drove them into their present territory, where the raiding continued but with less intensity.

The BaKwele ranged at will within the limits of their territory. Their subsistence was based upon the swidden (slash-and-burn) cultivation of the plantain, a crop that demanded little attention and thus allowed the BaKwele to move freely over the sparsely populated region into which they had been driven. The plantain economy and a minimal concern with land tenure allowed relatively intensive circulation of villages and village components.

The BaKwele are divided into a number of regional groups and, in precolonial times, these groups tended to maintain their territories against mass incursion by the others. Sibs were neither strongly organized nor significantly corporate. The largest operative unit of social organization, and the basic village component, was a lineage group composed either of a father and his sons or of brothers and their sons— and their women and children. The father had authority over lineage affairs, as well as the trusteeship of the lineage's wealth. This wealth consisted of iron money, livestock, and rare goods, usually of European manufacture. Wealth was primarily used in the system of marriage exchange.

Ideally, BaKwele marriage was polygynous; the acquisition of many wives made for a large and wealthy lineage. The scarcity of women— who were the most sought-after possession in the BaKwele economic order—led to keen competition in the marriage system.

In acquiring wives for themselves and their sons and younger brothers, family heads were expected to allocate family wealth equitably. In prac-

---

its plural form, and there is no equivalent of such singular forms as "MuKongo," "MuLuba," etc. The singular can be denoted by the construction *mooBeKwyel,* meaning "child of the BeKwyel." For this reason, I choose not to use the root form "Kwele."

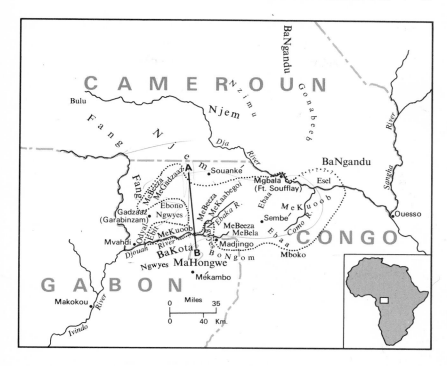

MAP 2. Distribution of the BaKwele and Culturally Related Peoples around 1900.
. . . . Approximate limits of the BaKwele-speaking people. Line AB: approximate division between the eastern and western BaKwele. (Map by University of Wisconsin Cartographic Laboratory.)

tice, however, the compulsion toward having a large family, and hence personal power in the village, drove many BaKwele family heads to spend the family wealth exclusively to acquire wives of their own.

Sons who despaired of getting wives soon enough through the help of their fathers split away from their lineage homesteads to seek wealth elsewhere. A strong, if informal, system of patronage and clientage existed, in which opportunists in search of wealth and wives became the followers of wealthy men who could fulfill their expectations. Such opportunists would usually settle in a patron's village without assimilating to his lineage. The patron could thus attain nominal control over a number of lineages, a more strategic arrangement in village politics than merely the support of his own sons and younger brothers.

BaKwele villages tended to consist of large chains of different lineages—often more than a dozen. A number of guardhouses were spaced out along the inner court of the village; each guardhouse represented a lineage and served as the focal point of its affairs.

Political power over the village was diffuse and transitory. In principle, decisions affecting the whole village were made by the consensus of all lineage heads. Yet these decisions expressed the interests of certain leaders who managed to prevail over the will of their peers.

The leaders who dominated consensus groups among the BaKwele usually had achieved certain informally acquired levels of status. The wealthy man (*kum*), who often founded the village, had the least distinctive status, though it was sometimes combined with others. There were various kinds of religious specialists (*begaa;* singular, *gaa*). The status of expert peacemaker (*tetep*) was a very important one, due to the prevalence of conflict in the villages and the difficulties in resolving these disputes. Many of these crises stemmed from the actions of men who held the status of war-leader or *gen* (plural, *begen*).

The *gen* was a man of violence who used his courage and martial skills to his best advantage in manipulating village affairs. In the BaKwele view, a lineage that did not have a *gen* to defend it against other lineages was virtually doomed. A *gen* could extort goods as damages and dominate lineages that had no *begen* of their own; at times his influence went so far as to give him virtual control of the affairs of a village or of a cluster of villages.

The greatest *begen* tended to avoid confrontations with one another. Yet armed violence frequently erupted in BaKwele villages, often between families whose leaders aspired to *gen* status. A lineage that had no *gen* but had been affronted by one would invoke—by a ritual formula—the aid of an unrelated *gen* who would then act as assassin in its behalf.

The informality and impermanence of status in BaKwele society kept the prevailing political condition of *primus inter pares* from becoming an institution. As resigned as the BaKwele may have been to the existence of *begen,* they were not resigned to a prolonged state of oppression or domination, which could have prevented them from fulfilling their own hopes of wealth and prestige. They tended to move out of villages in which life was made difficult, either to join or to found more congenial ones.

BaKwele lineages and villages thus divided and subdivided frequently as a result of men's quest for power, material gain, and more congenial neighbors. Yet this volatile quality in the life of the BaKwele ran counter to their view of an ideal society: a large village of long duration. The large and enduring village, apart from being a defensive necessity, served as proof of wealth and innate leadership, a testimonial to the excellence of the man who could attract and keep followers and friends together under his influence.

Men who had founded villages (or enjoyed considerable power or prestige in them) wanted these villages to cohere as long as they possibly could. In some cases, the founder's influence, although informal, was strong and pervasive enough to realize that aim. Yet the heterogeneity of village components—leaders with conflicting interests, clients of different patrons, disaffected sons and younger brothers—often generated fissive strains that were beyond the influence of those leaders to control.

At times of actual or impending crisis, a means of intensifying cooperation among antagonistic village segments was urgently needed. The main danger to each village lay in the direct and violent confrontation of its own components. Often a peacemaker tried to arrange a settlement between one and another of the disputants. Even then, however, the settlement usually fell short of reconciliation, and one of the disputants would move away, taking with him a number of friendly lineages.

The cohesion of the BaKwele village thus depended upon its leaders' ability to anticipate social crises, as well as upon having a means of diverting potential antagonists into interaction transcending the conflict of their personal interests. Such diversion was attained through the rites of the *beete* cult, the most spectacular and inclusive of BaKwele ceremonial occasions. Certain large-scale crises fell outside the range of explanation possible in BaKwele cosmological or religious principles. The most important of these crises were those brought on by the advent of epidemic diseases, the death of a great man or woman, or the threat of foreign invaders. The BaKwele attempted to cope with these disasters by using their own strongest available magical power, the *beete* rite. When the prospect of confrontation and violence seemed close at hand, the main leaders of the village would come together to decide how the crisis should be circumvented. The decision usually favored performing *beete*.[3]

The success of the *beete* rite depended upon the acquisition of effective quantities of witchcraft-imbued relics (particularly skulls of dead leaders) and magical substances. Frequently the relics owned by the village lineages were judged inadequate for the occasion, and the village leaders appointed a delegation to go to other villages in order to borrow notably powerful skulls owned by other BaKwele lineages. The chief

3. It should not be thought, however, that the rite was invariably a subterfuge for resolving, or rather diverting, personal conflicts. Occasionally, it is said, *beete* was held simply because the village had not yet experienced its magical benefits. An important village was expected to perform *beete* at least once during its relatively short duration.

magical substances used in the *beete* rite were the meat and intestinal contents of forest antelopes in addition to certain rare barks and leaves. These were put into a magic-imbued stew. Many of the younger men of the village went into the forest to mount a great net-hunt for antelope, an undertaking that forced them to cooperate with each other and built up a temporary esprit de corps. The hunt usually lasted at least a week.

While the various materials were being sought, the village also made preparations for the rite. The climax of *beete* consisted in the consumption of the magical stew, and the efficacy of this medicine was believed to depend upon the receptive condition of its consumers. At the proper time it was necessary that the village be animated by singing, dancing, and feasting, in other words, by intense and harmonious interaction. The women and children remained in the village, and some men also stayed back to defend it and oversee affairs. The pattern of *beete* made provision for the drawing together of all village segments, even highly disaffected ones, into the festivities.

The autonomy and the rivalry of the lineage groups that stayed in the village remained much the same as before. The most capable leaders were employing their skills elsewhere, but it is doubtful, even if they had been in the village, whether they could have led *all* the lineages into dancing together for any length of time. *Beete* itself had to provide leaders who could do this.

On each day of the *beete* period a messenger from the *beete* court— a clearing in the forest away from the village—announced that a *kuk* (plural, *ekuk*) would come to dance on the next day. The villagers dressed themselves richly, putting on new loincloths, arranging their hair elaborately, and reddening their bodies with palm oil and camwood powder. At approximately the appointed time, traditional songs of exhortation were heard coming from the trail leading to the village.

After a while, a strange face—large, sharp-edged, brightly colored, and impassive—appeared in the inner doorway of the guardhouse that separated the trail from the village court. Then the entire figure emerged, fantastically painted, wearing a mask and dancing in the BaKwele manner, the seed-shell rattles on its ankles clattering forth the rhythm. Followed by the singers and dancers who brought it in from the forest, the masked being came into the court and danced first down one side between the dwellings and the guardhouses and then down the other.

This dance-leader was a *kuk,* a "thing of the forest," who had come to dance with the BaKwele. It was part of *beete,* yet it belonged to no lineage and had nothing to do with everyday affairs. The villagers were quick to step into the dancing line behind the *kuk*'s troupe and to join in the singing. They danced within the village throughout the morning. Occasionally the *kuk* left, returning to dance on with new vigor. (The mask and body-paint were put onto another dancer of about the same size as the first.)

The dances continued during the days that the *beete* medicine was being obtained and prepared. Different *ekuk* appeared. The villagers became accustomed to dancing together and went on doing so even in the absence of the *ekuk*. The village became animated and ever more populous as leaders and hunters returned from their quests. Relatives and friends arrived from other villages to take part in the ceremony and to share in its benefits. At a certain point young men were led into the *beete* court and initiated into the secrets of the cult.

GON AND BEETE

One day the messenger from the *beete* court announced that *gon* would come to the village the next day. That evening all domestic animals that could be found were penned up indoors. On the appointed day an iron dog-bell was heard coming closer to the village, as were the voices of men singing a special song of exhortation asking *gon* to kill something for them. After a while the singing stopped, and only the increasing sound of the dog-bell was heard.

Gon came in at the end of the village. His mask-face was smooth and black; his body, the deep matte black of powdered charcoal (fig. 4.1). He looked out from under a steeply jutting brow. A sharp vertical crest ran the length of his head, and a pair of long, white-tipped teeth thrust down from his forward-sweeping jaw. He held five short spears in his hands. Only a small mongoose skin covered his nakedness. Around his chest was a thick rope, held like a leash by several of his followers. A dog-bell was tied under each knee. He did not dance but darted and ran about, straining against his leash and turning to menace his followers.

Eventually *gon*'s exertions prevailed, and he tore away from his keepers to run free in the village. He ran back and forth, throwing spears at his followers when they came too close to him and at doors that were slightly ajar. He ran through and around the village for hours in search of something to kill. Sometimes a straggling sheep or goat returning to the village or a dog that broke out of a house to run into the village court was transfixed by a spear thrown by *gon*. *Gon* threw

FIGURE 4.1. BaKwele. *Gon*-masker; painting by Gustav Dalstrom, Field Museum of Natural History, Chicago, based on data supplied by the author.

at anything that moved. His attendants had to be battle-wise warriors, able to dodge his shafts (in earlier times *gon*'s attendants carried shields).

Finally the strongest men in his retinue crept up to *gon*, pounced upon him and carried him to a stream, where immersion shocked him out of his blood-lust. Then the slain animals were gathered up by *gon*'s followers and taken to the *beete* court to be shared by lineage heads and other notables in a communal feast. The *beete* rite went on for several days after *gon*'s sortie. Other *ekuk* came in to dance with or perform before villagers. The rite ended when all participants assembled at a streamside, where the *gaa beete* sprinkled them with the juice of the magical stew. This they used in a symbolic scraping-off of dirt and evil into the water flowing past. The stew was then distributed and eaten. This ritual of purification and communion was believed to heal and strengthen the village.

Beete materials were then taken back to their hiding places. Most of the masks went into the forbidden chambers of lineage heads, to be kept with family relics until another *beete* rite. A few masks, however, might emerge during the interval. One *kuk*—never more—would be asked to dance to enliven the festivities accompanying circumcision or the event known as "speaking of the dead," a reunion of friends and relatives to settle the affairs of a recently deceased person. In these cases the entertainer was of the ordinary, dance-leading kind.

GON AS A POLITICAL IMPLEMENT

The BaKwele, it now seems clear, borrowed *beete* and its masks from the Ngwyes, a BaKele people nearby whom they encountered when they were being driven south (see map 2). The *beete* rite aided in maintaining, at least in principle, the dominion of a consensus group over the village by helping to prolong the duration of the village through the preservation of the status quo. However, the BaKwele also adapted *gon* to non-*beete* contexts in which they seemed to be striving toward another type of leadership, that of a family over its village, and sometimes nearby villages as well.

Although the concept of *gon* as part of the ritual system of *beete* came to the BaKwele from the Ngwyes, we cannot be sure that the form of the mask was also so derived. The model for the *gon* mask, according to the BaKwele themselves, was the upper part of the skull of an adult male gorilla (fig. 4.2), an animal which formerly abounded in BaKwele country. *Gon,* however, does not mean "gorilla" in BaKwele, nor are the people able to explain the etymology of the word. Nevertheless, before the introduction of guns, the gorilla was a frightening antagonist as well as a persistent raider of BaKwele plantations. The median crest that flares into two divergent ridges on the face of the mask is the most precise diagnostic link here with the gorilla's skull. The sculptural adaptations consisted in moving the crown of the head

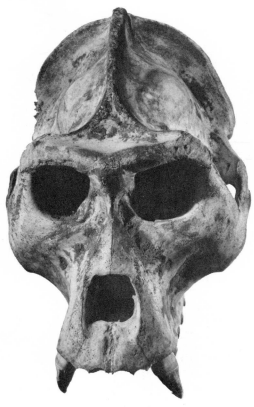

FIGURE 4.2. Skull of adult male gorilla (covered with camwood powder). MeKwa' village, Congo-Brazzaville. Author's collection. Ht. 11″ (27.9 cm). (Photograph: Field Museum of Natural History, Chicago.)

forward and the face under the brow-ridge backward, thus aligning all salient features more or less in one plane (fig. 4.3). The mask was usually carved in soft, light wood and darkened after completion by scorching it with a red-hot knife. The triangular depression on the brow was always reddened with camwood powder.

The relation a BaKwele mask had to the *beete* rite imbued that mask with sacred meaning and, when its use offended a villager, placed it beyond the reach of secular forms of redress. To reproach the action of such a mask was to question the worth of the medicine (that is, *beete* itself) which it represented. The harassment and loss individuals sustained at the hands of *gon* was considered part of the way in which the threatened village was to be saved; fighting back or remonstrating would have been tantamount to eliminating an essential element in the panacea.

Probably not long after the acquisition of the *beete* rituals by the BaKwele, the MeBeeza of the Gadzaaz (Garabinzam) region, the first group of BaKwele to associate with the Ngwyes, began to use *gon* to

FIGURE 4.3. BaKwele. *Gon* mask. MeSok village, Congo-Brazzaville. Author's collection. Ht. 15″ (38.1 cm). (Photograph: Field Museum of Natural History, Chicago.)

deal with problems that arose during the unsettled years following their sudden arrival in a new land. Much of the country to the south of the original home of the BaKwele was inhabited by the BaKota people (see map 2). When the BaKwele came into strange country as impoverished strangers, the BaKota welcomed them into their villages. Indeed, the MeBeeza subgroup settled in BaKota villages to such an extent that some villages became half-BaKota and half-BaKwele.

The MeBeeza sib of Ebagoona shared a village with a number of BaKota lineages. The Ebagoona, who had by then been introduced to *beete,* sent masks out to dance in the village. One day they sent out *gon,* and the BaKota men, unfamiliar with the nature of the performance, came out to watch. The masker threw spears at them and wounded some. The BaKota were terrified and fled, leaving the village to the BaKwele. Although the BaKwele do not say so explicitly, this stratagem probably enabled them to circumvent their solemn pledges to their BaKota hosts and thus to claim this area as their land and the inhabitants as their people. This is the first reported account of *gon* operating outside of the framework of *beete*. While the BaKwele do not state expressly that the episode was extraritual, it is reasonable to infer this since the rout of the BaKota would have been contrary to the objectives and procedure of the *beete* rite; in the early days the *beete* rites must have been observed in that particular region with even greater punctilio than they were later.

Gon's emergence in the *beete* sequence, intended to provide a fearsome thrill for the village, also involves an element of self-interest in the use of the mask. As the disguised slaughterer of livestock, *gon* did what no BaKwele would do in nonritual circumstances, for the killing of sheep and goats for gastronomic reasons would ordinarily be regarded as a meaningless squandering of the lineage's bride-wealth resources. During this time, when all wild game taken was put aside for feasting during the *beete* period and for the preparation of the *beete* medicine, the hunger for fresh meat apparently inspired leaders to adapt a ritual accessory to their own ends. Although *gon*'s part in the struggle for leadership need not have developed primarily out of its serving as victualler to the village leaders, the subterfuge does indicate awareness of the strategic value of the mask as a way around cultural deterrents.

One BaKwele informant observed that the *gon* Ebagoona was just like a *gen*. This remark underscores the circumstances that have taken *gon* out of the context of *beete* exclusively and into the field of competition for political power. Those who held the *gen* status must surely have seen the advantages and satisfactions implicit in working behind a disguise. Masked, an assassin could confront and surprise another *gen* without fear of losing stature; one could also kill domestic animals and even men without the customary consequences of recrimination, litigation, and indemnity. In the intervals between military action, one could play the role of *gen* without restraint, perhaps even more fully than was possible in battle.

The BaKwele state quite explicitly that the man who played *gon* could not be an ordinary person; he had to be imbued with witchcraft as well as bravery and ferocity to such an extent that he was thought somewhat mad. Some men, when being prepared to emerge as *gon*,

are said to have begun to tremble violently and to have gone into their
performance in a state of high excitement. Whether this condition was
purely psychic or partly due to the taking of a drug, *melaado*, made
from the bark of a shrub (*Alchornea floribunda*), is uncertain.

After the first instances of *gon* intervening in daily affairs, the
BaKwele seem to have capitalized on the situation. The immunity en-
joyed by the masked men allowed the playing of a war-game between
lineages of *begen;* this took the form of mock-raiding between BaKwele
communities, which, if performed unmasked, would have led to inter-
minable litigation and a perpetual state of war. To start the game, a
lineage that had a man who could play *gon* would have a mask made,
then send its *gon* out to test the mettle of other lineages, usually in other
villages. The initiating lineage normally waited until it heard that a rival
lineage, or village, was planning festivities in connection either with cir-
cumcision or with the settling of the affairs of a recently deceased villager.

When the festivites were under way, *gon* suddenly appeared, caus-
ing the celebrants to run for cover. The masker ran about the village
and, if he was fortunate, killed some animals, which were carried off by
the attackers when *gon* left. After *gon*'s departure, the celebration
would recommence, but its sponsors were aware of the raid as a chal-
lenge to their prestige and power. Moreover, they had to pay for the
losses inflicted by *gon*. The affronted lineage or lineages had to mount
a retaliatory raid by its own *gon* against the attackers in order to regain
self-respect. If they were unable to respond in this way, they had three
choices: (1) to submit to further raids, (2) to move away from the
lineage whose *gon* had raided them, or (3) to become clients of the
aggressor lineage. Any of these choices strengthened the leadership
position of the lineage that had used *gon*. Since *gon*'s followers were
undisguised and remained visible while the masker was in action, the
identity of the offending lineage, or at least of the village, was not a
mystery to the victims.

Respect for the *beete*-linked secret of the mask deterred direct con-
frontation between *gon* and those he harassed. The same principle of
protocol operated as strongly here as it did in the tacit understanding
that great *begen* do not come into open conflict. Similarly, a confron-
tation between two *gon* masks was unthinkable. Thus an effective
response through *gon* by the raided lineage would establish a balance
of power in the area, equivalent to that obtaining between great *begen*.

As the use of *gon* became more frequent among the BaKwele, its
institutional aspects came to resemble ever more closely those of the
gen status. Accounts of extortion by the masker multiply. The BaKwele
shrug off the depredations of *gon* as "*mezen*" ("amusement"), while

admitting that in some instances the threatened village was apprehensive enough to buy off the would-be raider with goods. These payments might amount to as much as three guns at one time, a windfall that must have considerably augmented the political power of the *gon*-owning lineage. On the other hand, since the increasing use of *gon* led to the diminishing patience of some lineages (and the sanction of *beete* could not always be relied upon), *gon*'s followers carried guns at the ready, in order to protect their masker against armed resistance.

The use of *gon* widened the *gen*'s field of action. Where a *gen* might ordinarily have been reluctant to confront another *gen* when ritually required to be his assassin, the availability of the masked disguise and its power to shock gave the *gen* an emboldening advantage.

The BaKwele groups in the Dja River region were settled in the last decade of the nineteenth century in country rich in rubber and ivory. They began a profitable trade with Europeans, whose goods—the highest form of wealth—soon entered the BaKwele economy in quantity. European trade provided new avenues to wealth for men lacking the traditional requisites for leadership. These new conditions also increased the competition for leadership. More guns led to more *begen*. The rivalry between parvenus increased the hiring of assassins. Increasing competition also must have led to an augmented use of *gon*. Today BaKwele elders speak of the *gon* of Ebagoona as unique, compared with which the *egon* used in their youth were commonplace. This suggests an increase in *gon*'s activity consonant with the expansion of the BaKwele economy.

A SUGGESTED RELATIONSHIP BETWEEN THE USE AND FORM OF THE MASK

Informants state that the *egon* of different lineages were distinguished from one another by their idiosyncrasies of appearance and behavior. The strategic advantages of imbuing the *gon* of one's lineage with distinctive attributes led to an awareness of the mask as an object in itself. This is implicit in the fact that the carving of the face of *gon* came to be done by master carvers rather than by a member of one's own lineage. That the skill and imagination of the specialist made a difference is indicated by the greater cost of the mask.

The *gon* mask became the second-highest-priced traditional mask of the BaKwele, reaching the sum of one anvil and one hammer, or twenty pieces of iron money, ten work knives, and one goat or dog. The price of the *gon* mask probably also rose along with its higher earning power: a period of affluence presumably increased the rewards of extortion and assassination. A dramatic-looking mask worn by a successful *gon*-masker might even be mounted as an ornament and remembrance upon the grave of the *gen* who had worn one.

Most dance-leading BaKwele masks are conceived in a plane parallel to the viewer, their features brought out in relief from a primary, relatively shallow block that the carver flattened fore and aft (fig. 4.4). The typical *gon* mask, on the other hand, impinges upon the viewer; the

FIGURE 4.4. BaKwele. *Ndyaadal*, a dance-leading mask. Aadyaala village, Congo-Brazzaville. Author's collection. Ht. 12″ (30.5 cm). (Photograph: Field Museum of Natural History, Chicago.)

alignment of its main plane is toward him; the brow and the jaw push forward beyond the plane of the upper part of the mask's face. The frame of the *gon* mask is lateral rather than frontal, and the carver seems to have been concerned with the illusion of depth. This concern was reflected in *gon* masks by a greater amount of carving and in the correspondingly high price of the mask.

FIGURE 4.5. BaKwele. *Gon* mask. Aa-dyaala village, Congo-Brazzaville. Author's collection. Ht. 13.3″ (33.6 cm). (Photograph: Field Museum of Natural History, Chicago.)

Nearly all of the *gon* masks in museum and private collections show a sophistication of conception and a skill in carving. They also show marked differences from each other, which, I believe, corroborate the implication in the BaKwele data that the individuality of the mask was a matter of concern to both its owner and its carver.

The extant examples indicate some of the ways carvers made *gon* masks distinctive objects while working within the limits of the conventionalized gorilla skull. The lower part of the face might be attenuated and extended beyond the plane of the brow (fig. 4.3). The brow, on the other hand, might be aligned with the plane of the tip of the jaw

FIGURE 4.6. BaKwele. *Gon* mask. The whitening of the entire mask is atypical. Museum of Primitive Art, New York (66.99). Ht. 15″ (38.1 cm). (Photograph: Museum.)

and extended upward almost perpendicularly (fig. 4.5). The eyes and nose might lie within a scooped-out face (fig. 4.6) or rise out of a level facial plane (fig. 4.5). The crest along the brow might be extended into a high wing-like form (fig. 4.7), or the entire shape might be condensed into a massive, almost crystalline arrangement of facets (fig. 4.8). It is noteworthy that this range of variation derives from analysis of the entire known corpus of *gon* masks—consisting of only twelve examples.

FIGURE 4.7. BaKwele. *Gon* mask. Office de la Recherche Scientifique et Technique Outre-Mer (ORSTOM), Centre, Brazzaville, Congo-Brazzaville. Ht. 18″ (45.7 cm). (Photograph: Henri Kamer.)

THE USE OF *GON* INFLUENCES OTHER BAKWELE PATTERNS OF MASKING

The variations in wealth, political competition, and importance found in the *gon* masks are paralleled elsewhere among the BaKwele. At the beginning of this century, new mask-types began to appear, and, like *gon,* these were "hot" masks, given to throwing spears and killing livestock. These masks are said to have been quite frightful looking but to have differed from *gon* in their form.

The Gothenburg Ethnographical Museum in Sweden has in its collection a round, deep mask from Souanké which has a relatively flat face,

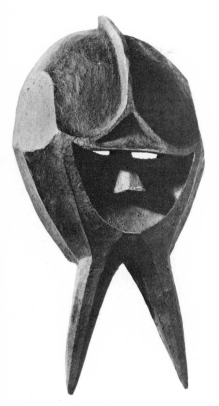

FIGURE 4.8. BaKwele. *Gon* mask. District of Souanké, Congo-Brazzaville. Collection Charles Ratton, Paris. Ht. 14.8″ (37.4 cm). (Photograph: C. Ratton, Paris.)

deep eye-holes, and long fangs extending downward from its chin (fig. 4.9). The last feature clearly recalls the *gon* mask, and it is likely that the behavior of this type of mask, if it is a traditional type, would have paralleled to a considerable extent that of *gon*.

Certain BaKwele mask-types that were not traditionally violent, but either mischievous or sinister instead, began at this time to perform with spears, throwing them at livestock and men. The proliferation of *gon*-like masks—both new and transformed—suggests that a number of individuals saw the political and economic advantages of this sort of masked performance, as well as the strategy of working outside of *gon*'s established system. The data indicate a cultural need both for *gon* and for masks of the kind that could appear more often than was required by the relatively infrequent demands of ritual. The increasing use of well-carved, relatively expensive disguises in activities designed to arouse antagonism or bring about submission indicates that the BaKwele recog-

FIGURE 4.9. BaKwele. *Gon*-related mask. Souanké, Congo-Brazzaville. Gothenburg Ethnographical Museum, Sweden (55.8.4). Ht. 13.8″ (34.9 cm). (Photograph: Museum.)

nized such masking as a serious part of the competition for political importance.

CONCLUSION

The abrupt end to the use of *gon* in political action occurred sometime after the consolidation of French power in the area in the early 1920s. This effectively prevents us from knowing whether *gon* could have become an instrument of established leadership, rather than a desultory stratagem with a minimal effect over time. It is known that a great *gen* sometimes gained control over his own village and might then influence a few neighboring ones (see von Elpons 1914, p. 65). But the transmission of a politically effective mask to his successors would have depended heavily upon a BaKwele lineage becoming closely affiliated with one particular settlement in one particular locus, a situation that never arose. To meet these hypothetical requirements, the behavior of the mask would probably have to change from an ephemeral show of brute force that could not be repeated too often for fear of losing its essential mystery and drama into a pattern more in keeping with the business of administration.

Studies of several peoples in Liberia, Ivory Coast, and Sierra Leone (Murdock's Kru and Peripheral Mande culture province; see Murdock

1959, pp. 259–264) indicate that dominant lineages or enterprising individuals can attain and keep power through the political use of masks. In some of these cases, the power is said to have been transmitted hereditarily, leading to the socially expected use of masks in the administration of village affairs (Holas 1952, pp. 79–80, 85, 88, and 1960, p. 70; Girard 1967, p. 80; Himmelheber 1960, pp. 146–147, 1963, pp. 232–233, and 1966, pp. 100–104).

Most of these West African institutions are described on one rather generalized level of time. Inquiry into the precise historical details of how masks in this area served to establish and sustain chiefships—or less formal but nonetheless transmitted political dominance—may enable us to learn whether a random, *gon*-like stage of political masking preceded the establishment of a system of masks fulfilling regulatory functions. The discovery of resemblances between the political uses of *gon* and the incipient patterns of "government by mask" among these West African peoples could tend to increase the chances of finding general correlations between certain types and uses of masks produced in villages composed of unrelated lineages during politically unsettled times.

REFERENCES

ELPONS, FRANZ VON
    1914   "Das Dschua-Becken oberhalb Madjingo." *Mitteilungen aus den deutschen Schutzgebieten, Ergänzungsheft* 9, suppl. a: 63–67.
GIRARD, JEAN
    1967   "Dynamique de la société ouobé." *Mémoires de l'Institut Fondamental d'Afrique Noire*. No. 78. Dakar.
HIMMELHEBER, HANS
    1960   *Negerkunst und Negerkünstler*. Braunschweig.
    1963   "Die Masken der Guéré in Rahmen der Kunst des oberen Cavally-Gebietes." *Zeitschrift für Ethnologie* 88, no. 2: 216–233.
    1966   "Masken der Guéré II." *Zeitschrift für Ethnologie* 91 no. 1: 100–108.
HOLAS, BOHUMIL
    1952   *Les masques kono*. Paris.
    1960   *Cultures materielles de la Côte d'Ivoire*. Paris.
MURDOCK, GEORGE P.
    1959   *Africa: Its Peoples and Their Culture History*. New York.

CHAPTER 5

Ibo Art and Authority

Herbert M. Cole

Although the Ibo of southeastern Nigeria occupy a continuous tract of land and speak dialects of the same language, they cannot be described in retrospect as having formed a unified people. The roughly eight million Ibo are socially and politically fragmented into several "tribes" which further subdivide into clans and then into village groups.[1] Unlike many of their neighbors to the east and west, the majority of Ibo have not developed centralized chieftaincy, hereditary aristocracy, or kingship. Leadership has traditionally been and still is most commonly vested in a village council among whose members are heads of lineage segments, elders, titled men, and others of wealth or position. Though one man may occasionally become nominal leader of the council, or "chief," he never transmits this position to his heirs; what little power he wields

Note: The field work and part of the additional research on which this chapter is based were made possible by fellowships awarded by the Foreign Area Fellowship Program and Columbia University. I am indebted to these institutions, as well as to the colleagues and friends who have helped in its various stages of preparation.

This chapter is set in an "ethnographic present" of about 1935. It discusses what may be called traditional Ibo culture prior in large measure to the changes brought by colonialism, nationalism, and other Western influences.

1. This study is not intended to include the Ibo living on the western side of the Niger or in those towns on its east bank, such as Onitsha and Oguta, which have been influenced by Benin in regard to their institutions of chieftaincy, title-taking, and other cultural matters.

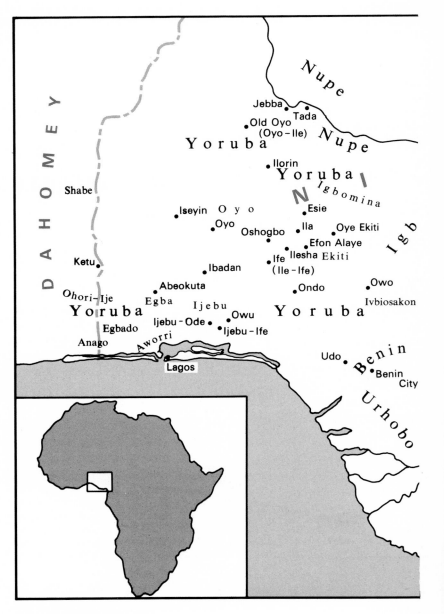

MAP 3. Southern Nigeria.

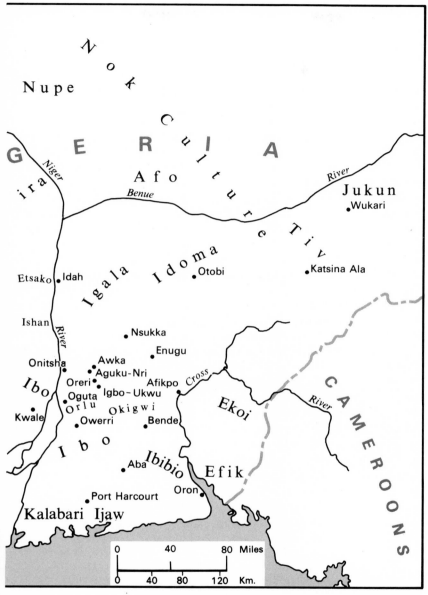

Map by University of Wisconsin Cartographic Laboratory.

is mainly as spokesman for the group. Local Ibo societies are therefore quite democratic and unstratified.

Before the introduction of European administration, lineage segments or individual villages were generally the largest effective political units found among the Ibo, though genealogical clan or subtribal identity was sometimes invoked for ritual reasons or in time of war. This political and social fragmentation, reinforced by the numerous dialectical differences in Igbo (the Ibo language), is paralleled by the diversity of kinship and land-tenure systems, religious beliefs, and art styles found in the area. In fact, few culture patterns or attitudes extend throughout the breadth of Ibo territory. Any attempt to make broad generalizations about the relationship of leadership and art for all the Ibo people is therefore unwise. Nevertheless, there are a variety of art forms that have served to reflect, uphold, and materialize social, political, and religious authority in comparable ways among certain Ibo groups. Examination of the role of art in two typical Ibo institutions—title associations and so-called "secret" societies—may therefore serve to show how art and leadership reinforce one another in a segmentary African society. These two institutions occur in different varieties in many parts of Iboland, sometimes side by side in the same community. In general, however, title associations are more typical of northern Iboland, while secret societies predominate in the south.

The Ozo title system may be regarded as a representative Ibo title society. Centered in Awka Division, it extends into Onitsha, Orlu, Okigwi, Owerri, and Nsukka divisions, with increasing variation toward the periphery. Secret societies in Iboland vary more in name, organization, and purpose than the Ozo title society; but the Ekpe society of Aba and Bende divisions in the southeast and the Omabe from the Nsukka area of the north may be considered fairly typical of this type of institution. The mere fact that the names Ozo, Ekpe, or Omabe extend over broad geographical areas does not indicate that any of them has an extensive sphere of influence. On the contrary, each society is a local entity, independent of other groups having the same name. Authority seldom extends beyond the boundaries of a village or town, though individual members of one group are peacefully received by their "foreign" counterparts.

Both title societies and secret societies in Iboland are groups made up of essentially the same sorts of people: elders, wealthy men, and other natural leaders. Thus, as has been pointed out, "although the society itself might have other interests, the fact that it brought together all the men that mattered in the community meant that it was bound to become involved in local government" (Jones 1955, p. 17). Nevertheless, title and secret societies differ from one another in their organization, in the kinds of authority wielded by their members, and in the types of art forms associated with their activities.

THE OZO TITLE SYSTEM

The Ozo system probably originated in Awka Division, where its most characteristic version is found and where, as in most of northern Iboland, local government was ostensibly vested in village council meetings open to all freeborn men. In actuality, these meetings were controlled by elders, the wealthy, and the personally forceful, many of whom were titled men (*ndi nze*). The qualities which combined to provide a man with social and political influence were diverse, but achievement of a high title was a socially recognized means of validating superior status. Once his right to hold such a title had been established, any energetic leader, with the help of his titled counterparts, could easily dominate the government in most of its administrative, legislative, and judicial aspects.

Important Ibo titles must be earned. Any free man who can afford the payments and meets the moral and ritual tests may take a title. The system is usually graduated into three major and several minor stages involving increasing expenditure and enhanced prestige. One of the titles in the final and highest stage is called Ozo, the name now given to the system as a whole.

The spiritual side of title-taking requires the candidate to undergo a ritual death and rebirth and a period of seclusion, and to participate in blood sacrifices, ceremonial washing, the taking of new names, and the establishment of a new personal god (*chi*). Title-taking is therefore analogous to graded initiation, with each successive stage bringing a man closer to the ultimate concerns of his community; passage through these rites confers an element of sanctity on Ozo men—they are closer to the gods and ancestors. Because of this, Ozo men are not allowed to tell lies, and having acquired a higher religious status than ordinary men, they are given more elaborate burials. As a group, however, the Ozo title-holders are concerned primarily with social and political problems; religious rituals figure prominently only in their initiation rites. Thus Ozo societies are almost entirely secular in effect, though they are spiritually sanctioned.

Lower titles, usually taken in childhood, are often financed by ambitious fathers who expect that their sons will later seek and pay for the higher titles.[2] Initiation fees consist of goods (yams, fowls, goats, palm

---

2. George T. Basden (1938, pp. 133, 135) notes that in some parts of Iboland lower titles were inherited, but never those which would have rendered a man forceful in local politics.

wine, etc.) and money, which are shared by the current title-holders; hence the Ozo system acts as a pension for those who have taken the higher, costlier titles and as an annuity for the title-taker. Since the first, inexpensive stages are reached by nearly all free men, effective socio-political authority at this level is practically nil. Real power is vested in the high grades that only relatively few men—skilled, energetic organizers and influential speakers for the most part—ever reach. Since the acquisition of a higher title is expensive and usually requires a man to mobilize economic resources from branches of his extended family, it is difficult for a man to achieve such status before middle age. In most communities, in fact, high-titled Ozo men are also elders in the chronological sense.

As an ambitious Ibo ascends the ladder of increasingly costly titles, he gains special privileges in his community, including gifts of goods and services from his extended family, a lightened work load, and a greater voice in council meetings. The right to speak—virtually limited to holders of high titles in some areas—constitutes the right to lead, since the decisions made in a meeting are in effect the constitution and laws of the town and are implemented by the authority of the meeting as a whole. In addition, each title brings to the earner the right to wear and use special insignia.

Title insignia, title names, perquisites, fees, and the regulations governing the system show considerable local variation. This variety doubtless stems, as George T. Basden notes (1938, p. 134), from the absence in Iboland of any overall central authority. Hence the descriptions of title paraphernalia that follow may be considered typical of, but by no means standard for, the many areas where Ozo-type titles are taken.[3]

Ozo insignia serve visibly to distinguish titled men from others and to differentiate between the members of various grades. Not all the Ozo paraphernalia are aesthetically pleasing; such articles of personal adornment as string anklets, red hats, feathers, animal skins, and carrying bags are included, none of which, taken separately, are really art forms, although together they contribute to the visible image of status. In the Awka area, entry into one of the lower grades requires the cutting of a distinctive type of facial scarification (*ichi*) consisting of deep parallel

3. A more complete, detailed description of several subdivisions of titles used at Awka, Onitsha, and Ogidi is to be found in Basden 1938, pp. 135–142. Basden (1938, p. 141) also notes considerable modification in title systems: "In past days, this order was undoubtedly a great power in the land. The members exercised a widespread influence, and they administered all the affairs of the community. They were treated with the utmost respect on the one hand, and were feared on the other. They had the power of life and death, and were the accredited despots of the town."

grooves on the forehead and upper cheeks (see Jeffreys 1948). While to Westerners scarification may not appear to be truly an art form, African peoples generally regard cicatrization, along with body painting, as a mark of beauty; most African scarification marks, like the Ibo *ichi,* are acquired during rites of passage to a higher social and/or spiritual status.

Among other prominent Ozo title emblems is a staff or spear which is used for swearing oaths. At the beginning of the colonial period in Awka, a wooden staff sufficed for the first title, a wrought-iron staff with brass-wire binding for an intermediate grade, and the highest rank required acquisition of an iron staff with twisted openwork decorations at the top and middle, the whole being bound at intervals with brass wire (Basden 1938, p. 139). Because so many men of the town of Ebenebe (north of Awka) achieved the highest Ozo rank, another higher grade was created there; its symbol became a staff decorated with four central baskets instead of the usual one (fig. 5.1). A wrought-iron staff having integral bells attached to its shaft also signifies the higher Ozo grades. These metal staffs were made by Awka blacksmiths who traveled the length and breadth of Iboland and beyond. This dispersion of Awka blacksmiths in some ways parallels the old custom— observed by priests of the adjacent Nri clan—of traveling to different parts of northern Iboland to help with the conferring of titles.[4]

Ozo stools are also important symbols. Not only is an Ozo man forbidden to sit on the ground, but also in some areas his stool accompanies him to the grave, where he is buried sitting on it. Traditionally, each titled man appoints a young nephew to carry his stool to the various meetings, where the Ozo men often sit according to rank. Several kinds of stools are known, but almost invariably the greater the elaboration, the higher the grade. Thus the stool for the low *chi* title is a simple narrow seat connected to a base by two plain struts. Common also is a round seat supported on a stem which splays into three or four legs (fig. 5.2). This type is sometimes associated with the highest Ozo rank, but where more elaborate stools are found it represents an intermediate grade. The most complex and elegant stools, those belonging to the highest grades, generally have a round base and seat with interior

---

4. The relationship between the Nri priest group and the doubtless old, yet apparently isolated and anomalous institution of Nri kingship (in Aguku Nri and in Oreri), and the possible relationship of the latter with the ancient bronzes discovered in Igbo-Ukwu (on land once belonging to Nri peoples) are questions too complex to discuss here. The three may well be related to the title system discussed here, although the points of intersection, especially with respect to Igbo-Ukwu bronzes, are by no means clear at this time. For further details, see Thurstan Shaw's (1970) study of the Igbo-Ukwu finds.

FIGURE 5.1. Ibo. Ozo title-society member with staff, stool, and tusk. Ebenebe village, Awka Division. (Photograph: author, 1966.)

supports carved in a variety of openwork designs (fig. 5.3). Ozo stools are carved from a single block of wood, and many are incised with geometric patterns which add textural interest to the forms.[5]

Elephant tusks (*okiki* or *ozara*)—also Ozo prerogatives—are rarely embellished with more than a few geometric patterns. Indeed they are

5. Made with a chisel and mallet, the carving on these flat surfaces consists of V-shaped incised patterns, usually geometric in character but occasionally including animal forms. This technique, known as "chip-carving," is frequently dubbed the "Awka style," although it is by no means confined to the Awka area.

FIGURE 5.2. Ibo. Stool associated with Ozo title-society. Umuduru Abagana, Awka Division. Ht. 16" (40.6 cm). (Photograph: author, 1966.)

FIGURE 5.3. Ibo. Stool associated with highest grades of Ozo title-society. Aguku Nri, Awka Division. Ht. 18" (45.7 cm). (Photograph: author, 1966.)

often left without any decoration at all. Occasionally, however, one is found with several motifs and rich geometric patterns in relief (fig. 5.4). The presence or absence of such decoration seems to have been a matter of personal preference. Embellished or not, these tusks are "badges of safe conduct" for Ozo men (and others who are lent them), when traveling in unfamiliar territory. Like the noises made by the small brass bells and belled staffs carried by titled men, a blast on one of these tusk-horns announces the presence of the man who carries it. Thus, sounds from instruments constructed of relatively scarce, expensive materials augment the titled man's total appearance.

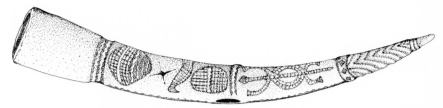

FIGURE 5.4. Ibo. Titled man's elephant tusk horn (*ozara*) from north Ibo village group Nrobo, Nsukka Division. Nigerian Museum, Lagos. Length: 17" (43.1 cm).

As a family and community leader and a person of status, a man of high Ozo rank needs an impressive compound and a place within it where he can meet with other men. In some areas, in the past, a man of Ozo rank was *required* to have two carved panels beside a carved door (fig. 5.5) at his compound entrance, and decorative relief panels on two of the walls of his meeting house (*obi*) (Jeffreys 1931, p. 36). Men of lesser rank were entitled to only one door without side panels and one decorated wall. In some communities, those without titles were denied the right to build an *obi* at all. These structures, with their lofty thatched roofs which are visible at some distance, are still the most impressive buildings in the traditional Ibo compound. The largest *obi,* those owned by the men of highest title in the Awka area, are decorated with carved openwork double panels that form the backs of the "altars" on which are displayed a man's *ofo* (staff), *ikenga* (personal shrine), *okpensi* (ancestral symbols), and other ritual objects, as well as various staffs and spears acquired by the owner and his titled predecessors.

In spite of the variations in the shapes and sizes of the paraphernalia associated with Ozo titles, these art forms have two notable traits: exclusiveness and increasing elaboration with higher rank. For a man without a title to wear or use one of the symbols is unthinkable. Whether the attribute is a stool, a staff, or an architectural feature, its formal simplicity or complexity reflects its owner's position in the title hierarchy. These art forms are fundamentally secular, scarcely being charged with spiritual content or symbolism except in so far as they refer to the status of a man and the group of which he is a part. Each man's title-attributes function, then, on two levels. They underscore the wealth and position of the individual, who by his use of them proclaims his own achievements and prestige as a leader. Yet they also call attention to the role of the title-holder as a member of a group, for the Ozo society, which conferred these privileges upon him, depends on its *corporate* identity to exert its force in social, judicial, and political affairs.

FIGURE 5.5. Ibo. Carved wooden compound entrance door and panels. Made by Edwin Agu of Nnokwa, Onitsha Division. Ht. about 6.8 ft. (205 cm). (Photograph: author, 1966.)

SECRET SOCIETIES: EKPE AND OMABE

Ibo secret societies, just like the title associations, served to institutionalize authority and to spread it among men representing different kindreds or interest groups. Secret societies were, if anything, more widespread. But secret societies differed ". . . from title societies in that the [secret] society was represented as being primarily concerned with the secret cult of a supernatural being or beings, whose propitiation was essential for the well-being of the community" (Jones 1955, p. 21). In parts of southern Iboland, secret societies (in contrast to any title groups) actually ruled the community; still, elders and men of wealth dominated both kinds of association: "The senior men of the [secret] society who were also the village elders were able to discipline other members of the community in the name of the society or rather of the supernatural being or beings to whom the society ministered, and the younger members carried out their orders with their identity concealed under masked or hooded costumes" (Jones 1955, p. 21). The art forms used in the society were employed primarily in masquerades which acted not for individuals, but corporately, for the cult; their effectiveness stemmed from spiritual sanctions, the tight security of the deliberations, and the fact that the actions of the society were collective. The various deities addressed by these cults were nature spirits, tutelary gods, or ancestral spirits, the latter predominating. In the minds of the Ibo, ancestors and important gods ranked as the true and ultimate rulers of the community. Though secret societies may have had, in part, recreational and political purposes, as indeed they did, fundamentally they were religious cults that periodically brought these ruler-deities into close proximity with the people, materializing the spirits or their messengers in the form of awe-inspiring masked figures.

Ibo secret societies differed from one another in name and function, not only from region to region but also within a single area. For example, in southern Iboland, where they reached their highest development, the Ekpe (Egbe, Ekpo, Egbo) society sometimes shared governing functions with other groups, such as Okonko and Akang; in other instances, towns had but a single all-purpose society. If some groups were graded rigidly, others were ungraded, while still others functioned in effect also as title and savings societies in which fees paid for admission to higher grades were shared among those already initiated. This marriage of title and secret societies was especially common among the Ibibio and Efik, from whom many of the southern Ibo secret societies are known to have diffused (Jones 1955, p. 22).

Before the advent of British rule the Ekpe society was the local government in several southern Ibo areas. By the 1920s, however, the

Ekpe had been supplanted by a colonial innovation, the warrant chief, who was given a hat, a staff, and a warrant to enable him to carry out executive and judicial functions. Warrant chiefs answered to and took their orders from a particular Native Court, with several towns and villages being grouped under one Native Court for administrative convenience by the colonial government. The powers theoretically vested in the warrant chief and the Native Court were in truth often still retained by secret societies; cases that were allegedly being adjudicated in the Native Court had in fact already been decided in prior Ekpe meetings. Secret societies were too firmly rooted to yield all authority to new courts or chiefs appointed by a foreign colonial regime.

The character of the Ekpe society before and during the early years of British rule is characterized by G. I. Jones (1956, p. 137) as follows: "The village elders . . . enforced their authority and punished and disciplined people in the name of the society, or rather, of the supernatural being to whom the society ministered. They could use its authority to support their legislative decisions, either by invoking the ban of Egbo [Ekpe] upon the offender himself or upon his property, or by sending the agents of the society sometimes in their own persons, sometimes disguised as Egbo spirits, to levy a fine or, in the pre-colonial period, to kill him." The precise relationship between these masked performances and the authority wielded by secret societies of the Ekpe type during the preadministration period is unfortunately not known from historical records. Clearly, however, masquerades were not the only or necessarily the most important sanctions of Ekpe. Yet Jones (1956, p. 137) adds that even the public festivals, while to some extent recreational, also performed political functions in disciplining and unifying younger society members, the potential leaders. Different age-grades were assigned the responsibility for providing music, dances, and masquerades, and the effort of organizing and executing such performances would naturally thrust youthful leaders to the fore.

By the 1930s, when anthropologists had begun to record data on Ibo masquerades, most of the performances sponsored by the various Ekpe groups were simply recreational displays—though some of them had probably had much more significance in earlier times. Among the masks worn in Ekpe (and other societies) which *may* have played a part in social and political control are skin-covered headdresses (of the sort generally labeled "Ekoi" in the literature on African art), which were worn by several southeastern Nigerian peoples. These masks are still considered powerful and mysterious; they may well have originated from trophy heads taken in headhunting raids. Another Ekpe play contrasts a relatively gentle, white-faced "maiden spirit" headdress with a harsh, fierce "elephant spirit" (Fagg 1963, pls. 120, 121). This juxtaposition may have been intended to express the conflict between the desirable, ordered, and secure world fostered by ancestors (beauty) and the dark, unknown world of unruly forces (the beast). Ekpe also employs a number of "runners," or lesser spirits in hooded net costumes that carry switches or machetes; they police the masquerade area and herald the arrival of more important spirits. Even today, in a time of peaceful plays, the "runners" are effective in controlling women and children. We can only guess that these and the other Ekpe masks were once more powerful and performed important duties in regulating behavior or adjudicating disputes.

In parts of Nsukka Division in northern Iboland, the Omabe cult formerly had the task of enforcing traditional governmental authority. Unlike Ekpe, however, Omabe was not a decision-making body. Actual government was in the hands of a council of lineage heads whose decisions were carried out by title-holders (*asogwa*) and their lieutenants (*ndishi iwu,* literally, "law leaders"). A secret male cult devoted to the propitiation of the tutelary and ancestral spirit which gave the society its name, Omabe nevertheless was ". . . used as an integral part of the system of law and authority" (Meek 1937, p. 75). The village councils made rules and preserved order generally without recourse to Omabe, which apparently was resorted to only when public secular authority had failed. Then Omabe was summoned to lend the weight of his authority to the council's decisions.

Thus Omabe was an agency for implementing authority only under unusual circumstances. If, for example, a man refused repeatedly to pay his debts, then some of the secular leaders were sent to his house ". . . accompanied by a masker impersonating the genius known as Omabe . . . to pillage the man's property" (Meek 1937, p. 147). Omabe apparently had more power over spiritual offenses, such as adultery (considered to be a pollution of the earth and therefore an offense against the powerful earth god) or the revealing of Omabe cult secrets to women. In the latter instance, after being tried by lineage heads and titled men, the offender was handed over to Omabe masqueraders who took him to the market place, drove away the women, and then shot him. Charles K. Meek (1937, p. 152) describes a confrontation between one such masker and his victim: "The approach of the masker caused terror to the culprit who, if he were wise, hastened out to meet the masker and buy himself off as cheaply as possible. Falling down before the masker, he saluted him by putting his hand to the ground and then to his forehead four times, murmuring, 'Ata, Ngwa Ala, Ata, Ngwa Ala,' i.e., 'Father, owner of the land.' "

A number of different masks were used by the Omabe society. One mask from Abbi (fig. 5.6), about sixteen miles from Nsukka town, is particularly interesting in the light of Meek's account of Omabe. Meek

FIGURE 5.6. Ibo. Ikorodo mask, perhaps associated with Omabe society. Abbi village, Nsukka Division. Author's collection. Ht. 33″ (83.8 cm). (Photograph: W. Swalling.)

(1937, p. 152) notes that many penalties were enforced in the name of the spirit Omabe: "The maskers of Omabe were indeed likened to the court messengers of the present [colonial] regime, and Omabe himself to the British District Officer." Though the mask illustrated in Figure 5.6 is removed in time (it was probably carved about 1945) and perhaps in space (Meek's data are unlocalized), the superstructure of this mask coincides remarkably with his account. There is no assurance, of course, that this mask was used to represent Omabe; informants gave Ikorodo as the name of its masking society, but would not state what the mask's specific name was. Questioned about the identity of the central equestrian figure, the men from whom the mask was purchased would say only "Eze," "king." Nor had they any reason to reveal the symbolic identity of Omabe (or a similar spirit) to an uninitiated white man. If the main figure, surrounded by four retainers (including two armed guards), is intended to be Omabe or a similar deity despite his guise as a colonial officer, the informants' answer is not inaccurate, for important gods are often addressed as "Eze." Following Meek, then, this imagery may be seen as a form of traditional authority in modern dress, stimulated by the force of British colonial rule and backed by its military power.

This melding of traditional and modern styles and functions has not until recently produced any diminution of artistic quality. Rather, the tendency has been toward a greater iconographic complexity, which in turn reflects changes that have taken place in the whole manner of Ibo life during the modern period. Significantly, the style of the figures and particularly of the mask itself *below* the superstructure is traditional in character. Many northern Ibo masks collected or photographed at the beginning of the European period have the same thin noses and lips on slender white heads, with black hairdressing, semicircular crests, and other details.

The successful marriage of traditional and modern or "imported" forms seen in Figure 5.6 is by no means unusual, for parallels are found in many parts of Iboland. In studying Ibo culture and art one is repeatedly struck, to use Simon Ottenberg's (1958) phrase, with "Ibo receptivity to change." In fact, artistic parallels abound in Iboland for the clothing of traditional religious authority in secular or modern dress derived directly from Western influence. In the Owerri area in southwest Iboland, where the Ozo title system is a relatively recent introduction, the most influential male deity, Amadioha, god of thunder, was represented in modeled-mud images with Ozo staff, tusk, and other attributes when these images were first found in *mbari* houses and recorded by Western observers. Soon after 1900, however, Amadioha figures begin to be dressed in prestigious European clothes in addition to their title insignia. In Awka and Onitsha divisions comparable wooden tutelary deity figures are also invested with title paraphernalia, and are attended by guards sculptured in early colonial military dress.

These examples suggest that Ibo imagery has long been accustomed to change. The precipitous alterations in the power structure wrought by colonialism were quickly followed by drastic iconographic changes in the art, even though the religious system remained substantially unaltered, at least during the first decades of colonial rule. There is some reason to believe that the Ibo welcomed the same kinds of change—artistic and otherwise—before the coming of the colonial era.

The embracing of change in the last sixty years has followed different courses according to the function and adaptability of the traditional leadership institution. In the case of all-purpose secret societies (in southern Iboland), the governing authority was *replaced* by colonial rule, and the associated art forms have tended to die out unless they could survive in secular entertainments with perhaps minor policing responsibilities and abbreviated leadership roles in truncated initiation rites. Many masks simply vanished. In northern Ibo areas secret masking societies were very numerous, and they never had, either individually or collectively, full political or social powers, for these belonged primarily to titled men. Many of these mask societies and their masquerades survive today. Like Ibo society as a whole, their art forms were resilient, for they came to image the power and authority of the modern world—gun-carrying policemen and figures dressed in European clothes. Title-taking, as a largely secular institution, was less subject to suppression by colonial fiat, and today it continues with diminished strength, moving away from political power as such and toward the expression of social status and prestige. The associated art forms survive in an equally diminished condition; stately traditional *obi* are replaced by concrete versions with tin roofs and bright paint, but lacking carved panels. These modern *obi* perfectly reflect the ambivalence of recent Ibo culture, which translates a traditional outward show of status in architecture into one that incorporates assimilated European forms. This happens in Iboland, perhaps, because Ibo and Western value systems are similar in their desire to dramatize status in architectural forms. Other title symbols are often retained, but they lack the vigor and careful craftsmanship of the earlier art objects that served essential traditional functions.

CONCLUSION

This study suggests that the art associated with Ibo leadership, though having its roots in the art of the common people, may nevertheless be distinguished from popular art. Of the attributes associated with titles, those in wrought iron may derive from prototypes in common Ibo weaponry. The exclusive use by title-holders of brass bells and ivory reflects the rarity of these materials, but the materials themselves may be intrusive elements. Carved panels, doors, and stools are aggrandized in size, number, and complexity from commonplace counterparts. Elaborate architecture houses dignitaries and thus draws attention to the ruling male group. Masks may well have originated with the people at large, but some of these objects have been elevated in function and imagery (if not in style) to higher status by Ibo leaders.

This process of elevating art objects that have lowly origins is entirely logical in a culture like that of the Ibo in which the leaders have been ordinary men for most of their lives. In the segmentary Ibo society, neither the leaders nor their arts have wide jurisdiction. Since no kings or courts exist here, naturally there are no courtly art forms.[6] Leaders' art forms must be at the same time village art forms; both the authority of the leaders and the forms of their art owe much to the people themselves.

Ibo art objects found in leadership contexts range from inactive secular objects to highly charged, spiritually sanctioned ones made and deputized in secret. They may be either privately or publicly owned; they may be worn or carried, or may consist of semipermanent buildings. Whatever their size, shape, or sanction, their fundamental purpose is to focus attention on authority and to command obedience to that power, whether vested in individuals or institutions.

6. A possible exception is the bronzes from Igbo-Ukwu mentioned above (note 4); this "hoard" includes a number of objects, such as sword hilts, pendants, tiny masquettes, and other forms that appear to have been the regalia of a political or religious leader of some consequence.

REFERENCES

ALLEN, J. G. C.
1933   "Intelligence Report on Ngwa Clan, Aba Division." Type-
            written. Enugu Archive, Nigeria.
BASDEN, GEORGE T.
1938   *Niger Ibos.* London. Reprinted, 1965.
ENNALS, C. T. C.
1933   "Intelligence Report on Ndoki Clan, Aba Division." Type-
            written. Enugu Archive, Nigeria.
FAGG, WILLIAM B.
1963   *Nigerian Images.* New York.
FORDE, DARYLL, AND JONES, G. I.
1950   *The Ibo and Ibibio-Speaking Peoples of Southeastern
            Nigeria.* Ethnographic Survey of Africa. London.
JEFFREYS, M. D. W.
1931   "Awka Woodcarvers." *The Nigerian Field* 2: 35–39.
1937   "Intelligence Report on Awka Division." Typewritten.
            Enugu Archive, Nigeria.
1948   "The Winged Solar Disk, or Ibo *Ichi* Scarification." *Africa*
            21, no. 2: 93–111.
JONES, G. I.
1955   *The "Jones" Report: on the position, status, and influence
            of chiefs and natural rulers in the Eastern Region of
            Nigeria.* Enugu, Nigeria.
1956   "The Political Organization of Old Calabar." In *Efik
            Traders of Old Calabar,* edited by Daryll Forde, pp. 116–
            160. London.
MEEK, CHARLES K.
1937   *Law and Authority in a Nigerian Tribe.* London.
OTTENBERG, SIMON
1958   "Ibo Receptivity to Change." In *Continuity and Change in
            African Cultures,* edited by William R. Bascom and Mel-
            ville J. Herskovits, pp. 130–143. Chicago.
SHAW, THURSTAN
1970   *Igbo-Ukwu: An Account of Archaeological Discoveries
            in Eastern Nigeria.* 2 vols. Evanston, Ill.
SOUTHERN NIGERIAN PROVINCES
1922   "Tribal Customs and Superstitions." In "Secret Societies."
            Pt. 1, chap. 16. Typescript compiled from reports of dis-
            trict officers. Enugu Archive, Nigeria.

CHAPTER 6

Humorous Masks and Serious Politics among Afikpo Ibo

Simon Ottenberg

Compared to their actions in ordinary life how do African men behave when they don masks and special costumes? Masking is behavior of a stylized and ritualized kind, and differs, therefore, from activity of a day-to-day nature. The question is more complex, it seems to me, than simply whether the man who puts on a goat mask is supposed to look and perhaps act like a goat or not. The same man wearing the same mask may be differently interpreted at various dances. The study of masking, then, forces us to look deeply into the specific behavior of the performers and into the relationship of their actions to crucial elements of the social structure of the society. For often the masked players symbolically represent both social tensions and political matters in their performances.

ETHNOGRAPHIC BACKGROUND

Afikpo, the subject of this study, is a village-group composed of twenty-two villages inhabited by some 30,000 persons in southeastern Nigeria.[1]

Note: Field research was carried out at Afikpo in eastern Nigeria between December 1951 and March 1953, while on an Area Research Fellowship from the Social Science Research Council, with the aid of an additional grant from the Program of African Studies, Northwestern University. Further research was conducted there between September 1959 and June 1960 on a National Science Foundation grant.

1. See Phoebe Ottenberg 1958, 1965; Simon Ottenberg 1955, 1965, 1968a, 1968b, 1968c, 1970, 1971; Simon and Phoebe Ottenberg 1962.

It is one of several hundred village-groups of Ibo (Igbo) who live in this portion of Nigeria and whose total population probably comprises some eight million. The Afikpo, like other Ibo, are sedentary horticulturalists with clearly delineated villages composed of well-defined social groupings. Like other Ibo, they have never formed themselves into a highly centralized political system; for many years the Afikpo village-group has had considerable autonomy in matters of traditional leadership and social control. The Afikpo are unusual for Ibo, however, in having double unilineal descent, each person belonging to corporate matrilineal groupings, which are nonresidential, dispersed, landholding descent groups, as well as to patrilineal groupings, residential groupings (associated with ancestral shrines) which form the basic units of the political system.

The typical Afikpo village is composed of several hundred to several thousand persons and generally consists of a number of patrilineages, often unrelated, each agnatic group living in its own compound more or less at the edge of the village common. Each village also has a distinct system of male age-sets, there being some twenty sets in all. Each set covers about a three-year span, the men being first formed into sets in their late twenties. Sets are grouped together into grades, the oldest forming the elders' grade, which rules the village; certain younger sets perform cooperative and communal labor at the elders' discretion. These age-sets form the basis of the authority system, in which age is a primary criterion, and they also help unite men of different descent groups into a common social organization.

The male elders rule the village by common agreement amongst themselves. There are no formal village chiefs or heads; consensus is the rule. Some elders, of course, are "more equal than others," because they are outstanding speakers, have influence through their wealth and the size of their landholding, or come from influential descent groups. Fundamentally it is an egalitarian situation for persons of the same age and sex, and an authoritarian one for younger and older individuals. Too much personal power among elders, or in any Afikpo for that matter, is frowned upon.

Each village has a secret society with its own secret initiation bush, its special spirit, and a host of rituals which its members carry out in the six months following the harvest season when the society is active. All village males join the society, generally before they reach adulthood. For men it is a universal association, since without membership a man is sociologically a boy and is excluded from most adult activities. The society is thus secret only with reference to women and children.

The tripartite authority structure of the Afikpo secret society must be mentioned briefly. The first unit includes the priest and assistant priest of the society's shrine, who are aided in carrying out sacrifices and other ritual activities by a small group of interested persons.[2] These persons are generally but not necessarily elders. The second unit comprises men who have taken senior titles within the society and who have the right to settle certain village disputes which the elders themselves cannot resolve. Again, many are elders, but there are exceptions. Third, the village elders as a group have some control over the society's activities. All three of these units—and some persons are members of two or three—act cooperatively to see that the various initiations, sacrifices, dances, plays, and the other activities of the society are effectively carried out. No highly centralized authority rules the secret society, just as there is none for the village.

Many of the society's activities are kept secret from noninitiates. These forbidden rituals include initiation ceremonies, title ceremonies of the society, the production of mysterious noises at night associated with mystical spirits, and sacrifices to the spirit of the society at its central shrine. But there is also a class of plays, dances, and musical performances carried out by society members which are open to the public; these affairs are extremely popular and well attended by men, women, and children. One of the more important types of play, consisting of a series of skits and dances, is the subject of this paper. The Okumkpa play, which lasts three to four hours or so, is performed in the village common and attended not only by local villagers but by many other Afikpo as well.

THE OKUMKPA PLAY

The Okumkpa is presented in the half of the year following the yam harvest (from about September to February), when the secret society is active in the villages. This half of the year is one in which the highly achievement-oriented Ibo of Afikpo (Simon Ottenberg 1958, 1971; LeVine 1966) turn their attention to realigning social relationships. It is the period when men take important titles by joining special title societies, thus raising their status and sometimes their power and influence. And it is the time when the elders have the opportunity to judge cases and disputes, especially in land matters. It is thus a period of productiv-

2. In some Afikpo villages there are no formal positions of priest and assistant priest, but there is nevertheless a similar type of ritual group.

FIGURE 6.1. Ibo, Afikpo. A dancer wearing the *nne Mgbo* (mother of Mgbo) mask. The raffia backing to the mask and the method of attachment to the face are visible. Mgbom village. Ht. 9″ (22.8 cm). (Photograph: author, 1960.)

ity in social relationships. In the other half of the year attention focuses on gaining material wealth and subsistence through farming and fishing. Social ties become less a focus of concern, the manual labor of individuals and groups more so. This work period provides wealth in foodstuffs which become resources for use in the ceremonial season; during this time new social tensions arise which are attended to in the following period. The secret-society play should be seen in this context.

As is true in virtually all of the public performances of Afikpo village secret societies, the players in the Okumkpa wear masks. They are believed to be spirits rather than people. Though most players are individually recognizable by their manner of dancing, walking, singing, and in other ways, the fiction is maintained that they are not really humans at all, but a general form of spirit (*mma* at Afikpo, *mmo* or *mau* elsewhere in Ibo country). If a wife sees her husband dancing in costume, she is not supposed to recognize him, nor to compliment him on his dress or dancing at a later time, though men can do so among themselves, as all are members of the secret society. But the crucial act of placing a mask on the face of a secret-society member changes his status from "mortal" to "spirit," and thus allows him to behave in certain ways with respect both to other players and to unmasked members of the audience.

FIGURE 6.2. Ibo, Afikpo. Another *nne Mgbo* mask. This is sometimes said to resemble a monkey or chimpanzee but is clearly female in character. *Nne Mgbo* is usually considered a very beautiful mask at Afikpo because of its whiteness and clearly delineated features. Mgbom village. Ht. 9" (22.8 cm). (Photograph: author, 1960.)

The masks themselves have a characteristic Afikpo style which differs from other Ibo mask styles.[3] Masks almost invariably have a vertical orientation and are narrower than the human head. Afikpo masks project forward from the face, the projection being markedly increased by bands of raffia which are tied to the back of the mask and hold it in front of the face, as seen in Figure 6.1. The masks are faces, not half or full heads, or helmets. Some are of animals—a goat, a monkey, a bird. Figure 6.2 depicts *nne Mgbo* (mother of Mgbo), often considered a monkey or chimpanzee mask by the Afikpo. Some are stylized human faces with additional designs and projections added to them. In this second group some are male, others female, and some represent either sex or no gender at all. A variety of these masks may be seen in Figure 6.3. One mask often represents a white person. A third group of masks consists of the ugly ones; they are distortions of human faces—something like the Iroquois False Face Society masks—with bulging cheeks, crooked noses and mouths, and ears that are out of line; these ugly masks are often dark or black in contrast to the other masks, which

3. For other Afikpo masks and related local styles, see Bravmann 1970, pp. 65–67; Starkweather 1968, nos. 1–66; Jones 1939.

FIGURE 6.3. Ibo, Afikpo. A group of the Okumkpa players sitting in the village common. Ugly masks (*okpesu umuruma*) are at the right front and left front and are about 12″ (30.5 cm) in height. There is an Ibibio-style mask at front center, which is about 11″ (27.9 cm) high, and a "queen" mask (*opa nwa*) toward the right, which is about 22″ (55.8 cm) high. Mgbom village. (Photograph: author, 1960.)

FIGURE 6.4. Ibo, Afikpo. The prayer beads and other aspects of the costumes of the actors are put on (and the beads played with) in ways designed to ridicule Moslems. Mgbom village. (Photograph: author, 1960.)

have brighter colors, making particular use of white. These ugly masks, which often represent old men, can be seen in Figure 6.4.

Some elements seem common to all the Okumkpa masks. Many have a human quality to them—even the animal masks—but they are almost as un-Negroid as one could make them. The noses have a high bridge. The faces lack everted lips, and in other ways do not look like actual Ibo people, as if the Afikpo wished to produce a clearly recognizable human face, yet one as distinct from their own as possible. They appear to be saying that these faces are, after all, not really theirs, but those of some other type of being. The masks are, of course, only a part of the total costume, though perhaps the most important part, for they make the man into a spirit.

The same "non-Afikpo" appearance prevails in the costumes. With the exception of khaki shorts, which have been adopted for general use, the costumes are not in any way like the usual dress of Afikpo men. This is evident from Figures 6.5 and 6.6. Animal skins worn on the back, porcupine-quill hats, and raffia shoulder-hangings and skirts indicate that this is the clothing of beings who are not Afikpo men. Red plastic waist beads, normally worn by unmarried girls, are often used as part of the costume, thereby confusing the sexual identity of the dancer.

A real social distance between the players and the audience is established through the use of mask and costume in Okumpka performances. In our society, when we watch a performance, the players are likely to be personally less well known to us and less involved in direct social relationships with us than is the case in Africa. Masks in Afikpo help to create an illusion of distance between player and audience—people who are otherwise on close social terms.

Each Okumpka mask has a name, and its wearer is expected to dance or play, at least at times, in character with the quality of the mask. But while masks are spirits, they are not particularly powerful; they do not give the wearer the right to try disputes, to judge cases, to wield every-day political power. There are no specific shrines associated with masks. Initiates may own, commission, or rent a mask for a play, or their part in the play may be assigned by the play leaders. Thus individuals do not have a close, personal relationship with a particular *mma* spirit.

Normally, Okumkpa consists of a series of skits and songs presented annually in some of the larger Afikpo villages, but the content of the plays changes every year, somewhat as variations on a recurrent theme. The play is led by two young men who volunteer for the work and who obtain the village elders' permission to prepare it. They gather their friends, peers, and relatives in the village and other volunteers in the settlement—generally it is men in their twenties and thirties that take

FIGURE 6.5. Ibo, Afikpo. The actors are playing out a skit. The main body of the performers is in the background. Mgbom village. (Photograph: author, 1960.)

FIGURE 6.6. Ibo, Afikpo. Two men dancing about between skits. They are allowed great freedom to dance in any style they wish, and sometimes, as here, do so grotesquely. Mgbom village. (Photograph: author, 1960.)

part. The players rehearse secretly at night in the bush for several weeks. Some older men who enjoy performing may also take part and will advise the players and judge the quality of the acts before the public performance. The play is kept secret from nonsociety members until it is given. Its two organizers lead the actual performance, wearing special masks which indicate their roles. Such masks can be seen in Figure 6.7 and on the two leaders in the background in Figure 6.4. After the play is presented the songs may be sung by secret-society members of any village who choose to do so; some popular ones are heard for many years afterwards.

In general the authority relationships among the Okumpka players are voluntaristic, cooperative, and not tied directly to the authority system of the secret society. If young men do not come forward to organize a play in a given year, none will be presented; the elders do not seem to pressure strongly for it. The players are not pushed by the elders to perform in a certain way, nor is their material censored. The young men are essentially free from the usual authority of the elders. This is so even though the latter decide on what day the play is to be given and may insist that members of certain younger age-sets take part, mainly as dancers, to make the play more impressive.

An Okumkpa play may involve over a hundred actors, singers, and musicians, all masked and costumed. They sit in the center of the village common facing the section where the village elders sit; the performers move out from there to act in the skits and to dance between the scenes. Part of such a masked group may be seen in Figure 6.3, and two dancers in Figure 6.6. Only the leaders stand apart. The players wear some ten different types of masks, which constitute the whole repertory for the Afikpo, with exceptions.[4] The Okumkpa masks blend together the history of Afikpo (Simon Ottenberg 1968a, chap. 2). Some are based on styles of the nearby Edda and Okpoha village-groups of Ibo, with which Afikpo has common historical ties; some are of Ibibio origin, an area with which the Afikpo have long had trading contacts, and some appear to be indigenous to the area, though probably of non-Ibo origin, coming from the general Cross River area of which Afikpo is a part. As we have seen, some represent animals, others male and female human-like spirits, one a white person; some are of older spirit-persons, some appear as younger beings. The masked

---

4. These exceptions include a special calabash mask worn during the initiation of a man's eldest son into the secret society, certain cloth masks, and masks that noninitiate boys make and use in play in the village.

FIGURE 6.7. Ibo, Afikpo. The mask of the senior of the two play leaders. Known as *nna okumkpa* (father of the Okumkpa), this mask is newly made. Often the leaders' masks a very old and are believed to have special spiritual qualities associated with them. Mgbo village. Ht. 12″ (30.5 cm). (Photograph: author, 1960.)

players as a group symbolize a totality of history, man, and nature at Afikpo. They are surrounded on all sides by an audience seated in the heart of the village—the group common—which also represents the totality of human life in the community.

The skits and songs are considered humorous by the Afikpo; they are intended to evoke laughter and other pleasurable responses from the audience, and they certainly do so. None of the Afikpo masks have movable parts. Their very immobility requires the careful and full use of vocal contrasts to handle subtleties, and the exaggeration of bodily movements in the skits to convey impressions of persons and indicate emotional states. These features accentuate the differences between the masked skits and songs on the one hand and everyday Afikpo behavior on the other. The masks become mobile only through the skillful use of the voice and body movement.

Although Afikpo do not distinguish sharply between the types of skits, we can group them into three basic varieties:

a. The first tells of single living individuals who have acted in foolish or greedy ways. Such persons may be men or women of any age. There are tales of men who are henpecked by their wives, who ask their wives' permission before doing things which are strictly male matters, such as taking titles. Tales tell of a man who always drinks too much at ceremonies and gets sick and vomits. As in all of these skits and songs the person is named, and specific details concerning him are often sung and acted out. The skit may tell of a man who performed an important ceremony, but was too cheap to hire a palm-wine tapper, and so climbed the tree himself, fell down, and broke his leg. Or of a person who became so interested in the nearby Catholic mission that he forgot how to speak his own tongue and now can say only English prayers— "Our Father who art in heaven, Our Father who art in heaven"—over and over again. Such commentaries seem to be reminders of how individuals in a wide range of social roles should behave. They comment on the need to follow proper procedures and etiquette, to act as persons of their particular sex and age are supposed to.

b. A second category of skits and songs concerns females, often groups of women rather than individuals. The men may sing that women should remember that if they wish to have children they should not sing the secret-society songs (which they are wont to do in modified form) or the spirit of the society will render them barren. Or that in the old days when the women went naked and fired their pots in the open, none broke; but now they wear clothes and shoes and their pots are not as good as they used to be and break in firing. This is because the women do not keep to custom nowadays.

The secret society is seen strictly as a male affair. In Afikpo the sex polarity in status and role is sharp: the economic and social activities of the sexes are clearly separated, and they spend little time together (Phoebe Ottenberg 1958). Nevertheless, in a culture which emphasizes individual achievement as this one does, and which is today under considerable pressure for social change, the traditional polarity is breaking down. Men admit that it is now hard to "keep women in their place." These songs and skits are attempts to reaffirm role differentiation. Men sing that women are after all women—they should not forget their natural functions of bearing children, raising them, and cooking, or try to change their ways. Women, for example, are not supposed to know any of the secrets of the secret society. If they do, it is thought that they will fail to bear children unless cleansing rituals are performed. Nor for similar reasons are they to touch the masked dancers. Wives of men who carve masks are not to know that their husbands, who do this work in secret, so occupy themselves, even though the women may grind some of the dyes used in decorating the masks for their men. In short, Afikpo men see these plays, as well as other aspects of the secret society, as reinforcing the distinctiveness of males in contrast to females, and as helping to maintain an authority structure in which men dominate the government and the decision-making in village and family affairs, while females play largely domestic roles.

c. A third category of skits and songs involves criticisms and ridicule of named leaders of the villages. These are generally elders or in some cases enterprising middle-aged men. The skits and songs generally involve a number of basic themes. One is about "palaver" men, those who engage in an argument or dispute for its own sake and so gather bribes and personal rewards at the expense of others, disrupting the normal tendencies toward cooperation and peace. Another theme criticizes the type of village leader who in a dispute sides with the group that he expects will give him the most money and food. One skit cites a man who collected money from Afikpo villages ostensibly to prosecute a court case between the Afikpo and the Nigerian government, but who actually used the money for himself. Or players may sing, again giving names, that certain elders are too shy to speak in public though they have no physical defects and can speak well, suggesting that they should come forward and give their views. In short, these brief dramas say that certain elders are foolish men who make unwise decisions for their own personal goals rather than for the whole community. They are enjoined to listen to what is being said at the plays, to help their own people, and to stop causing trouble, disruption, and dissension.

In a consensus society which also emphasizes individual achievement, there is always a tendency for some elders to try to usurp power, to go too far beyond the consensus principle. These men usually act on their own, and for personal gain, while appearing to represent their groups. Thus the consensus system of leadership at Afikpo makes for a sort of contradiction: men should be personally ambitious, but without disturbing the principle of group control. It is hard to regulate some elders and make them act as elders should. The contradiction at Afikpo is expressed both in the fear and in the admiration found there for the "big palaver man." For this reason too, elders themselves (who attend the plays in large numbers and enjoy many aspects of them) often think the dances, skits, and songs extremely funny—especially if they are about other elders, and more especially other elders whom they themselves think have acted inappropriately. The plays may also serve to articulate to some elders points that other elders find difficult to express directly themselves amongst their peers. The skits and songs therefore act as a sort of authority equalizer, just as wealth-distribution ceremonies, so characteristic of Afikpo, act to prevent any individual person from obtaining economic dominance. From the point of view of the elders, therefore, the plays have ultimately desirable goals. In another skit the leaders argue endlessly and foolishly in a divorce case. This is cleverly acted out, with side comments by the play-leaders about how some men love to talk. One skit concerns some Afikpo leaders who converted to Islam, allegedly for personal gains. This can be seen in Figure 6.4, where they are sitting together hoping for funds from the Moslems as a reward for conversion. The skit goes on to say that they were foolish to change religions for personal gain, and in the long run they lost money—that they are greedy men.

Another point brought out by Okumpka actors and singers is that when elders engage in foolish conflicts, they are liable to be killed by poison, sorcery, or other mystical means. The plays emphasize a point strongly believed in at Afikpo, namely, that disputes and conflicts by their nature kill persons, and that attempts should therefore be made to avoid them. Such disagreements kill good leaders as well as "palaver men" who stir up a dispute for personal reasons. One song, for example, tells of an argument between villages over ownership of a palm grove. The singers call upon certain named elders to give up the dispute because the grove belongs to a certain village. They sing of other prominent elders in Afikpo who died during the dispute; their deaths must be attributed to the conflict itself. This is, in fact, an old quarrel which has been going on for many years and which has cost the Afikpo a great deal of time and money without any settlement being reached. The players voice the anxiety of the public, that the elders should make peace with one another and not divert their strength into useless conflicts.

The kinds of comments these masked figures—young and middle-aged men—make concerning their leaders would be, Afikpo admit, impossible to utter, unmasked, in public. The political structure of the village is such that no young or middle-aged man would normally dare to make such statements at village councils. If he did so he would be quickly shouted down and probably fined by the elders. In fact, deferential behavior is invariably exhibited toward persons senior in age to oneself as defined by the age-set system. Younger brothers are expected to obey their older ones and not to try to outdo them in taking titles or in other political or commercial enterprises. Sons likewise may not speak up against their fathers at public meetings, nor may they take more titles than their fathers have taken while the latter are alive.

The comments about the leaders made by the Okumpka masked dancers are therefore of an unusual nature and are so recognized by the Afikpo. This is proved by the wide interest taken in them on the part of the audience, an interest shared by the elders and other leaders present. Names of offenders are freely given, and specific situations which have occurred, or are believed to have taken place, are acted out and sung about. If the named persons are in the audience, they are not allowed to become angry, for to show annoyance or disgust is considered very bad form. They are, in fact, expected to give the actors or singers pennies or shillings to show their approval of an act well done. In practice, however, criticized leaders react in a variety of ways. Some are so happy to have their names mentioned, even if in a derogatory manner, that they are not actually angered. They may be pleased at this recognition that they have special power or influence. Others are very upset and may privately try to take revenge on the play-producers at some future time through land-case litigation or other devices; but this is considered very bad form. Thus the pattern is generally maintained that the Okumkpa plays are very funny affairs and not to be taken too seriously. It is appropriate that the masked and costumed characters are light-hearted, amusing, and sometimes ridiculous. To become overly serious is to spoil the game—to invite factionalism. Even a mask carver was referred to as "that funny man who makes masks," as one who does not have a serious or major occupation, compared, say, to iron-smithing or palm-wine tapping. It is obvious, on the other hand, that carvers' services are indispensable, for masks are of vital importance to many activities of the secret society. But a kind of make-believe about the plays establishes them as effective devices for airing tensions in the village and for getting comments across that are otherwise difficult to articulate. Because people do recognize that the carver plays a serious and important role with high status, the content of the plays is more than make-believe or play-acting. In fact, I would argue that the play does have serious underlying intent.

For the young men *do* have honest grievances against the elders. Their comments are often serious, and they have no other effective ways of getting their complaints heeded short of refusing outright to cooperate with the elders, something which they rarely do. What in effect happens is that while elders normally make moral and judicial judgments on the behavior of the young men, in the plays the situation is reversed. Here the youths say to the elders: "Look, in such and such a situation you and you and you acted poorly and unethically." The characters who act out the misbehavior of the elders often use the dark ugly masks, with gestures and voices that are exaggerated and grotesque. They make fun of a leader who has a limp or speaks in a certain manner as part of their castigation of him. It is as if they are saying that the elders being portrayed are ugly, deviating, and foolish. The point is made indirectly at other times in Okumkpa, for all of the skits are about foolish people; generally, one skit is about the most foolish man in the village, and another about the most foolish woman. The latter skit usually involves a young dancer who wears the "queen" mask, *opa nwa* (carrier-child), which may be seen in Figure 6.3.

The spiritual forces of the Afikpo community are normally under the guidance of senior men who control and direct sacrifices and other religious rituals, in which young men play only supportive roles, supplying materials to be used in sacrifice and food for the feasts that accompany some religious activities. But in the Okumpka plays the younger men, as masked spirit dancers (*mma*), *are* the spirits and control and direct affairs. The elders, as ordinary members of the audience, sit passively, having only the secular role of reacting to the players. This is another aspect of the reversal of the leadership roles of elders and younger men that occurs through the masked plays.

FUNCTIONAL ANALYSIS

A tentative functional analysis of these plays may be in order. Functional theory is not by any means well established today, and between the earlier thinking of Emile Durkheim (1926), Alfred R. Radcliffe-Brown (1935), and Bronislaw Malinowski (1939, 1944) and the present day, it has been severely criticized (for example, Cancian 1960; Dore 1961; Erasmus 1967; Gregg and Williams 1948; Hempel 1959, Homans 1964; van den Berghe 1963) or developed in modified forms (Parsons 1951; Levy 1952; Merton 1949; Spiro 1952, 1961). Much anthropological writing on Africa has used functional analysis implicitly, and without making what was involved clear. I will try a somewhat more explicit formulation here.

First, the Okumpka plays stress normal and expected behavior by ridiculing deviancy; a wide range of deviant acts may be dramatized. The emphasis is on maintaining traditional roles, traditional forms of sex polarity, and traditional leadership. When the players are asked why they perform such skits and songs, they answer in specific terms. The manifest function of them, intended and recognized, is to make fun of and to ridicule that which the Afikpo consider to be the foolish acts of specific individuals and sometimes of specific groups. It is the anthropologist who generalizes the totality of actions as functioning in a latent manner to attempt to reduce deviancy, to uphold traditional custom, and to attack abnormality. Curiously, the young men are those who in Afikpo press for change the most, yet simultaneously they also are the ones who emphasize tradition in their plays. Why is this so? The leaders and style-setters of the plays seem quite traditionalistic compared with some other young men; those who are considered most "progressive" do not seem to play leading roles, although they often take part. Again, the young men as a whole—whether conservative or innovative—do not wish the elders to make the judgments about new conditions, for they do not feel that the elders understand them. Nor do the youths wish women to determine for themselves what changes to implement. Men today see changes in women's behavior as a threat to themselves. The Afikpo recognize that women are more independent and self-sufficient than they were formerly when they had to go to the farms under the protection of men and when they rarely traveled to distant markets or traded extensively in their own area. Afikpo women have a saying today: "When a woman has money, what is a man!" Thus, the young men see certain aspects of social change as desirable, but others as a threat to their position; in some ways they are conservative, in others they wish to play the controlling role in change.

A second major recognized and intended aim of some of the Afikpo skits and songs is to maintain sex polarity, the dominance of men over women and the restricted social and economic role of women in the face of changing conditions. Here the function of the play is seen in general terms, as many activities of the secret society are viewed, as a way of keeping women in their traditional roles. The means of coercion is the threat of barrenness in a society in which children are highly valued and where a person's status and prestige, male or female, is partly dependent on whether or not he or she has children, especially sons. The onus for failure to have children is placed on the women in Afikpo society, as can be seen in these plays and elsewhere and is associated with the angering of supernatural spirits through some form of female misbehavior.

Yet there also seems to be a latent function involved at the psychological level which the Afikpo do not verbalize. The fact is that men are extremely anxious about their failure to produce offspring even though the women are generally blamed for this, at least at first. A man must have at least a son to have status and to perform certain ceremonies and titles. Many children bring him considerable prestige and publicly symbolize his sexuality. The plays and skits, like other aspects of Afikpo life, operate to project strong, though rarely expressed, male anxieties about childlessness upon the women, particularly upon "mis-behaving" females who are identified by a male definition. Women who have passed menopause sometimes flaunt the secrecy of the society. They may say: "I am an old woman now, what can the secret-society spirit do to me. I will die anyway!" The extent to which men are some-what annoyed and bothered by such acts may be contrasted with their real displeasure if women of childbearing age do the same. This greater annoyance suggests that male anxiety over childlessness is a serious problem in Afikpo society.

A third major function of Okumpka plays centers around the use of the theatrical situation to air anxieties and aggressive feelings that the young men hold concerning the elders. Here again the Afikpo see as a manifest function the fact that the plays and songs ridicule the elders who do not behave as elders should, who are greedy, foolish, bribe-takers, and so on. This is quite obvious, but we have to go further to see some latent functions as well. I take it that egalitarian gerontocracy in Afikpo inevitably leads to younger men developing some resentments and hostilities toward their elders. In one sense the system of political authority in these villages is a projection of the family situation. The psychological features in man which make the young rebel against their fathers in the home context also operate by extension at the village level. Criticisms of the elders' actions in the village are a very limited and ritualized working out of youths' feelings against the authority of their fathers at home. Plays provide a way of handling aggressive feelings without changing the form of village social organization. The young men apparently do not really want radically to alter this form of government, and are in fact committed to it. They see long-term rewards in the status quo, even though they are restless with it.

The question why such aggressive tendencies, such criticisms, cannot be brought out openly at public meetings in the village, except in a highly circumspect manner, is crucial to the analysis here. I suggest that such tactics would be highly disruptive. The few attempted cases that I have seen were put down with short shrift by the elders, whom the youths both respect and fear, and whose place they desire some day to take themselves. I do not think we could postulate that village unity or Afikpo society would disintegrate or disappear if direct public aggres-sion by clearly identified youths took place, although changes would occur. The theme of "social collapse unless aggressions are strongly displaced" is an old one in functional analysis, but is also moot. The fact seems to be that the young men, on the whole, are committed to the system to which they themselves sometimes object (Simon Otten-berg 1955), and they are not interested in radically altering it. Further, they are well aware that the elders hold the ultimate sources of power— the control and regulation of supernatural forces. Those "progressive" individuals who are not happy in this system of authority generally live outside the villages or elsewhere in Nigeria and take only a limited part in village matters.

The criticisms of the Afikpo elders also serve other latent functions, which are occasionally recognized in specific cases. One purpose is to reduce individualism among the elders and thus to maintain egalitarianism by criticizing those who draw too much power to themselves. Some elders support this view as well, for the ideal of consensus as a basis for decision-making and the fear of village domination by single individuals are both strong sentiments. In this sense the skits and songs concerned with the elders are a functional equivalent of the witchcraft accusations among the Tiv, which are directed toward powerful individuals (Bohannan 1958). Both are attempts to reduce and contain such power. Conflict among the elders seems to stir anxiety among many persons in the Afikpo village, and attempts through the plays to reduce factionalism and get the elders to pose as a cooperative group may reduce such feelings.

A further function, again one that is mainly latent and that needs little comment, is that the Okumpka plays seem to help develop or maintain a sense of pride and accomplishment in the village as a unit, to maintain a sense of the whole, of persons acting and working together regardless of individual kinship and residential ties. Many other Afikpo come and see these plays and persons remark on which villages have produced good plays in a given year and which have not. Intervillage rivalry, which also finds expression in wrestling and whipping contests and in other secret-society plays and dances, is enhanced and maintained by this particular form of play. The theater becomes a symbolic and public statement of the state of village organization.

The use of masks and costumes as "screens" helps to facilitate the outlet of anxieties and aggressive feelings without fear either of counterattack or any reorganization of the authority structure. I take it that here, as in the case of mother-in-law jokes in our own society, the humor expressed is related to some anxiety and tension. I do not mean to imply, however, that there is a natural tendency for a society to maintain itself or for equilibrium situations automatically to assert themselves in a society through such plays. Following Homans (1964), I suggest that individuals in the village are not anxious, in terms of their goals, to change its organization drastically at this point in time; they are interested in it as it is, and their orientation toward it is what maintains it, rather than there being any natural tendency toward equilibrium or stability.

The plays also can be looked at as dysfunctional, though I think to a relatively small degree. They may lead to anger on the part of elders and others who have been ridiculed and criticized. Such anger is often directed toward the leaders of the play, with consequent gestures of noncooperation toward the men involved (for example, pressuring to oust them from land they are using on loan). Thus every play seems to leave some residue of ill-will in the village, though this does not seriously affect the operation of the village organization and usually occurs between individuals rather than groups.

It is also worth noting that the rather free-floating authority structure of the players' group within the larger authority system of the secret society and the village is no accident. This autonomy gives players the freedom to act as they would not be able to if they were directly under the authority of the village elders, the priests' group, or the titled group of the secret society. Such functional autonomy (Gouldner 1959) is necessary for the effective preparation and performance of the plays. In order to be prepared and performed, a play and its creators must be in a certain structural arrangement vis-à-vis society at large, here one of relative freedom to create, independent from the elders.

Three queries concerning this sort of analysis may now be considered. The first question is: what sort of things are *not* acted or sung about in these plays? I see two major omissions: matters having to do with the secret-society's priests (and other religious officials at Afikpo) and sexual references. Plays may criticize the priests of Afikpo's spirit shrines and diviners, but only indirectly—for example, by reminding priests in general that other priests who have failed to perform their work effectively in the past have died before their time. Beyond this, there seems to be no attack on religious leaders, probably because of their direct association with very powerful spirits. As *mma* spirits, the masked actors are free to criticize elders in their role as secular leaders, but not as religious heads. This fits well with the Afikpo view. Spirits are guardians of morality, but as a rule they are not believed to be critical or hostile to other spirits.

With regard to sexual matters, it is interesting to note that apart from an occasional reference, such matters are generally not treated in Okumpka plays, though there is plenty of deviation from sexual norms at Afikpo which could be used as material. Rather, certain unmasked public song and dance festivals are held annually which do treat the actions and misbehavior of individuals, again giving names and details.

The singers are young people—male and female—of certain ages. We have to ask why these performances can be given openly and not through the use of masked plays, and why women can take an active part in them. The answer is in a sense a test of the fitness of the analysis presented above. At this moment I cannot provide a fully satisfactory explanation, but I suggest that a primary factor is that sexual deviancy from the norm is not taken very seriously in Afikpo unless it involves a few special forms, such as sexual relationships between members of the same matrilineal clan. In fact, virtually everyone in Afikpo is involved in nonnormative sexual acts, assuming it is even possible to determine accurately what normative sexuality is for this area. Further, many of these cases involve persons in different villages—which cases are therefore not purely internal matters—and also matrilineal groupings which do not have a residential base; thus the frictions that arise over these affairs often cut across villages, rather than merely affecting intravillage relationships. Hence the authority structure of the village is generally not involved, even if the violators of sexual norms are elders.

A second problem arises out of the fact that we are basing at least part of this analysis on hypotheses concerning individual anxieties and aggressive feelings. I have imputed these to the young men in terms of a general theory of father-son ties and some known facts about young men and elders at Afikpo and in other societies. But I really lack proof for Afikpo. We might learn more by using psychologically sensitive data, or, if a village in Afikpo could be found which did not carry out such plays, or did so very rarely, an examination of its authority structure and sex polarity and a careful search for functional equivalents of the masked plays might be made. A few small villages in Afikpo do not produce Okumpka plays, but at the time they were investigated, I did not have this question in mind.

A third problem is that of evaluating what the plays really *do* to people, other than amusing and pleasing them. How are persons actually affected by them, what really is their impact on the audience—on a short-term or long-range basis? As we have seen, songs from the plays may be sung by many persons for months, even years, after the original performance, and both songs and skits are discussed in the village and elsewhere for a long time afterwards; their influence clearly extends beyond the day they are first presented, and beyond a second neighboring village where the play is sometimes given again a few days after its original performance. I have mentioned the attempt in Okumpka plays to maintain sex polarity and egalitarian leadership. I would add that the plays seem to be primarily tension-reducing devices; they point up moral and ethical standards, they attempt to reduce individualism in leadership, they help to give a village a sense of identity and unity as against other villages, and so on. But it seems that in the analysis I have presented, and in others of like kind, we have yet to develop techniques for accurately gauging how effective the plays actually are in accomplishing these tasks. We do not, at present, have sensitive field tools to achieve this purpose. Furthermore, traditional field work techniques are inadequate in this context, so that new and more accurate tools of a different order will have to be devised. Functional analysis of the sort presented here is at a very simple and crude level operationally. It can indicate manifest intentions and latent functions, but it has few techniques for measuring actual consequences.

In any case, while the Afikpo plays themselves are humorous, popular, well attended, and very much enjoyed, much of the subject matter clearly is serious and directly tied to questions of authority and control in the village. The secrecy of the dancers, achieved through the use of masks and costume as concealing forms, is a method of publicly revealing what persons gossip about privately, or simply do not know. The masked players, through a ritual role reversal of leadership, become devices through which the secrets of the "other world" are revealed and explained. Thus masked secrecy is a mechanism to undo secrets.

REFERENCES

BATESON, GREGORY
      1936   *Naven*. Cambridge, England.
BOHANNAN, PAUL
      1958   "Extra-Processual Events in Tiv Political Institutions."
                      American Anthropologist 60, no. 1: 1–12.
BRAVMANN, RENÉ A.
      1970   *West African Sculpture*. Index of Art in the Pacific North-
                      west, no. 1. Seattle.
CANCIAN, FRANCESCA
      1960   "Functional Analysis of Change." *American Sociological
                      Review* 25, no. 6: 818–827.
DORE, RONALD P.
      1961   "Function and Cause." *American Sociological Review* 26,
                      no. 6: 843–853.
DURKHEIM, EMILE
      1926   *The Elementary Forms of the Religious Life*. 2d rev. ed.
                      New York. Translation of *Les formes élémentaires de la
                      vie religieuse*. Paris, 1912.

ERASMUS, CHARLES J.
    1967   "Obviating the Functions of Functionalism." *Social Forces*
                    45, no. 3: 319–328.
GOULDNER, ALVIN W.
    1959   "Reciprocity and Autonomy in Functional Theory." In
                    Symposium on Sociological Theory, edited by L. Gross,
                    pp. 241–270. New York.
GREGG, DOROTHY, AND WILLIAMS, ELGIN
    1948   "The Dismal Science of Functionalism." *American Anthro-
                    pologist* 50, no. 4: 594–611.
HEMPEL, CARL G.
    1959   "The Logic of Functional Analysis." In *Symposium on
                    Sociological Theory*, edited by L. Gross, pp. 271–307.
                    New York.
HOMANS, GEORGE C.
    1964   "Bringing Man Back In." *American Sociological Review*
                    29, no. 6: 809–818.
JONES, G. I.
    1939   "On the Identity of Two Masks From S. E. Nigeria in the
                    British Museum." *Man* 39, art. 35: 33–34.
LEVINE, ROBERT A.
    1966   *Achievement Motivation in Nigeria*. Chicago.
LEVY, MARION J., JR.
    1952   *The Structure of Society*. Princeton.
MALINOWSKI, BRONISLAW
    1939   "The Group and the Individual in Functional Analysis."
                    American Journal of Sociology 44, no. 6: 938–964.
    1944   *A Scientific Theory of Culture and Other Essays*. Chapel
                    Hill.
MERTON, ROBERT K.
    1949   "Manifest and Latent Functions." In *Social Theory and
                    Social Structure*, edited by R. Merton, pp. 21–81. Glen-
                    coe, Ill.
OTTENBERG, PHOEBE
    1958   "The Changing Economic Position of Women Among the
                    Afikpo Ibo." In *Continuity and Change in African Cul-
                    tures*, edited by William R. Bascom and Melville J. Her-
                    skovits, pp. 205–223. Chicago.
    1965   "The Afikpo Ibo of Eastern Nigeria." In *Peoples of Africa*,
                    edited by James L. Gibbs, Jr., pp. 1–39. New York.
OTTENBERG, SIMON
    1955   "Improvement Associations Among the Afikpo Ibo." *Africa*
                    25, no. 1: 1–28.
    1958   "Ibo Receptivity to Change." In *Continuity and Change
                    in African Cultures*, edited by William R. Bascom and Mel-
                    ville J. Herskovits, pp. 130–143. Chicago.
    1965   "Inheritance and Succession in Afikpo." In *Studies in the
                    Laws of Succession in Nigeria*, edited by J. Duncan M.
                    Derrett, pp. 33–90. London.

1968a   *Double Descent in an African Society: The Afikpo Village-Group.* American Ethnological Society, Monograph 47. Seattle.

1968b   "Statement and Reality: The Renewal of an Igbo Protective Shrine." *International Archives of Ethnography* 51: 143–162.

1968c   "The Development of Credit Associations in the Changing Economy of an African Society." *Africa* 38, no. 3: 237–252.

1970   "Personal Shrines at Afikpo." *Ethnology* 9, no. 1: 26–51.

1971   *Leadership and Authority in an African Society: The Afikpo Village-Group.* American Ethnological Society, Monograph 52. Seattle.

OTTENBERG, SIMON AND PHOEBE

1962   "Afikpo Markets: 1900–1960." In *Markets in Africa*, edited by Paul Bohannan and George Dalton, pp. 117–168. Evanston, Ill.

PARSONS, TALCOTT

1951   *The Social System.* Glencoe, Ill.

RADCLIFFE-BROWN, ALFRED R.

1935   "On the Concept of Function in Social Science." *American Anthropologist* 37, no. 3: 394–402.

1957   *The Natural Science of Society.* Glencoe, Ill.

SPIRO, MELFORD

1952   "Ghosts, Ifaluk and Teleological Functionalism." *American Anthropologist* 54, no. 4: 497–503.

1961   "Social Systems, Personality and Functional Analysis." In *Studying Personality Cross-Culturally*, edited by Bert Kaplan, pp. 93–127. Evanston, Ill.

STARKWEATHER, FRANK

1968   *Igbo Art: 1966.* Museum of Art, University of Michigan, Ann Arbor.

VAN DEN BERGHE, PIERRE L.

1963   "Dialectic and Functionalism." *American Sociological Review* 28, no. 5: 695–704.

CHAPTER 7

Royal Sculpture in the Cameroons Grasslands

Suzanne Rudy

Although they number several millions and are divided into hundreds of socio-political units, the peoples of the Cameroons Grasslands share remarkably similar economic, political, and religious institutions. The hilly plateau they inhabit provides adequate soil for root crops and cereal cultivation, as well as forest patches where palm trees, fowl, and wild game flourish. Various socio-political institutions, such as chieftain-ship, hieratically organized courts, title-holding, and secret societies, as well as patrilineal descent and patrilocal residency, are widely shared in the Cameroons. Grassland polities vary greatly in size, however, from tiny *chefferies* of no more than a few hundred people to large kingdoms of tens of thousands.

Leadership in most Cameroons societies is vested in a chief or king who is responsible for the prosperity and well-being of his people. In most instances the chief (or king) not only conducts the major sacri-fices and propitiatory rites directed toward the maintenance of fertility (Malcom 1925, p. 373), but also acts as the titular head of the local secret society which, for this reason, often becomes the instrument of his military power. As a man of wealth and influence, the ruler is also the major patron of the arts; he is usually surrounded by elaborate, often monumental, sculptures and architectural reliefs which silently but

Note: The Reverend Dr. Paul Gebauer kindly criticized an earlier version of this paper in the light of his vast knowledge of Grasslands life and arts. I wish to offer my thanks for his encouragement and assistance.

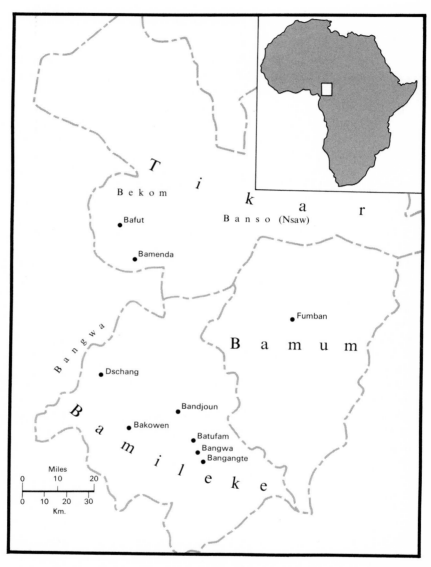

MAP 4. Central Cameroons. (Map by University of Wisconsin Cartographic Laboratory.)

eloquently proclaim his economic, socio-political, and religious ascendancy.

This chapter will deal with a single aspect of Cameroons Grasslands sculpture, but one that bears directly on the relationship between art and leadership—the depiction of sovereign beings and nobility. In some African arts it is easy to distinguish images of leaders from those of inferiors, but this is not true of sculpture in the Cameroons. For here we are dealing with a congeries of styles and a diversity of forms, only a few of which are precisely attributed and documented. Wars, migration, and market exchanges have further fragmented and confused the information, so that even if we know where an object was collected, we cannot be sure where it was made. Often we cannot even tell who is represented in a given sculpture because of the paucity of collection data and the practice of making replicas of important pieces. Nor are stylistic distinctions particularly useful in this regard, though the existence of three main style clusters in Cameroons art—the Tikar group, the Bamum around Fumban, and the Bamileke—may be recognized. But by taking the evidence from these centers collectively, we may hope to shed some light on Cameroons Royal imagery.

At the apex of the leadership hierarchy is the chief or king, through whom are channeled appeals to the ultimate spirit powers—the ancestors. Next to the chief in importance are titled persons of high rank, mainly members of the Royal household. In many areas the Queen Mother or the chief's first wife is accorded extraordinary respect and privilege; she may even assume authority in the chief's absence. Other wives, sons, and daughters born into the chiefdom enjoy distinct prerogatives. Special attention and favors are given to Royal twins. Of somewhat less importance are subchiefs who act as the ruler's viceroys in managing the affairs of the far-flung tribe, counsellors in court, and such various functionaries as messengers, attendants, and bodyguards. Although many of these individuals are servants, most of them are granted titles and consequently take their place in the highly stratified society of the court.

Office holders of every level are represented in Grasslands sculpture. Among the Bamileke, for example, a newly installed chief commissions an effigy of himself and another of the mother of his first daughter (Lecoq 1953, p. 117). In the Batufam area several generations of rulers and their wives and retainers are represented in facade sculpture, forming a sort of courtly tableau on permanent display in the village (see Lecoq 1953, figs. 92–95, and Paulme 1956, pl. xvii). Often, though, we do not know what rank or office is associated with a particular image or symbol. Many Cameroons chiefs were accustomed to grant members of their retinue the right to use emblems similar to their own, which further complicates the problem of iconographic interpretation. In general the more numerous the adornments and implements linked with a figure, the greater the likelihood that the image depicts a sovereign leader. Even the presence of a few attributes usually means the person represented is a member of the nobility. Of course a distinction should be made between an image which *depicts* a ruler and those which he simply owns as means of reinforcing his power. In the Grasslands, leaders often surrounded themselves with retainers *in sculptural form* as well as in person. Raymond Lecoq (1953, figs. 17, 103) illustrates two subservient figures, one of which makes the hand-over-mouth gesture of obeisance, while the other proffers the royal pipe. Yet since these carvings are covered with cowrie shells (a clear indication of chiefly ownership[1]), the images must originally have been made for and used by the leader and belong, therefore, to the elite tradition in Cameroons art.

What, then, are the functions of these aristocratic images? In many cases, figures that represent elite beings can be considered a sort of portraiture. As with other African "portraits," however, there is no attempt at a highly individualized rendering of human features, but rather there is a generalized realism within the canons of local style. Nevertheless, the Grasslands people refer to these images as depictions of specific individuals and tend to treat them accordingly.

The "portrait" seems to have been regarded primarily as a receptacle into which the ancestral spirit of a dead leader might be precipitated. Libations and sacrifices were offered to the carved figure to placate and propitiate the spirit so that it would favor and benefit the living descendants. The role of ancestor figure, therefore, is perhaps the part most frequently assigned to Cameroons sculpture and one of the more important it performs in the lives of the people. Another role played by certain Grasslands figure carvings is that of preserving the tribe's historical associations, genealogies, and legends. This narrative function explains why many of the figures are placed over or near doorways of houses, especially that of the chief, who symbolizes both the origin and destiny of his people.

The overriding significance of Cameroons *elite* sculpture, however, seems to have been prestige. Symbols of status occur here almost as frequently as in the well-known aristocratic styles of Nigeria. An impressive array of costume details and personal ornaments enhance these carvings, including caps, hats, loincloths, waistbands, bracelets, anklets,

---

1. Paul Gebauer (oral communication) reports that virtually all Cameroons images covered with beads, shells, and appliqué metals belonged to important chiefs.

necklaces, and earrings. Some images are further individualized by means of beards and relief cicatrization, while in others the status of the ruling class is telegraphed visually by means of such symbolic objects as staffs, weapons, skulls or trophy heads, calabashes, drinking horns, pipes, and bowls. In particularly elite examples the figure sits on a stool, the single most important Grasslands status symbol. A carving of a Bakowen chief (fig. 7.1) illustrates a number of these symbols com-

FIGURE 7.1. Bamileke group, Bakowen chiefdom. Seated chief holding pipe and calabash. [In order to locate Bakowen it was necessary to consult Paul Engo of the Cameroon mission to the United Nations and Dr. Hans Becher, Director, Department of Anthropology, Niedersächsisches Landesmuseum, Hannover. Dr. Paul Gebauer finally located this area on the M. Moisel map published by Dietrich Reimer (1913) on the basis of information supplied by the museum. Eds.] Collected by Second Lieutenant von Frese, military station Dstzang (Dschang), Kamerun, 1910. Niedersächsisches Landesmuseum, Hannover, West Germany (IV/5541). Ht. 44.2″ (112 cm). (Photograph: Museum.)

bined in a highly sophisticated manner. In this work the chief carries three important emblems of rank—calabash, drinking horn, and pipe. Besides having a utilitarian purpose, each of these objects also has a ritual and symbolic value which will now be described.

Throughout the Grasslands the calabash is used as a container for palm wine, a sacred drink to Cameroons people who believe it has fertility-giving properties (Gebauer, oral communication). Since palm wine is essential to the annual agrarian rites, the calabash, as its container, symbolizes the ritual powers which ensure the well-being of the community. Royal calabashes are often elaborately beaded, and, unlike the plain gourd type, are also sometimes used as containers for the cranial bones of defunct chiefs (Lecoq 1953, p. 171). Everywhere in the Grasslands area skulls of important ancestors are carefully guarded and preserved, since a dead leader's skull, like a wooden ancestor figure, is thought to contain some of his vital essence. Conversely, if the ancestral skulls of an enemy people are captured in war, the power of that group is accordingly diminished. Thus Royal calabashes, whether in themselves or in sculptural rendering, are richly endowed with symbolic meaning.

The drinking horn, either attached to the calabash or carried in the hand (figs. 7.1, 7.2, 7.3), is among the most frequently seen objects in aristocratic Grasslands figure sculptures. Its use parallels that of the calabash, and as a palm-wine container it is an important utensil in social and ritual life of the Grasslands nobility. Like the calabash and other attributes appearing in sculpture, actual drinking horns were often decorated with figural or abstract designs. In sculptured images, however, these attributes are usually simplified or unadorned.

A third emblem of status seen in Cameroons elite sculpture is the ceremonial pipe smoked by the chief while presiding over important rituals or social occasions. Made either of fired clay or of *cire perdue* cast brass, the actual smoking-pipe bowls often show a mastery of lacy forms and intricate shapes. The Bakowen carving (fig. 7.1) illustrates an unusually faithful, if not unique, translation into wood of one of these pipes. The pipe bowl consists of a human figure with a large head and a drastically reduced torso. In the more usual type (figs. 7.2, 7.3) the head and bowl are reduced to a simple rounded form. In other carvings male figures hold shorter pipes in the smoking position.

Although the calabash, drinking horn, and pipe are the attributes most prevalent in aristocratic Grasslands sculptures, some figures also carry staffs, scepters, heads or skulls, or bowls. Two famous Bekom stools, one in Berlin and the other in Frankfurt (Fagg 1965, fig. 63),

FIGURE 7.2. Bangwa subgroup (probably Fontem) (West Cameroon). *Fosia* (?). Chief carrying a drinking horn in right hand and a long tobacco pipe in the left. Museum für Völkerkunde, Berlin-Dahlem (III C 10514). Collected 1899, Conrau. Ht. 33.5" (85 cm). (Photograph: Museum.)

have as backs standing figures that carry a staff and a scepter. Fortunately the identity of these figures is known; the collector's notes indicate that the stools belonged to the Bekom king and queen who reigned in 1900, while the carved figures represent the king's great-grandfather and great-grandmother (Vatter 1926, p. 177). Staffs and scepters here are clear expressions of Royal authority. The holding of heads or skulls, on the other hand, may be intended to underline the military role of the ruling class. Sometimes a chief or nobleman is shown as a victorious warrior brandishing a sword or other weapon in one hand and a severed head in the other. Rather different from these conquering-warrior

FIGURE 7.3. Tikar group, Bafut chiefdom. Chief seated on a "spider" stool, with amulets on necklaces. Museum für Völkerkunde, Berlin-Dahlem (III C 14606). Ht. 39.8" (101 cm). (Photograph: Museum.)

images are other carvings in which the figure holds a calabash in addition to the head or skull. Perhaps these sculptures depict the chief at the time of his investiture, since in some Grasslands groups the chiefdesignate was required to elevate the skull of his predecessor, thereby illustrating the passing of authority and assuring the continuity of leadership from generation to generation (Jeffreys 1950, p. 40).

The numerous Grasslands figures that hold bowls are more problematical. Some of these bowls are apparently intended merely to support calabashes; yet throughout the Grasslands, bowls are regarded as spirit containers, and sacrifices and presents are placed in them to propitiate the supernatural or ancestral powers that reside there. Figure

FIGURE 7.4. Tikar group, Banso (Nsaw) chiefdom. Large seated figure holding a bowl. His head is covered with a sheath of tinfoil, while his body and the bowl are covered with cowrie shells. Museum für Völkerkunde, Berlin-Dahlem (III C 15017). Collected 1902, Pavel. Ht. 31.5" (80 cm). (Photograph: Museum.)

7.4 represents such a figure, which we know belonged to a ruler, since the body is completely covered with shells and the face is sheathed with a thin metal foil. Only chiefs' figures could be embellished in this way. It may well represent the ruler himself.

This brings us to the most clear-cut diagnostic of Royal or noble figures: the seated posture. In the Grasslands, as in several other African areas, the seated position indicates power and authority. To this day a Cameroons chief's audience always maintains a subservient position—kneeling or crouching—or if allowed to sit, by doing so at a level

FIGURE 7.5. Bamileke group, Bangangte chiefdom. Seated female, a chief's wife or mother, with child. Musée de l'Homme, Paris (34.171.607) Ht. 24.4" (62 cm). (Photograph: Museum.)

lower than his. In some areas this custom applies even to burial practices; the chief is interred seated on a traditional stool, whereas commoners are buried in the usual horizontal position (Jeffreys 1950, p. 39). The stool is important not only in sculpture but also as a symbol in itself. The leader's stool is always the largest and most elaborate one in the community; often it is adorned with leopards, panthers, pythons, or other motifs symbolizing his sovereignty, and frequently is covered with beads or shells. If a chief grants members of his court the right to use lesser stools, the designs and sizes of these will reflect their owner's status in the court hierarchy. Lecoq (1953, p. 199) reports five ranks of stools for the Bandjoun, but there appears to be considerable variation in this regard from area to area. Sometimes the stool is elaborated into a throne, as at Fumban, where the powerful and colorful Sultan Njoya sat on a beaded throne with his feet resting on a footstool.

The stools depicted in Grasslands figure sculpture are inevitably some-what simplified in form, yet almost all the main stool-types are repre-sented, including those with central stems, tripod legs (fig. 7.1), sup-porting animals as bases, and hollow cylindrical forms. Only the type with elaborate caryatid figures or animals supporting the seat appears to be lacking in sculpture. Figure 7.3 illustrates a male figure sitting on a replica of a cylindrical stool which is decorated with conventionalized spider designs, a favorite motif in Grasslands sculpture. The spider, used for divining the future, symbolizes wisdom (Bascom and Gebauer 1953, p. 61; see also Gebauer 1964). Since the figure here also wears magic-working amulets around his neck, he may represent an important diviner or sorcerer/leader of his tribe.

In addition to the many male figures in seated postures, seated female images exist (fig. 7.5), the majority of which represent a woman tend-ing or nursing a child. Though precise information is lacking, these women probably represent the chief's wives or his mother. A number of seated pregnant female figures from Cameroons also appear, and while this theme is relatively rare in African art, the representation of pregnancy here perhaps illustrates the notion of the Cameroons chief as the father of his people and the source of all fertility.

Apart from iconography, certain stylistic properties distinguish Cam-eroons Royal figures (figs. 7.1, 7.3, 7.4). In almost all of these statues the forms are unusually bold and massive, suggesting the dignity and power of the sovereign. Some figures seem to be in a state of command and composure; others appear restlessly aggressive. Invariably, though, they convey authority. Cameroons Royal statuary may also be distin-guished by its use of other aesthetic devices. Hieratic scale appears, for instance, in a remarkable Bangwa figure of high rank (fig. 7.6, probably representing a priest), which is flanked by two smaller figures (twins). This image, as well as most other aristocratic Grasslands figures, conveys a feeling of monumentality strongly reinforced by the use of large, weighty forms often sharply constricted at the joints. In nonaristocratic figures such forms are less clearly articulated and tend to be chunky and ill-defined. They also lack the careful descriptive detail character-istic of noble figure carvings and are generally smaller.

Cameroons Royal figures contrast with those of most other African areas by virtue of their extraordinary vivacity and energetic movement. These sculptures are often dramatically asymmetrical, with heads and bodies that twist and turn in spiralling rhythms. The thrust and counter-thrust of opposing forms create a baroque manipulation of space, of which Figure 7.5 represents one of the most plastically expressive exam-

FIGURE 7.6. Bangwa subgroup (West Cameroon). *Aini* (parent of twins, priest of the earth), seated male figure flanked by two children, one male, the other female. Provenance unknown. Museum für Völkerkunde, Berlin-Dahlem (III C 10521). Collected 1899, Conrau. Ht. 35.1″ (89 cm). (Photograph: Museum.)

ples. Although Grasslands art is often regarded as a provincial style, the aristocratic figures from this area must be described as sophisticated images. The artists' finesse in combining rounded forms with angular rhythms rivals or surpasses that seen in more "refined" courtly styles, while a preference for rough, faceted surfaces adds boldness to the presentation. Postures and gestures of command and obeisance contribute to the power and grandeur of these figures and serve as an index to the ideas held about nobility in the Grasslands region.

REFERENCES

ALBERT, ANDRÉ [S. C. J.]
1943   *Bandjoun.* Montreal.
ANKERMANN, BERNARD
1910   "Bericht über eine ethnographische Forschungsreise ins Grasland von Kamerun." *Zeitschrift für Ethnologie* 42: 288–310.
BASCOM, WILLIAM R., AND GEBAUER, PAUL
1953   *Handbook of West African Art.* Popular Science Handbook no. 5. Milwaukee Public Museum.
EGERTON, F. CLEMENT G.
1939   *African Majesty.* New York.
FAGG, WILLIAM
1965   *Tribes and Forms in African Art.* New York.
GEBAUER, PAUL
1964   *Spider Divination in the Cameroons.* Milwaukee Public Museum Publications in Anthropology 10.
HUTTER, F.
1902   *Wanderungen und Forschungen im Nord-Hinterland von Kamerun.* Brunswick.
JEFFREYS, M. D. W.
1950   "The Bamum Coronation Ceremony as Described by King Njoya." *Africa* 20, no. 1: 38–45.
LECOQ, RAYMOND
1953   *Les Bamiléké.* Paris.
MALCOLM, L. W. G.
1925   "Notes on the ancestral cult ceremonies of the Eyap, Central Cameroons." *Journal of the Royal Anthropological Institute* 55: 373–404.
PAULME, DENISE
1956   *Les sculptures de l'Afrique noire.* Paris.
SYDOW, ECKART VON
1926   *Kunst und Religion der Naturvölker.* Oldenburg.
VATTER, ERNST
1926   *Religiöse Plastik der Naturvölker.* Frankfurt a/M.

CHAPTER 8

The Symbols of Ashanti Kingship

Douglas Fraser

Within her national boundaries, Ghana incorporates many diverse traditional societies, each of which has its own history and distinctive character. Among the best known of these societies is that of the Ashanti, an Akan group, numbering over a million, who occupy the forested fringes of southern Ghana centering around Kumasi. The leader of the Ashanti is the Asantehene, currently Nana Opoku Ware II, a lineal descendant of Nana Osei Tutu, who reigned about A.D. 1697–1731 and was the founder of the Ashanti Confederacy. The Asantehene is elected from among the members of the Royal lineage by a council consisting of certain privileged chiefs of the Kumasi Division of the confederacy. Associated with the Asantehene and symbolic of his supreme office are innumerable ritual objects and regalia. To understand the function and meaning of these, it is necessary to know something about Nana Osei Tutu and the origins of the Ashanti Confederacy.

HISTORICAL BACKGROUND

During the seventeenth century, increased trade in what Europeans then called the Gold Coast seems to have encouraged the emergence of various local kingdoms. Of these, perhaps the most powerful was

Note: This chapter was compiled from information supplied by the Honourable A. A. Y. Kyerematen, Ph.D., Director, Ghana National Cultural Centre, with the kind permission of the late Asantehene Otumfuo Nana Sir Osei Agyeman Prempeh II.

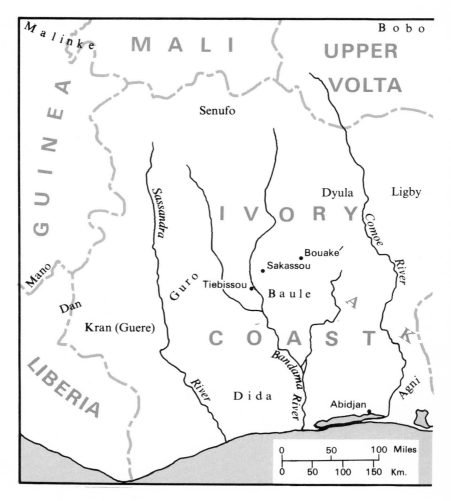

MAP 5. Central Guinea Coast.

Denkyira, founded near the coast about 1620. In subsequent decades
Denkyira expanded its influence until by 1700 it controlled most of the
forest belt of southern Ghana. But about 1701, employing newly learned
military tactics, the Kumasi leader Osei Tutu defeated Denkyira in a
battle at Feyase; thereupon many independent city-states, including
Mampon, Juaben, Kokofu, Nsuta, Kumuwu, Asumegya, and Bekwai,
banded together to form the Ashanti Confederacy. To seal their union,

Okomfo Anokye, chief priest, adviser, confidant, and paternal nephew of Osei Tutu, promised the king and the nation that he would call down from the skies a supernatural stool of solid gold which would enshrine and protect the soul of the nation. As a precondition to fulfilling his promise, however, he demanded that the ancestral (blackened) stools, state shields, state swords, and other regalia of all the member states be surrendered to him. This was done, and he buried them in the bed of

FIGURE 8.1. Ashanti. The Golden Stool enthroned on the Hwedomtea or throne-chair which rests in turn on the elephant-hide rug known as Banwoma. Attached to the stool (which is of solid gold) are cast gold effigies, used as bells, along with one gold and two brass bells and precious beads (*suman*). Kumasi. Ht. 18″ (45.7 cm). (Photograph: Embassy of Ghana.)

the Bantama River in Kumasi. The purpose of this action was twofold: to ensure that no item of regalia in the new kingdom could have a longer history than the Golden Stool and hence take precedence over it, and, by depriving the formerly independent states of the relics of their respective pasts, to pave the way toward a new and broader union.

Finally on a certain Friday (Fiada Fofie), after performing some magical acts in the presence of the king, paramount rulers, and assembled Ashanti people, Okomfo Anokye summoned the Golden Stool from heaven, whence it fell, alighting on the lap of the king. Okomfo Anokye then proclaimed the latter the Father and Supreme Ruler of the people. The Golden Stool, he stipulated, must be treated with the utmost respect and was to be fed at regular intervals, for if it should become hungry, it might sicken and die; with it would perish the soul of the Ashanti nation. To make certain that all the subgroups accepted the Stool, Okomfo Anokye ordered that locks of hair, nail-parings, and rings belonging to the principal chiefs present be surrendered to be driven into the Golden Stool, along with such mystical objects as the skin of a viper. He also spelled out a formal constitution for the government of the Ashanti and outlined a code of moral laws to be observed throughout the country.

THE GOLDEN STOOL OF THE ASHANTI

During the last two and a half centuries, the power of the Ashanti Confederacy has waxed and waned, but the potency of the Golden Stool (fig. 8.1) in the eyes of the Ashanti has not diminished. The Stool is recognized as a common heritage of all the Ashanti, which they must unite to preserve. It is regarded as a supernatural object, enshrining the essence of the nation and capable of protecting the people in time of need; it is the symbol of their nationhood and the ultimate sanction for

FIGURE 8.2. Ashanti. The late Asantehene Otumfuo Nana Sir Osei Agyeman Prempeh II and the Golden Stool reposing in state at a major ritual event. The Asantehene is dressed in *kente* cloth of two traditional, named patterns and rests his feet on the footstool of his office. Flanking the Asantehene are rows of chiefs and courtiers who hold state swords, linguists' staffs, and umbrellas. Kumasi. (Photograph: Embassy of Ghana.)

their code of moral behavior. The most important ritual object in the Asantehene's custody, the Golden Stool is exhibited only at his installation, at *durbars* (royal receptions) for the highest leaders, and at recurrent ceremonies such as the Adae and Odwira festivals, occasions for the formal presentation of the king to his people, which provide them with assurances of the Stool's safekeeping and an opportunity to enjoy the hospitality and munificence of the leader (fig. 8.2).

The honors accorded the Golden Stool are, broadly speaking, those rendered to an individual of the highest rank. The Stool must never touch the bare ground, and, when it is exhibited on state occasions, it rests on its own special throne, the silver-plated Hwedomtea, an elaborate chair. The term *hwedom* means "facing the fold of the enemy," and chairs of this type are used by rulers when declaring war against another group or when presiding over court sessions involving capital offenses. Not only does the Golden Stool have its own throne, it also has its own set of regalia, including state umbrellas, elephant-skin shield and rug (Banwoma), a gold-plated drum, a lute, and its own bodyguard and attendants. Indeed its name, Sikadwa (or Adwa) Kofi, "The Golden Stool That Was Born on Friday," conforms to the Akan custom of naming people, in part, according to the day of the week on which they are born. The Stool is viewed as a living person, a sacrosanct being that houses the soul and spirit of the Ashanti people.

ASHANTI STOOLS

The responses accorded the Golden Stool parallel in microcosm the expressions of Ashanti religious and political values observable on a broader level. In Ashanti, as in most Akan communities, an extraordinary intimacy is believed to exist between a man and his stool. As the Ashanti put it, "There are no secrets between a man and his stool." The first gift a father gives his child when the latter begins to crawl is a stool. A young girl undergoing the rite (*bra goro*) that signals her attainment of puberty is placed on a stool; and it is customary for a bridegroom to present a stool to his new-wed wife to be sure of keeping her. At death the deceased is bathed on a stool before being laid out in state. The close association between an individual and his stool is established long before death, for a man's soul is believed to inhabit his stool. In daily life, too, this principle obtains; when a person vacates a stool, it should be tilted on its side to prevent some other spirit, particularly an evil spirit, from occupying it. The stools of a chief are identified not only with the man but with his office as well. Stools of political leaders therefore symbolize the unity of the state and the authority of the ruler. The Queen Mother's high status is signaled by a finely decorated stool with silver sheathing. Stools are in fact the *sine qua non* of Ashanti leadership (fig. 8.3).

Ashanti leaders use three kinds of stools: domestic ones for dining (*did dwa*) and bathing (*adware dwa*); Black Stools (*nkonnwa tuntum*), which represent past rulers and are preserved in their memory; and a ceremonial stool (*adamu dwa*). The latter is the reigning king's personal stool, which he usually occupies when sitting in state. If he dies while still king, his ceremonial stool is smoked or blackened all over with soot mixed with the yolk of an egg. It thus becomes a Black Stool and is kept in the stool house (*akonnwafieso*) along with those representing his predecessors. The personal stool of a king who is deposed, however, may be retained for use as a ceremonial stool by succeeding rulers. After blackening, a stool is believed to be possessed by the soul of the dead

FIGURE 8.3. Ashanti. Man's ceremonial stool (*kotokodwa*) decorated with silver sheathing. British Museum, London (neg. no. LXXX½). Ht. 16" (40.6 cm). (Photograph: Museum.)

leader. Black Stools, being the abode of the spirits of past rulers, function as the foremost sacramental objects in the state ancestor cult. On appointed days, food and drink are placed on each of these stools as an offering to the soul, and prayers are addressed to the soul for the peace and prosperity of the community.

In most Akan states, one of the Black Stools (usually that of the founder or most successful leader) is the principal stool and stands for kingship—past, present, and future—and for the nation as a whole. In a few instances, such as that of the Stool of Precious Beads of the Denkyira people, this all-representative stool is believed to have come from the Supreme God as a miraculous gift. The principal stool of the Ashanti is, of course, the Golden Stool; although not blackened, it is regarded as the Black Stool of Nana Osei Tutu and hence a memorial to him.

In the case of ceremonial stools (which may eventually become Black Stools), great interest attaches to the symbolic meanings conveyed by their shape and ornamentation. As soon as a candidate for the throne has been chosen, it is customary for him to decide on the design and ornamentation of his personal stool in order to convey a message to his people. This message may appear in the form of the column (*sekyedua*) that supports the seat of the stool, or, more commonly in Ashanti, in the ornamental patterns which, for the Asantehene, are fashioned in gold leaf. The St. Andrew's cross (*apodwa*) design selected by King Osei Bonsu, for example, expressed the idea that he would consolidate the accomplishments of his predecessors. The message of King Kwaku Dua I, a circular chain (*kontonkrowie*), meant that the ruler would make his power felt by all peoples (though in fact he was the least pugnacious of kings). The moon and stars (*sanee ne nsroma*), the design on Nana Prempeh I's stool, signified that during his reign the fame of the Ashanti would spread far and wide like the moon and stars, which are seen all over the world. The design chosen by the recently deceased Asantehene Nana Prempeh II, a reef knot or knot of wisdom (*nyansapo*), conveyed the notion that he would solve the nation's problems by sagacity rather than by the power of the sword.

OTHER REGALIA

Next in importance to stools as symbols of Ashanti leadership are gold-hilted state swords (fig. 8.4). These are symbolic of a chief's authority and are used when swearing oaths of allegiance to a superior chief and at the installation ceremonies when the leader promises to serve his subjects well. Such swords are also essential in the chief's periodic "soul-washing" or soul-purification ceremonies. Indeed the Ashanti word for one type of chief's sword is *akrafena* (sword of my soul). Other swords (*asomfofena*) are used as tokens of credibility when sending messages by courier or delegate. If the messenger is to address a subordinate chief, he will take with him the sword on which that chief originally swore allegiance. Should the message be received contemptuously, a declaration of war (in the form of another sword having a gun and keg of gunpowder represented on its blade) will be dispatched. Other designs depicted on sword hilts may convey peaceful messages. A cluster of palm-nut kernels with a heart, for example, depicted on one of the late Asantehene's personal swords indicated that he would serve his people—who spring from a common stock (as do palm nuts) —with all his heart.

The principal state swords of the Asantehene are known as *keteanofena*. They may be divided into two groups, the *akrafena* and the *bosomfena*, which are carried respectively on his right and left sides in state processions. This division is explained by the Akan belief that a person is both a corporeal and a spiritual being. A man inherits his biological nature (*mogya*) and hence his civic status from his mother, but his spiritual nature comes from his father. The spiritual being of man is made up of his ego or personality (*sunsum*) and his soul or life-force (*kra*), both of which derive from his father. The *kra* or soul is regarded as a small bit of the Creator that dwells in every living person. At death the *kra* departs and returns to the Creator whence it came (*kra ko nakyi*). The Asantehene's two groups of swords refer to these two sets of spiritual elements inherited from his father. Those on the right (*akrafena*) represent his soul or life-force (*kra*); those on the left (*bosomfena*), his ego, spirit, or personality (*sunsum*).

The Asantehene has a large number of state swords (see chapter 9, fig. 9.2), but the four principal ones in order of importance and seniority are the Bosomru, Mponponson, Bosompra, and Bosomtwe. The Bosomru, first made for King Osei Tutu, is the sword with which, at the most solemn part of his installation, every Asantehene dedicates himself to the service of the nation. It represents Osei Tutu's *sunsum* and is one of the *bosomfena,* or left-hand swords. On it is cast a gold image of a chimpanzee's jawbone that symbolizes one believed to have magical powers, that was caught by Okomfo Anokye from the skies. The Mponponson sword belonged to Osei Tutu's immediate successor, Nana Opoku Ware. *Mponponson* means "responsibility," and the sword was given this name because Opoku Ware was required to succeed his granduncle Osei Tutu, following the latter's death on the battlefield during the war against Akim-Kotoku (1731). On this sword the leaders of the Ashanti states swear their loyalty to the Asantehene. It is the largest sword and the foremost example of the *akrafena,* or right-hand swords.

After the reign of Opoku Ware, it became the custom for each ruler to have two swords, a *bosomfena* and an *akrafena,* made for himself. Nana Kwaka Dua I, for example, had the third most important sword, the Bosompra, fabricated as his *bosomfena* and the Kraku sword as his *akrafena.* The former is decorated with a treasure container (*kuduo*) signifying the responsibility of the king for his people's material needs. It is associated with the proverb, "The big pot provides for many" (*"esen kesee gye adededoo"*), and is used when the Asantehene sends a message to the Queen Mother. The fourth most important sword is the Bosomtwe, which, having an image of a crocodile on it, is linked with a deity that resides in Lake Bosomtwe.

Another important type of attribute associated with the ruler in Ashanti is the state umbrella (fig. 8.4). Made of richly colored materials, these huge objects are both practical sunshades and symbolic, quasi-architectural, space-defining forms that help express the chief's role as ruler. State umbrellas, like other Ashanti regalia, are often topped with wood carvings sheathed in gold leaf and intended to communicate a meaning. On one belonging to the Asantehene, there appears a repre-

FIGURE 8.4. Ashanti. Detail of an engraving of a "Yam festival" (Odwira) first published by the traveler Bowdich in 1819. The umbrellas are topped with gold emblems of the sort

sentation of a certain fruit called *prekese,* which has a very strong smell. This signifies that the Asantehene is omnipresent: like the *prekese,* he is to be sensed even where he is not seen; in other words, no gossip or plotting can evade his hearing.

Arab visitors to the ancient Mali empire in the fourteenth century. (From Bowdich 1819, ng p. 275.)

The Asantehene owns no less than twenty-three of these state umbrellas, each of which serves him on a particular occasion. The Boaman umbrella made for King Osei Bonsu and topped with *babadua* plant signifies that he is the destroyer of nations. It is used when rebellious or enemy states are being tried in absentia by the Asantehene and his councillors. The Akokobatan Ne Ne Mma (fig. 8.5), with its top depicting a hen and her chicks, is used when he is trying to achieve a peaceful settlement of a dispute arising among chiefs or between a chief and his subjects; for the mother hen, it is said, steps on her chicks not to kill them but to put them on the right path—in other words, the purpose of punishment is to correct, not to harm, miscreants. The rainbow-colored Nyankonton umbrella is employed when the Asantehene wishes to resolve disputes between himself and members of the Royal House. The rainbow colors are supposed to remind people of their obligations to the ruler. Other umbrellas, such as the Nsaa Kyiniye and Nhwehwe Kyiniye, are used to shelter the Golden Stool at the Adae festival.

Among an Ashanti chief's regalia are also to be found various containers (*kuduo*) for his treasures (figs. 8.6, 8.7). These containers are, for the most part, elaborately worked, cylindrical metal vessels designed to hold gold dust (*suruboo*) and precious beads (*bota*) which are offered in religious rites. In the Asantehene's treasury, one of the most important insignia of office is the Dwete Kuduo (a silver bowl), which was captured by Nana Osei Tutu from Bodwesango Adu Gyamfi of Adansi state. This vessel is formally handed over to the new incumbent at the installation ceremonies, for without this bowl the king is not properly installed. In it are kept articles which the Asantehene needs to have with him, particularly gold dust which is required for gifts. This bowl is always with him and is placed on his right when he sits in state.

Only the Asantehene and certain chiefs are privileged to have spokesmen or linguists whose staffs are decorated all over with gold leaf (see chapter 11). Like umbrellas, these staffs are often topped with carved

FIGURE 8.5. Twifo State. The hen and her chicks (Akokobatan Ne Ne Mma). This is the top of a staff carried by the linguist of Nana Amponrenfie II, but it illustrates the same theme as the Ashanti versions. Twifo-Mampon town. Carved by Kwaku Adae, who was active between 1900 and 1940. Ht. of carving 10″ (25.4 cm). (Photograph: George Preston, 1970.)

naturalistic images that convey a proverbial meaning. One of the finest of these staff-tops is that carried by the linguist of the Asumengyahene (the head of the left military wing), which represents a large fish floating in the middle of a stream with a number of water snails clinging to the banks. This alludes to the idea that the Creator first made the water snails and placed them in the stream, then the fish, coming along later, occupied the middle of the stream. Underlying this image is the notion of the primacy of the common people, among whom the chief is but a recent arrival. Other staff-tops make still subtler points: for instance, a carving representing a hand holding an egg advises the leader to be neither a weakling nor a tyrant; the egg symbolizes the power of the state which, if it is clutched too tightly, will be crushed, while if it is held too loosely, will slip from his grasp. The Asantehene's own linguist, the Akyeamehene, carries a staff called Asempatia, which means, "True evidence given in court is always brief."

In addition to the foregoing, the power of Ashanti rulers is expressed through many other kinds of objects, including palanquins; such military accoutrements as shields, breastplates, and gold-plated guns; the personal clothing of the leader; ornaments; and musical instruments, such as drums, lutes, trumpets, flutes, horns, gongs, and rattles. All of these play a significant part in enhancing the ambiance of the ruler and in calling attention to his authority.

SIGNIFICANCE OF ASHANTI REGALIA

The symbols used by Ashanti leaders function on several distinct levels, although in actual practice it may be difficult to distinguish these roles from one another. Clearly, regalia have an aesthetic and artistic purpose expressed in the interplay of colors, surfaces, textures, and shapes independent of any meaning that may attach to the objects themselves. The dramatic appearance of an Akan chief in full regalia, preceded by dozens of subordinates who bear his treasures, is a thrilling spectacle and enlivens the day for all who behold it. At the same time, spectators may take pleasure in the sheer skill and craftsmanship manifest in the symbols themselves. Anyone who has seen the magnificent *kente* cloths, *kuduo*, gold and silver-sheathed wood carvings, and metal castings of the Ashanti can testify to the technical excellence of these artists' work.

Apart from this, however, there are other functions which Ashanti regalia perform, roles which may be categorized as historical, religious, and political. Items of regalia are chronicles of the incidents of Ashanti history; each object was made for or acquired by a specific monarch in

FIGURE 8.6. Ashanti. Treasure container (*kuduo*) to hold gold dust and precious beads. Musée de l'Homme, Paris (65.17.1). Ht. 11.4″ (29 cm). (Photograph: Museum.)

connection with a particular event. These insignia, therefore, are intimately identified with the historical events that help to give them historical meaning and which they in turn serve to recall and validate. Such

FIGURE 8.7. Ashanti. Detail of Figure 8.6 showing courtly scene on top of vessel. Hieratic images of a large king flanked by smaller attendants such as this are reminiscent of the art of Benin. Musée de l'Homme, Paris (65.17.1). (Photograph: Museum.)

objects, moreover, remind a chief of the achievements of his predecessors and invite him to emulate the success of earlier leaders. By making it possible to recall exploits from the past, regalia also instill in the ordinary people a sense of pride in their collective accomplishments.

Paraphernalia also express the relative political status of individual leaders. This enables those in authority to conduct the business of state in an orderly fashion and to delegate responsibility to and through subordinates where necessary. For a chief, promotion is signaled by his accession to new regalia, the public possession of which serves as a means of authenticating his newly acquired status. Other kinds of regalia lend credence to the words of envoys or authority to the utterances of royal spokesmen.

Yet in the final analysis it is probably the mystical values adhering to these objects that are most instrumental in securing the obedience of the subjects to the wishes of a leader. Virtually all important Ashanti regalia have at root religious functions that are epitomized by their appearance in state rituals. At the center of everything is the Golden Stool, the focal point of the national cult. This Stool transcends in importance and takes precedence over even the person of the Asante-hene. There was no rebellion, for instance, when King Prempeh I was exiled by the British in 1896; but when the governor, Sir Francis Hodgson, demanded the right to sit on the Golden Stool, the Ashanti uprising of 1900 ensued. Such a symbol, then, is more than a rallying point for the people. It is a value in itself and the fulcrum around which Ashanti society organizes and disposes the bulk of its energies.

CHAPTER *9*

The Diffusion
of Ashanti Political Art

René A. Bravmann

A highly conspicuous feature of both centralized and acephalous politi-
cal systems in sub-Saharan Africa has been the use of art forms as
validating symbols of leaders' prerogatives. Within highly centralized
states such as the kingdoms of Benin and Dahomey, the number of such
objects is truly impressive; yet even among relatively unstructured (or
even acephalous) societies, the visual arts exist, in part, to define and
delimit leadership and its responsibilities.

To date, no study of the arts that are linked to African politics has
touched upon the role of such objects in the expansion of political units;
but it seems obvious that political developments may well have led to
the diffusion of leaders' art forms. Considering the vitality and impor-
tance in Africa of political expansion movements, their study in this
light might well add a dynamic dimension to scholarship in the art field.

A particularly cogent example of the use of the visual arts in the
process of state formation comes from the Ashanti kingdom (map 5),
where gifts of regalia were distributed throughout its various terri-
tories in a conscious attempt to meld together disparate cultures under
the aegis of the Asantehene in Kumasi, the Ashanti capital. This chapter
deals with the diffusion of Ashanti political hegemony and art to one
non-Akan-speaking culture—the Nafana of western Brong-Ahafo (map

Note: The research on which this publication is based was made possible by a
fellowship awarded by the Foreign Area Fellowship Program. A special note of
thanks is due Mr. Kofi Ofori Ansong and Mr. Kwesi Pipim for invaluable assis-
tance rendered during my period of field work.

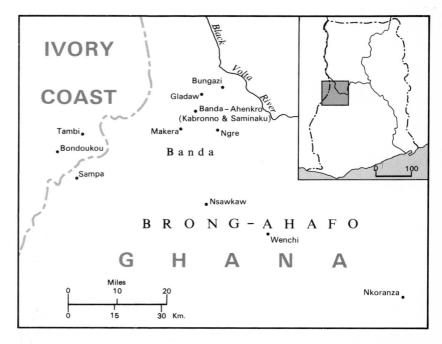

MAP 6. Banda Area. (Map by University of Wisconsin Cartographic Laboratory.)

5)—a group brought under control between 1710 and 1715, very early in the Ashanti expansion toward the rich gold-trading centers of the northwest.

THE HISTORICAL BASIS FOR DIFFUSION OF THE ARTS

Kwame Arhin (1967) has written an article entitled "The Structure of Greater Ashanti," in which he attempts to delineate the various methods by which Ashanti managed to incorporate and consolidate its far-flung possessions. Although Arhin retains Joseph Dupuis's (1824) distinctions between provinces, tributaries, and protectorates as a means of classifying the varied relationships of Ashanti to its numerous subject states, Arhin goes beyond Dupuis, who appears to have based his categories on the twin factors of "political distance" and "participation in Ashanti wars."[1] Arhin includes as criteria such factors as the commonality of cultural features, similarities and differences in historical experiences,

1. See Arhin 1967, p. 67, and Dupuis 1824. According to this approach, provinces include peoples speaking Akan languages yet lying immediately outside of

and the frequency and nature of the interactions between Kumasi and the various peoples under its control.

For Arhin, Ashanti was able to realize its efforts to integrate newly acquired territories most fully in the case of the nearby provinces. This was due, in his opinion, not only to the geographical proximity of these areas to Ashanti proper, but also to the fact that the inhabitants were all Akan peoples sharing similar political and cultural institutions. For these provinces, then, assimilation did not imply a major break with past traditions; rather it demanded full participation within the new and larger political framework of the Ashanti state and a reorientation of allegiances toward Kumasi (Arhin 1967, p. 78). Also according to Arhin, certain Ashanti officials known as the *adamfo* helped to bridge the gap between the rulers and the ruled. As representatives of the Asantehene they served as advisors to local chiefs and, more important, as communication links between local states and the ultimate seat of the government in Kumasi.

Great state occasions such as the Adae and the Odwira festivals played equally vital roles in further integrating the provinces with nuclear Ashanti:

There was enforced attendance of provincial chiefs at the Ashanti annual *Odwira,* yam festival, at Kumasi. . . . The point of these festivals in their rituals, drama, and pageant was to re-enact, re-interpret, and transmit Ashanti history; renew communion between dead and living Ashanti; and to emphasize the unity of greater Ashanti. Those who took part in them were theoretically united in their allegiance to the occupant of the Golden Stool [the Asantehene], the centre of the festivals. (Arhin 1967, p. 82)

The Odwira served as the paradigm of the state, legitimizing in dramatic ritual form the political reality of Ashanti and strengthening the ties between Kumasi and the neighboring provinces.

In the case of the more remote protectorates and tributaries, however, Arhin concludes that these subject peoples and states were treated very differently by the Ashanti. Measures of integration were only superficially and unevenly applied in the case of protectorates, and not at all in the areas that were merely tributary to Ashanti. Protectorates such as Accra, Nzima, Aowin, and Banda (map 5) were considered to be politically part of Ashanti, since they contributed both financially and

---

Ashanti proper. Tributaries include not only more distant Akan speakers but also peoples such as the Kulango and Mo (Degha) who belong to other language subfamilies (in this case Gur). Protectorates are the groups farthest removed geographically, linguistically, and historically from core Ashanti; examples include Gonja, Dagomba, and Mamprussi.

physically to the cycle of Ashanti wars and came under some measure of administrative and judicial control through the agency of Ashanti representatives. Nonetheless, they proved to be too refractory to be assimilated fully within the expanding frontiers. Distant tributaries such as Gonja and Dagomba remained virtually untouched by Ashanti attempts at political and cultural integration. They served primarily as political, military, and economic outposts of the state and as vital communication links between Ashanti and the north (Arhin 1967, p. 77).

According to Arhin, then, it was really only in the provinces that Ashanti succeeded in its policy of political and cultural integration. Yet even he calls attention to the Nafana state of Banda, located just south of the Black Volta at the northern fringes of the western Brong region (map 6), as a case where Ashanti did in fact try to impose its policy of assimilation upon one of its protectorates: "In Banda, it appears that there were attempts to 'Akanize' as Dr. Goody puts it, to introduce the material symbolisms of kingship as a prelude to what shall be asserted in relation to her provinces, her assimilation into Greater Ashanti" (Arhin 1967, p. 78). Arhin goes no further in dealing with the implications of this example, even though it certainly suggests that the areas outside the provinces are where one would expect to find Ashanti's most vigorous efforts toward integration. Assimilation was never very difficult to achieve within the provinces, since Ashanti was dealing with other Akan peoples who, for the most part, already shared a number of basic culture patterns. Beyond the provinces, however, Ashanti was confronted with a very different ethnographic situation, that is, with non-Akan societies having diverse historical experiences which in turn meant much greater resistance to enculturation. In the western Brong area, for instance, Ashanti expansion encountered a highly mixed cultural situation, with Mande-speaking peoples such as the Dyula and Ligby (Ligbi) and representatives of the Gur language family such as the Kulango, the Mo (Degha), and the Nafana. As an expansionist state Ashanti had somehow to weld all these peoples into its political system, especially since they controlled the gold trade routes to the northwest that were so vital to Ashanti interests.

By 1710 Ashanti had succeeded in establishing a foothold in western Brong, and began applying its policy of "Akanization" throughout the region. "Akanization" was particularly successful among the Nafana of Banda, in part as a result of the introduction and acceptance of Ashanti art forms. As object types related to politics, Ashanti regalia[2] were central to this process.

2. The use of Ashanti regalia among non-Akan cultures in western Brong is not restricted to the Nafana; it also occurs among the Kulango and Mo (Degha).

ASHANTI REGALIA AS AN INTEGRATIVE FACTOR

Before dealing with Ashanti relations with the Nafana and the use of regalia in the process of state formation, it is necessary to recognize that this is but one instance of many that could be cited; the evidence overwhelmingly demonstrates that Ashanti used the bestowal of regalia time and again as an integrative device, especially in the non-Akan regions under its control. East of the Volta River, for example, where Ashanti influence now appears to have been far more extensive and massive than had previously been suspected, there are many indications that Ashanti regalia were employed by some Ewe as well as by Guan splinter groups (from the area of Central Ghana) living in southeastern Ghana. Ashanti regalia were seen in this region in the late nineteenth century by the German officer Hauptmann Kling, and by George Ekim Ferguson, a member of the government service of the then Gold Coast, who served on the Anglo-German Boundary Commission in the 1890s (Johnson 1965, pp. 35–39). According to Kling, the chief of the eastern Adele, who was called Lapoda or Jaopura, was also the priest of the shrine of Fruko and owned a number of items of Ashanti regalia. Among his paraphernalia were several state umbrellas, an Ashanti stool, and a leopard drum, all pointing to his former close connections with the Asantehene (Johnson 1965, p. 35). Kodjo of Dutukpeme, another chief in the eastern Adele area, also surrounded himself with a sizable collection of Ashanti objects, as Kling noted:

. . . a great gay umbrella of about three metres in diameter, and a palanquin elegantly woven from bamboo, an arm chair with brass ornaments [clearly an example of the Ashanti *asipim* chair] . . . a valuable cloth of Ashanti workmanship made up of small pieces of coloured cloth decorated with hand embroidery [*konin?*], whose price in the interior is about 100 marks, but almost double at the coast, a finely carved wooden native stool decorated with cowries [decorated stools with an overlay of cowries not being an Ashanti type, this stool was probably from elsewhere] . . . a filigree gold plate of Ashanti workmanship [the description seems to fit the Ashanti *akrafokonmu*, or "soul washer's" badge, carried by the "soul washers" of the chief in all Ashanti states]. (Johnson 1965, p. 35; bracketed additions are mine)

Similar items were seen by Kling at the Shrine of Buruku at Siade, where the priest had as part of his regalia a cowrie-studded elephant's tail, a common item of regalia at Ashanti courts and important state shrines. Kling also observed a gold-handled state sword, which was identical to the Ashanti state sword (*akofena*) and was kept in the shrine itself in order to signal the importance of the deity (Johnson 1965, p. 35). How these items were procured by the chiefs and priests so far from Ashanti is not known, but many of the objects may have been gifts from various Asantehene for temporal or spiritual services rendered the Golden Stool. This assumption gains support from the statement of Ferguson, who notes that "The King of Kumasi distributed honours and court decorations to the various Kings of his Kingdom" (Johnson 1965, p. 35).

Such gifts were not limited to political chiefs. Priests and shrines of important deities were always considered to be of vital interest to the Ashanti. Indeed the creation of the Nsumankwa stool of Ashanti was made possible by the fact that the priests of foreign shrines could be enlisted to promote the prosperity and expansion of Ashanti. In this way, particularly important non-Ashanti deities were placed under the aegis of the Nsumankwahene and his stool, enabling the Ashanti state to exert a measure of control over its subject peoples even in the spiritual sphere (Agyeman-Duah 1962).

North of the Black Volta all of the major states included by Arhin within the "tributary" classification show signs of having adopted a number of Ashanti cultural features. As John R. Goody (1966b, p. 22) has noted, in such states as Gonja and Dagomba the *ntumpani* drums found in the compounds of major chiefs announce the arrival of ". . . each subordinate chief as he comes to pay his respects to his political superior. The close connection of these drums (*ntumpani*) with the Ashanti is brought out by the fact that 'they speak Twi.' "[3] Such Ashanti regalia as state umbrellas and swords occur frequently in the various divisions of Gonja, being brought out at important state festivals such as Damba. According to the Bolewura, chief of the Bole division of Gonja, umbrellas have always formed a part of the regalia of his court but have never been made locally. Formerly they were gifts bestowed upon the "skin" of Bole by the Asantehene (the "skin" is equivalent to the state stool among the Akans and is an index of elevated political rank), but this practice ceased with the advent of the colonial period. Most of the present collection of state umbrellas owned by the Bolewura were purchased from itinerant Ashanti who represent the umbrella-makers, goldsmiths, and carvers in and around Kumasi, and who ply the motor road from Kumasi to Wa carrying these prestige items with them. On the other hand, clients sometimes travel to Kumasi for the express purpose of commissioning a piece of regalia, especially if the objects brought by the traders are of inferior quality or too costly. The last state umbrella purchased by the present Bolewura was acquired in this

3. The language spoken by the Ashanti is Ashanti-twi, a branch of the Akan subfamily.

manner. Such efforts demonstrate the high esteem in which these items of Ashanti regalia are held.

As in other areas such items of regalia are not necessarily limited in the north to politically important individuals; examples are found, for instance, at Senyon-Kupo, the major shrine in the Bole division in the western part of Gonja province of northern Ghana. Here, Ashanti paraphernalia is an important feature of the annual Den festival of purification for the deity. The priest of the shrine, the Kibiriwura, receives devotees and numerous Gonja chiefs while sitting on an *asipim* chair, which is alleged to have been an Ashanti gift to the shrine.[4] Gold-handled state swords and linguist staffs from Kumasi are also said to constitute part of the Kibiriwura's regalia, but it is not clear whether these items were political gifts to the deity or personal rewards given to the spirit of Senyon-Kupo. Granted that one finds a more limited range and sparser distribution of Ashanti objects in the north than south of the Black Volta, political and religious gifts of regalia were clearly a significant aspect of Ashanti relations with the north. Cultural and geographical distances obviously did not act as a serious barrier to the dispersion of such art forms.

ASHANTI AND THE NAFANA OF BANDA

The relationship between Ashanti and the Nafana state of Banda is the clearest and most complete example known of the use of regalia in the process of Ashanti state formation. In the attempt to reconstruct this phenomenon, a number of sources have proved invaluable; the data recorded by Louis-Gustave Binger (1892), Maurice Delafosse (1908), and Louis Tauxier (1921), although extremely fragmentary in nature and concerned almost exclusively with the Nafana of the adjacent Ivory Coast, provide the earliest specific documentation. The writings of Eva L. Meyerowitz, from the late 1940s, contain the first in-depth studies on the Nafana in the then Gold Coast, but her findings are fraught with inconsistencies and her theories of the origins and migrations of the group, at best confused (1952, 1958). Only with the recent work of John Goody (1954, 1964) and Ivor Wilks (1961) does the ethnographic and historical picture of western Brong become clarified. Another useful source in attempting to elucidate the internal features of Nafana history is the minutes of sessions of the Banda Traditional Council. Finally, oral traditions collected among the Nafana and

4. This particular item of regalia was first noted by H. M. Tomlinson in the 1930s and cited in his later paper (1954, p. 18).

a systematic inventory of the art forms related to politics help create a base line from which to deal with the diffusion of Ashanti regalia into this region.[5]

Oral traditions of the Nafana state of Banda, collected at the capital town of Banda-Ahenkro and at such subordinate villages as Bungazi, Ngre, and Makera, point to an early migration of a large group of the Nafana into the western Brong region. All these traditions are consistent in their claims that the Nafana came from Jimini, the southeastern section of the Senufo country located just to the west of the Comoe River in the Ivory Coast. Prompted by a succession dispute, the Nafana left Jimini under the leadership of Kralongo, who brought them eastward across the Banda Hills to the land they now occupy. Exactly when the Nafana arrived in the western Brong region is difficult to determine, but the available evidence tends to place this movement in the latter half of the seventeenth century. The reign of Kralongo was a peaceful one. Under his leadership the Nafana established their capital town, founded a number of smaller villages, and brought several Mo (Degha) settlements south of the Black Volta under their control.

The Nafana claim to have come into contact with the Ashanti during the reign of their third Mgono, or chief, Sielongo. According to local tradition the chief of Nkoranza, Baffo Pim, defeated the Nafana in a war and took Sielongo to Kumasi to pay homage to the Asantehene Osei Tutu.[6] A treaty of friendship was then established between Osei Tutu and Sielongo, as a result of which the Nafana were placed under the jurisdiction of the Adumhene of Kumasi and were required to pay a yearly tribute of seven sheep at the annual Odwira festival in Kumasi. In return for Banda's recognition of the paramountcy of Kumasi, Osei Tutu rewarded Sielongo with a gift of salt, gourds of palm wine, and a white Ashanti stool that was to serve as Sielongo's symbol of friendship with the Asantehene.

The Nafana claim that the tradition of blackening the personal stool of the Mgono of the Banda state began with Sielongo's death. Stools called *kulugon,* consisting of a flat seat and a handle with four rudimentary legs (fig. 9.1), had been a feature of earlier Nafana culture, but the concept of blackening ancestral stools in the Akan manner was to

5. Nafana oral traditions collected by Kwabena Ameyaw (1965) have served as valuable corroborations of the histories I recorded on three different occasions between October 1966 and January 1968.

6. Ameyaw's transcription does not mention a war during this period. The version I collected receives some measure of confirmation from traditions collected at Nkoranza, Wenchi, and Nsawkaw which tell of a war between Baffo Pim and Banda.

FIGURE 9.1. Nafana. Kwaku Sorma, the head of the Sorma family pouring a libation of gin to the *kulugon* (stool) owned by his family. A typical family *kulugon*, it is appreciably smaller than the *kulugon* owned by the paramount and sub-chiefs. The ancestral stool of a family is not blackened, this being restricted to the stools of the Royals. There is only one *kulugon* for each family (unlike the tradition among Royal families); it is named after the founder of the family—in this case, Togba. All other family heads are remembered, however, and are propitiated along with Togba whenever the *kulugon* is in ritual use. The present *kulugon* was carved about twenty years ago by Sa Kwabena, a member of the Sorma family. Makera, Banda. Ht. 8″ (20.3 cm); length, 13″ (33 cm). (Photograph: author, 1966).

them totally foreign.[7] Sielongo's stool was placed in a temporary shelter until a stool room could be completed, whereupon it was formally blackened and consecrated as an ancestral stool of the state. The *kulugon* of Kralongo and his successor, Gyara, the first two chiefs in the Banda regnal list, were enshrined at the same time.

Among the Nafana the *kulugon* stools of all previous Mgono who had died a natural death while in office were traditionally honored by having them retained by each chief's successors. Since all chiefs' stools were highly venerated and since Sielongo's had now been blackened, it was logical to the Nafana to blacken the stools of Sielongo's predecessors as well. To blacken the stools of *all* dead chiefs is, of course, not an Ashanti tradition; only their most outstanding political leaders were, and are, accorded such an honor. This modification by the Nafana of an imported Akan concept illustrates the need for adaptability in the receiving group if a cultural transfer is to be achieved.

The newly adopted custom of blackening ancestral stools appears to have spread rapidly among the subchiefs of the Banda state; it was adopted by the heads of even the smallest and most insignificant villages. Initially the use of the Ashanti-type stool was restricted to the Mgono of Banda, but subsequently Banda paramounts began presenting these stools to certain lesser chiefs for meritorious services rendered in wars.[8]

During this period the Banda Nafana state also adopted the Ashanti pattern of military organization, with certain village heads being nominated as war captains. All the military titles found in Ashanti proper, including even their Twi names, were assumed in Banda. Thus, by 1750, when Sielongo died, a number of Ashanti features had already become fully assimilated into the context of politics—and art—in the Banda Nafana state.

Sielongo's successor, Sakye (known in Ashanti history as Worosa), rebelled against the authority of Kumasi, claiming that the Nafana of Banda were independent and would no longer serve the Golden Stool. The Nafana then murdered a number of Ashanti traders at the village of Gladaw, which infuriated the Asantehene Osei Kwadwo and touched off a war in which the Ashanti were led by the Dadiesoabahene of Kumasi. Banda traditions tell of the desperate nature of the struggle, which was fought almost exclusively on Banda soil, and of the death of Sakye on the battlefield. With his death the Nafana surrendered. The renewed oath of allegiance to Ashanti, administered by the Dadiesoa-

7. The broad sequence of events is confirmed by Ameyaw 1965, p. 3, although details vary slightly.

8. Data collected at Makera and at Bungazi from the Kydomhene of the state, October 1966.

bahene Atobra Kwesi, was duly sworn by the subchiefs of Banda.[9] The annual tribute paid to Ashanti was reinstated, and Sakye's head was taken back to Kumasi as ultimate proof of the surrender of the Nafana. Osei Kwadwo, the Asantehene, then ordered that a miniature copy of Sakye's head be cast in gold and placed on the sheath of a state sword to serve as a permanent reminder of the war. The Banda refer to the sword as Sakye-po, while the Ashanti call it Worosatiri. This piece of regalia is part of the collection of state swords owned by the Asante-hene, and it is carried at all major state occasions just in front of the Golden Stool. During these festivals it forms part of a group of five swords known collectively as the messenger swords (asomfofena); the name of each sword derives from a cast-gold object (abosodie) attached to its sheath. Together these objects symbolize a number of political and historical associations and ideas familiar to all who attend the important state festivals of Ashanti (Kyerematen 1961, p. 8). For Mgonos of Banda required to come to the annual Odwira at Kumasi (an obligation met only sporadically after the death of Sielongo), the sight of the Worosatiri must have been a strong deterrent to thoughts of rebellion.

The list of Banda Nafana chiefs for the last half of the eighteenth century mentions the reigns of Mgonos Pehzo, Petele, and Habaa. Shortly after 1801 the Nafana participated as an ally of Ashanti in the Gonja war, and as a reward for this, the Mgono Habaa received a gold-handled state sword from the Asantehene Osei Bonsu. Banda-Ashanti relations were then cordial, and the situation remained relatively peaceful.

In 1807 Osei Bonsu requested that the Nafana aid the Ashanti in their war against the Fanti. The newly enstooled Mgono Wulodwo led a contingent of Nafana to Kumasi. Although the Nafana fought nobly in this war, the Adumhene of Kumasi, who headed the division in which the Nafana were included, accused the Bandahene of having retreated during the battle—an act tantamount to treason. With the war successfully completed, the charge of treason was brought against Wulodwo in the presence of the Asantehene and his court. The Adum-hene's accusations were found to be unjust, and the Nafana were removed from the jurisdiction of the Adum stool and placed under the leadership of the Dadiesoabahene. For services rendered in the Fanti war Wulodwo received from Osei Bonsu a palanquin (apakan, called gba by the Nafana), six gold-hilted state swords, and a set of arm ban-gles (bemufena). In addition to augmenting the regalia of Wulodwo, Osei Bonsu conferred a white stool upon Akuadapa, the Queen

9. Nafana tradition is clearly supported in this matter by accounts of the history of the Dadiesoaba stool. See Agyeman-Duah 1963.

Mother of Banda, as thanks for her spiritual assistance during the war, which consisted of supplying the exceptionally powerful charms sewn on the warcoat of the Adumhene of Kumasi.[10] The munificence of Osei Bonsu is emphatically acknowledged in the oral histories of Banda, where he is remembered particularly for his many gifts of regalia.

For the remainder of the nineteenth century, however, Banda-Ashanti relations were plagued by conflicts and rebellions. Banda assertions of independence, particularly her frequent alignments with the Bron state of Gyaman, weakened her ties with Kumasi. With the defeat of the Ashanti in the Anglo-Ashanti war of 1874, the entire western Brong region was thrown into a state of turmoil, and the already fragile links between Kumasi and Banda virtually disappeared. Nafana traditions claim that the annual Odwira in Kumasi was almost never attended and that no gifts of regalia were given to Banda after 1874. With the British occupation of 1900, Banda was placed in the northwestern district of the colony of Ashanti by the colonial administration, and all previous political and economic connections with Kumasi were severed.

What appears most striking in Nafana oral traditions about art and leadership is the emphasis Ashanti placed on distributing gifts of regalia to subordinate states. The number of these gifts was directly related to the closeness of the relationship between the areas in question: the more intimate the political and military connections with Kumasi, the greater the flow of regalia from the Asantehene to the Mgono of Banda. The first Ashanti contact with Banda was to a considerable extent initiated in this way, as seen in the case of the stool given to Sielongo by Osei Tutu; thereafter, allegiance was encouraged by recurrent displays of generosity.

The diffusion of certain Ashanti object-types to the Nafana led to wider patterns of cultural borrowing. With the acceptance of regalia came the adoption of a number of festivals within which these objects functioned. The enstoolment of the paramount chief of Banda as well as the annual yam festival—a period during which the state is purified—are now also occasions when the ancestral black stools are propitiated. The Ashanti language, Twi, spread rapidly throughout the Nafana state. It quickly became the second language of the Banda people and was always used in rituals employing imported Ashanti regalia. The political and military organization of Banda was also patterned after Ashanti practices, and the right to use official regalia was delegated downward to include the many chiefs under the paramountcy. When Banda-Ashanti relations deteriorated in the nineteenth century and items of regalia were no longer presented by Kumasi, Nafana chiefs

10. Interview with the Nifahene of Banda, the head of the Kabronno family.

FIGURE 9.2 Nafana. Of the eight state swords in the possession of the Kabronno family, the six largest represent pieces given by Asantehene Osei Bonsu to Mgono Wulodwo. The *dangapo* is the fourth sword from the left and the one upon which all wing chiefs of the Banda state will take their oath of allegiance to the next paramount from the Kabronno family. The two small swords were fashioned at Ashanti-Obuasi about thirty years ago at the request of the last Kabronno para-mount, Kwesi Bako Senapim. Kabronno, Banda. *Dangapo* ht. 37" (94 cm). (Photograph: author, 1966.)

traveled south to Ashanti to commission artisans to produce these objects, which had become a necessary part of Nafana culture.

An interesting corollary to the diffusion of these Ashanti cultural features is the manner in which the Nafana accepted them. Art forms, like other aspects of culture, are subject to reinterpretation as they travel through space and time. In Banda there is a rotational system of government with two royal families, Saminaku and Kabronno, alter-nately contributing candidates to the paramountcy.[11] Each royal family

11. For an excellent discussion of various forms of rotational political systems, see Goody 1966a.

has, therefore, to have its own set of regalia, including ancestral stools. Each now has a special room in which are kept the blackened stools of all the former paramount chiefs from that particular family. In the Kabronno family's room are five blackened stools—those of Petele, Sakye, Wulodwo, Sakyame, and Senapim; at Saminaku there are stools in memory of Kralongo, Gyara, Sielongo, Sakyi, Pehzoo, Habaa, Dabla, Yaw Due, and Yaw Sielongo. The three Ashanti-type stools (called *tegon* in Nafana) at Kabronno honor the memories of Sakye, Petele, and Wulodwo, while the *kulugon* are in honor of Sakyame and Senapim. At Saminaku, *tegon* preserve the memories of Sielongo, Dabla, and Yaw Sielongo. The stool of Sielongo, the original gift from Osei Tutu, was of course an Ashanti *tegon,* but according to the elders of both royal families, each successive Mgono was free to choose either a *tegon* or a *kulugon* to be his own sacred stool.

All the black stools of a particular family were supposed to remain in the memorial room belonging to that family. The only exception is Kralongo's stool, which, having been owned by the founder of the state, alternates between the two families. At present Kralongo's stool is with the Saminaku family because the current paramount is a Saminaku. At his death it will be transferred to the stool room of the Kabronno, since it is upon this stool that all Banda Mgonos are invested. The Kralongo stool will then become part of the regalia of Kabronno and will only be returned to the Saminaku family at the enstoolment of the next Saminaku chief. In 1965, however, Kofi Dwuru made an attempt to prevent the continued circulation of the Kralongo stool under the pretext that the newly built concrete stool room at the Saminaku compound was the most fitting permanent repository for this sacred item. A heated controversy arose between the two royal families, and the case was finally settled by the Traditional Council of Banda, which ruled against the chief (Dwuru 1955).

All the items of regalia presented to the paramounts of Banda by various Asantehene have been retained, as custom dictates, by the respective royal families to which the Mgono belonged. The six gold-hilted swords that Osei Bonsu gave to Mgono Wulodwo still serve as the messenger swords for the heads of the Kabronno family (fig. 9.2). The largest of the six (known as *dangapo* in Nafana, or *mponposon* in Twi), is also used for swearing allegiance; all wing chiefs of Banda pledge their support to the next Mgono from the Kabronno family while holding the *dangapo*. In addition, the *dangapo* is held by the paramount-designate from the Kabronno family when he is about to be enstooled; thus this particular sword functions at three different levels. The multiplicity of roles played by the *dangapo* is unlike any-

FIGURE 9.3. Nafana. Stool (the Mma Gwa) which was presented by Osei Bonsu to Akuadapa after the Fanti war of 1807; note its decoration of cowrie shells and the silver medallion. This particular stool is the most important of the three in the possession of the elderly women of the Kabronno compound. It was carved about fifteen years ago in Ashanti and is the fifth replacement for the original stool. Kabronno, Banda. Ht. 14" (35.6 cm); width, 22" (55.9 cm). (Photograph: author, 1966.)

thing found in Ashanti, where each of the many state-sword types has its own well-defined function. In Banda, however, where relatively few state-sword types (see chapter 8) are owned by the royal families, that a sword such as the *dangapo* would have many roles to perform seems entirely natural.[12]

Three white stools are in the possession of the female elders of the Kabronno family. The most significant of these is certainly the stool presented by the Asantehene Osei Bonsu to the Queen Mother Akuadapa after the Fanti war of 1807. What survives today is not the original stool itself, but a replacement (made in Ashanti) which conforms to the original design. The Nafana refer to this stool by its Twi name, Mma Gwa, literally "the woman's stool," and claim that its importance derives not only from the auspicious circumstances under which it was acquired but also from the fact that it is an exceptionally powerful object (fig. 9.3). The silver medallion decorating the center of the seat

12. The gold-leafed handles of the swords were said in 1966 to have been replaced several times, although it was claimed that the blades were the originals.

FIGURE 9.4. Nafana. Photograph of a chief and, to his right, the foremost linguist of the town. The young boys holding the state swords of the town are members of the chief's family. All of the regalia depicted—the royal fillets worn about the head, the cloths worn by the chief and his linguist, the arm bangles, the gold bracelets, and the rings—were fashioned in Ashanti or in the Brong region to the northwest of Ashanti proper. None of these objects are produced by the Nafana and must therefore be imported. Tambi, Cercle de Bondoukou, Ivory Coast. (Photograph: author, 1966.)

FIGURE 9.5. Nafana. The *akonkromfi* chair of Kofi Dwuru, the present Mgono of the Banda state. This particular example of a typical Ashanti brass-studded *akonkromfi* chair is used by the Mgono of Banda when he is seated in state, in the manner of paramounts in Ashanti. Kofi Dwuru purchased this chair in 1942 at Kumasi in order to augment the regalia of Banda and thereby to increase the prestige of the state. The openwork design on the back of the chair and the use of the *nyansapo* (wisdom-knot motif) bridging the legs of the chair are typical Ashanti stylistic and iconographic details. Saminaku, Banda. (Photograph: author, 1966.)

and the ring of cowries tied to the base of the central column were gifts from Osei Bonsu and were attached to the original stool. Talismans given by the Nsumankwahene of Ashanti—and placed in the supporting column of the original stool—have also been preserved; they too help to give this object its heightened efficacy and power. The next Queen Mother from the Kabronno family will sit upon this stool when it is her time to reign.

Although almost all types of Ashanti regalia are found among the Nafana, they accord special significance to objects which were given as gifts by specific Asantehene. These items are historical documentation of the ties established between Kumasi and the state of Banda. In addition, they generally are the first examples of each particular type of imported object known to the Nafana. To be sure, most items of regalia found in Banda (including those commissioned by "unrewarded" paramounts or wing chiefs) are imports from Ashanti and its environs, since the tradition of *making* regalia never really took root among the Nafana (figs. 9.4, 9.5). Though prized for their beauty and valued for the roles they play, these other pieces are clearly of secondary importance; oral traditions relating to them are hazy at best and often all but forgotten. By contrast, the retention of data concerning Ashanti regalia received as rewards, honors, and gifts is in all cases still remarkably vivid. These oral traditions constitute in essence a well-annotated history of Ashanti-Nafana relations and thus serve to perpetuate a dynamic instance of the visual arts functioning as an adjunct to political and cultural expansion.

REFERENCES

AGYEMAN-DUAH, J. A.
    1962   "Nsumankwa Stool History." Institute of African Studies, Ashanti Stool Series, no. 22. Mimeographed. Legon, Ghana.
    1963   "Dadiesoaba Stool History." Institute of African Studies, Ashanti Stool Series, no. 12. Mimeographed. Legon, Ghana.

AMEYAW, KWABENA
    1965   "Tradition of Banda." Institute of African Studies, Brong/Ahafo Series, no. 1. Mimeographed. Legon, Ghana.

ARHIN, KWAME
    1967   "The Structure of Greater Ashanti." *The Journal of African History* 8, no. 1: 65–85.

BINGER, LOUIS-GUSTAVE
   1892   *Du Niger au Golfe de Guinée.* 2 vols. Paris.
DELAFOSSE, MAURICE
   1904   *Vocabulaires comparatifs de plus de 60 langues ou dia-
               lectes parlés à la Côte d'Ivoire et dans les régions limitro-
               phes.* Paris.
   1908   *Les frontières de la Côte d'Ivoire, de la Côte d'Or, et du
               Soudan.* Paris.
DUPUIS, JOSEPH
   1824   *Journal of a Residence in Ashantee.* London.
DWURU, KOFI
   1955   Nana Kofi Dwuru v. the Nifahene of Kabronno. Banda
               Traditional Court Record Book. December. Banda-Ahen-
               kro, Ghana.
GOODY, JOHN R.
   1954   "The Ethnography of the Northern Territories of the Gold
               Coast, West of the White Volta." Mimeographed. Colonial
               Office, London.
   1964   "The Mande and the Akan Hinterland." In *The Historian
               in Tropical Africa,* edited by Jan Vansina, Raymond
               Mauny, and L. V. Thomas, pp. 193–218. London.
   1966a   "Circulating Succession among the Gonja." In *Succession
               to High Office,* edited by John Goody, pp. 142–176. Cam-
               bridge, England.
   1966b   "The Akan and the North." *Ghana Notes and Queries,*
               no. 9, pp. 18–24.
GOODY, JOHN R., AND ARHIN, KWAME, EDS.
   1965   *Ashanti and the Northwest.* Legon, Ghana.
JOHNSON, MARION
   1965   "Ashanti East of the Volta." *Transactions of the Historical
               Society of Ghana,* no. 8, pp. 33–59.
KYEREMATEN, A. A. Y.
   1961   *Regalia for an Ashanti Durbar.* Guide to Durbar in honour
               of Her Majesty Queen Elizabeth II. Kumasi, Ghana.
   1964   *Panoply of Ghana.* New York.
MEYEROWITZ, EVA L.
   1952   *Akan Traditions of Origin.* London.
   1958   *The Akan of Ghana.* London.
TAUXIER, LOUIS
   1921   *Le noir de Bondoukou.* Paris.
TOMLINSON, H. M.
   1954   "The Customs, Constitution, and History of the Gonja
               People: an essay." Mimeographed. Institute of African
               Studies. Legon, Ghana.
WILKS, IVOR
   1961   *The Northern Factor in Ashanti History.* Institute of Afri-
               can Studies. Legon, Ghana.

CHAPTER 10

Kwahu Terracottas, Oral Traditions, and Ghanaian History

Roy Sieber

The Kwahu of Ghana live on an escarpment (known as the Kwahu Scarp, situated some one hundred sixty kilometers east of Kumasi) and on the Afram plains north and west of the scarp. They share many cultural traits with the Ashanti and for more than a century were closely identified with the Ashanti Confederacy. Kwahu oral traditions record a series of migrations, which probably took place about A.D. 1700, to the scarp from Adansi, an area south of Kumasi. The leaders of this migration, together with those of another from Adansi about a half century later, apparently laid the foundations of the present Kwahu aristocracy. For Kwahu "Royals," as they are now called, are identified as descendants of the leaders of these migrations and/or the founders of Kwahu villages. In other respects the aristocratic structure of Kwahu society is analogous to that of the Ashanti;[1] chiefs, while they must come from Royal lineages, are chosen by popular selection; army cap-

Note: I am grateful to Mr. Kwabena Ameyaw, research assistant at the Institute of African Studies, University of Ghana, for his assistance in the field and for his help and advice, which is based on several years of intensive study of Kwahu traditions. The basic research for this paper was undertaken while the author was Visiting Professor at the Institute of African Studies, University of Ghana, under an African-American University Program grant. Partial support for research was granted by Indiana University. I am also grateful to Ivor Wilks for his advice in the preparation of this paper.

1. Or for that matter other Twi groups such as the Agni, who migrated southwestward from a point not far distant from the origin of the Kwahu.

FIGURE 10.1. Kwahu. Funerary terracotta representing a priest of Bruku, tutelary deity of the tribe. Lid constitutes a "portrait" showing plaited hair. Vessel has three figures: center, carrier of priest's stool; right, palanquin bearer; left, figure representing soul of deceased. In low relief between the figures are a sword (left) and a tortoise and snail (right). Made by Akosua Foriwa of Mpraeso in 1962. Brass-covered *asipim* chair on which terracotta rests was the property of the priest; it was made in 1929. The ground cloth is Hausa. Kwahu-Tafo. Ht. 19" (48.2 cm). (Photograph: author, 1964.)

tains, counsellors, treasurers, chief priests, and others assist the chief in governing his people.

In the course of studying Kwahu traditions and institutions, I have come to believe that many of the traits we generally identify with the Ashanti, particularly the accoutrements of leadership, must have been in existence before the foundation of the Ashanti Confederacy about 1701. While I cannot discuss the full data here, the following may be cited in support of this view.

It is clear from a variety of evidence that the Golden Stool, the principal symbol of the unity of the Ashanti states, was conceived by the priest Okomfo Anokye and employed by the first Asantehene, Osei Tutu, within an existing context wherein stools were both symbols of leadership and the repository of the owner's soul. Similarly, Ashanti architectural forms and decorations dating from the mid-1700s appear to be far too complex to have been evolved in a half century. Moreover, a weapon of the so-called "state sword" type, now in the National Museum in Copenhagen, has been in Europe since 1640, more than a half century before the Ashanti Confederacy was formed. In other words, though far from complete, the data would seem to demonstrate the existence of a complex of Royal symbols predating 1700 and, in some instances, predating the historical separation of other Akan groups such as the Agni and the Baule, who probably migrated to the Ivory Coast in the seventeenth and eighteenth centuries.

The art form I propose to discuss here—the funerary terracottas of the Kwahu—also almost certainly predates the Ashanti Confederacy. Whether or not the older ceramic forms were exclusively a prerogative of Royals, I have been unable to ascertain. But since the use of terracottas is limited to Royals nowadays, the same may well have been true in the past. Before we turn to the historical aspects of this art, however, some basic description is in order.

The most commonly seen type of Kwahu terracotta consists of a thin, flat, solid face or head mounted on a cylinder which is sometimes hollow in part (fig. 10.1). The face (reminiscent of the heads of the Ashanti dolls generally known as akua'ba) has eyebrows, eyes, nose, mouth, and occasionally other details in high relief. One or more of these features is often broken off cleanly, indicating that the features were modeled separately and later attached to the images. The ears, placed low on the sides of the nearly circular face, are often created merely by making curved incisions in the clay. The neck cylinder is ringed and, at times, the larynx is indicated as a boss (fig. 10.2, right). The head, which ends in a flattened disc-like base, often serves as the lid of a

FIGURE 10.2. Kwahu. Terracotta heads from a shrine. The hollow head (left) was made about the mid-1880s. Solid head (right) was made about 1944 by a potter, to be used at his own funeral. White lines were recently applied to these and other heads in the shrine. Aduamoa. Ht. approx. 12″ (30.5 cm). (Photograph: author, 1964.)

pottery vessel (fig. 10.1). To the vessel are sometimes attached a number of half figures which spring free from the body of the pot and touch the rim. Between these figures occur various low relief devices. Less frequent is a second type of terracotta, the head of which is hollow (fig. 10.2, left). In other respects these are similar to the flat type. I saw no example of the hollow type which also served as the lid of a vessel, although such a terracotta might well have done so.

In both the flat and hollow examples, the flattening of the head is a reference to beauty. After birth the heads of Kwahu infants are massaged at dawn for three days to assure a high, flattened receding forehead. Similarly the ringed neck is a sign of a beautiful woman or a handsome, successful man; these rings are not wrinkles, but rolls of fat, which are equated with prosperity. Individualized features are used to indicate sex and the portrait aspects of the heads: women's ears are

FIGURE 10.3. Kwahu. Terracotta of woman and child from a cemetery. A few specimens of this substyle were rescued by Kwabena Ameyaw before the cemetery was inundated by water from the new Volta Dam. From Nkami on the Afram Plains. Collection of the Institute of African Studies, University of Ghana, Legon. Ht. 13″ (33 cm). (Photograph: author.)

pierced; a man may have worn a beard, a chief a particular crown, and a priest most certainly would have had plaited hair, indicative of his office (fig. 10.1). This seems to support the contention, heard time and again, that these images were portraits of the dead. The figures on the sides of the vessels, however, seem to have no fixed iconography. In some instances they are said to represent the children of the deceased, in others his soul, stool bearer, or palanquin carriers. The low relief

FIGURE 10.4a. Kwahu. Grave of a priest (also of Bruku) who died in 1908, with terracotta *in situ*. The grave, once inside a house, is exposed because the walls have collapsed. Kwahu-Tafo. Ht. of head approx. 9″ (22.9 cm). (Photograph: author, 1964.)

devices refer to parables, particularly those suggesting virtues of the deceased.

Kwahu terracottas were made after the death and actual burial of an important person of Royal (that is, aristocratic) lineage. They were made for the subsequent formal funeral of the deceased and were exhibited under a palm leaf shelter next to a specially constructed hearth where food for the dead was cooked. After dark on the last day of the ceremonies, the hearth, the pottery and wooden cooking

FIGURE 10.4b. Kwahu. Close-up of head in Figure 10.4a.

vessels and utensils, the shelter, and the terracottas were all taken to the royal cemetery and placed on the grave. If the deceased had been buried under the floor of his house, a surrogate "grave" was made in the cemetery. At times the terracottas were kept in the village or in the house of the owner. Some became shrine pieces.

There are, to my knowledge, no specialist makers of Kwahu terracotta images; rather, potters—men or women—are commissioned to model one of these objects when the occasion arises. Because potters make very few during a year, or even a lifetime, there is much variation in style and details. Although the makers are aware of the basic traditional forms, they have had little opportunity (in recent years, at any rate) to examine many older examples. As a result there seems to have been a good deal of style drift.

Having given this general description, I should like to turn to historical considerations. I have seen and photographed Kwahu funerary terracottas that date from every decade of this century, as well as other specimens from the last half of the nineteenth century (fig. 10.2, left). A number of pieces from the cemetery at Nkami on the Afram plains may stem from the late nineteenth century (fig. 10.3). Figures 10.4a and 10.4b illustrate a somewhat damaged head (dating from 1908), which, although now exposed, was originally kept in a room in the house of the deceased. Among other specimens worthy of note is an extremely abraded head with fragments of eggshell adhering to it; this work is

FIGURE 10.5. Kwahu. Fragmentary head formerly owned by Nana Amoo Asenso, the Krontihene of Asakraka. Said to have been brought to Kwahu from Asumengya in Adansi (only a few miles from Ahinsan) in the late eighteenth century. Collection of the Institute of African Studies, University of Ghana, Legon. Ht. approx. 6" (15.2 cm). (Photograph: author.)

reported to have been brought from Adansi during the late eighteenth century (fig. 10.5).

Of particular interest is a complete figure now in the collection of the Institute of African Studies of the University of Ghana[2] (fig. 10.6). It is said to be a portrait of Adua Adwesawa, the first Queen Mother of Asakraka village; if true, this would date the image to the early or middle years of the eighteenth century. It is almost certain that this example is not the original figure, for important pieces, if broken, were replaced. But whether or not this is the original representation of Adua Adwesawa, the existence of this image and the tradition that surrounds it indicate that the Kwahu were making and using funerary terracottas within a few years of the time of their arrival in their present territory.

Archaeological material found elsewhere in Ghana, particularly in the Adansi area south of Kumasi, whence the Kwahu are believed to have migrated, offers support for this hypothesis. A number of terracotta heads, most of them hollow, have been discovered at Fomena, in Adansi, reputedly near an old cemetery (Wild and Braunholtz 1934). Although the age and use of these objects is uncertain, they would seem to date at least from the nineteenth century. More important still is the work undertaken by Oliver Davies at Ahinsan (in Adansi, near Fomena). Davies has excavated a series of terracotta heads and frag-

2. The head and one leg were rejoined to the body. Some small damage exists. It was collected through the joint efforts of the author and K. Ameyaw, who arranged for a replacement to be made, and through the kindness of Nana Kwabena Afram, Asakrakahene.

FIGURE 10.6. Kwahu. Terracotta representing first Queen Mother of Asakraka. May date to the early or mid-eighteenth century. It was kept in front of the Queen Mother's consecrated (blackened) stool. Collection of the Institute of African Studies, University of Ghana, Legon. Ht. approx. 16″ (40.6 cm). (Photograph: author.)

ments of vessels which he dates to the last half of the seventeenth century. These heads, though most are smaller than those found at Fomena or currently observable in the Kwahu area, are both hollow and flat. In techniques and basic style they are closely comparable to the funerary terracottas of the Kwahu. The vessel fragments discovered by Davies at Ahinsan are extremely close (if not nearly identical) to those found at Kwahu (Davies 1964, pp. 46–47; 1956, p. 147; and Kofi 1964, figs. 36, 37).

It seems probable, therefore, that the tradition of making funerary terracottas was brought by the Kwahu Royals with them on their migration from Adansi. Nor is this likely to be an isolated ethno-historical event. Fragments of terracotta heads have been found south and east of the Kwahu area on the Accra plains, in the Shai Hills, and at Dawu on the scarp.[3] All of these objects were found in contexts assigned provisionally to the seventeenth century. Other more recent terracotta traditions also deserve mention. Among the many Ghana-centered peoples that use terracotta funerary images, the Ashanti,[4] the Fanti,[5] and other related groups such as the Krinjabo of the Agni[6] are particularly prominent. Further research will be needed to establish the full geographical and temporal distribution of this terracotta tradition. As far as I know, this is the oldest datable African sculptural tradition still functioning in a traditional context, the roots of which can be located archaeologically.

3. The Dawu specimens and one example from Wodoku (near the Accra airport) are illustrated in Shaw 1961. Alexander found another specimen at Wodoku; Ivor Wilks found one at Larteh, and myself one at Adwuku in the Shai Hills.

4. Rattray 1927, fig. 66, shows an Ashanti "family pot" seemingly related to the Kwahu examples. There is in a private collection in New York a brilliantly executed vessel, probably Ashanti, which is most likely a "family pot."

5. A number of "Fanti" terracotta heads are in German museums.

6. Despite Davies' feelings that "the Kringabo [Agni] group is not closely related" (1964, p. 46), Agni terracottas probably stem from the same tradition as the Ahinsan and Kwahu examples. Not only do the Agni have a tradition of migration from what is now Ghana, but their terracottas are used in an almost identical manner and are limited to Royals. See, for example, F. J. Amon d'Aby (1960), Pere Monezy (1942), and L. Tauxier (1932). I am grateful to René Bravmann for pointing out these parallels to me.

REFERENCES

AMON D'ABY, F. J.
1960   *Croyances religieuses et coutumes juridiques des Agni de la Côte d'Ivoire.* Paris.

DAVIES, OLIVER
1956   "Human Representation in Terracotta from the Gold Coast." *South African Journal of Science* 52: 147–151.
1964   "The Archaeological Evidence for the Iron-Age in Ashanti." In "Ashanti Research Project: First Report." Mimeographed. Legon, Ghana.

KOFI, VINCENT
1964   *Sculpture in Ghana.* Ghana Information Services, Accra.

MONEZY, PERE
1942   *Histoire et coutumes du pays d'Assinie et du Royaume de Krinjabo.* Paris.

RATTRAY, R. S.
1927   *Religion and Art in Ashanti.* Oxford.

SHAW, THURSTAN
1961   *Excavation at Dawu.* Published for University College of Ghana. Edinburgh.

TAUXIER, L.
1932   *Religion, moeurs et coutumes des Agnis de la Côte d'Ivoire.* Paris.

WILD, R. P., AND BRAUNHOLTZ, H. J.
1934   "Baked Clay Heads from Graves near Fomena, Ashanti." *Man* 34, art. 1: 1–4.

CHAPTER 11

Gold-Plated
Objects of Baule Notables

Hans Himmelheber

In Ghana (formerly known as the Gold Coast) and on the Ivory Coast, the notables of the Akan tribes own wooden objects which are covered with gold plate of local manufacture. In Dahomey, silver is also used. I have seen these objects being made and in use among the Baule during my eight field trips there between 1933 and 1971 and on one visit to Ghana.

It is a strange fact that these objects, so highly valued by the people who create them, enjoy no appreciation at all on the part of Western connoisseurs of African art. When I first brought a collection of seventeen objects to Germany in 1933 and exhibited them at the Frobenius Institute in 1934,[1] the consensus of the experts was that they were fakes, although at that time postcards of Agni chiefs parading these objects were on sale at Abidjan, and Maurice Delafosse had previously described them in the year 1900. To this day I know of no collector who owns one of them, no museum which exhibits them (except for an occasional single piece), and, apart from my own books, no studies of African art that mention them.

I have myself described and illustrated both objects and technique in my books *Negerkünstler* (1935) and *Negerkunst und Negerkünstler*

1. This exhibition at the Institut für Kulturmorphologie in Frankfurt a/M was accompanied by a small catalogue containing descriptions of my Baule objects, compiled by Heinrich Wieschhoff from information provided by me. See Wieschhoff 1934.

(1960), and discussed the technique especially in an article in *Abhand-lungen und Berichte des Staatlichen Museums für Völkerkunde, Dresden,* 1968, entitled "Die Technik des Vergoldens bei den Baule, Elfen-beinküste."[2] In the present chapter I propose to describe them as *objects of art,* giving an account of their use and of the technique of making them. A. A. Y. Kyerematen, in his book *Panoply of Ghana* (1964), has described and pictured gilded regalia of Ghanaian chiefs. His information on the use and significance of these objects certainly applies to those of the Ivory Coast chiefs as well.

The Baule belong to the Akan peoples who inhabit Ghana and the Ivory Coast. They originally lived in Ghana as part of the Ashanti and emigrated westward some three hundred years ago to what is now the Ivory Coast. Today they form the westernmost outpost of Akan-speak-ing peoples. Their neighbors are the Kru-speaking Dida, the Mande-fu-speaking Guro, the Mande-tan-speaking Malinke, and the Senufo. The history of their migration is still well remembered; the male descen-dant of the queen who led the exodus still lives in the residence (Sakas-sou) which she founded, and he is respected by all Baule as their nominal king (Himmelheber 1951, pp. 137–156).

The Baule live in savannah country. They plant yam, and some corn, and today coffee and cocoa for export as well. Hunting is no longer of any importance, but when I first visited them in 1933, elephants and buffalo were still numerous.

From Ghana the Baule brought with them the technique of casting works of art in metal by the lost wax process—gold weights from brass and various ornaments from pure gold—and probably also the tech-nique of plating wooden objects with gold.

When in state, a Baule notable holds in his hand a fly whisk made of a long horsetail which is nailed onto a gold-plated wooden handle (fig. 11.1). This handle has quite an extraordinary "un-African" shape; on a bulbous base rises, somewhat like the Egyptian papyrus column, a flower-like form (fig. 11.2). Such chiefs or kings also wear a kind of crown, made from a ribbon or cap of black cloth, onto which small gold-plated pieces of wood are sewn. These may be just little squares, or they may have a human face or the figure of an animal carved on them (fig. 11.1).

Around a greater chief stand or squat his followers, holding more gold-plated objects. Most frequent are swords with double-globe han-

---

2. In 1965 I took a film of the entire manufacturing process in the village of Asabonou.

FIGURE 11.1. Baule, subtribe Atutu. Carver Tanu with gold-plated fly whisk and crown, both carved by him. Akoue Kouadiokro village. (Photograph: author, 1963.)

dles (fig. 11.3, middle). They are of no practical use, for the blade is blunt, and sometimes two blades even run parallel to each other.[3] From Kyerematen (1964, p. 33 et seq.) we know that the swords had various

3. These double-bladed swords were previously reported by Paul E. Isert, a Danish doctor who traveled on the Gold Coast in 1783–1787: ". . . oftmals sind zwei Schneiden zusammen in einen Griff gefaßt." (1788, p. 37—". . . frequently two blades are contained in one handle").

FIGURE 11.2. Baule, subtribe Uarebo. Figures on fly-whisk handles: left, young leopard, 7.5″ (19 cm); center, bird on nest, 3″ (7.5 cm); right, horse, 7.5″ (19 cm). (Photograph: author.)

functions and, accordingly, various shapes: they were used in swearing allegiance, in the ritual for purifying the chief's soul, and as a badge of credence for those going on the ruler's errands. R. S. Rattray (1927, p. 280) reports that the king of Ashanti had four hundred sword-bearers. Another object pertaining to chieftainship is a staff which is carried by the chief's linguist. The linguist, according to Kyerematen (1964, p. 92), is

a member of the class of elders through whom an Akan chief speaks and is spoken to at both public and private meetings. He is the mouthpiece or spokesman of the chief. . . . Linguists also have other duties. They advise on traditional law and customs, being regarded as experts in these matters; they are sent as ambassadors to other states to declare war, negotiate for peace or convey some important message; they act as chiefs of protocol for visiting potentates; in courts of law they pronounce judgment on behalf of the chief; and at ritual ceremonies they are present to support the chief in the offering of prayers. . . . His office is denoted by a staff or mace.

Among the Baule this staff is usually subdivided into sections, some of which are gold-plated, others being covered with black cloth. On top is a figure of a man or animal (Wieschhoff 1934, fig. 7). These Baule staffs are more modest than those of the eastern Akan tribes, who cover entire staffs with gold and place *groups* of figures on top. The Baule king also has a spear with two points (fig. 11.3, left; compare Schilde 1930, p. 93) whose staff is partly gold-plated, and there are

FIGURE 11.3. Baule, subtribe Uarebo. Anoubli, king of Baule (center). Followers are holding gold-plated objects: (left to right) fly whisk, two-pointed spear, sword, solid imitation of shotgun. Sakassou village. (Photograph: author, 1933).

gold-plated signal horns, knives with gold-plated handles, and also free-standing figures of men and animals (Himmelheber 1960, fig. 168).

Quite surprising, though not unique in African art, are gold-plated *solid* objects representing items of daily use, such as an ointment bowl or a bugle (Himmelheber 1935, pl. XII). These may be wooden imitations of *natural* objects (such as a calabash), wooden imitations of something which is otherwise made in a different material (such as an iron musical instrument), or wooden imitations of objects which are normally also made in wood; the only difference in this last case is that the imitation is solid so that it cannot be used and is covered with ornaments. I own an imitation of a wooden hammer used for beating the above-mentioned iron instrument (fig. 11.4); the only difference

FIGURE 11.4. Baule. *Laule*, a two-part musical instrument consisting of wooden hammer and hollow iron, and an imitation of same for gold-plating. From left to right: wooden hammer used in playing the instrument; imitation of hammer for gold-plating, covered with ornaments; hollow iron, to be beaten with hammer; imitation of hollow iron, in wood and solid, covered with patterns for gold-plating. Wooden hammer ht. 10.3″ (26 cm). (Photograph: author.)

between original and imitation hammer is the overall ornamentation of the latter. Analogous "imitations" are found among the Kuba of the Congo: their *bongotol* are objects formed from red camwood dust mixed with sand and water. Here too there are also independent figures of animals and solid, nonfunctional objects of daily use, such as baskets (Himmelheber 1960, figs. 287, 288).

Important Akan princes own an incredible number of gold-plated objects—hundreds of them! I received a vivid impression of the importance attached to their quantity when I saw several chiefs parading at a state fair in Abidjan in 1934. Each one showed his treasure of gold-plated objects—except that the king of the Baule, whom I knew to be quite wealthy, appeared to own only a modest number. When I later visited him in his residence, Sakassou, he showed me many more. Asked why he had not taken them to Abidjan, he replied that he had done so once before, but that two Agni chiefs had threatened to poison him if he again stole the show.

Nowadays chiefs from the non-Akan areas of the Ivory Coast have also begun to buy and wear crowns with gold-plated pieces of wood as a sign of their high position. This applies especially to the Guere, a Kru tribe. They send messengers to purchase such things from the Baule.

Two neighboring Baule villages specialize in the manufacture of gold-plated objects: Asabonou and Kongonou, some ten miles north of the administrative post of Tiebissou. Both belong to the Atutu subtribe. Nearby is another Atutu village, Ngattatorkro, where objects of pure gold are cast in the lost wax process. Asabonou and Kongonou are so well known for their gold-plated objects that I have seen messengers from the kings of faraway eastern Agni tribes ordering such objects in these two villages.

The practice of this handicraft is a family matter: each family compound in Asabonou has a workshop with built-in bellows and another with anvils. The younger men, and even boys, do the work. The gold is washed out of alluvial deposits on river banks by women. They use flat wooden pans exactly like those of the gold prospectors in Western countries (Himmelheber 1968, figs. 2, 3). One of the young men then melts the gold dust into a lump about the size of a small pea, using a crucible which is placed in the charcoal in front of his bellows. This lump is then hammered on the anvil into one sheet about the size of the palm of a hand and approximately 0.05 millimeters thick, which is to say about three hundred times the thickness of our commercial gold leaf (fig. 11.5, and Himmelheber 1968, figs. 5–12). The wooden carvings to which these gold sheets are applied are made by one of the "goldsmithing" families or by carvers from other towns (Himmelheber 1935, p. 25).

Originally the gold plate was fastened to the wood by miniature gold staples. Then different kinds of glue came into use: a starch paste, as Delafosse reports (1900, p. 438); resin, as I was told in 1935, and white man's glue, as I saw in 1965. The metal is applied in small pieces or strips. Then it is pressed and smoothed onto the glue-covered wood with the fingers and the splinter of an ox femur (fig. 11.6). It does not easily come off after that, but objects are not touched on their gilded parts and after use they are carefully wrapped in lengths of native cotton cloth (Delafosse 1900, fig. 2).

The wooden objects are carved in much greater numbers than can ever be plated with gold. Carvers appear to enjoy showing their talent and imagination in creating these ornate things, the more so because they carve them leisurely while gossiping under the village tree. This applies particularly to fly-whisk handles. I have seen not hundreds, but

FIGURE 11.5. Baule, subtribe Atutu. Artisan hammering out the gold leaf on a small anvil. Asabonu village. (Photograph: author, 1965.)

thousands, of these during my trips to Baule country, and they are still there, and still more are being carved. Only a small percentage of them will ever be gold-plated and given a horsetail (which is imported from the Western Sudan, for there are no horses in Baule country) so as to actually serve as a fly whisk. The public manufacture of such objects contrasts with the making of masks and figures, which, because of their religious significance, are produced at a secret workplace in the bush.

FIGURE 11.6. Baule, subtribe Atutu. Artisan pressing gold leaf into grooves of the ornaments with a splinter of an ox's femur. Asabonu village. (Photograph: author, 1965.)

As art objects, these gold-plated articles of the Baule differ in several respects from what we otherwise know as Baule art. We might even enlarge this statement to say: from what we know of *African* art, Baule art is usually restrained in form, attitude, and decoration. Gold-plated objects are rather at the other extreme: they are covered all over with varied ornamental patterns, and are often crowned with groups of animals whose bodies are densely patterned and which sometimes even show action. A description of these characteristics follows:

TWO-DIMENSIONAL ORNAMENTATION

Whereas other Akan tribes who practice gold-plating cover the wood with only a few grooves, the Baule adorn it with a dense network of patterns. I know of only one other African people similarly fond of and gifted in ornamenting wooden objects: the Kuba in the Congo and their relatives, the Kete. Kuba ornaments are quite different from those of the Baule, however, since the Congolese groups employ curved lines and continuous ornamental figures like the meander, which they cut deep into the wood, and also accord much space to the individual line or motif. Baule ornament stays more on the surface and consists entirely of straight lines; curved lines never occur. Whereas the Kuba only rarely insert a natural motif, such as a human face or a duiker's horn, into their decoration, the Baule make ample use of naturalistic motifs. Kuba ornamentation has more force, more ingenuity; Baule ornamentation is more delicate.

LINEAR DESIGNS

These patterns are the same on all gold-plated objects. The artist seems to want to show as many designs as possible on one object, which is therefore subdivided into a number of fields. In some cases the subdivisions pay heed to the form of the object, in others they do not. Thus on the handle of a fly whisk, the round edge of the upper part is usually marked by concentric circles (fig. 11.2, left, center), and the top part is subdivided into symmetrical fields starting from its center. Yet the designs on the main, ascending part of the handle show no such functional arrangement. This part is horizontally subdivided into two to four belts, each of which is again vertically subdivided into five to ten small vertical sections (fig. 11.2, left). An unfinished handle in my collection shows that the carver had first subdivided this part of the handle into fields of the same size, then filled the fields with different patterns (fig. 11.2, right). The patterns of various fields have no symmetrical or other relationship to one another.

Linear geometrical patterns consist of:

a. straight-cut lines, leaving about one millimeter of the original surface between them; I know of sixteen different patterns of this type (figs. 11.7–11.12[4]);

---

4. I am indebted to Miss Christina Schäublin, of the Museum für Völkerkunde in Basel, for making the drawings shown in Figures 11.7–11.32, after objects in my possession.

11.7

11.8

11.9

11.10

11.11

11.12

FIGURES 11.7–11.12. Baule. Designs used in gold-plating.

b. a design in which one half may be deeply incised, the other half remaining raised (figs. 11.13–11.16, the black part in the illustrations signifies raised areas);

c. a combination of straight lines and zigzags, leaving *raised* triangles or rhomboi between them (fig. 11.17);

d. parallel lines slanting off like a range of parallel mountain slopes (figs. 11.18, 11.19);

11.13   11.14   11.15

11.16   11.17

11.18   11.19   11.20

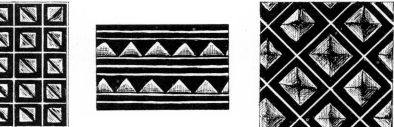

11.21   11.22   11.23

FIGURES 11.13–11.23. Baule. Designs used in gold-plating.

e. cut-in squares, rhomboi, or triangles within which little pyramids rise to the original level (figs. 11.20–11.23);

f. only rarely, some overlapping within the pattern, suggesting a ribbon-like continuity, such as is quite frequent in Kuba and Benin ornamentation (fig. 11.24).

Figure 11.25 shows a combination of several of the aforementioned kinds of patterns. I do not know whether these geometrical patterns have any significance or even names.

RELIEFS OF ANIMAL OR HUMAN MOTIFS

Parts of the human body and animals appear in relief, set between the geometrical designs. They are always symmetrically arranged.

a. Human motifs. The human face is shown in relief on the two globes of sword handles, on the bulbous part of fly-whisk handles, and on chiefs' staffs (figs. 11.26–11.28). In an oval or square shape are set eyes, nose, mouth, and sometimes the hair above the forehead, all in a very stylized fashion. The eyes are sometimes oval, sometimes half-oval as we know them from Baule masks and statuettes; the nose is long, with pronounced, broad wings; the mouth is usually just a little cut or not indicated at all, as in Figure 11.27.

Only one object in my collection, a fly-whisk handle, shows a human *hand* carved in relief (fig. 11.29). Its location is also unusual, being placed in the middle of the ascending part of the handle where normally there are just linear patterns. Another fly-whisk handle (illustrated in Wieschhoff 1934, fig. 8) ends in a human hand with the thumb pointing upward, which, according to Kyerematen (1964, p. 93), signifies that only God matters. This again has a parallel in Kuba ornamentation, for the Kuba carve a hand on the lid of a cosmetic powder box as a sign that its owner has killed an enemy (Himmelheber 1960, fig. 280). On Benin bronzes, too, the human hand can be seen. As the means by which men do their deeds, the hand is a symbol of life-force. The Oba has "an altar of the hand" to which he sacrifices to strengthen his life-force (Bradbury 1961).

b. Animals are shown only from above, for symmetry is required. This is another parallel with Kuba ornamentation. Therefore, those animals on which one ordinarily looks down are preferred. In Baule designs we often find the crab alternating with the human face on the bulbous part of the fly whisk, and occasionally a spider (fig. 11.30), a tortoise, a crocodile (fig. 11.33), or a frog. A curiosity from the Occidental point of view is the relief of a bird, strongly stylized, as seen from above, and therefore symmetrical (figs. 11.31, 11.32). As far as I know, this "point of view" toward a bird is not taken by any other African tribe; the

11.24

11.25

11.26

11.27

11.28

11.29

FIGURES 11.24–11.29. Baule. Designs used in gold-plating.

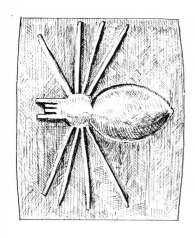

11.30   11.31   11.32

FIGURES 11.30–11.32. Baule. Designs used in gold-plating.

FIGURE 11.33. Baule. Relief of crocodile
on a sword handle. Ht. 7.5″ (19 cm).
(Photograph: author.)

199

Senufo, for example, with all the birds they carve in relief on porches and drums, always show them in profile.

Specific *parts* of animals are not carved on gold-plated objects, with the exception of an occasional duiker's horn. The duiker horn is a receptacle for magic mixtures all over West Africa, and again occurs in Kuba ornamentation.

c. Masks rarely occur as parts of the decoration. An occasional exception is the Dje (steer) mask. It is surprising that the mask motif is so rarely used, for the Baule carve miniature masks quite frequently on their weavers' heddle pulleys and on the little hammers for the iron musical instrument known as *laule*.

FREE-STANDING FIGURES OF ANIMALS
SINGLE FIGURES WITHOUT ACTION

These occur mainly on the tops of fly-whisk handles and on chiefs' staffs (fig. 11.2). On fly whisks, the animal is most often a bird: a duck, shown swimming (therefore without legs; Himmelheber 1960, pl. VIII), a cock, or an eagle. One fly whisk in my collection shows a bird meant to be sitting on its nest (fig. 11.2, center). Less frequent are elephants and leopards. Another of my fly whisks shows a horse, an animal practically unknown in Baule country (fig. 11.2, right). It is strangely clad in a long gown and has a curious pointed head like that of an insect-eater. If it were not for the saddle and bridle, the animal could not be identified as a horse, yet the object is quite a work of art. Figures of such animals as tortoises, birds, and elephants are also carved without making them part of any other object (Himmelheber 1935, pl. VI).

I have not yet found a Baule who could elucidate any of these animal figures, either those on objects or free-standing. But the Akan in Ghana attribute some meaning—or even several meanings—to carvings of single animals on chiefs' staffs. Thus a parrot indicates: "If you see a parrot all by himself, don't throw a stone at him, for it might belong to a flock which will then attack you." Similarly, a porcupine warns: "If you attack me, thousands will stand up to defend me" (like the quills of the porcupine which suddenly stand up to defend their owner). A monkey: "The monkey sees his medicine with his eyes" (you should *see* before you *believe*). A bird precariously perched on a linguist's staff looking backward: first meaning: "Let not bygones be bygones"; second meaning: "Take up what falls behind you—it isn't much trouble"[5] (corresponding to the German: "Wer den Pfennig nicht

5. Oral communication from Mr. T. A. Aketua, guide in the Accra Museum.

ehrt, ist des Talers nicht wert"—"He who does not honor the penny does not deserve the shilling.")

ANIMALS SHOWING ACTION, SINGLY OR IN GROUPS

Movement, so rare in African art, is shown by a baby leopard on a fly whisk (fig. 2, left). It turns its head as if in astonishment at something it has not seen before.

Also unusual in African art are scenes showing two animals interacting; these are often seen on Baule fly whisks, with one animal freestanding, the other in relief. One example shows an eagle on the top, bending his neck down to grasp a snake crawling up the handle as if to fight the bird (Himmelheber 1960, fig. 167). One of my fly whisks depicts a free-standing bird which has just grasped a lizard and is keeping it tight under his claws, while greedily feeding on a mouse (fig. 11.34). Animals clutching their prey are not uncommon motifs in African art: for example, a crocodile grasping a fish on a Benin tusk, a snake grasping a frog on a Senufo drum. These little scenes, however, are *stationary;* they do not show *action,* whereas the scenes on the Baule objects are *dramatic.*

FIGURE 11.34. Baule. Fly-whisk handle: bird keeping a lizard under its claws, feeding on a mouse. Ht. 9.1″ (23 cm). (Photograph: author.)

FIGURE 11.35. Baule. Gilded fly-whisk handle. Crocodile, creeping up the handle, bites the trunk of an elephant standing on top. Ht. 9.1" (23 cm). (Photograph: author.)

Another of my fly whisks shows a rare scene: a crocodile creeping up its handle and biting the trunk of an elephant which stands on the top (fig. 11.35).

Animal scenes are also carved as independent sculptures. In 1934 I acquired a fine group (about 12 in., or 30 cm. in height) of an eagle standing on a tortoise and hacking away at it.

The Akan in Ghana lend meanings to these scenes: The eagle biting a snake means "All depends on who is most alert, for the snake can blind the bird by spitting poison into his eyes" (which of course it cannot). But if the snake catches the bird: "Nature is so full of wonders that even though the snake can only crawl on the ground, it can catch the bird which flies freely in the air."

On the top of another of my fly whisks three birds sit facing one another. In Ghana this is interpreted as meaning, first, "One man alone should not make an important decision," and second, "Fighting with words amounts to nothing." A hen on her nest, as is shown on another

FIGURE 11.36. Baule. Gilded fly-whisk handle. The varying kinds of feathers on the different parts of the bird's neck, body, and wings are indicated by appropriate patterns. Ht. 6.3″ (16 cm). (Photograph: author.)

fly whisk (fig. 11.2, center) means: "He who stays with his mother will get better food."[6]

The designs on these animal carvings often imitate natural characteristics of the animals, but they can be purely fanciful as well, as I have shown in my book *Negerkünstler* in the section on the ornamentation of two carved tortoises (1935, fig. 15). Thus the feathers of the different parts of a bird's body are characteristically stylized in linear patterns (fig. 11.36): the long feathers of a duck's wings by unbroken parallel lines, the little ones at the front part of the wings by lines crossing at small intervals; the small feathers on a cock's chest are indicated by small angles, but those on the neck below the beak by long lines meeting at a sharp angle. The elephant's tough, wrinkled skin is imitated by a pattern of deep cuts crossing at right angles, leaving tiny pyramids between them (fig. 11.37).

6. Oral communication from Mr. T. A. Aketua, guide in the Accra Museum. Further information on the meanings of figures on linguists' staffs, state umbrellas, and swords is given by Kyerematen (1964, pp. 34, 37, 90, 93–97).

FIGURE 11.37. Baule. Head of linguist's staff. Wrinkled skin of elephant is indicated by rows of little pyramids. Ht. 4" (10 cm). (Photograph: author.)

HUMAN FIGURES

Sometimes a fly-whisk handle does not have the papyrus shape described above. Instead it is formed like a human hand (Wieschhoff 1934, fig. 8) or like a human head and neck (fig. 11.38, left), or, in exceptional cases, like an entire seated human figure (fig. 11.38, right). The neck and body are densely covered with patterns of many types, and the hairdress shows the braids of the old Baule, still worn by the women. Traditional tattooing is shown on the face.

Free-standing human figures may also be gold-plated. When this is done, the figure is closely covered with many patterns (Himmelheber 1960, fig. 168)—unlike the normal, well-known Baule figures.

HISTORY AND PARALLELS

How old is the technique of gold-plating? No mention is made of it at all in Thomas Astley's *Allgemeine Historie der Reisen zu Wasser und Lande,* published in 1749, where Akan objects of *solid* gold are described in several places (vol. 4, bk. 8, pp. 21, 44, 112 et seq., 117, 145, 146). Thomas E. Bowdich, who visited the king of Ashanti in 1817, accurately describes the manufacturing of *solid* gold ornaments (1819, pp. 36, 47, 259, 260). He pays much attention to the splendor of Ashanti gold; thus when describing his reception in the capital,

FIGURE 11.38. Baule. Fly-whisk handles: left, human head, ht. 9.25″ (22 cm); right, seated human figure, ht. 10.3″ (26 cm). (Photograph: author.)

Kumasi (pp. 34–35): "The sun was reflected, with a glare scarcely more supportable than the heat, from the massy gold ornaments, which glistened in every direction . . . arms and swords of gold . . . wolves and rams heads as large as life, cast in gold, were suspended from their gold handled swords, which were held around them in great numbers; the blades were shaped like round bills, and rusted in blood." Bowdich expressly states that what he saw was solid gold. I think, however, that he took some objects for solid gold which were actually only gold-plated, for example, the "gold handled swords, which were held around them in great numbers."[7] Kyerematen never mentions handles or tops of umbrellas or linguists' staffs of solid gold, but only gold-plated ones. The oldest mention of gold-plating I can find is the above-mentioned treatise by Delafosse (1900, pp. 438–439, 545, fig. 2). Willy Schilde, in his extensive article "Die afrikanischen Hoheitszeichen," 1930, does not mention these gilded objects.

Since the Baule have no active relationship with their faraway Ashanti cousins, yet both practice gold-plating, it is likely that the Baule brought

7. When French President Pompidou visited the Ivory Coast in February 1971 and was met at the airport by Agni chiefs in full regalia, Western journalists also reported seeing "swords and fly whisks with handles of solid gold"; in fact, these were all of gold-plated wood.

this knowledge with them when they emigrated from the Gold Coast. This would accord the technique an age of at least three hundred years.

It might be supposed that gold-plating was a lesser people's imitation of solid gold objects made for the wealthy. Gold *is* connected with rank. A. B. Ellis writes (1887, p. 262) that Akan chiefs of the first rank have emblems of solid gold on their state umbrellas, while for chiefs of the second rank these objects are made of wood, and Kyerematen expressly connects gilded objects with rank in the case of linguists' staffs: "The staff is of wood and privileged chiefs wrap their linguists' staffs with silver or gold leaf" (1964, p. 92). Solid gold objects exist among the Akan peoples, including the Baule, in enormous numbers. A family's wealth is in fact judged by its possession of such rich and costly objects. On certain occasions these are displayed in public (Niangoran-Bouah 1964, p. 143). However, these objects are of an entirely different nature from the gold-plated objects discussed here. They are mainly small pendants, rarely weighing more than one pound. It is hard to imagine the weighty handles of fly whisks or swords ever having been made of pure gold. Besides, chiefs, not lesser men, own the gold-plated objects, so I think this technique sprang from the chiefs' desire to make their appearance as resplendent as possible.

In view of the great number of objects which are ornamented in this manner but *not gilded,* it may be questioned whether gilding is actually the cause for this ornamental art, or whether this ornamental art developed independently of the gilding technique. Patterned carving does not seem to be technically necessary to make the gold leaf stick to the wood, because of the old technique of nailing gold leaf onto the wood and the more modern glueing method. Figure 168 in *Negerkunst und Negerkünstler* (1960) shows a statuette gilded in the glue technique, with a face largely unornamented, yet gilded. This, however, is an exception. Most gilded objects are patterned all over. Never have I seen a normal, unpatterned Baule sculpture plated with gold. So there *is* a connection between gold-plating and this ornamentation.

I see two possibilities for this connection: First, that the ornamentation might be an imitation of metal engraving. Yet objects in solid gold, so numerous among the Akan peoples, do not show engraved patterns. Second: that the ornamentation might be meant to enhance the brilliance of the gilded surface by the play of light on its edges. This latter interpretation seems the more probable to me.

The difference between these objects and "normal" Baule sculpture is not only in the ornamentation. For it is only in this branch of Baule carving that animals are abundantly sculptured and even appear as independent, free-standing objects. On heddle pulleys, where they might just as well be carved (the neighboring Guro do so), they are rare. More important, animals are carved in a style which differs from those appearing in "normal" Baule sculpture, where they are strongly stylized and of a certain stiffness. In ornamental sculpture, on the other hand, they are more naturalistic, and, as we have seen, often in graceful or dramatic action, sometimes two or more of them combined in little scenes.

In conclusion, then, this art of gold-plating wooden carvings was probably created among the Akan peoples of the Gold Coast more than three hundred years ago to add rich and visible splendor to the offices of their nobility. The Baule have developed it into a specific genre, distinct from their other sculpture, characterized by ornamentation which covers the entire object, by unusual forms like the flower-like fly-whisk handle, by scenes with animals showing dramatic action, and by the imitation of objects of daily use.

REFERENCES

Pages on which metal-covered objects or objects made of solid gold are mentioned are set within brackets.

ADANDÉ, ALEXANDRE
1962   *Les récades des rois du Dahomey*. Institut Français d'Afrique Noire, Catalogues et Documents no. 15. Dakar. [pp. 13–15]

ASTLEY, THOMAS
1745–47   *A New General Collection of Voyages and Travels*. 4 vols. London. Translated as *Allgemeine Historie der Reisen zu Wasser und Lande*. Vols. 1–7. Leipzig, 1749. [vol. 4, bk. 8, pp. 21, 44, 112 et seq., 117, 145, 146]

BOWDICH, THOMAS E.
1819   *Mission from Cape Coast Castle to Ashantee*. London. [pp. 36, 47, 259]

BRADBURY, R. E.
1961   "Ezomo's *Ikegobo* and the Benin Cult of the Hand." *Man* 61, art. 165: 129–138.

DELAFOSSE, MAURICE
1900   "Sur des traces probables de civilisation égyptienne et d'hommes de race blanche à la Côte d'Ivoire." *L'Anthropologie* 11: 431–451, 543–568, 677–690. [pp. 438–439, 545]

ELLIS, A. B.
1887   *The Tshi-Speaking Peoples of the Gold Coast of West Africa*. London. [pp. 245, 262 et seq.]

HIMMELHEBER, HANS
    1935   *Negerkünstler.* Stuttgart. [pp. 25, 47–50, pls. IV, VI, XII]
    1940   "Art et artistes 'Bakuba.' " *Brousse* 1: 17–30. Léopoldville.
    1951   *Aura Poku.* Eisenach.
    1960   *Negerkunst und Negerkünstler.* Braunschweig. [pp. 219 et seq., pl. VIII, figs. 167–169, 288]
    1968   "Die Technik des Vergoldens bei den Baule, Elfenbein-küste." *Abhandlungen und Berichte des Staatlichen Museums für Völkerkunde, Dresden* 28: 83–90.

ISERT, PAUL E.
    1788   *Reise nach Guinea und den Caribäischen Inseln.* Berlin. [p. 37]

KYEREMATEN, A. A. Y.
    1964   *Panoply of Ghana.* New York.

LABOURET, H.
    1914   "Notes contributives a l'étude du peuple Baoulé." *Revue d'Ethnographie et de Sociologie* 5: 73–91, 181–194. [p. 183]

NIANGORAN-BOUAH, GEORGES
    1964   *La division du temps et le calendrier rituel des peuples lagunaires de Côte d'Ivoire.* Institut d'Ethnologie. Paris. [p. 143]

RAMSEYER, F. A., AND KÜHNE, O.
    1875   *Vier Jahre in Ashanti.* 2d ed. Basel. [p. 281]. English ed.: *Four Years in Ashanti.* London.

RATTRAY, R. S.
    1923   *Ashanti.* Oxford.
    1924   "Arts and Crafts of Ashanti." *Journal of the African Society* 23, no. 92: 265–270.
    1927   *Religion and Art in Ashanti.* Oxford. [pp. 124, 126, 130, 277, 280]

REINDORF, C. C.
    1895   *History of the Gold Coast and Ashanti.* Basel. [figure, p. 187]

SCHILDE, WILLY
    1930   "Die afrikanischen Hoheitszeichen." *Zeitschrift für Ethnologie* 61: 46–152. [pp. 83–106]

WIESCHHOFF, HEINRICH
    1934   "Goldgegenstände der Baule." *Beiblatt 5 zu den Mitteilungen des Forschungs-Instituts für Kulturmorphologie,* December, pp. 71–72. Frankfurt a/M.

CHAPTER 12

Ife, The Art of an
Ancient Nigerian Aristocracy

Frank Willett

THE ARISTOCRACY OF THE CROWN

Yoruba society unquestionably rests on ancient aristocratic foundations that go back, as the people see it, to the origins of the world. In the view of the Yoruba, the world was created out of the primordial ocean at Ife, where Oduduwa, accompanied by fifteen other gods, descended from heaven by means of an iron chain. He had obtained the wherewithal to make the dry land (a calabash of sand and a five-toed chicken) from Orishanla on the way down, when the latter had fallen asleep after drinking too much palm wine. Oduduwa emptied the sand into the sea and set the chicken down, whereupon it scratched at the sand and scattered it across the face of the deep, thereby forming dry land. Eventually the other gods acknowledged Oduduwa as their ruler and he became the first king (or Oni) of Ife. In this capacity he is still worshipped at the grove of Igbodio in the center of the town. Later Oduduwa sent out his sons to found kingdoms for themselves, giving each a beaded crown with a veil-like fringe which partially hid the wearer's face. These sons are known as the original crowned kings of Yorubaland, but exactly how many of them there were is difficult, if not impossible, to establish; accounts vary as to the number and identity of the kingdoms which are entitled to claim foundation by a son of Oduduwa.

Note: This paper has benefited from discussions with John Picton and Douglas Fraser, to whom the author is grateful.

209

To attempt to sort out the truth from the conflicting accounts, even if this were possible, is not our problem. What matters here is that throughout Yorubaland it is the ambition of each Oba (king) to wear a fringed beadwork crown known as *ade*[1] (fig. 12.1) and to claim descent by direct line from Oduduwa.[2] The beaded crown, with its implications of royal lineage, is the greatest mark of honor for a Yoruba Oba and also the most powerful sanction for his authority, for the crown is considered to have power in its own right. Those Obas who are not entitled to wear the *ade* must be content with an *akoro,* or coronet, a simpler headdress without a bead fringe, which is also worn by crowned Obas on less formal occasions. The ruling monarch, then, takes an aristocratic pride in the descent of his lineage, his title, and his emblems from the god-man Oduduwa.

Today most Yoruba kings are elected by a group of king-makers (consisting of the inner and outer chiefs, court and town leaders, respectively), who choose the new Oba from among the members of certain royal lineages. In the case of Ife there are four such families, all descended from the Oni Lajamisan of More quarter, the other branches having taken the names of the Ilare, Ilode, and Otutu quarters of the town. Each family puts up a candidate in turn until the king-makers agree to accept one. If all the first choices are rejected, the lineage's second candidate may then be selected. Members of lineages that have the right to put up one of their members for election usually bear names which include the word *ade* (a crown) either alone or in a compound (such as Ademiluyi, who was Oni of Ife from 1910–1930). They consider themselves to be royal families, though most of their members work at ordinary jobs—farmers, teachers, clerks, even laborers—and they intermarry with nonroyals. This, then, is the hereditary aristocracy of Yorubaland—the members of royal lineages who claim title to a crown instituted by Oduduwa and are recognized by their crown names.

CHIEFTAINCY TITLES

In Ife there is also a lower grade of aristocracy. Certain lineages own particular chieftaincy titles. The lineage decides which of its members is best suited to hold the title and to look after its interests; the candidate has also to satisfy the other chiefs of his suitability. Chieftaincy

1. Other examples of Yoruba crowns are illustrated in Ogunba 1964 and Ajayi 1965, p. 22. See also chapter 13 in this volume.
2. H. Ulli Beier (1956, p. 31) gives an example of how the desire to claim a beaded crown has led to an obscuring of the real history of Yorubaland.

FIGURE 12.1. Yoruba. King's beaded crown, with fringe. Ht. of crown 12″ (30.5 cm). British Museum, London (1954-AF 23 262). (Photograph: author, 1960.)

titles fall into two groups: those concerned with duties in the royal court (the inner or *modewa* chiefs) and those concerned with the administration of the town (the outer or *Ife mefa* chiefs, literally "the six Ife chiefs"). The inner chiefs have free access to the Oni at all times. Their titles are Lowa (who is the senior of them), Jaran, Aguro, Shanire, Lowate, Ladin, and Erebese. I was told that they number only these seven, but Roy C. Abraham (1958, under Ife, 6 [K]) says they number eight, and William Bascom (1969, p. 35) gives Arode as the eighth title. The outer chiefs in theory are each responsible for a quarter of the town, and their selection has to be approved jointly by the inner and outer chiefs. Since originally each major lineage lived in its own quarter, it is natural that political office and kinship organization should coincide. The senior of the outer chiefs at Ife is Orunto, who is primarily responsible for the Iremo quarter; but in the old days, when the Oni only appeared in public two times a year (for the feasts for Ogun and Orishanla), the Orunto was responsible for the general running of the town, whence his nickname Obalufe (King of Ife). The other chiefs are Obajio (More quarter), Obaloran (Ilode quarter), Washin (Ilare quarter), and Jagunoshin and Ejesi (who have no quarters). To these six have been added Akogun, formerly a war-chief, now responsible for Okerewe quarter, and Obalaiye, who is responsible for the strangers in the town. There is also a separate title, Ogunsua, for the chief of Modakeke, which is the large part of the town in which the Oyo refugees from the Fulani wars were allowed to settle in the mid-nineteenth century.

Each of these outer chiefs has a group of lesser chiefs below him who help to administer the quarter. There are supposed to be seven of these lesser chiefs in each Ife quarter;[3] one of these subchiefs in Ilode quarter, Balale, is said to have a further seven chiefs under him. These subchiefs are nominated by the people of the quarter and are approved by the chief. Together they form a local council for the quarter. Many of them are in charge of shrines; for example, Oshogun of Ilode quarter is in charge of the principal shrine to Ogun, and Olokore of Ilode quarter is responsible for the grove of Obameri. There are also other titles which are independent of this series; the Apena, for example, is appointed by the Ogboni Society and is responsible to them, while Obadio, the priest/chief of the Oduduwa cult, is appointed by his family.

PATRONAGE TODAY

The aristocracy has relatively little effect on the arts of present-day Ife. The Oni himself has commissioned sculptures for the Council Chamber

---

3. Ideally the chiefs seem to be grouped in sevens. I was told that there were seven inner chiefs and six (plus one) outer chiefs, Ogunsua being a nineteenth-century creation and not counting for this purpose; each outer chief is supposed

—wooden house posts and doors which were carved by Agbombiofe of Efon Alaye, an Ekiti town about forty miles from Ife. The house posts, however, are not functional; they are fastened with metal strapping to the substantial brick columns which support the palace roof. The back gate-house of the palace, now used as the motor taxation office, reflects patronage jointly by the Oni, in his modern function as chairman of the Divisional Council, and a European district officer. They arranged for doors and house posts to be commissioned from three carvers, George Bandele, Lamidi Fakeye, and Fayo, who worked together at the Oye Ekiti Crafts Centre. Another house post, representing a woman with children, is in a style I have not been able to identify; but there is also an older door with motifs of the thunder god carved upon it, presumably for Oramfe, the Ife equivalent of the Oyo god Shango. These, however, are all merely examples of modern patronage by leaders, not of an aristocratic style of art, even though Yoruba kings are represented among the motifs.

Probably the only exclusively aristocratic arts left in Ife (although the actual manufacture seems to be done by craftsmen from Efon Alaye) are those concerned with the emblems of royalty and chieftaincy: the manufacture of beaded crowns and coronets (of which the Oni has a great many), beaded fly whisks for the Oni and his chiefs, and badges and leather-embroidered hats for the chiefs. Usually the badges and hats have the chief's title worked into the designs. Figures 12.2 and 12.3 show some of the beaded insignia of the chief who is in charge of the shrine of Akire in the center of Ife. His hat bears the inscription: *A ju won ko se wilejo: ija ilara ko tan boro M. A. Kayode 1951: Chief Moses Ade-Ayode Kayode—Oba Kire.* The first part is a proverb: "Thinking to oneself 'they're no match for me' does not entitle one to bring a suit against them": that is, jealousy and pride give no one peace. This is followed by his name and year of accession, with his full name and title below. His badge is inscribed with his name, *Ade Ayo Kayode,* and title, *Oba Akire.*

There are, of course, two or three woodcarvers still practicing in Ife, and one brass-smith. The former for the most part carve *egungun* masks and second-burial effigies for hunters (Willett 1959b and 1965, and William Fagg 1959); the brass-smith produces a variety of small castings, mostly to the order of Ogboni society members (but also for

---

to have seven subchiefs under him. Unfortunately my data on the chiefs are not complete, and I have not been able to check the validity of this notion. William Bascom (1969, p. 33), however, writes that in 1937–1938 each of the five ward-chiefs had five subchiefs.

FIGURE 12.2. Yoruba. Chief Obakire wearing his chief's hat. Ife. (Photograph: author, 1962.)

European visitors). There is no question nowadays of obtaining royal permission to have a brass cast. In modern Ife, then, apart from the specific insignia of title-holders, no art form is restricted to the royal and chiefly classes.

FIGURE 12.3. Yoruba. Badge of Chief Obakire. Ife. (Photograph: author, 1962.)

The present Oni of Ife, Sir Adesoji Aderemi, has been a major patron of the arts, however, in a different and uniquely important way: soon after he ascended the throne in 1930, he began to have ancient works of art brought into his palace for safekeeping, and later he gave land at the front of his palace to be the site of the Museum of Ife Antiquities. His care in protecting the antiquities of Ife has been the principal reason for the richness of the collections in the museum now, for without these precautions, most of these objects would have been sold to museums and private collectors all over the world. As it is, a visit to Ife these days is much less trouble than a trip round the greater part of Europe and America would be, and one has the advantage of seeing these sculptures all together, where they can be easily compared. Most important, however, is the fact that this cultural heritage remains readily accessible to Nigeria's own citizens, who are rightly proud of it.

CLASSICAL IFE ART AND THE ANCIENT ARISTOCRACY

As regards the ancient arts of Ife, which are now mostly preserved in the museum, there can be no doubt that they played aristocratic roles. Of the human figures represented, nearly all are royal beings, court attendants, or sacrificial victims. To be sure, figures in Benin often actually represent gods conceived as kings and queens, which con-

FIGURE 12.4. Ife. Brass head no. 4 found in Wunmonije Compound. Ife Museum. Ht. 12.8″ (32.4 cm). (Photograph: Francis Speed, 1962.)

stitute, one must suppose, a hyper-aristocratic art (Bradbury 1957, pp. 52–53). Even though certain ancient works of art are still employed in various shrines at Ife, the historical and religious traditions of the current worshippers are unfortunately of no help in determining whether a god or a king is represented, since the intentions of the artists are lost in antiquity. In one sense, of course, to distinguish between god and king is pointless, since the Ife king was, and for some still is, divine. Yet if we are to understand the purposes of the artists who made the sculptures, we must try to establish what these artists' intentions were and what functions their sculptures would have performed in the old Ife society. These matters are not easily settled because so little is remembered. We are compelled, therefore, to rely chiefly on analogy.

Approximately thirty ancient brass-castings from Ife are known, together with several hundred terracotta fragments, representing several scores of distinct sculptures (see figs. 12.4–12.6). By contrast, from Benin we have several thousand brass-castings but only a score or two

FIGURE 12.5. Ife. Brass figure of an Oni of Ife. The badge on the chest probably corresponds to the one shown in Figure 12.3. Found at Ita Yemoo, Ife, in 1957. Ife Museum. Ht. 18.8″ (47.6 cm). (Photograph: author, 1958.)

FIGURE 12.6. Ife. Upper part of the chest of a terracotta sculpture of a queen. Excavated at Ita Yemoo, Ife, in 1958. Ife Museum (1.Y.30). Ht. approx. 10″ (25.4 cm). (Photograph: author, 1964.)

of terracotta sculptures. Fortunately for our study, Benin historical traditions seem to have been built on a reasonably sound basis (Bradbury 1957, 1964); among the most persistent of these traditions are those describing the close connections between the royal families of Benin and Ife, including links between their brass-casting.[4] Some inferences about the art of Ife will therefore be made later from an examination of the social factors affecting Benin art.

At the same time, there is increasing evidence of a connection between the art of Ife and recent Yoruba sculpture. Indeed the ritual importance of the Oni of Ife as the ruler of the place of origin of the whole Yoruba world is recognized over the greater part of Yorubaland. The social and artistic practices of the present-day Yoruba, therefore, may throw light on the Ife past. And because the Yoruba and Bini peoples have remained in contact since the legendary days when Oronmiyon set out from Ife to establish a Yoruba dynasty in Benin, these

4. Alan F. C. Ryder's (1965) attempt to discredit these traditions relies chiefly on demonstrable misunderstandings of the material evidence, as is pointed out in Frank Willett (1969b). Radiocarbon dates from Orun Oba Ado in the center of Ife, where the heads of the kings of Benin were buried up to 1888, range between the sixth and tenth centuries A.D., while dates from Ita Yemoo range from the ninth to the fifteenth centuries A.D. (see Willett 1969a). Ife was certainly in its present location in the period to which Benin traditions refer.

two cultures have continually influenced each other. Since both are groups belonging to the Kwa-speaking language family, their ultimate roots were at one time much closer,[5] and it is quite possible that customs of considerable antiquity were retained in one group, yet lost in the other.

One custom still found in Benin in a form which allows its full significance to be observed is the practice of making wooden second-burial figures known as *ako* for the final rites for deceased incumbents of certain important offices, specifically for the king himself, his mother, the Ezomo (one of the principal war chiefs), and the Ihama (the priest of the cult of royal divinity). R. E. Bradbury, some years ago, discussed the significance of these ceremonies with me and kindly allowed me to make use of his conclusion that the effigy represents the *dignitas* of the office itself, which is immortal and continues through each successive office-holder; the chief may die, but the chieftaincy goes on. A comparable situation exists in Britain, where central authority is referred to as the Crown and is regarded as enduring, even though the head on which it rests may change. So too in Benin (and in a great many other African societies), the succession of office-holders is seen as one continuous line handing on the unchanging power of the office from generation to generation. The *ako* effigy in the Benin ceremonies wears the emblems of the office, and the successor is bare of them until the rite is completed, whereupon he is invested with them.

A similar ceremony is conducted at Owo, a Yoruba town eighty miles north of Benin, whose art styles and regalia have been influenced by the latter center. Here the second-burial effigy is also called *ako,* but its application is not so restricted as in Benin. The Owo *ako* has become in part a display of wealth and affection on the part of the mourners, who increase their own prestige by performing the expensive sacrifices associated with it; they are afterwards allowed to wear a specially patterned sash, *ashigbo,* as a mark of this prestige.[6] These *ako* figures are life-size wooden sculptures with the heads, feet, and hands carved in naturalistic fashion. The remaining parts of the body are roughly made, since they

5. The now discredited technique of glottochronology suggested a date of 4000 years ago for the separation of these two languages (Bradbury 1964, p. 150).

6. These remarks are based on field work done in Owo in 1958 and 1961. In 1948–1949, Justine Cordwell (1953) was told that the purpose of the ceremonies involving *ako* figures was to raise the status of the deceased in the afterworld, and thereby to ensure his continued benevolence. Evidently in about a decade there had been a considerable relaxation of attitude toward the ceremony and a significant loss of social meaning.

are hidden by the figure's clothes. Justine Cordwell (1953, p. 223) shows photographs of one of these figures dressed and undressed.

The life-size ancient brass heads of Ife were probably also originally attached to wooden bodies, since all have large nail holes in their necks (fig. 12.4). Around the foreheads are rows of small holes which follow the shape of the crowns represented on the smaller castings. These apparently permitted the attachment of real crowns, probably by means of nails, for one nail has survived in position on the temple of head Number 4 (fig. 12.4).[7] When mounted on wooden bodies, these heads must have looked remarkably like the *ako* figures of Owo, and it seems likely that they were used in a similar way to represent the continuing *dignitas* of the office of Oni in the second-burial ceremony. Many of these brass heads bear signs of having been dug up twice, once from their original graves, the second time when they were rediscovered in Wunmonije Compound, where they had apparently been brought together after they were first discovered.

The brass images from Ita Yemoo (Willett 1959a) shed additional light on Ife society. Three represent royal figures, while the others depict victims of human sacrifice. One of the royal figures portrays a standing Oni in his regalia (fig. 12.5). (Part of a similar figure was found with the heads at Wunmonije Compound.) The second consists of a pair of figures, an Oni and his queen with their arms and legs intertwined. The third brass illustrates a queen curled round a pot which is set upon a pair of stools, probably ceremonial seats if not royal thrones (Fagg and Fagg 1960, Willett 1967). Stools form an important element in the art of Ife and appear to have been made both in wood (with brass and glass decoration) and in stone; stools are also depicted in objects of brass and terracotta. The royal character of all these brasses suggests that the Oni of Ife may have exercised a monopoly over brass-casting similar to that enjoyed by the Benin king.[8]

Although naturalistic art seems to be closely associated with royalty in Ife, another mode of depiction appears here which is much more

7. The nail can be seen in Leon Underwood's illustration (1949, fig. 19) in front of the left ear on the head turned away from the camera.

8. The majority of Ife terracotta sculptures also represent royal figures similar in appearance to those depicted in the brasses (fig. 12.6). Elsewhere in this volume Roy Sieber (chapter 10) describes the Ghanaian use of terracottas in post-mortuary funeral rites; it is not impossible that Ife terracottas were used in a similar way. On the whole, though, Ife pottery sculptures are more likely to have served as shrine furniture. A number of them lack crowns and appear to depict attendants (Willett 1967, pls. 12 and VIII); two have their hair half shaved off in the manner of present-day court messengers (*emese*) at Ife (Frobenius 1912–13, 1, pl. VII, opp. p. 344, top left and top right; and Willett 1967, pl. 60).

conceptual in character. An outstanding example of the conceptual mode is a large fragment of a monstrous horned head with snakes or elongated fishes issuing from its nostrils (Willett 1967, fig. 35). In conception this object is akin to the unusual Benin heads illustrated by Philip Dark and W. and B. Forman (1960, figs. 78, 80) and in William B. Fagg (1963, figs. 18, 19). There are also a number of highly stylized heads which are little more than symbols of faces with holes for the eyes and a slit for the mouth (fig. 12.7). Round the top of each head is a series of points which seem to represent crowns. Other examples in this group are conical in shape, but one specimen in this group has quite naturalistic features (see, for example, fig. 12.8), thus combining the two modes in a single sculpture. We cannot therefore equate the naturalistic mode with an aristocratic demand and the conceptual mode with more plebian tastes, since not only are both styles of sculpture found in association (for example, at Abiri; see Bernard Fagg 1949), but also in some cases they are combined in the same sculpture. A group of rustic-looking terracotta sculptures (fig. 12.9) from a site just outside Ife on the Ondo Road are clearly copies of both the naturalistic and the highly stylized modes of classical Ife sculpture. This group, even if it is late rather than rustic, adds further confirmation of the coexistence of the two strands of representation. In 1963 Oliver Myers excavated examples of both styles in the grove of Obameri, but in a secondary, not a primary association; that is to say, the various fragments of sculpture had been brought together perhaps from several places and put into the grove. Although the surviving examples of the two modes appear to be contemporaneous, the roots of the stylized mode may well go back to a period before the increasing sophistication of the court and priesthood overcame the inhibitions which had previously restricted naturalism to the representation of animals.

Some art historians have difficulty in believing that the Ife artists could have developed their naturalistic art without influence from Europe. Yet the earliest European visitors to Benin in 1485 recorded that the Oni of Ife used to send a staff, a pectoral cross, and a hat, all made of brass, to confirm each succeeding king of Benin in office (see de Barros 1552, 1, iii, cap. iv). Thus, although heads and figures are not mentioned in this account, brass-casting was certainly going on in Ife when the first Europeans arrived. William Fagg's studies have further demonstrated that the Benin brasses develop from a stage of relative naturalism which could well have derived from that of Ife through increasing stylization, ending in the heads known to be of nineteenth-century date (Fagg 1963, pp. 32–38). There can be little doubt, then, that the casting of life-sized naturalistic brass heads was flourishing in Ife in the fourteenth

FIGURE 12.7. Ife. Stylized heads in terracotta. The three on the left are from Abiri, nine miles from Ife; the fourth belongs with the group illustrated in Figure 12.9. (Abiri Abraham site, 171/61). Ht. of tallest 6.5" (16.5 cm). (Photograph: author, 1962.)

FIGURE 12.8. Ife. Three conical heads. Left, from Abiri; center, from the grove of Osangangan Obamakin, Ife; right, from Oranmiyan Memorial College, Ife. (Abiri S. F.; 29; 65/61). Ht. of largest 7.9" (20 cm). (Photograph: author, 1962.)

FIGURE 12.9. Ife. Group of terracotta sculptures found in 1955 on a cocoa farm about four-teen miles from Ife. They are somewhat rustic in character and include copies of naturalistic royal figures like those seen in Figures 12.5 and 12.6 and of stylized heads such as that shown in Figure 12.7. Ife Museum (171/61). Ht. of largest 11.2″ (28.3 cm). (Photograph: R. A. Farquharson, 1964.)

and fifteenth centuries before the advent of the Europeans.[9] Moreover, the brass figures from Ita Yẹmoo were in a layer corresponding to that in which terracotta sculptures lay with charcoal, which produced radio-carbon dates indicating a twelfth-century date for the occupation (Willett 1971, pp. 72–73, 269).

NATURALISM IN ART AS A RESPONSE TO SOCIAL NEED

For a long time it has been customary to distinguish between European or "civilized" art and "primitive" art, though the latter term is now being abandoned by scholars because of its misleading implications. The first of these arts is usually equated with a naturalistic mode, and the second

9. As William Fagg has pointed out (Fagg and Willett 1960, pp. 31–32), the naturalism of Ife art is restricted to the facial features and does not include the form of the head or the proportions of the body. The head occupies about a quarter of the overall height (see fig. 12.5), a phenomenon which Fagg has called "African proportion," although it occurs in other arts outside the European canon.

with a conceptual or stylized mode. This contrast, however, expresses no more than tendencies—statistical expressions, one might say, of the mean in these two categories of art. In fact the opposition of these two concepts is quite misleading. Ernst Gombrich (1960) has clearly shown that all art is stylized in varying degrees; each artist has his own schemata through which he represents the real world around him. No matter how realistically he may try to represent his subject, the artist is working always through those conventions which compose his individual style. It would be more meaningful, then, to visualize all art, whether European or not, as varying in emphasis between two extremes of minimum and maximum stylization. The art of tribal societies usually employs a considerable degree of abstraction from reality, but the degree varies considerably even within the same society. Many tribal societies regularly produce naturalistic sculpture, particularly when the purpose is to commemorate a deceased person. The portraits modeled on skulls in New Guinea and the New Hebrides (Leenhardt 1947, pp. 23, 41; Linton and Wingert 1946, pp. 115, 157) are excellent examples. Less portrait-like, but in a more general way naturalistic, are the wooden figures of the Kuba kings (see chapter 3 above). As long ago as 1897 Franz Boas drew attention to the existence of naturalistic sculptures alongside highly stylized designs in the art of the North Pacific coast of America.

It is clear, then, that naturalistic sculptures are quite often made in tribal societies, most frequently in association with ideas of commemoration of the dead. There can no longer be any grounds for insisting on the non-African character of Ife naturalism. Very realistic representations of animals appear in the terracotta sculpture (for example, Willett 1967, pl. XIII) of the Nok culture of northern Nigeria, which dates from the last few centuries before Christ. The development in Ife of an aristocratic society with its need to commemorate and glorify divine kings and their courtiers no doubt encouraged the shift of emphasis to naturalism in human representation in their sculpture. Most of these works of art appear to have been used in practices associated with the cult of royal ancestors, an institution deeply rooted in African tradition. Indeed their religious content is so clear that we might reasonably characterize the art of Ife as hieratic rather than aristocratic, especially since the majority of Ife leaders had priestly functions.

REFERENCES

ABRAHAM, ROY C.
   1958   *Dictionary of Modern Yoruba.* London.
AJAYI, ADETAYO
   1965   "Olosunta Festival." *Nigeria Magazine,* no. 84, pp. 17–30.
BARROS, JOÃO DE
   1552   *Da Asia.* Lisbon.
BASCOM, WILLIAM
   1969   *The Yoruba of Southwestern Nigeria.* New York.
BEIER, H. ULLI
   1956   "Before Oduduwa." *Odù; A Journal of Yoruba and Related Studies,* no. 3, pp. 25–32.

BOAS, FRANZ
   1897   "The Decorative Art of the Indians of the North Pacific Coast of America." *Bulletin of the American Museum of Natural History* 9, art. 10: 123–176.
BRADBURY, R. E.
   1957   *The Benin Kingdom and the Edo-speaking Peoples of South-Western Nigeria.* Ethnographic Survey of Africa. London.
   1959   "Chronological Problems in the Study of Benin History." *Journal of the Historical Society of Nigeria* 1, no. 4: 263–287.
   1964   "The Historical Uses of Comparative Ethnography with Special Reference to Benin and the Yoruba." In *The Historian in Tropical Africa,* edited by Jan Vansina, R. Mauny, and L. V. Thomas, pp. 145–164. London.
CORDWELL, JUSTINE
   1953   "Naturalism and Stylization in Yoruba Art." *Magazine of Art* 46, no. 5: 220–225.
DARK, PHILIP
   1960   *Benin Art.* (With W. and B. Forman.) London.
ELISOFON, ELIOT, AND FAGG, WILLIAM B.
   1958   *The Sculpture of Africa.* London.
FAGG, BERNARD
   1949   "New Discoveries from Ife on Exhibition at the Royal Anthropological Institute." *Man* 49, art. 79: 61.
FAGG, BERNARD AND WILLIAM
   1960   "The Ritual Stools of Ancient Ife." *Man* 60, art. 155: 113–115.
FAGG, WILLIAM B.
   1959   "Another Yoruba Hunter's Shrine." *Man* 59, art. 335: 216–217.
   1963   *Nigerian Images.* New York.
FAGG, WILLIAM B., AND WILLETT, FRANK
   1960   "Ancient Ife, An Ethnographical Summary." *Odù, A Journal of Yoruba, Edo and Related Studies,* no. 8, pp. 21–35.

FROBENIUS, LEO
   1912–13   *Und Afrika sprach.* 3 vols. Berlin. Translated as *The Voice of Africa.* 2 vols. London, 1913.
GOMBRICH, ERNST
   1960   *Art and Illusion.* London.
LEENHARDT, MAURICE
   1947   *Arts de l'Océanie.* Paris. Translated as *Folk Art of Oceania.* New York, 1950.
LINTON, RALPH, AND WINGERT, PAUL S.
   1946   *Arts of the South Seas.* Museum of Modern Art. New York.
OGUNBA, OYIN
   1964   "Crowns and Okute at Idowa." *Nigeria Magazine,* no. 83, pp. 249–261.
RYDER, ALAN F. C.
   1965   "A Reconsideration of the Ife-Benin Relationship." *The Journal of African History* 6, no. 1: 25–37.
UNDERWOOD, LEON
   1949   *The Bronzes of West Africa.* London.
WILLETT, FRANK
   1959a   "Bronze and Terra Cotta Sculptures from Ita Yemoo, Ife." *The South African Archaeological Bulletin* 14, no. 56: 135–137.
   1959b   "A Hunter's Shrine in Yorubaland, Western Nigeria." *Man* 59, art. 334: 215–216.
   1965   "A Further Shrine for a Yoruba Hunter." *Man* 65, art. 66: 82–83.
   1966   "On the Funeral Effigies of Owo and Benin and the Interpretation of the Life-size Bronze Heads from Ife." *Man,* n.s., 1, no. 1: 34–45.
   1967   *Ife in the History of West African Sculpture.* London.
   1969a   "New Radiocarbon Dates from Ife. *"West African Archaeological Newsletter,* no. 11, pp. 23–25.
   1969b   "New Light on the Ife-Benin Relationship." *African Forum* 3, no. 4/4, no. 1: 28–34.
   1971   *African Art: An Introduction.* London.

CHAPTER 13

The Sign of the Divine King:

YORUBA BEAD-EMBROIDERED CROWNS WITH VEIL AND BIRD DECORATIONS

Robert F. Thompson

The bead-embroidered crown with beaded veil, foremost attribute of the traditional leaders (Oba) of the Yoruba people of West Africa, symbolizes the aspirations of a civilization at the highest level of authority (fig. 13.1). The crown incarnates the intuition of royal ancestral force, the revelation of great moral insight in the person of the king, and the glitter of aesthetic experience.

The Yoruba provide an appropriate setting for the study of art and authority on the African continent. Chieftaincies remain important here, and, as half of the population of Yorubaland (southwest Nigeria and parts of Dahomey and Togo) lives in towns over which such leaders preside, traditional loyalties are strong (Legum 1966, p. 213).

According to tradition it was none other than Oduduwa himself, awesome maker of land upon water and the father of the Yoruba, who initiated the wearing of the beaded crown with veil as the essential sign

Note: A Ford Foundation Foreign Area Training Fellowship enabled me to study Yoruba sculpture in the field from October 1962 to January 1964. I am also extremely grateful to the Concilium on International Studies at Yale for a grant to continue field studies during the summer of 1965 and during December 1967/ January 1968. The essay has profited from conversation with William Bascom, George Kubler, Leonard Doob, Frank Willett, the Araba of Lagos, and his Highness the Alaperu of Iperu. Unless otherwise indicated, all statements attributed to informants are direct quotations from my field notebooks.

Although my essay on this subject was originally prepared for the symposium out of which this book grew, a slightly different version of it has been pre-

227

of kingship (Mellor 1938, p. 154). He placed a crown on the head of each of his sixteen sons.[1] These sons journeyed from the site where the traditional Yoruba believe Oduduwa lived—Ile-Ife (Ife) in the forests of what is now southwest Nigeria—and established separate kingdoms. In time these kingdoms became the modern Yoruba states.[2] The rulers of these ancient provinces all claim descent from Oduduwa,[3] and are honored as seconds of the gods (*ekeji orisa*).

Yoruba gods long ago chose beaded strands as emblems. The fact that the crowns of the Yoruba leaders are embellished with bead embroidery therefore immediately suggests godhead. Indeed, the prerogative of beaded objects[4] is restricted to those who represent the gods and with whom the gods communicate: kings, priests, diviners, and

viously published in *African Arts/Arts d'Afrique* 3, no. 3 (1970): 8–17, 74–80. I am indebted to the editors of both publications for allowing me to publish it in this dual form.

It is a pleasure to thank Douglas Fraser for many kindnesses, most especially a thoughtful editing of an earlier version of the present essay. Warmest thanks are extended to Kenneth Murray for allowing me to consult his invaluable unpublished manuscripts on Yoruba art and to John Picton for facilitating study of the holdings of the Nigerian Museum, Lagos, in 1963 and to Ekpo Eyo for subsequent similar courtesies. Afolabi Ojo and Richard Neal Henderson were kind enough to read the manuscript and offer useful suggestions.

This essay is dedicated to the traditional chiefs of Yorubaland and their ancestors.

1. According to an Oyo Yoruba myth, the original crowns of Oduduwa were owned by the rulers of Benin, Ila, Ketu, Owu, Oyo, Popo (Alladah?), and Shabe (Johnson 1921, pp. 7–8). An Ijesha Yoruba myth, on the other hand, associates ten original crowns with the following ancient towns: Aramoko, Benin, Efon-Alaye, Igbajo, Ijero, Ila, Ilesha, Ondo, Otun, and Oyo (Johnson 1921, p. 23). G. J. Afolabi Ojo (1966, fig. 19) has published an interesting map showing some thirty-four Nigerian Yoruba "crowned towns" (*ilu alade*) linked to the foundation of Yoruba kingship. To his list ought to be added Ila-Orangun, Ketu, Shabe, and other important settlements.

2. The largest of these states are the Oyo, Igbomina, Egba, Ijebu, Ife, Ijesha, and the Ekiti. West of the Egba and the Ijebu are the Egbado, Aworri, Anago, Ohori-Ije, and Ketu Yoruba.

3. Peter C. Lloyd has written that "one could, I think, write a textbook on comparative political systems, drawing almost all one's examples from the Yoruba." The remarks of the present writer therefore apply to most northern Yoruba kingdoms where chieftaincy titles tend to be hereditary within the lineage. Lloyd shows that elsewhere chiefly titles are obtained through title association, such as the cult of the earth among Egba Yoruba. In Ondo the king selects the chiefs. Kabba Yoruba groups, in the far northeast of Yorubaland, are without kingship. For details, see Lloyd 1960.

4. Privileged royal beaded objects include slippers (*bata ileke*), staffs (*opa ileke*), fly whisks (*irukere*) with beaded handles, and gowns (*ewu ileke*). A fine

native doctors. The beaded crown therefore connotes power sustained by divine sanction. Formerly, it is reported, red jasper beads were imported from Litingo in Upper Volta and fashioned and polished at Oyo-Ile (Old Oyo), the ancient capital of the Oyo Yoruba (Ojo 1966, p. 260). These formed the main material of royal bead embroidery, although in antiquity beads of different colors were made at Ile-Ife. Today crowns are embellished with imported colored beads.

Bead embroidery is practiced at a number of centers, especially at Efon-Alaye, Ile-Ife, Oyo, Ilesha, Abeokuta, and Iperu-Remo. The men who work in this tradition must be extremely skilled. Their task entails the stringing together of beads to form a strand of a single color, and the tacking of these strands (length and color determined by design) to the surface of the crown until the visible portion of the object has been completely covered.

The bead embroiderer begins with the making of a wicker-work or cardboard frame. At Efon-Alaye, one of the leading centers of the crown-making industry, the shape of the frame is an almost perfect cone. The cone towers over all other forms of Yoruba headgear. The embroiderer or his helper stretches wet starched unbleached muslin or stiffened cotton over the frame, providing the base for the embroidery, and allows the object to dry in the sun. A frontal face, a Janus design, or a circular band of frontal faces are often molded in relief over the lower portion of the frame, with shaped pieces of cloth dipped in wet starch. The actual embroidering then follows, after a choice of surface pattern. Some crown-makers hold up small cardboard silhouettes—Afro-Islamic interlace patterns, flowers, crosses, and so on—then mark their outlines on the canvas with chalk or pencil. Efon-Alaye masters are said to waive this procedure at times and work from memory or inspiration. A gifted artist sometimes experiences agony at this point. "I do not tell people," an Ijebu Yoruba crown-maker confessed to Justine Cordwell (1952, p. 227), "but sometimes I have great difficulty in arranging designs and colors on crowns. When this happens I go to my room and take out the [image of the god of native medicine] that has been in our family many years . . . I make a sacrifice . . . that night when I dream I see the crown as it is when complete, with all the colors and designs as they should be."

The basic unit of the work is the single strand of beads. These may be extended vertically, diagonally, or horizontally to form geometric out-

---

example of royal beaded treasure is the collection of the paramount chief of the Aworri Yoruba, who has some twenty beaded crowns, many with fly whisks, staffs, canes, and slippers beaded to match.

lines, and they may be cut in diminishing or increasing lengths to fill in patterns. A single strand may form a circle, or coil around the trunk of a miniature elephant, or hook back upon itself to complete an interlace motif. Outwardly simple, the string of beads is actually an aesthetic instrument of subtle expressive power.

The craftsman normally sews small representations of birds fashioned in the round onto the sides of the crown. These birds are also covered with beading. There are cases where other beaded figures (chameleons, elephants, human figures) are attached to the crown. A beaded bird often surmounts the summit of the crown. In some instances the bird seems to peck the frontal side of the crown.

Choice of bead color serves the intensification of relief elements. Horizontal and vertical pink strands define the frontal face which forms the main design element of the crown of the present traditional ruler of the Ijebu settlement of Ijebu-Ife (fig. 13.1). Black beads strung on these strands at precise points represent vertical and horizontal facial marks associated with a particular descent group. The projection of the eyes is rendered more impressive by the framing of black beads with white. And beaded red strands emphasize the formation of the lips in relief.

The details of the structure of the crown may be modified by individual creativity, but the basic forms, linked to ancient canons, must be honored. Thus traditional crowns are either cone-shaped or a vertical stem-on-cone structure characterized by the elongation of the cone so that a long, narrow cylinder is created. A bird presides over the top of this cylinder, and the sides are often ornamented by subsidiary birds arranged as an inward-facing circle. Another kind of crown, having an "elliptical helmet" shape, from the front resembles a cone but is actually shaped not unlike a bishop's mitre (see Talbot 1926, 3, figs. 191, 140). Traditional crowns—as opposed to casual royal headgear (ori-ko-gbe-ofo) which is without sacred implications—must include (1) a beaded fringed[5] veil (iboju) for state occasions when the king incarnates divine powers and it is dangerous to stare at his naked face, (2) frontal faces

---

5. There are different kinds of fringework: (1) *Continuous fringe*, the simplest and perhaps oldest variety, decorates the rim with a curtain of parallel beaded strands. Parallel brass chains hang from old Ijebu brass crowns and probably indicate relative antiquity as to the use of continuous fringe. (2) *Netting-over-fringe*, as in an important crown worn by the paramount chief of the Ijebu and documented by P. Amaury Talbot (1926, 3, p. 141). Beaded mesh here decorates the rim and from this mesh hang parallel strands. (3) *Netting-between-fringes*, of which the royal headgear of the ruler of Ogere is a good example, has netting at the front to veil the face of the wearer while parallel fringes cover the sides and back of the face and neck.

FIGURE 13.1. Ijebu Yoruba. Beaded crown with veil worn by the ruler. Ijebu-Ife. Ijebu Province. (Photograph: author, 1968.)

rendered in relief or partial relief, and (3) beaded birds rendered in the round.

Remove the beaded veil and the crown is devoid of full significance. According to tradition (Johnson 1921, p. 24), the first king of the city of Ilesha severed some of the fringes from the crown of a nobleman of Ile-Ife, a terrible act, not unlike attempting enforced abdication.

Frontal faces may be applied to ordinary royal headgear, such as a beaded cap worn by a certain titled chief of the city of Ikere-Ekiti, but almost without exception they appear on ceremonial crowns with fringes. The same point applies to beaded birds. It is the veil, however, which lifts the object to the highest level of significance.

An important sanction distinguishes the fringed crown from lesser forms of head covering. The gaze of the king must not fall upon the inside of his fringed crown, for there are believed to be magical forces within the object (what they are may never be revealed to commoners) that have the power to blind a careless wearer. In my presence, the king of Otta accidentally saw the inside of his crown, whereupon he immediately whispered in Yoruba, "My eyes have seen and may my eyes remain." The Araba of Lagos, a high-ranking priest of the Yoruba cult of divination, maintains that long ago a despotic king might have been forced by the elders to look inside the fringed crown as a hint that he should "go and rest"; this served notice on the despot that he had but a brief interval during which he might commit suicide or face certain execution. The crown thus serves, in part, as a kind of supernatural check against the conduct of the king.

The visual effect of the beaded veil in ritual context is extremely impressive (fig. 13.1). The vaguely perceived outlines of the face of the ruler match, in a sense, the generalized qualities of the frontal faces on the crown. Veiling diminishes the wearer's individuality so that he, too, becomes a generalized entity. Balance between the present and the past emerges. No longer an individual, the king becomes the dynasty. He is concealed behind his beaded netting in a way not unlike the manner of concealment traditional in the Egungun cult, whose principal devotees impersonate the dead. The crown becomes a mask. The use of the veil extends a tradition in force since at least the sixteenth century,[6] when João de Barros reported that ambassadors were only allowed to view curtains of silk, behind which sat the king of Ile-Ife, "for the king is regarded as sacred" (Crone 1937, p. 126).

HISTORICAL EVIDENCE

The origin of the crown in its present form is obscure. The sculpture of Yoruba antiquity (A.D. 960 to 1160), found at the site of the city of

6. J. Bertho (1950, p. 73) mentions that the king of Bornu is veiled in modern times on certain occasions. It would be interesting to make a further study of the distribution of this custom.

Ile-Ife, does not yield an exact concordance. Archaeological evidence does show, however, the use in ancient times of beaded crowns, some with frontal emblems. Some smaller-than-life-size Ife heads are depicted wearing especially elegant beaded headgear, but these do not match the modern crown; they are without birds and frontal faces. Some life-size metal heads have rows of holes running along a line which might be the outline of the bottom rim of a crown. Frank Willett (1966, p. 42) suggests that these heads carried the real crowns worn in life by the persons commemorated by the sculptures. We can only speculate as to their form.

Four hundred years later clues to the rise of the crown in its modern form begin to emerge. First of all, there is the so-called Gara image,[7] one of a group of seven metal sculptures found at the small village of Tada on the Niger, not far from the site of the old imperial capital of the Yoruba (fig. 13.2). This image represents a traditional ruler in regalia. He wears a garment extending to his knees. Upon the surface of this garment appear various motifs—crosses, interlace, zigzag, and frontal birds with strangely coiled wings. The figure wears a textured outer vestment covered with the depiction of cowrie-shell embroidery. The wealth of the man is communicated by the use of cowries, an ancient form of currency, as the overall embroidery of the vestment. Over the embroidery hang two narrow sashes. And over the sashes, at the chest of the figure, hangs an arch-shaped medallion of a ram's head flanked by long-beaked birds and with a third long-beaked bird above the beast.

The elaborate helmet of the ruler is of great importance. Two large medallions, one frontal (fig. 13.3), one facing back, are fixed to the helmet, and these bear a horned face with nostrils from which issue serpents (or fish). The mouth of the face is open, the teeth are bared, and the tongue protrudes. These faces are like a sign of wrath. Between them two powerfully wrought tresses emerge, perhaps suggesting radiating might through magic hair. At the top of the ruler's headgear, four metal birds once stood on long legs (in the passage of time the birds have been bent down until they are now almost obscured). The birds once crowned the image in harmony with the Janus disposition of the frontal faces: two faced forward and two faced the rear. Each bird is carefully modeled, although we cannot be certain that a specific

7. Informants in Tada used this term, which is linked with the legend of the coming of the seven metal sculptures from Igala (Igara) country in the sixteenth century; they called the famous seated figure "Danboroko image." Frank Willett (1966 personal communication), however, was told that the name of the latter image was "Tsoede."

FIGURE 13.2. Tada. Middle Niger River, Nupe. Standing bronze figure of a traditional ruler, called by one informant "the Gara image." Allegedly brought to Tada from Igala country in the first quarter of the sixteenth century. Possibly of Yoruba origin. Ht. 46″ (116.8 cm). (Photograph: author.)

species was intended. The length of the egret-like legs of the birds may reflect care that their position be commanding.

Of importance here is that classic elements of the modern crown—frontal faces under birds—have emerged. The date of the sculpture is consequently crucial to regalia history, but accessible information permits only guesswork. Stephan F. Nadel (1942, p. 406) relates a legend which tells of the arrival of these sculptures from Idah in conjunction with the flight of Tsoede, the founder of the Nupe kingdom, about A.D. 1523. But the main Nupe settlements are found across from the Yor-

FIGURE 13.3. Tada. Detail of chest and head from Figure 13.2. Crown medallion diameter 5.5″ (14 cm). (Photograph: author.)

uba on the left bank of the Niger and in the contiguous hinterland. The legend does not explain why these metal sculptures were left in a small and isolated village incommensurate with their evident urban aristocracy.[8]

8. One might consider the possibility of their removal, either for safekeeping or as abandoned booty, from the former imperial capital of the Yoruba, Oyo-Ile (Old Oyo), during the early nineteenth-century wars. The ruins of Oyo-Ile are less than sixty miles from Tada, but two hundred miles upstream from Idah in Igala country. Perhaps the arrival of these objects was blended with the legend

Some stylistic details of the Gara image, the birds with coiled wings and the frontal face with serpents issuing from the nostrils, suggest a measure of relation to the art of Benin. But the latter motif also occurs in Yoruba antiquity. In addition, a metal figure of a bowman at Jebba, near Tada, very much in the style of the Gara image, has on its forehead a bird with coiled wings that has upward-bent legs analogous to those of the image of the Benin king in a divine state—that is, the king with legs which have become upward-bending mudfish (chapter 14, fig. 14.4). Perhaps the coiled-wing bird with upward-bending legs is an alter ego of the divine king.

The chronology of Benin metal sculpture (Fagg 1963, pp. 24–38) sheds some light on the history of Yoruba crowns that are comparable to Benin styles. One example of the beaded-crown type (von Luschan 1919, 2, pl. 12), from the "Middle Period" of Benin art history, has been dated approximately by William Fagg to the era extending from the midsixteenth to the late seventeenth century. Here a ruler wears a crown of arch-like contour reminiscent of the shape of the chest medallion worn by the Gara image. The headdress bears a horned frontal face, also recalling Tada. In addition, another Benin metal plaque (von Luschan 1919, 2, pl. 8, no. III C 8392) shows frontal eyes and mouth on a high conical hat. A most extraordinary example is a bronze Benin head which is surmounted by four metal birds and tentatively dated to the midsixteenth to late seventeenth century (fig. 13.4; Fagg 1963, pl. 18). Serpents issue from the nostrils and tear-ducts of this image. Many beaded crowns with beaded vertical shafts are also shown on Benin plaques, suggesting relation with the Yoruba stem-on-cone mode of chiefly headgear. Although the dates of the Tada/Jebba finds remain to be established, related Benin images suggest that the bird-over-the-frontal-face was present as an important motif in the art of Yoruba regalia by the sixteenth century.

The chest medallion of the Gara image depicts a probable metal prototype. The stylistic closeness between this medallion and those forming part of the headgear of the Gara image and the Jebba bowman raises the question of whether there were metal crowns in existence in Yoruba antiquity. The answer is affirmative. João de Barros, who commanded the Portuguese fortress of São Jorge da Mina from 1522 to 1525 and monitored information collected from farther east, mentions

---

of Tsoede by the people of Tada for reasons of their own. The beautiful seated figure at Tada is unquestionably ancient Yoruba in origin, and another figure, bringing hands together before his chest, has facial traits which seem Yoruba.

FIGURE 13.4. Benin. Bronze head surmounted by four metal birds. Tentatively dated mid-sixteenth to late seventeenth century. Museum für Völkerkunde, Berlin-Dahlem (III C 10878). Ht. 10.4" (26.3 cm). (Photograph: Museum.)

the use of metal crowns in sixteenth-century Yoruba or Yoruba-related territory:

. . . to the east of Beny at twenty moons' journey there lived the most powerful monarch of these parts, who was called Ogane. Among the pagan chiefs of the territories of Beny he was held in as great veneration as is the Supreme Pontiff with us. In accordance with a very ancient custom, the King of Beny, on ascending the throne, sends ambassadors to him with rich presents to request confirmation. To signify his assent, the prince sends the king a staff and a headpiece of shining brass, fashioned like a Spanish helmet. (Crone 1937, p. 126)

Oghene (*Ogane*) is the term used in Benin City for the king of Ile-Ife (Bradbury 1957, p. 20). The text suggests that brass crowns were in use before the sixteenth century. It is significant that brass crowns are still found in Yorubaland and that their use is linked to ancient cults and kingships. At the Ekiti settlement of Ogotun there is a brass crown, associated with the worship of Obanifon (Obalufon),[9] one of the original followers of Oduduwa. Willett (1966 personal communication) photographed a brass crown for Obanifon at Obo Aiyegunle itself. And Philip A. Allison (1960) documented a tiered brass crown, somewhat resembling a pagoda, at Agbanda in Igbomina Yoruba territory. These may be modern brass crowns or relatively recent work dating from the last century.

But certain Ijebu settlements conceal the existence of important brass crowns, some of which may be several centuries old. The king of the city of Ijebu-Igbo has an ancient brass crown.[10] There are three large brass birds near the base of the crown, and presumably a frontal face, but the customary chain fringe is said to have disappeared.

The ruler of the Ijebu-Remo settlement of Ogere inherited a brass crown of stem-on-cone shape. The crown is made of curved brass sheets clamped together. Six ornamental chains hang from a projecting circular edge near the top of the crown. Three small brass face-masks, attached by studs, ornament the crown. Opposed crescent markings are visible on their foreheads, a sign associated with brass figural sculpture for the Yoruba cult of the earth. A chain veil is said to have once hung from the bottom of the crown. Comparison with a brass crown in the neighboring town of Iperu (fig. 13.5) suggests the Ogere object is relatively recent, stemming perhaps from the second half of the last century.

The Iperu crown is closer in form to the stem-on-cone headgear of the Benin Middle Period. The name of this crown, "Crown-from-the-beginning" *(ade isheshe),* suggests its relative antiquity. The writer would guess that the object is three to four hundred years old by analogy with related headgear of Benin. According to Iperu tradition the object is more than five hundred years old. There are four frontal faces on this crown, and some of its surface is pierced with lattice-like openwork. The frontal faces bear the opposed crescent markings. The "Crown-from-the-beginning" is used in the worship of the departed kings of Iperu.

The chameleon, called *agemo* in Yoruba, has been used as a metaphor of extraordinary leadership since time immemorial. One of the ancient followers of Oduduwa (Forde 1951, p. 37) took the name of this remarkable creature. And there is an ancient cult, associated with

9. Ojo (1969 personal communication) recently brought to my attention the full name of the deity, "Obalufon who became very old and tough as iron" *(Obalufon ogbo d'irin).*

10. I have not seen this crown and base the description on remarks made by Roy C. Abraham (1958, p. 292).

FIGURE 13.5. Iperu. Remo Yoruba. Brass ceremonial crown (*ade isheshe*) for the worship of the ancestors of the present ruler. According to local tradition, more than five hundred years old. Ht. approx. 9.8" (24.7 cm). (Photograph: author, 1964.)

the use of brass crowns, which takes the same name. Agemo is virtually the national cult of the Ijebu. Priests of the cult are attributed awesome faculties; they are, for example, believed to have the power to fell trees and destroy buildings by the force of their curse. Each priest of Agemo is alleged to own a brass crown.[11] The chief priest of Agemo at Imosan said in 1968 that at least one of the sixteen ministers of Agemo, Lijagbori of Imosan, did not have a brass crown because his role of throwing kola in honor of Agemo was secondary, and I suspect that another priest, the Moko of Okun-Owa, does not have one. Some priests will only wear their crowns in ritual context or in time of dire emergency; as a result only one has been visually documented (Abraham 1958, p. 292). This is the brass crown of the Agemo priest of Odo-Nopa, a village to the east of the city of Ijebu-Ode (fig. 13.6). An

11. Tami of Odogbolu; Lumoro of Imoro; Petu of Ishiwo; Lashen of Orun; Posa, Ija, and Lijagbori of Imosan; Onugbo of Okenugbo; Bajelu of Omuku; Sherefuse of Igbile; Nopa of Odo-Nopa; Idebi and Lubamisan of Ago-Iwoye; Ogbegbo of Obonwon; Mogodo of Aiyepe; and Moko of Okun-Owa (MacKenzie 1938; Odukoya 1960; Ogunba 1965).

FIGURE 13.6. Ijebu Yoruba. Brass ceremonial crown of the local priest of Agemo. Perhaps made in the late nineteenth century. Odo-Nopa. Ht. approx. 16″ (40.5 cm). (Photograph author, 1964.)

extraordinary bird with plumage rendered in sheet brass surmounts the stem at the top of the cone of the crown. The bird has an exponentially curved double crest. A short forked tail continues the curve of the crest, and the body of the bird is ingeniously fashioned in openwork. The bird stands on a small disk from which hang small brass pendants. At the bottom of the stem the crown flares into a cone embellished with relief designs with fine passages of openwork. Two small birds, cast in the round, seem to peck the bottom portion of the stem. Brass chains hang from the bottom of the crown and form a metallic veil which effectively blurs the countenance of the wearer when in use. A number of birds are fashioned in low relief on the surface of the conical portion of the crown. But the most visually arresting elements are the Janus faces with schematized limbs and body. The eyes of the faces are bi-faceted and projecting, and their diagonal placement is striking. The nose is heavy and descends from a swelling above the eyes, from which flare a pair of horns. The small body is separated from the face by openwork, and from the body extend zigzag arms in "ladder" pattern and hands grasping an object (leaf? fan? ceremonial sword? Compare fig. 13.1). The legs of the image are fish with tails ending in a knobbed-cross motif outlined by openwork. Here the royal frontal face is associated with the fish-legged figure, ancient motif of sacred leadership in Yorubaland and Benin.[12] The faces are to be compared with figural brass staffs *(edan)* for the cult of the earth. Let us take, for example, a body of six earth-cult staffs (Williams 1964). The Agemo crown shares with these a number of traits, such as swollen forehead, obliquely positioned bi-faceted eyes, and fine ladder-like ornament. The suggested dating of these six brasses is broad, midseventeenth to midnineteenth century. The Agemo crown at Odo-Nopa was perhaps made near the end of this period if not later, for flaws in the casting suggest debasement of earlier craft excellence. This priestly object may have been closely copied from a vanished original which itself reflected stylistic affinity with the ancient brass crowns of the Ijebu.

A collection of old beaded crowns at Idowa, an ancient and important Ijebu kingship, also has a bearing on the problem of crown history. One group of three or four of these crowns is given as presixteenth-century work, while a second group includes specimens said to have been made after the settlement of Idowa in the sixteenth century. The earlier crowns are said to have been brought from the capital of the Ijebu at the founding of Idowa. "One of the oldest crowns," a beaded

12. The famous Efon sculptor Owoeye Oluwuro stated in 1964 that the fish-legged motif which he carved on one of the royal portals of the palace of the Oni of Ile-Ife represented Oduduwa.

cap surmounted by vertical beaded shaft with double-knobbed finial, bears fragments of beaded fringe dangling from a ruined rim (Ogunba 1964, p. 253). There is a certain concordance between this crown and the stem-on-cap beaded crowns depicted on Middle Period Benin plaques. The handsome use of polychromy in the organization of design qualifies the common assumption that all old Yoruba crowns were entirely covered with carnelian. O. Ogunba (1964, p. 250) explains the lack of frontal face and birds thusly: "in pre-sixteenth century times . . . the [ruler] was more . . . priest-king than a secular king . . . content with a symbolic crown [rather] than a gorgeous one."

It is possible that sixteenth-century and perhaps earlier Ijebu crowns reflected Benin influence. Certainly sufficient evidence exists to prove the impact of Benin culture upon the urban Ijebu peoples. But the mode of Benin might have derived from Yoruba antecedents. Cordwell (1952, p. 210) feels that the original Yoruba crown was a close-fitting cap with a small conical elevation[13] to the rear and cites the indigo wax head covering of priestesses of a prominent riverain spirit (also associated with kingship) as a modern continuation of the mode. The likelihood is that the crown-making traditions of the ancient Yoruba interwove with those of Benin. Willett (1966 personal communication) says this is confirmed by the Ile-Ife corpus.

Two allegedly eighteenth-century Idowa crowns recall modern styles. Perhaps the finest of the two has been attributed by local priests to the reign of King Anowoneyo. This crown is covered almost entirely with gleaming cowrie-shell embroidery. A stem-on-cone type, it has a con-

13. It is possible that the high conical shape of brass and beaded crowns stems from Islamic sources, a suggestion which fits the known impact of Islamic embroidery patterns on the costumes of the Yoruba. In the Saray Museum of Istanbul there is a Persian helmet dated 1528 which is of interest because its chain mail neckpiece recalls the continuous chain fringe of the Ijebu brass crowns. However, the chains of the former are, of course, much more tightly spaced for defensive purposes (Kühnel 1963, figs. 160, 162). References might also be made to an inlaid steel helmet, dated 1625–1626, from Persia (Barrett 1949, pl. 39) and a conical helmet in the Louvre of the Circassian Mamluk period, dated to the reign of the Sultan al-Ashraf Barsbay (A.D. 1422–1438). We know from the Kano Chronicle that iron helmets and chain mail were in use to the north of Yorubaland in the cities of the Hausa by A.D. 1410 (Palmer 1908, p. 73). If the fringed, beaded crown does prove to represent a reworking of Islamic armor in the medium of bead embroidery, the form was probably elaborated in the two ancient Yoruba cities of Ile-Ife and Oyo-Ile, where native beadworking industries existed in precolonial times. Oyo-Ile, especially, was in contact with the cities of the Hausa—perhaps with Gao and Djenne on the upper Niger—suggesting possible avenues of diffusion of the form from the north.

tinuous fringe and four ingenious cowrie-embroidered birds. A bird at the top of the stem is clearly senior in terms of position, dimension, and imaginative elaboration of tail plumage. The birds seem to peck the crown with long beaks, recalling the birds on a beaded crown in the Wellcome Collection at the University of California in Los Angeles. Ogunba's remark (1964, p. 251), "As the [king] carried this cowrie crown about at a public ceremony, he must have appeared to the average citizen as the very fountain of their prosperity," recalls the impact of the sumptuous vestment of cowries at Tada.

Frontal faces and more complicated gatherings of birds emerge on those crowns at Idowa believed to have been made in the nineteenth century and more recently. The gist of the iconography of the Yoruba crown, for several centuries, is the frontal face under bird or gathering of birds. It is now appropriate to examine these themes in some detail in order to probe their iconological depth.

THE FRONTAL FACE

The frontal face is generic as a rule but is sometimes linked to actual descent groups by virtue of facial markings. Some faces show, like the Tada medallions, bared teeth. This is rare in the sculpture of the Yoruba, where the normal concern is to represent the lips closed as an aspect of dignity. The open mouth, on the other hand, implies a different kind of condition and, as we have seen at Tada (not to mention Ile-Ife), the baring of teeth is associated in certain cases with the snakes-issuing-from-nostrils motif, as if to emphasize doubly the unleashing of extraordinary powers. These powers illumine the present with the past: such powers come from the dead. L. Kevin Carroll (1950, p. 353) was told that the frontal faces on the crown represented skulls. This fits the suggestion of an aura of ancestral force. In keeping with this idea, one might note that Yoruba artists sometimes carve single faces to represent the decapitated heads of felons (as seen on a drum for the spirit of the earth at Odo-Nopa), the decapitated heads of witches (as on circular boards worn by ancestor-impersonators in Ibarapa Yoruba country), or slain enemies (as along the highest register of the brass door for the king of Ilesha). As a unit these heads suggest victory over evil.

The frontal face is not always correlated with morally instructive horror, however. The serene visage which embellishes the Yoruba divining board represents the mercurial spirit who accompanies the god of divination as trickster and messenger. In addition, the frontal face may simply stand for a human being. Thus the bottom line of faces on one of the doors of the palace of the king of Ile-Ife represents, according to the artist who carved them, a group of royal messengers (*emese*). But the majority of frontal faces in Yoruba art have to do with the extraordinary.

As for the frontal faces on the crown, the combination of exaggerated human traits and specific descent-group markings suggests a synthesis of the world of the dead and the world of the living—the king as living ancestor. This seems to be the primary meaning of the frontal face,[14] the plausibility of which is supported by native testimony. The ruler of the capital of the Aworri Yoruba says that the frontal faces represent, as a Janus, Oduduwa himself. The Araba of Lagos extends this by asserting that the Janus is an allusion to one of the magical characteristics of Oduduwa, believed to have had both an earthly and a spiritual face. An echo of this belief, in wood sculpture, may be seen among the Ibarapa Yoruba, where a two-headed standing male figure for Oduduwa has been documented (Idowu 1962, pl. 3a). A most interesting apparent validation of the depth of the belief comes from the Yoruba of Cuba: "Oduduwa has two faces—one facing forward, towards life, the other backwards, towards death" (Fabelo 1960, p. 60).

14. There is a stylistic relationship linking Yoruba conical beaded crowns and the *omo* face-bells of Ijebu-Ode and at least one Ekiti settlement. Both are conical and bear the representation of a human face. *Omo*, like crown faces, represent ancestors. At Ijebu-Ode, they are the privilege of the chiefs of the royal lineage: the Awujale, Olisa, Egbo, and Apebi (Murray 1949–1954). The lord of the Ijebu, the Awujale, by tradition has inherited some thirty-nine brass *omo*. However, although it is reported by Murray that a certain Mr. W. Smith, resident at Ijebu-Ode, has seen this extremely important collection, they were not divulged either to Murray in 1954 nor to the present writer in 1962–1963. Talbot (1926) illustrates the *omo* of the Olisa of Ijebu-Ode. The present Olisa has emphasized that although most *omo* represent remote ancestors, each incumbent has a face-bell made to be later worn by his son over the right shoulder with the bell coming to rest at the left hip of the wearer.

The present Egbo of Ijebu-Ode has inherited a face-bell which is shaped in the form of an expressionistic visage, the face of Yaduwa, the first Egbo, who came to Ijebu-Ode during the reign of the tenth Awujale from a site "near Benin" called Ijamo. The Egbo suggests that the date of the object is presixteenth century. This does not take into consideration the possibility of intervening replacement of the actual original. The ferocity of the glance of this remarkable sculpture recalls the protruding eye of the crown frontal face. *Omo*, both in form and function, seem related to the role of the frontal faces on brass and beaded crowns as communication of ancestral power. The power, as appropriate to rank, seems restricted to a single person in the case of *omo*, whereas crown faces may be multiple and of infinite suggestion.

The ruler of Iperu-Remo maintains that crowns with multiple faces (fig. 13.5) allude to the "all-seeing" gods, attesting the power of the king to view by supernatural means all that occurs in his domain. The king of Ijebu-Ife was told that the face on his inherited crown stood for the first king of his settlement. Basing his ingenious interpretation on field work among Ijebu Yoruba, Ogunba (1965, p. 258) feels that an image with bared teeth on one of the Idowa crowns implies the transformation of the king at his coronation from a human being into a spirit. This dramatic extension of the notion of divine kingship can be related to the testimony of an Ijebu ruler: the king wearing the ceremonial crown with fringe may not stand upon the naked earth, but must stand on a mat or cloth of suitable quality. This recalls the fact that certain Yoruba possession priests must stand on wooden mortars when the deity is manifest in their flesh. The Dagburewe of Idowa explains: the king is deified at this moment.

Frontal faces communicate this belief. The king behind the veil incarnates the most awesome powers a mortal can possess. He is both impregnated with godhead and subject to the morally watchful gaze of the gods. His own face has vanished and the countenances of his ancestors have become his own at a higher level of vision. Thus the meaning of the frontal face on the beaded crown seems to be: the union of the living king with the deified royal dead.

THE GATHERING OF THE BIRDS

The representation of birds on beaded crowns is normally generalized. It is pointless to seek exact depictions of species unless feathers from an actual bird have been added to the representation as identifying ornamentation. In the Yoruba-related metal art of Benin the emblem of the bird is said to represent the ibis, and a frequent downward-curved beak makes the attribution seem plausible. Precise species have in fact been suggested (Schüz 1969). On the other hand, long-billed birds also appear in Benin art in aggressive settings, such as astride horned beasts, and this is of course far removed from the nonpredatory, relatively placid quality of the actual species. And what if the length of the beak has to do with expressionist distortion, at the threshold of the supernatural, based upon but transcending strict mimesis? This anticipates an argument that beak shape and other details are items of a magic biology that converges upon the real.

In Yorubaland, variant interpretations of species attest to the generalized nature of the original. One Egbado ruler asserted at Oke-Odan in

1962 that the birds represented pigeons, emblems of victory, while a neighboring king insisted the intention was to convey the impression of a gathering of cranes. Still another mentioned the vulturine fish-eagle. Extremely interesting was an identical opinion voiced independently by two sources: a priestess of Obalufon at Ogotun-Ekiti and a high-ranking member of the cult of the earth at Oluponon (Oyo), both of whom alleged that the birds on the crown are egrets (*okin*). The high rank and traditional learning of these informants made their testimony merit close attention. Hence I reproduce the statement by the latter informant in full:

The earth spirits whom the men of the cult of the earth [Ogboni] worship were the first to wear crowns. This was before the Yoruba kings. These spirits put egret feathers on their crowns, just as some Yoruba kings do today, because the egret is the bird of decorum. The egret is the sign of orderliness which is the mark of our cult. And, long ago, when animals talked, it was the egret who had the power to settle disputes arising among the creatures of the world.

The Araba of Lagos ties the Egbado and Oluponon versions together by his own assertion that the commanding bird at the top of the crown is an egret and the minor birds a group of pigeons, the image of political power. Tail feathers of white cattle egret are attached to the summit of some Yoruba crowns today.[15] This custom extends into the realm of sculpture at Igogo-Ekiti, where the local priest dresses an image of a mounted dignitary by adding white feathers to the carved bird which surmounts the representation of a ruler's bonnet.

The lordly aura which surrounds the gathering of the birds is further communicated by their arrangement, as master and entourage, whereby a senior figure overlooks a circle of followers. The vision is hieratic, ordered, and at the same time mysterious. A striking detail is the frequent positioning of the minor birds parallel to the stem or cone of the crown, so that they recall the West African grey woodpecker (see Abraham 1958, p. 759), which alights parallel to the trunk of a tree, preparatory to hammering the bark with his beak. Even more interesting is the fact that some minor birds, and occasionally the one at the summit, are positioned so that they actually seem to peck the sides of the crown. This does not mean that a straightforward allusion to the

15. See Ojo 1966, p. 219: "The rarity of the egret gave it a value out of proportion to its size: the long white feathers were formerly presented to the [rulers] of Yorubaland who used them to adorn their crowns. Nowadays the feathers are sold rather than presented."

woodpecker is intended—no informant ever mentioned this—but that, perhaps, something to do with the *action* of the woodpecker, the piercing of an object, is recalled. The imaginative use of color in the beading of these birds makes it clear that a systematic denotation of the woodpecker is not intended. But the fact remains: the birds are ordered and imply hierarchy, yet something in their positioning hints of the unleashing of unnamed, penetrating powers, just as the frontal faces fuse qualities of terror and decorum.

Native interpretations of the number of birds on the crown reveal conflict that conceals hidden unity. W. F. Mellor (1938, p. 154) documented a prevailing Ijebu belief that the sixteen birds on the crown of the paramount chief stand for the sixteen founders of the Yoruba states, the sixteen original sons of Oduduwa. Southeast of the territory where Mellor did his research, the ruler of the town of Agbowa-Ikosi said in 1963 that the birds were a practical measure of the rank of the wearer: the crown of a minor ruler bears four, that of a great chief twelve, that of the great paramount chief sixteen or twenty-four birds.

Interpretations change when one moves from the kingdoms of the Ijebu to Oyo and Ijesha territory. Thus D. W. McCrow (1953, p. 306, caption to illustration) at Oshogbo writes that the "ceremonial bead hat represents traditional Yoruba system of government. Large birds at base represent Chiefs of various wards of the town. Vertical lines of small birds are subjects being led upwards to the chiefs of the compound, the larger birds surrounding the King himself." Here the birds directly reflect the distribution of power in Yoruba civilization. Diagrammatic political structure becomes cryptic civic geography at Ilesha where Fagg (1962 personal communication) was told each bird signifies a ward of the town.[16]

The persistent theme is the measure of the might of the king, whether by quality of descent (scion of one of the sixteen original sons), quality of influence (the king, the ward chiefs, and their followers), or quality of domain (the particular wards and hence the size and importance of his city). And running through the versions is the consistent association of the bird with the elders and the king, men who have lived life long and who, because of their accumulated riches of mind, are therefore

16. The conventional numbers of the beaded birds—four, twelve, sixteen, and twenty-four—in important instances do not match actual urban geography. Thus the imperial capital of the Oyo by tradition had eleven quarters: Oke Eso, Modade, Molaba, Nsise-Ogan, Ntetu, Ondasa, Onse-awe, Aremu, Ile-Ologbo, Ajofa, and Isale-Ogede (Johnson 1921, p. 281). Moreover, the supreme leader of the Ijebu rules over a city divided into twenty-five quarters.

charged with maintaining order. The careful disposition of the birds, subject to a major figure, mirrors the point.

There is a kind of suggestive momentum to these symbols which carries us deeper into the problem of multi-variant meaning. Herta Haselberger (1964, p. 139) has stressed the different levels of significance which attach to the relief sculpture of Kumasi in what is now Ghana, in which she finds a secular and condensed meaning for the common man and a rich, spiritual meaning for the initiate. Similarly, James Fernandez (1965, p. 905) has observed that the iconographic themes of Bwiti cult ceremonies in Gabon exist not serially, but simultaneously, demanding the consideration of several levels of meaning at any given point of the ritual. There is an analogous depth of allusiveness to the gathering of the birds.

The theme reappears in the medium of iron sculpture as the primary emblem of cults having to do with divination or healing, or both. Nor is this the only artistic form shared by kings, diviners, and native doctors. All three of these groups of leaders (including some special, highly titled priests of other cults) as noted are the only men in traditional Yorubaland who share the right to beaded objects. The distinction is clear—the king may enjoy the widest latitude in beaded objects, from beaded slippers to beaded canes, but the diviner may possess a beaded bag and the officiant for the spirit of medicine owns a beaded bottle. The latter object may be observed among some Efon Yoruba settlements.

The links between kingship, healing, and divination are perhaps more powerfully extended by the sharing of the bird emblem. The native doctor is often identified by the possession of a wrought-iron staff surmounted either by a single iron bird or a circlet of minor birds under a commanding bird at the summit. Similar staffs are also made for the cult of a riverain spirit, Eyinle, who has marvelous powers of healing. Southwest Yoruba medicine staffs often have roughly horizontal radial bars near the top of the staff a short distance underneath the senior bird at the top. These bars sometimes end with miniature iron implements (sword, arrow, machete, and so forth) associated with the "hot" iron god Ogun, together with cryptic emblems of other deities associated with heat and witchcraft (Thompson 1970, fig. 5; Nigerian Museum, Lagos, no. 48.25.27). Their siting suggests control by a superior force manifest in the spirit of the bird or, alternatively, the bird as messenger. In Aworri and Anago settlements the writer has observed staffs of this "candelabra" type surmounted by two birds in iron, heraldically opposed. The Nigerian Museum also has related iron medicine-staffs attributed to the northern provinces of Yorubaland (nos. 46.9.44;

48.9.129; 54.8.1). The basic form of these derives from the placement of the major bird over an inward-facing circle of minor birds, the latter spirits standing on an iron circle secured to the staff (which passes through the center of the described circle) by means of horizontal cross-bars.

The Yoruba cult of divination has its own kind of iron staff with bird motif, the diviner's staff (*osun*) (Thompson 1970, fig. 14). This is a vertical iron stake with a number of small, hollow, inverted iron cones which are attached to the shaft near the top so that they appear to radiate from the staff. The open inverted bottom portion of these cones is covered with a flat iron disk over which an iron bird is normally centered. Conical iron bells are often hammered right side up in one or more rows the length of the staff.[17] The form of diviner-staff morphology therefore is: bird over disk over inverted cones over bells.

Benin medicine staffs are related to Yoruba medicine and diviner staffs, but are heavier, being virtually baroque elaborations. They are embellished, not only with iron bells, but also with representations of animal horns, chameleons, human royal figures, chains, and so forth. Three documented staffs show virtuoso expressions of the mode, with ferociously beaked senior birds mounted on horseback (fig. 13.7) or astride a horned beast or enveloped by a circlet of birds. These staffs do not have the circular disk of the diviner staff and show the bold departure of vertical, human-like arms in some cases. The presence of the alternation of serpents and miniature iron implements around the senior bird bespeaks close connections between the iconography of Yoruba and Benin medicine.

The diviner staff in Yorubaland and in the Yoruba sectors of Bahia, Brazil, is associated with the representation of ancestors (dos Santos 1967, p. 79). The cognate *asen* of Dahomey are iron stakes surmounted by flat disks in iron. These are kept for the ancestors. The bird at top sometimes vanishes, leaving the disk unadorned or serving as a platform for emblematic allusions to the special qualities of a ruler.

Iron sculpture for divination and medicine intersects with brass sculpture for the cult of the earth with the appearance of the bird. Birds are sometimes shown pecking the human figure represented on earth-cult brass staffs, hence the iconography seems closer to the crown in the sense that the bird sometimes is shown engaged in an active role. The

17. Decorative detail varies with the particular area of Yorubaland. For example, Ekiti versions are often embellished with wrought-iron chameleons, perhaps an allusion to the fact that the chameleon is an important ingredient in the compounding of certain types of medicine (Ojo, 1969 personal communication).

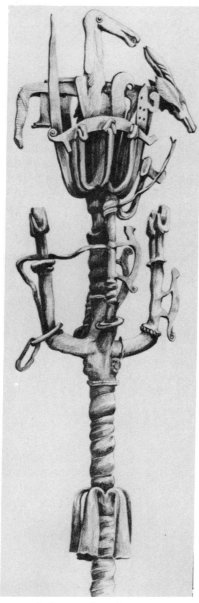

FIGURE 13.7. Benin. Medicine staff. Mounted bird with long beak surmounted by a circle of miniature iron implements. Candalabrum-like "arms" are attached to the staff beneath the principal figures. (After von Luschan, 1919, 3, pl. 109.)

men of the earth cult are in many cases the same elders we have met before as heads of city wards and advisors to the king, so their sharing of the emblem of the "bird of the elder" with the king is not surprising and leads us deeper into an evermore interconnected world of symbolism. Indeed we have seen that one earth-cult member claims that the society owned the bird motif before the Yoruba system of kingship existed.[18]

Oral literature provides some further clues. A myth collected by Lydia Cabrera among descendants of Yoruba slaves in Cuba tells of an evil figure who closed the roads of the world. He thereby threatened humanity with absolute destruction until he was tricked into dancing by a pair of twins (Yoruba believe all twins possess special powers), in which vulnerable position he could be killed in order that the world be saved. The description of the dance is interesting: "Birds of darkness came down to dance with the Devil. They flew in shadowy flocks, spinning around his knotted hair, a circle of owls and bats that revolved about him in lugubrious flight" (Cabrera 1948, p. 23). The characterization of the spirit in terms of the absolutely evil "Devil" may reflect Westernization of Yoruba thought in Cuba, for some Yoruba priests in Nigeria say that there is no such thing as categorical evil. Nevertheless, the honoring of a central figure (here seen as evil) with a circle of birds recalls Yoruba iconography. Indeed one may further cite a tale from the Yoruba side of the Atlantic wherein the noisome retinue is recreated in a similar context of sinister honor: "As [the old woman] paused, all of her birds perched on her shoulders and head . . . Then she said: 'My name is Jungle Witch. I am the owner of this jungle from the beginning of the earth' . . . But immediately she mentioned her name to us, Jungle Witch, all of her birds flew round her and then perched again on her body. That showed us that they honored her" (Tutuola 1962, p. 16). Here we are very far from the exemplary dignity of the Yoruba court, but a kind of visual resonance alerts us to dark associations attaching to the theme of the gathering of the birds.

In another Afro-Cuban myth, a single bird is cast in a role consistent with the notion of the positive magic of kingship. Again the world is threatened with total destruction (resulting from a dispute between heaven and earth). This time the pied crow (*kanakanna*) flies beyond the stars with a message of reconciliation that saves mankind from death. The bird becomes sacred and takes perpetual shelter in the spreading arms of the *iroko* tree. Here the bird symbolizes communication with the gods, the very substance of divination and kingship, and one clue to the understanding of the sharing of the bird emblem

18. Cf. Lloyd (1968, p. 47): "Much as they may, as individuals, stand in awe of the kingship, the council of chiefs see in the reigning ruler a man selected by themselves." Thus it seems logical that the power of the elders to check the powers of the king might be reflected by the sharing of certain artistic motifs.

between kings and diviners emerges. Although the role of the bird has been reversed in the latter myth, from destroyer to redeemer, the theme of mortal conflict with forces of destruction remains.

What are these "forces of destruction"? The Yoruba believe that there exist on earth certain people who reveal themselves by their intemperate reactions to such jealousy-provoking situations as blatant wealth. These people, largely old women with magic powers, are architects of doom and death. They transform themselves into birds, bats, or owls, creatures which come into their own at night, "for witchcraft is a nocturnal thing, the witches being most active between twelve and three A.M. in the realm of dream and nightmare" (Prince 1961, p. 797). The ancient Yoruba image of the witch, to use the dramatic term which does not carry in Yorubaland the notion of absolute evil, is the bird.

This bird, known by the euphemism "bird of the elder," takes certain forms: "a white bird with a long red beak and red claws," and "a brown bird like a bush fowl with a long red beak" (Prince 1961, p. 797). The mention of the long beak immediately recalls many depictions of royal birds, and the whiteness of the first type is like a parody of the association of the egret with kingship. More to the point is the belief that the witch bird damages its victim by pecking the head or neck and sucking out the blood. This fits the positioning of birds on crowns so as to suggest the pecking of the sides of the crown, as well as that of birds on earth-cult objects which seem to peck the sides of the head of a human figure. Direct comparison between the bird of the witches and the penetrating beak of the woodpecker is made in singing for the witches documented in the Yoruba sector of eastern Dahomey (Beier 1958, pp. 10–11):

Our mother kills quickly without a cry
To prick our memory suddenly
Quickly as the woodpecker pecks the tree on the farm
The woodpecker who hammers the tree while words rush forth from his mouth
Large, very large mother at the top of the *iroko* tree.

Many elements seen in enigmatic expression elsewhere seem to coalesce in this passage. Not only is the association of the bird with the witch sharpened by partial allusion to the woodpecker's piercing of wood, but the witch presides, like the messenger who saved mankind, at the summit of the *iroko,* a tree sacred to traditional Yoruba. Descendants of Yoruba slaves in Bahia, Brazil, maintain that the metal staff with bird finial for the god of medicine represents an iron bird in an iron tree.

The radiating supports of minor birds on some types of Nigerian medicine staffs strongly recall the Bahian metaphor.

Deepening the implications of the imagery, an important priest of the god of medicine in the capital of the Anago Yoruba, a man of great traditional erudition at the center of a Yoruba subgroup, testified in 1963 that the birds fashioned in iron on medicine staffs not only represented witches but honored them and made them fear the owner of the staff. Raymond Prince (1961) has shown that the diviner honors witches by sacrificing to them at the base of an *iroko* tree whenever a patient seems struck by an illness beyond normal medical understanding. It may be that the medicine staff serves as a surrogate for the *iroko* tree whenever the diviner or native doctor is unable to make a journey into the forest.[19]

In any event, the gathering of the witches in the night at the top of the *iroko,* the positioning of the iron birds at the top of the medicine staff, and the gathering of the birds at the summit of the headgear of the ruler suggest parallel idealist metaphors of the transformation of doom into human survival. The witch, after all, is an elderly person, susceptible to the pleasures of honor and entourage. As the ruler may be praised and at the same time be reminded of his obligations to the people, so the witch may, upon being honored and recognized, become responsible. Respect assures continuity.

But there is another factor. One of the verses of Yoruba divination tells of the refusal of the trickster deity to grant witches the power to kill until they agreed to accept certain signs as a means by which men might protect themselves from them (Prince 1961). The gathering of the birds is surely one of these ancient signs. This recalls the testimony of the priest in the capital of the Anago: one places the iron birds on the staff to honor the witches and make them fear the owner of the staff.[20]

19. The suggestion that the medicine staff serves as surrogate for the *iroko* tree is, however, but one of various possible interpretations.

20. Pierre Verger (1965) has written an important study of Yoruba witchcraft. He corrects the degenerate image of the witch as absolute evil with evidence showing that the "witch" is actually a fallen deity to whom the creator of the world had granted power over all deities, the power symbolized by the bird and the gourd, the latter image standing for the world. The Anago testimony, that the bird on the iron staff honors the witches and makes them fear the owner of the staff, might be rephrased in the light of Verger's materials to the effect that the herbalist strikes through to the positive factor in witchcraft for the good of his client. It is believed that the central bird of the staff with sixteen iron birds is a bird capable of neutralizing witchcraft (Ojo, 1969 personal communication). The concept seems consistent with the argument that the king is supreme among men in the arts of discovering and harnessing positive witchcraft for the good of his people.

Crowns and staffs, where so embellished, may form joint altars to the witches. The emblem of the famous familiar of the witch, the bird, may remind those who in feathered form kill by night of the limits placed upon their propensities by the positive magic of good government, medicine, and divinatory action. No man is more responsible for the protection of the people from witchcraft than the traditional ruler; hence the bird would seem to confer an aura of supernatural fluency and arcane mastery. And the men who wear the "bird of the elder" are, in many cases, elders themselves. This leads to the conclusion that the king, in order to neutralize witchcraft with authority, must himself assume powers of witchcraft.

This does not impugn the humanity of the king, but means he knows by intimate association the proper medicines by which to wreak supernatural havoc when it is necessary to save his people. He can destroy by positive force those enemies whose unchecked actions might lead to the ruin or death of the ruler and, hence, by a logical sequence, to the destruction of the state and the people.

Transmission of force and ethics in the person of the king must therefore be protected by magic set about his body. We have seen that there are probably active powers concealed in the crown with fringes, and it might be added that on ceremonial occasions in Benin, skulls are mounted on staffs to deflect evil from the king. Leather-wrapped charms may be observed hanging from the ceiling of the audience porches of the palaces of some Yoruba kings. A legend exactly in point with the thesis of the bird as motif of royal witchcraft is found among the Yoruba-influenced Fon of Dahomey. There Dada Sagbadjou Glele, living representative of the royal families of Dahomey, explained the symbolism of a certain bird-mounted staff (asen) from the capital of the Fon, now in the collection of the Museum of Primitive Art in New York: the bird represents the victory of the king of Dahomey over the witchcraft of the Mahi, a people living to the north of the Fon capital. The story goes that as the Fon king and his army marched north against the Mahi, they observed a bird associated with the power of the Fon ruler devour another bird associated with the head of the Mahi. This was a sign that the witchcraft of the Fon king had overcome the witchcraft of the Mahi and shortly thereafter supernatural suggestion was translated into practical military accomplishment. The legend recalls the traditional opinion of the Suku of Congo (Kinshasa) that it is imperative to have a leader who can operate fluently within the sphere of the witches on behalf of his kinsmen (Kopytoff 1965, p. 469).

Magic aggression is consequently another possible dimension of the meaning of the gathering of the birds on Yoruba crowns. The greater the number of birds, perhaps, the stronger the royal supernatural power; the greater the wards and domain, the mightier the royal ancestors, the more numerous the vicissitudes which the king can master. Kings probably invoke their royal ancestors in time of emergency to help wage counter-witchcraft. It is interesting that the Yoruba deities of war and uncertainty, Ogun and Eshu, provide in their program of sculptures two possible links between the bird, as crown motif and as emblem of medicine and ancestor worship. A wrought-iron sculpture of the god of iron, allegedly found at Zagnanado in Dahomey,[21] supports an unmistakable wrought-iron altar to the ancestors, or *asen* (Sieber and Rubin 1968, addendum to catalogue). Eckart von Sydow (1954, pl. 16b) illustrates a mud image of the trickster from the Ewe of Ghana. The head of this image also supports a small iron altar to the ancestors. These altars derive from the Yoruba divination staff which bears the image of the bird. The metaphor which has been suggested, that the king's crown is an altar of political power to which medicine and ancestor worship are incidental, here becomes an actuality.

The argument is strengthened not only by the fusion of ancestor staff and crown traditions in the Dahomean and Ewe field but, more importantly, by the fact that the pendants hanging from disks near the top of the old Ijebu brass crowns are more explicable when compared to the pendants hanging from the disk on the staff which surmounts the head of the deity of iron from Zagnanado. Perhaps the Fon synthesis of the rival iconographies derives from an earlier Yoruba solution. We know that Yoruba divination was active at Alladah in Dahomey before 1659 and that the king of "Haarder" (Alladah) practiced divination at that time in the Yoruba manner (von Luschan 1919, 1, p. 493). Possibly a relationship between the symbolism of kingship and divination existed before the seventeenth century, for we have observed the confrontation of the fish-legged motif of the king in a divine state with the bird since Tada and the Middle Period of Benin.

The gathering of the birds on the crown of the Yoruba king converges in several ways with the gathering of the birds in the iconography of Yoruba medicine and divination. The notion of the beaded crown with birds as an altar of royal authority enlivened with allusions to the ancestors and their power to wage counter-witchcraft on behalf of

---

21. But even without the Zagnanado figure one might make reference to the more firmly documented image of the Dahomean war god in the Musée de l'Homme in Paris. This god is crowned with various iron implements in miniature form, some precisely of the type and shape seen on some iron staffs for the Yoruba god of medicine in the Yoruba kingdoms to the east of the Fon. It is as if the deity were wearing a modified medicine staff as headgear.

mankind, begins to look plausible. And the bird as ancestral forc merges with the idea of the ancestral frontal face. Indeed we havc witnessed the association of the two images since antiquity.

CONCLUSION

The beaded crown with veil blends the terror and splendor of kingship. A ruler must face evil dreadful beyond human imagination. Birds suggest evil and the neutralization of evil, flying out to destroy enemies foreign and domestic and even the king himself should he prove to be fundamentally wicked. The senior priest of Agemo at Imosan was firm on the punitive powers of the crown: "The crown brings evil to the head of the man who does evil." The shape of the ancestral frontal faces on the crown extends the vision of moral vigilance and wrath.

The birds symbolize the splendor of communication with the gods, with the spirits of departed kings, and with the king himself in full ancestral panoply. The faces of his ancestors bear witness to his earthly grandeur, the fall of the veil lifts his glory to their level of ontological purity. The review of the documents, visual and written, suggests a series of oppositions: summit of tree as site of force—head of king as seat of judgment; flight of bird or piercing with beak—royal communication or magic incisiveness; transformation of the generic into the vaguely individual—transformation of the individual into the vaguely generic; the coming of night when unseen forces are unleashed—the fall of the veil when unseen forces are absorbed. The meaning of these oppositions might be simply interpreted: the king can uphold the aspirations of civilization only if he embodies within an essential goodness the understanding of evil.[22]

22. This article is an exploratory essay which proffers possible explanations for the main themes of the crown of the Yoruba kings. However, the interpretive passages, although based on extensive field data, are essentially subjective. Comparison of the iconographies of Yoruba medicine, divination, and kingship yields the recurrent image of the bird and the prerogative of beaded objects. These apparent structural links, within the religious and political life of a single African people, have suggested to the writer a generalized interpretation of motifs in the final paragraph which is meant to stimulate further exploration. Apropos of the work which remains to be done, one might repeat the words of the priest of Agemo at Imosan who, when shown a drawing of a crown with veil, birds, and frontal faces, immediately exclaimed: "The very history of the Yoruba."

REFERENCES

ABELL, A. F.
1935   "Notes on the Ijebu-Remo District of Ijebu Province."
                Typewritten. Nigerian Museum. Lagos.
ABRAHAM, ROY C.
1958   *Dictionary of Modern Yoruba*. London.
AJAYI, J. F. ADE, AND SMITH, ROBERT
1964   *Yoruba Warfare in the Nineteenth Century*. Cambridge,
                England.
ALLISON, PHILIP A.
1960   "Field Reports on Yoruba Ethnography and Art." Type-
                written notes. Nigerian Museum. Lagos.
AVEZAC-MACAYA, ARMAND D'
1845   *Notice sur le pays et le peuple des Yébous en Afrique.*
                Paris.
BARRETT, DOUGLAS
1949   *Islamic Metalwork in the British Museum*. London.
BASCOM, WILLIAM R.
1949   Manuscript notes (mainly on Ife). Cited in Forde (1951,
                p. 85).
1961   "Odu Ifa: The Order of the Figures of Ifa." Institut
                Français d'Afrique Noire, *Bulletin* 23, nos. 3–4: 676–682.
BEIER, H. ULLI
1956   "Before Oduduwa." *Odù, A Journal of Yoruba and Re-
                lated Studies*, no. 3, pp. 25–32.
1958   "Gelede Masks." *Odù, A Journal of Yoruba and Related
                Studies*, no. 6, pp. 5–24.
BERTHO, J.
1950   "Coiffures-masques à Franges de Perles chez les Rois
                Yoruba de Nigéria et de Dahomey." *Notes Africaines*, no.
                47, pp. 71–74.
BIVAR, A. D. H.
1964   *Nigerian Panoply: Arms and Armour of the Northern
                Region*. Department of Antiquities, Lagos.
BRADBURY, R. E.
1957   *The Benin Kingdom and the Edo-speaking Peoples of
                South-Western Nigeria*. Ethnographic Survey of Africa.
                London.
BRINKWORTH, I.
1958   "The Crown Makers of Effon Alaye." *West African
                Review* 29: 729–732.
CABRERA, LYDIA
1948   *Porqué . . . cuentos negros de Cuba*. Havana.
CARROLL, L. KEVIN
1950   "Yoruba Craft Work at Oye-Ekiti, Ondo Province."
                Nigeria Magazine, no. 35, pp. 345–354.
CLAPPERTON, HUGH
1829   *Journal of a Second Expedition into the Interior of Africa,
                from the Bight of Benin to Soccatoo*. London.

CORDWELL, JUSTINE
    1952   "Some Aesthetic Aspects of Yoruba and Benin Cultures."
                Ph.D. diss., Northwestern University. Microfilm. Evan-
                ston, Ill.
CRONE, G. R., ED.
    1937   The Voyages of Cadamosto . . . . London.
DARK, PHILIP J. C.
    1960   Benin Art. (With W. and B. Forman.) London.
    1962   The Art of Benin. Catalogue. Field Museum of Natural
                History, Chicago.
DAVENPORT, CYRIL
    1897   The English Regalia. London.
DENNETT, R. E.
    1906   At the Back of the Black Man's Mind; or Notes on the
                Kingly Office in West Africa. London.
FABELO, T. D.
    1960   Olórun. Havana.
FAGG, WILLIAM B.
    1963   Nigerian Images. New York.
FAGG, WILLIAM B., AND WILLETT, FRANK
    1960   "Ancient Ife: an Ethnographical Summary." Odù, A Jour-
                nal of Yoruba, Edo, and Related Studies, no. 8, pp. 21–35.
                Reprinted in Actes du IVe congrès panafricain de pré-
                histoire 2 (1962): 357–374. Tervuren.
FERNANDEZ, JAMES
    1965   "Symbolic consensus in a Fang reformative cult." Ameri-
                can Anthropologist, n.s., 67, no. 4: 902–929.
FORDE, CYRIL DARYLL
    1951   The Yoruba-Speaking Peoples of South-Western Nigeria.
                Ethnographic Survey of Africa. London.
FROBENIUS, LEO
    1913   The Voice of Africa. 2 vols. London. Translation of Und
                Afrika sprach. 3 vols. Berlin, 1912–13.
    1949   Mythologie de l'Atlantide. Paris.
HASELBERGER, HERTA
    1964   Bautraditionen der westafrikanischen Negerkulturen. Vi-
                enna.
IDOWU, E. BOLAJI
    1962   Olódùmarè: God in Yoruba Belief. London.
JOHNSON, SAMUEL
    1921   The History of the Yorubas. Lagos.
KOPYTOFF, IGOR
    1965   "The Suku of Southwestern Congo." In Peoples of Africa,
                edited by J. L. Gibbs, Jr., pp. 443–477. New York.
KÜHNEL, ERNEST
    1963   Islamische Kleinkunst; ein Handbuch für Sammler und
                Liebhaber. 2d ed. Braunschweig.
LEGUM, COLIN, ED.
    1966   Africa: A Handbook. 2d ed. New York.

LLOYD, PETER C.
  1960   "Sacred Kingship and Government among the Yoruba."
          Africa 30, no. 3: 221–237.
  1968   "Conflict Theory and Yoruba Kingdoms." In *History and
          Social Anthropology*, edited by I. M. Lewis, pp. 25–61.
          London.
LUSCHAN, FELIX VON
  1919   *Die Altertümer von Benin.* 3 vols. Berlin.
McCROW, D. W.
  1953   "Oshogbo celebrates Festival of Shango." *Nigeria Maga-
          zine*, no. 40, pp. 298–313.
MACKENZIE, J. A.
  1938   "Notes on the Idowa District of Ijebu Province" (with
          appendix on the Agemo Cult). Typewritten. Nigerian
          Museum. Lagos.
  1940   "Notes on the Ijebu-Igbo Area of Ijebu Province." Type-
          written. Nigerian Museum. Lagos.
MELLOR, W. F.
  1938   "Bead Embroiderers of Remo." *Nigeria Magazine*, no. 14,
          pp. 154–155.
MORTON-WILLIAMS, PETER
  1960   "The Yoruba Ogboni Cult in Oyo." *Africa* 30, no. 4: 362–
          374.
MURRAY, KENNETH C.
  1938(?) "Native Minor Industries in Abeokuta and Oyo Pro-
          vinces." Typewritten. Nigerian Museum. Lagos.
  1949–54 "Notes on the Arts and Crafts of the Ijebu." Typewritten.
          Nigerian Museum. Lagos.
NADEL, STEPHAN F.
  1942   *A Black Byzantium.* London.
ODUKOYA, A.
  1960(?) "Odun Agemo." *Olokun, Iwe Atigbadegba Ni Atata Yor-
          uba* [*Yoruba Historical Research Scheme*]. Ibadan. Vol. 2.
          [Irregular, ceased publication.]
OGUNBA, O.
  1964   "Crowns and Okute at Idowa." *Nigeria Magazine*, no. 83,
          pp. 249–261.
  1965   "The Agemo Cult in Ijebuland." *Nigeria Magazine*, no. 86,
          pp. 176–186.
OJO, G. J. AFOLABI
  1966   *Yoruba Culture.* London.
PALMER, H. R.
  1908   "The Kano Chronicle." *Journal of the Royal Anthro-
          pological Institute* 38: 38–98.
PRINCE, RAYMOND
  1961   "The Yoruba Image of the Witch." *The Journal of Mental
          Science* [*British Journal of Psychiatry*] 107, no. 449:
          795–805.

ROTH, H. LING
1903   *Great Benin; Its Customs, Art and Horrors.* Halifax, England. Reprinted, New York, 1968.

SANTOS, D. DOS
1967   "West African Sacred Art and Rituals in Brazil." Mimeographed. Institute of African Studies, University of Ibadan. Ibadan.

SCHÜZ, E.
1969   "Der problematische Ibis der Benin-Bronzen." *Tribus* 18: 73–84.

SIEBER, ROY, AND RUBIN, ARNOLD
1968   *Sculpture of Black Africa: The Paul Tishman Collection.* Los Angeles.

SYDOW, ECKART VON
1954   *Afrikanishe Plastik.* New York.

TALBOT, P. AMAURY
1926   *The Peoples of Southern Nigeria.* 4 vols. London.

THOMPSON, ROBERT F.
1970   "The Sign of the Divine King: An Essay on Yoruba Bead-Embroidered Crowns with Veil and Bird Decorations." *African Arts/Arts d'Afrique* 3, no. 3: 8–17, 74–80.

TROWELL, MARGARET
1960   *African Design.* New York.

TUTUOLA, AMOS
1962   *Feather Women of the Jungle.* London.

VERGER, PIERRE
1957   *Notes sur le culte des Orisa et Vodun.* Institut Français d'Afrique Noire, Mémoires, no. 51. Dakar.

1965   "Grandeur et décadence du culte d'iyami osoronga (ma mère la sorcière) chez les Yoruba." *Journal de la Société des Africanistes* 35, no. 1: 141–243.

WILLETT, FRANK
1960   "Ife and Its Archaeology." *The Journal of African History* 1, no. 2: 231–248.

1966   "On the Funeral Effigies of Owo and Benin and the Interpretation of the Life-size Bronze Heads from Ife, Nigeria." *Man,* n.s., 1, art. 1: 34–45.

WILLIAMS, DENIS
1964   "The Iconology of the Yoruba *edan Ogboni.*" *Africa* 34, no. 2: 139–166.

CHAPTER 14

The Fish-Legged
Figure in Benin and Yoruba Art

Douglas Fraser

"Oba Oguola wished to introduce brass casting into Benin so as to produce works of art similar to those sent him from Ife. He therefore sent to the Oni of Ife for a brass-smith and Iguegha was sent to him. Iguegha was very clever and left many designs to his successors, and was in consequence deified, and is worshipped to this day by brass-smiths. The practice of making brass-castings for the preservation of the records of events was originated during the reign of Oguola."

With these words first written some thirty-five years ago, Chief Jacob Egharevba (1960, p. 12), the Benin court historian, set forth his people's traditions concerning the origin of their royal art. On the basis of this information, anthropologists and art historians have constructed a series of hypotheses—and this is really all that anyone can do—about the origins of Benin art and its relation to that of Ife. To be sure, there have been some recent modifications; Egharevba's date of ca. A.D. 1280 for Oguola's reign has been brought forward about a hundred years by R. E. Bradbury (1959, p. 286), placing the advent of metalworking

Note: Many friends and colleagues have generously shared their knowledge with me. In particular I should like to thank A. A. Barb, R. E. Bradbury, Otto Brendel, Richard Brilliant, Herbert M. Cole, Philip Dark, Ekpo Eyo, William Fagg, Alfred Frazer, Friedolf Johnson, Helge Larsson, Thorsen Lundbeck, Jean Mailey, Peter Morton-Williams, Edith Porada, Roy Sieber, Robert Farris Thompson, Deborah Waite, Frank Willett, and Rudolf Wittkower. I wish also to thank the Institute of African Studies at Columbia University and the Ford Foundation, for a Faculty Fellowship which made it possible for me to visit Nigeria in the summer of 1966.

in Benin ca. 1400. Recent radiocarbon dates from Ife indicate that that style was established as early as the twelfth century (Willett 1971, p. 43, and above, chapter 12, p. 223). Unpublished excavations by Ekpo Eyo (1971) still in progress at Owo, a Yoruba town some eighty miles north of Benin City and one hundred miles east of Ife, have disclosed evidence suggesting that Benin and Ife stylistic influence were present simultaneously in Owo from the end of the fourteenth to the end of the fifteenth centuries. If true, this would mean that Ife could hardly be ancestral to Benin.

Those who accept the Benin oral traditions as valid—William Fagg, Frank Willett, and Philip Dark, for example—have used this as a starting point to develop a chronology for Benin art that has won widespread approval. First, Benin specimens that most resemble Ife heads are attributed to the early period, while others are placed at lesser or greater remove in time according to their degree of similarity to Ife castings. To allow time for the initial divergence between the Ife and Benin styles to occur (following the transfer of the technique ca. 1400), the earliest *extant* Benin art objects are usually dated not before 1500 (see, for example, Fagg 1963, pl. 11).

It is not my intention here to discuss the authenticity of Benin oral traditions, which Alan Ryder (1965, 1969), Arnold Rubin (1970), and Frank Willett (1969) have recently done. What I hope to indicate instead is the possibility of expanding the limited information given in the traditional accounts by making use of visual evidence extant in the art itself. Everyone who works on the problems of Nigerian art history has felt the need for such expansion because of the discrepancies— some of them serious—that exist between the historical evidence and what the art forms tell us.[1] For example, the majority of the motifs represented in the Benin plaques have no parallels in Ife; nor do ground lines, the symmetrical flanking of a central figure, or hieratic scale (in which the size of the figure indicates its rank)—all characteristic Benin features—play any significant part in Ife art. How, then, are we to account for these differences? Should we regard them as a later evolution of the style carried out by Benin casters after the end of initial Ife influence? Can some of these developments be the result of Portuguese or Dutch influence which did not reach Ife? Are we dealing with technical decline, decadent virtuosity, or social change, as some have suggested? Or are there better art-historical methods of interpreting

1. Paul Wingert (1950, p. 36), for example, points out that many differences exist between the Ife and Benin styles. More recently, Denis Williams (1964, p. 163, note 1) has suggested that the transfer of influence, if it took place, may have affected only the tradition of casting memorial heads.

the available sources that do not place so much of the burden on a single oral tradition?

SOME UNUSUAL MOTIFS IN BENIN ART

In searching about in Nigerian art for motifs that might yield art-historical evidence, I have often been impressed with certain Benin (and Yoruba) images that appear to have extra-African parallels. Prominent among these is the depiction of the Oba holding the tails of a pair of crocodiles or leopards, one on either side of his head (for example, fig. 15.4; von Luschan 1919, 1, pl. I, fig. 742; Fraser 1962, pl. 49). This motif, known as the "Animal Master" or *dompteur,* is widely distributed in Western art, where it dates back to at least 3000 B.C., occurring in the Ancient Near East and Egypt in the Protoliterate and Protodynastic periods (Fraser 1966). The essential feature of the dompting image is the symmetrical controlling by a central human figure of a pair of ani-mals—whether horses, lions, snakes, leopards, crocodiles (see Egyptian example of ca. 660 B.C., Brooklyn Museum 1960, pl. 15, no. 36), or other creatures. Such groupings seem to have been designed in general to express graphically the idea of a leader's control over various forces, good as well as evil. In Benin, the design serves in part to underscore the Oba's own power, because the leopards he holds are symbolic of himself (Dark 1960, p. 35). Since the theme of the Animal Master occurs also in Classical, Early Christian, Medieval, Renaissance, Chinese, Indian, and many other art styles, this image only illustrates the exis-tence of extra-African parallels and cannot be used to date any possible contacts.

A companion theme to the Animal Master is the image of the ruler standing erect on the back of an animal. This is the so-called "vehicle" motif seen in Hittite, Neo-Hittite, Romano-Hittite, and later in Indian and Sassanian art. Like the Animal Master, the "vehicle" figure re-emerges in Romanesque times, particularly in Lombardy, thereafter entering the heraldic-decorative vocabulary of European art. In Benin, the beast is the royal elephant (Pitt Rivers 1900, pl. 11, figs. 66–68; von Luschan 1919, 3, pls. 79–80). Here, the image appears mainly on scepters, which were among the most sacred Benin symbols and were handed down from one generation to the next, suggesting the antiquity of the motif. Once again, though, precise dating is prevented by the long history of the motif in the West.

Another telling symbol, perhaps the most monumental imagery in all African architecture, appeared on the lofty pyramidal turrets that for-merly adorned the roofs of the palace buildings in Benin. These turrets

FIGURE 14.1. Benin. Detail of brass plaque showing pyramidal
turret over entrance to royal palace. Museum für Völkerkunde,
Berlin-Dahlem (III C 8377). (From von Luschan 1919, 2, pl. 40.)

were topped with a giant bronze bird and/or a huge snake that wrig-
gled down the facade[2] (fig. 14.1). This juxtaposition of bird and ser-
pent on the steep pyramidal roofs is probably no accident. Rudolf Witt-
kower (1938) has shown that the linking of bird and serpent with a

2. Olfert Dapper (1668), D. van Nyandael (1705), John King (1823), and
J. F. Landolph (1823) all mention one or the other of these creatures on the
pyramidal turrets, while the combined form is represented on several other Benin
castings (see, for example, Dark 1960, pl. 1; von Luschan 1919, 3, pl. 90).

FIGURE 14.2. Benin. Brass bell with snake running down front. Museum für Völkerkunde, Berlin-Dahlem (III C 8375). (After von Luschan 1919, 1, fig. 136.)

high place became a widely distributed symbol after its beginnings in the Ancient Near East. Often a metaphor for the cosmic opposition of sky and earth, of light and darkness, of good and evil, the bird-serpent confrontation frequently takes place on an elevation representing the world-mountain. With its eschatological content, the symbol is linked with divine kingship throughout most of its history. The prominence of the symbol in Benin and its physical links with the Oba is clearly illustrated by Montserrat Palau Marti's (1964, p. 67) reconstruction of the palace plan. Our only difficulty is that, as before, there is no way of dating the image other than to indicate that it probably predates Portuguese contact.

Some indication of antiquity comes, however, from an ancillary form, the brass bells known as *eroro* (Dark 1960, pl. 15; von Luschan 1919, 1, p. 94). These are usually of pyramidal shape, and the serpent shown wriggling down the front of some of them (fig. 14.2) indicates they are miniature versions of the pyramidal roof turrets. The antiquity of these bells, as Dr. Bradbury kindly pointed out to me, is proved by a sixteenth-century portrait of Captain Thomas Wyndham wearing one (Tong 1958, opp. p. 55), although Wyndham in fact never actually reached the city of Benin! One of the few metal objects allowed to those of lesser rank, *eroro* were rung at altars to contact the ancestors in time of crisis and seem also to have been used to summon the people to a human sacrifice. Pyramidal bells appear in many of the brass plaques, primarily as warriors' ornaments (von Luschan 1919, 1, pp. 368–374), and, according to Bradbury, *eroro* still have definite military associations. All of these functions are consistent with the eschatological symbolism suggested for the roof turrets. Placing one's soldiers under the aegis of such powerful emblems serves to identify their efforts with the ultimate cosmic struggle, for upon their success or failure depends the fate of the sovereign state.

Apart from their shape, the *eroro* bells illustrate several themes that have important extra-African parallels. One is the frontal face (some-a   b   c   d   e   f   g

FIGURE 14.3. Benin. Motifs appearing on various brass bells. Dark suggests that 14.3f and 14.3g are derived from the long side-curls worn by European faces such as 14.3a. (After Dark 1957, fig. 5.)

times of a Portuguese) framed by means of a double-spiral ornament (fig. 14.3a); Dark (1957, p. 205, and 1962, p. 46) has suggested that spirals 14.3f and 14.3g evolved from the side-curls worn by European heads such as 14.3a. There is, however, considerable evidence that the isolated double-spiral and framing spiral forms existed side-by-side in the Ancient World. The double-spiral alone appears between the breasts of the well-known twelfth-century B.C. fertility goddess from Beirut (Frankfort 1954, p. 150, pl. 144), where it symbolizes the life-giving power of the uterus. Throughout the Ancient World the double-spiral form was synonymous with fertility (Frankfort 1944, pp. 198–200); today, Egyptian women still wear the isolated double-spiral for protection in childbirth. When used to frame the frontal human face, the spiral becomes the omega- or Hathor hairdress, an apotropaic and propitious coiffure, traceable from the earliest Sumerian images that represented Nintu (literally, "Our Lady of Births"; see Frankfort 1954, pl. 58C) directly down to the first known Christian Madonna, that in the Priscilla Catacomb in Rome. Here, too, the problem is an embarrassment of riches, for such a motif can have reached Benin from any of a hundred sources.[3]

3. Besides appearing on the bells, the omega motif is seen in Benin art on certain altar pieces, probably representing a Queen Mother (Pitt Rivers 1900, fig. 240, pp. 324–325) and a prisoner about to be sacrificed (von Luschan 1919, 3, pl. 82). The double-spiral occurs also on ivory sistra struck by the Oba at ceremonies (Roth 1903, fig. 227) and on the foreheads of three unusual brass hip masks worn by the chief brass-caster (Dark 1960, pl. 81; Fagg 1963, pl. 19; and Fagg and Plass 1964, p. 106). These contexts appear to be consistent with the potency imputed to the respective individuals. Metal ornaments of this shape are used as hair and body decoration elsewhere in Africa (Nuer, Bari, Mamvu, Chokwe, Ngbaka, Daba *inter alia*) and indeed in many Bronze Age cultures (for example, the Koban culture of the Caucasus, the Andronovo culture of central Asia, the Dongson culture of Southeast Asia [with modern survivals in Sumatra and the Philippines], and the early metal-working cultures of Peru and Ecuador. See Heine-Geldern 1954).

Still another Benin motif of interest is that known to the Greeks as the Uroboros, a snake that holds its own tail in its mouth. Again a cosmic symbol, this creature usually represents the world snake who circumscribes the ocean surrounding the earth and is equated with the rainbow by day and the Milky Way by night. According to the Roman authors Macrobius and Claudian, the Uroboros came to be interpreted as a symbol of the zodiac and eternity, illustrating the ceaseless destruction and regeneration of Time the self-devourer (Deonna 1952, p. 168). Known in Egypt since at least 1100 B.C., where the self-biting snake served as a cartouche frame in reliefs, the image later appears in Graeco-Egyptian Gnostic gems and in Mandean metalwork deriving from these forms. The Benin examples of this motif (von Luschan 1919, 1, fig. 693, and 2, pl. 104e; Pitt Rivers 1900, no. 102; and a similar example now in the Nigerian Museum) appear to be relatively late works. A comparable motif, however, a mudfish biting its own tail, is seen on plaques (Dark 1960, pl. 27), bells, ivory tusks (von Luschan 1919, 2, pl. 46, and 1, fig. 746), kola-nut boxes, and ritual staffs (*uxurhe*) (Dark 1962, p. 47) used exclusively by the Oba and "the most direct symbol of the power of the god or spirit" (Bradbury 1961, p. 132). Self-devouring snakes are also known in Yoruba art (Frobenius 1913, 1, pp. 134, 249), in Dahomey wall reliefs and metal staffs (Verger 1957, pls. 133–134), and in Dogon cosmology (Griaule 1938, fig. 15), but there is no precise way of localizing the source of any of these motifs.

Several other elements of Benin culture also suggest outside influence, such as the supporting of the Oba's hands, which Meyer Schapiro notes corresponds to the Biblical ritual mentioned in the battle of the Israelites and the Amelikites (Exod. 17 : 8–13), the depiction of confronting felines, rosettes, and so on. But these are matters best discussed at greater length than is possible here.

THE FISH-LEGGED FIGURE IN BENIN ART

There is one motif, however, present in Benin but even more articulated in Yoruba art that does afford evidence of its pedigree, namely the fish-legged figure (fig. 14.4). This extraordinary image appears in Benin art on ivory tusks, bracelets, sistra, and on plaques, pectorals, and other metal objects,[4] and on specimens of non-Benin origin ascribed to the "Lower Niger Bronze Industry," a term coined by William Fagg for this unlocalized material. Fish-legged figures also occur on ivory brace-

4. Philip Dark has kindly informed me that fish-legged figures appear on 137 items in the Benin corpus he has compiled.

FIGURE 14.4. Benin. Oba figure. British Museum, London (After von Luschan 1919, 1, pl. K, fig. 745.)

lets, containers, and other objects from the Ijebu and Owo Yoruba areas, where the royal art style often closely resembled that of the Benin court (Fagg 1951, pp. 73–74). The image also figures prominently in most other Yoruba areas, particularly on ivory bracelets, large wooden drums (*agba*) and a few metal figures (*edan*) used by the Ogboni society, wooden mortars (*odo*), doors and staffs (*oshe*) linked with the Shango cult, and elsewhere (see Thompson 1969, p. 131). A single brass bracelet illustrating a snake-footed figure (Willett 1967, fig. 33) and the property of the Kukunu (king) of Wukari (Jukun), though probably of Yoruba manufacture, is the sole example of this motif in Africa that cannot absolutely be ascribed to Yoruba- and Benin-influenced art. Thus the fish-legged figure forms a decided link between the two areas.

Just who or what the fish-legged being represents is a matter of uncertainty. The best known and most consistent version, that seen in Benin, invariably occupies the central position on sistra, tusks, plaques, or bracelets and hence can only be a god or deified Oba. Always dressed elaborately, the figure frequently wears baldrics or crisscross straps which, Bradbury confirms, were a mark of very high rank:[5] in traditional Benin art only the fish-legged figure (and occasionally two of his immediate attendants) are ever depicted wearing these straps. The Benin people sometimes interpret the fish-legged being as Olokun, the god of the sea, human fertility, and wealth (Bradbury 1957, pp. 52–53); the mudfish feet are said to be symbolic of Olokun's aquatic nature. At the same time, the Benin people do not fully accept this interpretation. They state that they describe this figure as Olokun because they do not enjoy referring to its real meaning, which, as we will see, involves physical deformity; since ordinarily the Benin people are not reluctant to speak of physical handicaps, Bradbury (1965 personal communication) regards this as an odd reaction.

The other, less readily forthcoming explanation for the fish-legged figure given in Benin is that the image represents Oba Ohen, who reigned ca. A.D. 1334, according to Egharevba 1960, or early in the fifteenth century in Bradbury's view (1959). According to Egharevba (1960, p. 13), after reigning for about twenty-five years, Ohen had the misfortune to become paralyzed and, being a divine king whose health reflected that of his people, was in danger therefore of being put to death. To conceal his infirmity, the Oba had himself carried into the council chamber before the arrival of his chiefs and later required them to leave before he did. But the Iyashe (the leader of the town chiefs) concealed himself in the room and discovered the Oba's weakness, whereupon the king had him executed. Here the stories diverge. According to one version, the people then rebelled against Ohen, eventually stoning him to death with pieces of chalk (Egharevba 1960, pp. 13–14) or forcing him to commit suicide (Talbot 1926, 1, p. 158). Talbot adds that the ceremonial costume worn by the Oba and his courtiers is said to have originated in this reign. Other accounts hold that Ohen was able to evade being executed for his deformity by giving out that he had become possessed by the god Olokun and that his legs, now resembling mudfish, were sacred and ought never to be exposed

5. The restrictions governing the wearing of these straps were enforced almost until the twentieth century; in the 1890s Oba Ovonramwen, wishing to placate a man to whom he was very much indebted, conferred on him the right to use these bands. Leaders of the man's lineage still wear the baldrics to the present day (Bradbury, 1966 personal communication).

(Waugh 1961, p. 198). According to this version, Ohen is honored as the promoter of Olokun worship.

Apart from the visual aspects of the narrative, the Oba Ohen story has, as Dr. Bradbury has kindly informed me, important religious and political connotations. The incapacity of the Oba, an intolerable defect in a divine king, poses a threat to the well-being of the entire community. His death by stoning with chalk is therefore an act of ritual purification; chalk plays a major role in post-mortuary cleansing rites (Bradbury 1957, pp. 50–51). A second point made in the story is a rejection of political absolutism. The execution of the Iyashe is considered atrocious because he embodies and symbolizes the power of the town chiefs (many of them self-made title-takers) and, by extension, that of the people at large; these powers ought always to counterbalance that of the Oba and his entourage of hereditary palace chiefs.[6] The murder of the Iyashe, in other words, represented an offense against both piety and polity.

It seems likely, therefore, that the depiction of the fish-legged God-Oba in Benin functioned in large part as a cautionary image designed to remind the living Oba of the need to respect the power of the people and to guarantee his continuing good will to his councillors. What remains obscure is why the Oba should have fish legs in the first place. Paralyzed people are a common sight in African towns, and it takes a remarkable imagination to see such misfortune as having anything to do with mudfish. Indeed, the image might just as well precede the story, the latter being an after-the-fact interpretation.

YORUBA FISH-LEGGED FIGURES

Turning now to Yoruba art, here too the role of the fish-legged figure is exalted but perplexing. Closest in style and context to Benin examples are figures on ivory bracelets, beakers, and other objects from Owo and Ijebu whose true provenience has only recently been ascertained, thanks primarily to the efforts of William Fagg. Like Benin ivories, virtually all of which belonged to the Oba (Bradbury 1957, p. 26), these Owo and Ijebu objects were surely restricted to the use of sovereigns. On the other hand, fish-legged figures are also represented on the sides of *agba* drums (fig. 14.5), which were beaten to announce funerals

---

6. This balance of opposing forces is also graphically represented in the division of Benin City into two halves, on one side (*ogbe*) of which live the Oba and the palace chiefs, and on the other (*ore n'oxwa*), the town chiefs (Bradbury 1957, p. 34; Fraser 1968, ill. 59).

FIGURE 14.5. Yoruba. Ijebu. Oshugbo (Ogboni) society drum. University Museum, Philadelphia (29-93-39). Ht. 32″ (81.3 cm). (Photograph: Museum.)

and meetings (and formerly, executions) of the Ogboni society (Fagg 1963, pls. 90–91; Williams 1964, p. 141, note 2); the designs carved on these drums could be viewed only by members of the society (Morton-Williams 1960b, p. 371). The fish-legged image also appears on boards, doors, ritual mortars (*odo*), and staffs (*oshe*) associated with the Shango cult (Frobenius 1913, 1, pp. 204, 207, 213). Palace doors of Yoruba kings are often decorated with fish-legged figures, one of which is said to represent Oduduwa himself, the founder of divine kingship at Ife (Thompson 1969, p. 131, note 21). An example atop a brass casting (*edan Ogboni*) from Odo-Nopa has kindly been brought to my attention by Robert F. Thompson, who adds that in northern Oyo the motif is sometimes associated with Erinle, a deity linked with hunting, herbalism, and rivers. William Fagg (1963, pl. 98) has seen a wooden specimen in Ilesha that formed a part of the equipment of an Ifa divination priest, while the motif is sometimes depicted on divining trays (*opon Ifa*). Thus, the fish-legged figure is both widely dispersed and functionally varied in Yorubaland.

With regard to the meaning of this image among the Yoruba, there are clearly many analogies with Benin. Its links with aristocracy and public function are evident in the bracelets and other ivories (see Fagg 1963, pl. 98) as well as on the palace doors, where, in one instance, the figure is said to represent Oduduwa, the first monarch of the Yoruba. On the other hand, the image appears in a secretive manner on the drums (fig. 14.5; Hall 1928) of the Ogboni society, a cult of elders dedicated to the veneration of the Earth, the mother of all life, to which man returns at death (Morton-Williams 1960a, p. 38, and 1964, p. 245). The fish-legged figures carved on *agba Ogboni* are often "explained" by reference to the modern deity known as "Mammy Water." Popular today throughout much of coastal West Africa (see, for example, Himmelheber 1965, pp. 116–117), this deity is believed to inhabit rivers and to confer prosperity on men. Her functions are very similar to those of Olokun in Benin, who also dwells in the waters that surround the earth and bestows rewards on mankind (Bradbury 1957, pp. 52–23). The other main symbol, besides the fish-legged figure, normally seen on the *agba* drums is the head of a horse with snakes coming out of its nostrils (Morton-Williams, 1965 personal communication); this image also appears on royal objects of ivory from Owo and Benin. The political, judicial, and ritual functions of the Ogboni society stem largely from their control of the Earth spirit (Onile) who is the conceptual counterpart of the Sky God (Olorun) from whom Oduduwa and all Yoruba kings are descended (Forde 1951, pp. 18–23; Morton-Williams 1960b, pp. 363–367, 371, 1964, pp. 245, 248). Thus the role of the Ogboni society vis-à-vis Yoruba kings is to some extent a cautionary, counterbalancing one analogous to that of the Iyashe and the town chiefs in Benin.

Just what significance the fish-legged figure has in the Shango cult is uncertain. Possibly it has simply attached itself to this art because Shango was a great king. Similarly, there is no clear way of accounting for its use in Ifa divination. Nevertheless, there can be little doubt that the motif is one of central importance in Yoruba art and that it forms one of the chief bonds with the royal style of Benin.

EXTRA-NIGERIAN PARALLELS

This still leaves us with no adequate explanation for the mysterious fish legs. If there were no extra-African parallels to this motif, one would have to abandon the search at this point. But innumerable counterparts to the Yoruba, Benin, and Lower Niger examples exist, as H. Ling Roth (1903, p. 50) and others have pointed out. Fish-legged figures are so frequent in European and West Asian art, however, that no conclusions can be based on this data. I propose therefore to limit the discussion to one extraordinary subtype of fish-legged figure, the *self-dompting* beings that grasp their own legs, elevating them on either side of their torsos. This type of image is not found in Benin or Lower Niger art but is restricted to the Yoruba. It appears in three distinct versions: in the first, the figure holds fish-like tails aloft (fig. 14.6); in the second, the fish tails have heads that converge towards the figure's groin (fig. 14.7); in the third, instead of fish tails, the person's legs end in the form of torsos of reptiles, probably crocodiles or lizards (fig. 14.8). Stylistic differences notwithstanding, the majority of these Yoruba self-dompting figures show marked affinities with the better known Benin fish-legged being, including the depiction of the bands worn baldric-fashion on their chests. A number of these figures also wear a sort of scalloped skirt and have deep navels. Although individual specimens vary from one another in detail, they are all obviously interrelated, forming a cluster of complex variations on an extremely arbitrary theme.

For this is indeed an extraordinary image. The chances of the self-dompting fish-legged figure having been derived from the observation of nature are nonexistent. No such composite human-animal form exists nor is it physically possible to elevate one's legs outward in this position. That these are arbitrary conceptions of the human mind is surely the preferable interpretation. If this is true, our three versions can be seen as imaginative, yet systematic, elaborations of a central theme. While there are no known African parallels, the image in many ways resembles the European mermaid.

The possibility of comparing the European mermaid to Benin and other fish-legged figures occurred many years ago to Felix von Luschan (1919, 1, pp. 402, note 1, 406), though only as a general correspondence due to convergence. To show this, he illustrated (1, p. 522, fig. 889) a Nuremberg grave plaque dating from about A.D. 1540 which depicts a mermaid clothed to the neck in a tunic having a scalloped skirt; she grasps her own scaly legs, wears a crown and broad necklace, and has a deep navel. Known as Melusine, this image appears fre-

FIGURE 14.6. Yoruba. Owo. Detail of ivory armband. Museum für Völkerkunde, Berlin-Dahlem (III C 4882). (After von Luschan 1919, 1, pl. C, fig. 614.)

quently in European art from the twelfth century onward. Its role after 1300 is primarily in heraldry (Boutell 1907, p. 228), where it is identified particularly with certain German families (Moule 1842, p. 213).

Fortunately we need not concern ourselves with the post-Renaissance period, for it can be shown that the self-dompting figure existed in Nigeria in substantially its contemporary form prior to 1674. Two Owo Yoruba ivory bracelets now in the Nationalmuseet, Copenhagen, mentioned in the royal Kunstkammeret records at that date, each depict

FIGURE 14.7. Yoruba. Ijebu. Detail of ivory armband. Whereabouts unknown. (Not in Egerton Collection, as stated by von Luschan.) (From von Luschan 1919, 1, fig. 623a.)

FIGURE 14.8. Yoruba. Owo. Detail of ivory armband. British Museum, London (1920 11-21). (Photograph: author.)

one female and five male figures grasping their own legs, one of which ends in a crocodile or lizard, the other in a simplified mudfish head. In Figure 14.9, all the figures appear to wear a brief loincloth and identical necklaces. In the other example (not illustrated) the torsos of three of the male figures have circular depressions indicating nipples and navels; two male figures are inverted, and a different pair lack necklaces. Although not quite symmetrical, these early specimens demonstrate fully an awareness of the motif in its thoroughly African form by the midseventeenth century. If these self-dompting Yoruba images owe anything to extra-African sources, the influences must date from the Renaissance period or earlier.

The transmission of the self-dompting concept to Nigeria by a Renaissance agency is not difficult to imagine. Europeans who traded in West Africa or Africans returning home owned textiles, metal objects, wood carvings, books, engravings, furniture, and the like from which designs could easily have been appropriated as symbols of African leadership. Such a synthesis occurred in the case of two Afro-Portuguese ivory carvings, one in Denmark since at least 1743 (fig. 14.10), the other from Newcastle on Tyne now on loan to the British Museum,

FIGURE 14.9. Yoruba. Owo. Ivory armband known to have been in Denmark before 1674. National Museum, Copenhagen (EDc 26). Ht. 4.8″ (12 cm). (Photograph: Museum.)

which depict semi-nude female figures with fish tails. However, since these single-tailed mermaids do not grasp their tails, they are not self-dompteurs; judging by their style, moreover, both objects were made in Sherbro, Sierra Leone.

Nevertheless, Renaissance European examples of self-dompting are not difficult to find: a fifteenth-century Spanish engraving (Cirlot 1958, p. 384), an Italian engraving of ca. 1465–1480 (Hind 1938–1948, 2,

FIGURE 14.10. Sierra Leone. Sherbro. Detail of Afro-Portuguese ivory vessel known to have been in Denmark before 1743. National Museum, Copenhagen (EDc 67). (Photograph: author.)

pl. 147), a sixteenth-century Neapolitan textile (Museum of Fine Arts, Boston, no. 13.138.1), and Rumanian ceramics (Nicolescu 1955/56, fig. 5) of the end of the fifteenth century all depict the theme, indicating the breadth of its distribution, which is not surprising since the image goes back to the Medieval period. Nor is the tail-grasping version the only variant found in Europe at this time. Frescoes at S. Giustina in Padua, painted about 1540–1546, include a female triton whose legs turn into dolphins that converge toward the figure's lower torso (Volkmann 1923, abb. 19), an idea derived from Classical antecedents. This type may be seen also in modern heraldic imagery. But I have been unable to locate any European example from Renaissance or modern times that parallels the third variant, in which the upheld legs terminate in animal heads, nor do we anywhere see the crisscross baldrics so characteristic of the Nigerian examples. Of course, some of these motifs might have been independently invented in Africa but this seems unlikely since, as will be shown, the whole ensemble constitutes a coherent formal system that normally travels together.[7] Thus on formal grounds I conclude that Renaissance art was not the inspiration for the fish-legged figure in Nigeria.

There are other good reasons for rejecting the Renaissance possibilities. The fish-legged figure, as we have seen, is deeply imbedded in the very core of both Yoruba and Benin iconography, for it occupies the place of honor on ivory sistra, bracelets, and Ogboni drums. Could the Nigerian artists with their strong traditions have assimilated alien motifs so rapidly that the Benin ivory sistra, thought to date from the sixteenth century, would show no evidence whatsoever of foreign derivation, whereas ivory masks of the same period clearly depict the intrusive in the form of Portuguese heads? If the fish-legged figure had been taken over from Europe, we might expect to see coronets, mirrors, blazons, and the like; but instead we are impressed with the absolute Africanness of the form and style. Extraordinary selectivity would be required, moreover, for the Nigerian artists to single out Melusine from the thousands of heraldic and ornamental devices circulating in Renaissance Europe, not one of which, to my knowledge, appears in traditional Benin or Yoruba art. Incredible, too, is the notion that the Nigerian cultures would be so permeable (or gullible) as to adopt for their most sacrosanct symbols, images transmitted publicly by foreign adventurers. Not even the past century of intensive exposure to Western ideas has succeeded in displacing the peoples' traditional imagery and values. Nigerian depictions of Dutch and Portuguese traders (Dark 1960, pls. 44–53, 55–56) always betray the intrusiveness of these individuals, most of whom had no direct access to the highest leaders, still less to religious institutions such as the Ogboni society. And how could the highly arbitrary self-dompting figure have become so thoroughly diversified in function in so short a time? There simply is no logical explanation. Thus three important canons of art-historical authenticity (degree of centrality to the culture, agreement with local style, and duration as shown by breadth of dispersal and functional differentiation) strongly indicate that the fish-legged figure in Nigeria predates the advent of the Portuguese to West Africa.

MEDIEVAL PARALLELS

The Renaissance and modern examples of the fish-legged figure discussed so far actually represent stereotyped late versions of a theme

7. Of course the missing versions may yet appear in Renaissance art, having simply escaped my attention despite a lengthy search. Their presence is well documented in pre-Renaissance art and, once evolved, an image can always recur either as a survival or revival.

having a longer and much more meaningful history. The immediate source of the imagery is to be sought in Romanesque art of the twelfth century where we find the full range of types observed in Nigeria, including those with upheld fish tails (fig. 14.11), groin-biting fish (fig. 14.12), and the animal heads at the ends of the legs (fig. 14.13). Once again the images are widely distributed: Italy (Bernheimer 1931, no. 138), France (Adhémar 1939, p. 184; Baltrušaitis 1931, figs. 249, 252–256, 262), Germany (Troescher 1954, abb. 27, 32), and Spain (Cirlot 1958, opp. p. 33, p. 384). From Switzerland and elsewhere come examples which have scalloped skirts (fig. 14.11). However, the crisscross bands are lacking in all the Medieval specimens known to me.

The origin of the Romanesque figures has become clearer as a result of recent studies. The form almost certainly is *not* of purely ornamental origin, derived from doubling the single-tailed figure, as Jurgis Baltrušaitis (1931, p. 109) once suggested. Nor is it a purely Medieval creation, resulting from the borrowing or misunderstanding of Sassanian forms, as A. Kingsley Porter (1924, p. 20) and Richard Bernheimer

FIGURE 14.11. Switzerland. Geneva. Romanesque figure. Cathedral of St. Peter. (After Deonna 1928, fig. 1.1.)

FIGURE 14.12. Italy. Parma. Romanesque relief. (After Baltrušaitis 1931, fig. 262.)

(1931, pp. 144–146) have argued. All the variations and details can be traced back to Antique prototypes, although most scholars have relied on Mediterranean art styles which do not illustrate all the details.

The meaning of the fish-legged image in Medieval times was essentially negative. Interpreted as sirens and temptresses, such figures were often juxtaposed with symbols of the eight principle vices (Troescher 1954, pp. 36–38). A male version at Remagen was probably identified with *superbia* (pride), while at Münchsmunster, fish sirens seem to have been symbols of avarice and *luxuria* (unchastity). These interpretations stem mainly from association with the Classical figure of Scylla, whose iconography is similar, though not identical, to that described above (Adhémar 1939, pp. 182–184). Waldemar Deonna (1928, p. 18) also has suggested that the crowned masculine version of Gothic date (fig.

FIGURE 14.13. France. Poitiers. Romanesque figure. Notre Dame la Grande. (After Baltrušaitis 1931, fig. 256.)

FIGURE 14.14. Switzerland. Gothic relief. (After Deonna 1928, fig. 1.2.)

14.14) relates to the "bishop of the sea" or "king of the fish" of popular legend.

The possibility that influences spread from Romanesque Europe to Nigeria must be taken seriously. Except for the baldrics, all of the details and variants existed equally in both areas. Romanesque objects, moreover, have been found in China and other regions much more remote from Europe than West Africa. But if visual influences did reach Nigeria from Romanesque Europe, it is extraordinary that no specifically Christian motifs were included among them, or if they were, that these have since vanished from Africa without leaving a trace. None of the standard themes of Medieval Christian iconography appear, to my knowledge, in either Benin or Yoruba art. All the parallels between Romanesque and Nigerian art, in actuality, involve elements of an older, pagan origin that happen to have been revived in the Medieval period.

Certain medieval images (fig. 14.14) are, however, reminiscent of the fish-legged figure in Benin art, including the scalloped skirt and the expanding central pendant form below the groin, which in Benin art (fig. 14.4) becomes a crocodile or hand. But none of these features is a Medieval invention, nor are they necessarily even of European origin, since the models on which they depend are scattered throughout western Asia as well as the Mediterranean world. Thus while we cannot rule out the possibility of Romanesque influence in Nigeria, in the light of the available evidence such an occurrence seems highly improbable.

THE ANCIENT POSSIBILITIES

Both the Medieval and Renaissance fish-legged figures descend from Antique prototypes. The ornamental version, revived in the Renaissance and consisting usually of a male figure grasping foliate, curling tails (for example, Göbel 1923–1934, 2, no. 367), springs from Roman sources.[8] But these Roman versions completely lack significant variation, so much so that Porter, Bernheimer, Jean Adhémar, and other specialists in the transmission of Classical motifs into the Middle Ages have been unable to find sources for the full range of Medieval forms in Roman art. Moreover, if the Romans had employed the variants that interest us, Renaissance artists almost certainly would have employed them too. Although the scalloped skirt is a well-known Roman motif, it is only when we look to earlier Antiquity that we find even approximations of the full series of themes.

One of the closest visual parallels to the Nigerian images is that provided by a Hellenistic-Etruscan triton of ca. 300 B.C. (fig. 14.15). Here the legs end in serpent heads, and the figure wears clearly marked baldrics. These bands, it should be noted, are a distinctive Hellenistic trait and are not characteristic of the later Roman art in the Mediterranean West. Almost invariably, in Antiquity, such crisscross straps appear only on nonhuman, demonic water-beings, especially the serpent-legged tritons. Thus, baldric-wearing, both in the Classical world and in Nigeria, is strongly linked with demonic snake- or fish-legged beings, suggesting a relationship between the two areas. The Mediterranean region, however, lacks some of the systematic variations seen in Nigeria.

The ultimate origin of the fish-tail-holding figure may lie in the Ancient Near East. A unique and therefore not yet fully authenticated

8. For example, at Herculaneum, Lesbos (Adhémar 1939, p. 183), and southern Russia (Reinach 1908, 4, no. 249–3). I am especially indebted to Otto Brendel, Jean Mailey, and Mrs. Howard Sachs for sharing with me the fruits of their own work on this theme in Antiquity.

FIGURE 14.15. Italy. Hellenistic-Etruscan. Triton. (After Reinach 1908, 2, pt. 1, fig. 411-4.)

specimen from Luristan in Iran (fig. 14.16) suggests that the theme, though perhaps not all the versions, dates from at least about 700 B.C. According to Bernard Goldman (1960, pp. 53–57), this figure with its fish legs, prominent breasts, and navel synthesizes the idea of the water goddess with that of the so-called "Animal Mistress," the fertility and war goddess. The image also wears the previously discussed omega- or Hathor hairdress, a sign of her association with birth goddesses. But since we have, as yet, no other comparable Luristan specimen, it would be rash to place too much reliance on this single figure.[9]

By far the closest resemblances to the Benin and Yoruba fish-legged figures that I have been able to discover are found during the period of about 100 B.C.–A.D. 300, in the art of the Eastern Roman Empire. This art was one in which Hellenistic and Roman influences mingled

9. As I have previously done (Fraser 1962, pp. 100–103, and in an unpublished paper read at the annual meeting of the African Studies Association in Washington, October 13, 1962).

FIGURE 14.16. Iran. Luristan. Bronze figure. (After Goldman 1960, fig. 1.)

with older concepts derived from the Ancient Near East; together these composite ideas spread eastward as far as India and Chinese Turkestan. Figures 14.17–14.19 illustrate respectively the being with fish-tailed legs, the person whose legs become creatures that converge toward the groin while he holds their tails, and the figure whose legs end in zoomorphic monsters. To be sure, the animals in this case are *makara* (fish-tailed water monsters of Indian origin) and Near Eastern leogriffs, and there are slight differences in the manner in which the animals are controlled; but the structure of the images is the same as that seen in Nigeria. The central beings are clearly tritons of Mediterranean origin.

FIGURE 14.17. India. Mathura. Figure. (After Combaz 1937, 2, pl. 86.)

FIGURE 14.18. Afghanistan. Begram. Triton. Ivory. (From Hackin 1954, fig. 522.)

To add to the similarity, the being in Figure 14.18 wears an abbreviated scalloped skirt, a necklace, and baldrics. Comparing the image of a related creature holding *makara* (fig. 14.20) with an Owo Yoruba detail (fig. 14.21), we 'see extraordinary similarities of detail in the deep navel, segmented necklace, waistband, and coffered decoration of the

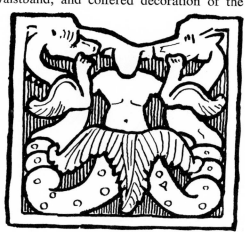

FIGURE 14.19. India. Mathura. Figure. (After Combaz 1937, 2, pl. 86.)

FIGURE 14.20. Afghanistan. Begram. Triton. Ivory. (From Hackin 1954, fig. 177.)

FIGURE 14.21. Yoruba. Owo. Detail from ivory beaker. Museum für Völkerkunde, Berlin-Dahlem (III C 4883). (After von Luschan 1919, 1, pl. W, fig. 827.)

scalloped skirt, despite the fact that three thousand miles and two thousand years separate these two images. Can there be any doubt that both derive from some common ancestry?

As it happens, all of the images in Figures 14.17–14.20 come from an area farther from Rome than Nigeria is. These specimens were collected in Afghanistan and India, particularly at the sites of Begram and Mathura, which were major trade route stations for the caravans plying between the Roman world and India. In these outposts of the Eastern Empire, Mediterranean, Ancient Near Eastern, and Indic influences fused together readily. Thus the Classical triton grapples in the Near Eastern manner with monsters that are of Indian origin (Stern, in Hackin 1954, pp. 32–33, and Viennot 1958, p. 204). These Indian monsters, of course, were merely local replacements for the comparable Classical fish or serpents.

In citing these parallels, I am in no way suggesting that the Nigerian forms came directly from India or Afghanistan. The motifs seen here, being well known and widespread, could easily have been introduced from any of a dozen Eastern Empire centers. Nor can a specific date be assigned to the event.[10] But the visual evidence strongly suggests that the Nigerian images were influenced by concepts stemming ultimately from the Eastern Empire, probably in the first millennium A.D.

ALTERNATIVE EXPLANATIONS

While the conclusions advanced above have much to recommend them, there will inevitably be scholars who disagree and who prefer alternative explanations. Three main possibilities present themselves: transmission from modern or Renaissance sources, Medieval inspiration, or independent invention in Nigeria. The first two theories have already been discussed above and discarded; but the theory of independent invention deserves consideration. It is possible, I suppose, to imagine the independent invention of fish-legged figures, conceivably even of self-dompting ones in the three variants discussed here; but how, short of repealing the laws of chance, can we allow for these images to be

10. The impetus for making figures of this sort did not come to an end with the decline of the Eastern Empire. Examples dating from the seventh and eighth centuries A.D. have been found in Chinese Turkestan (Dyakonova and Sorokin 1960, no. 199) which, while they are not fish-legged, still wear the scalloped skirt and baldrics. Rather than their own legs, these figures elevate garlands in the Coptic and Sassanian manner (Bernheimer 1931, Porter 1924). The revival of the skirt motif in the Romanesque period (fig. 14.11) also demonstrates that these forms must have persisted in the East throughout the 1st millennium A.D.

combined with the scalloped skirts, waist bands, deep navels, segmented necklaces, and baldrics? The latter feature is especially telling because in Benin the baldrics are emphatically associated both *orally and in the art forms* with the fish-legged Oba, just as these straps are specifically identified in the Ancient World with fish- and serpent-legged beings. Nor are the baldrics, scalloped skirts, deep navels, and segmented necklaces merely isolated individual parallels; a complex of forms, they cluster together in Antiquity as well as in Nigeria. Had the Nigerian ivories and wood carvings been found almost anywhere else, their family resemblance to the Eastern Empire examples would probably have been recognized long ago.

It may be argued that the enormous temporal and spatial gaps between the Antique objects and those made in Benin and Yoruba would have prevented the retention of any significant similarities. This objection can be answered in one of several ways. First, we may note that the criticism itself involves an *a priori* judgment of what is or is not possible before proceeding to test the issue. Secondly, the persistence of motifs and ideas through time and across great distances is documented in other non-Western traditions, as, for example, in China, Mexico, and Peru, even though we are unable there, too, despite extensive archaeology, to fill in many of the spatial and temporal gaps. Thirdly, we may note the great stability of symbols in societies in which the manipulation of power stems largely from controlling those symbols. Finally, it may be pointed out that the gaps separating Benin and Yoruba art from the Eastern Empire are scarcely greater than those that intervene between the latter and the Romanesque period. Yet few will deny that links exist in the second instance, although as yet we have absolutely no proof of the connection (see Hackin 1939, p. 86). But if we can accept the distant kinship of first-century Indian examples with twelfth-century Romanesque specimens, there is no good reason for not entertaining at least the possibility of similar connections with pre-Portuguese Nigeria. To do otherwise is simply logically inconsistent.

Just how Eastern Empire influences may have reached Benin and Yoruba is a matter for speculation. A clue to the problem may lie with the Nok culture, which flourished in northern Nigeria from perhaps 500 B.C. to A.D. 200 (Fagg 1963, p. 23). Along with its famous clay heads, Nok also yields some of the earliest evidence of iron-working in West Africa. The casting of nonferrous metals, on the other hand, seems to have been diffused to West Africa at a much later date (Shaw 1970; and Williams, quoted in Forde 1965, p. 62). The absence of a pre-ferrous Bronze Age in West Africa makes the early appearance of iron there all the more significant. Metalworkers do not simply set off at random to transmit their technology to foreigners. There must already have been trade contacts, perhaps for gold, ivory, and slaves, even before 500 B.C.; in the case of Nigeria, these trade routes may well have crossed by way of the upper Nile to Egypt and the Ancient Near East. Thus the subsequent transmission of Eastern Empire ideas may have followed long-established avenues.[11] The quest for ivory in particular may have been a significant motive for contact, since ivory was in great demand in the Ancient World. Until the eighth century B.C., there were still elephants in Syria which may have supplied some of this demand; but African and Indian sources must have been known by then, as ivory work continues without interruption down through the centuries. In Benin, moreover, there is perhaps reason to believe that ivory carving predates the adoption of brass-casting by the Iguerovo (Iguneromwo) or brass-smiths guild. The making of the first wooden heads and stools and iron objects in Benin is ascribed to Ere, a culture hero who antedates Oba Oguola by a considerable margin (Egharevba 1960, p. 2). Wood and ivory carving were both the work of the Igbe-sava (or Igbesamwan) guild, a term derived from the root "to carve ivory." Thus wood and ivory carving may well preserve an older style, in contrast to metal heads, the casting of which might possibly reflect Ife influence. Many of the compositional groupings and artistic devices used on the Benin plaques are, in my opinion, visual quotations taken over by the brass-smiths from ivory carving.

The suggestion that Benin and Yoruba iconography have been in part influenced by Eastern Empire ideas in no way derogates the significance and importance for African art history of the Nigerian centers or the accomplishments of the leaders and artists of these areas. On the contrary, an attempt should always be made to clarify the past and thereby place the achievements of art and artists in a just and rational perspective. For to attribute a virtually autonomous development to all African art, as many scholars have done in a sort of crypto-nationalistic fashion, is just as counterproductive as the opposite course of ascribing everything African to outside influences. The comparative method stipulates no arbitrary geographical or intellectual limits, only the testing of data by juxtaposition and analysis. Africa's art is distinctly African,

11. Recent excavations in Nubia have unearthed evidence of late Classical influence there, most of which appears to stem from the Eastern Empire.

and there can be no doubt of its unique, beautiful, and wholly African properties. But we cannot hope to specify these features, nor to grasp their nature and significance without making an effort to discover what Africa has accepted as well as given.

The suggested Eastern Empire influences are not in fundamental conflict with Benin and Yoruba origin traditions, whatever value these may have. Both groups hold that their forefathers came ultimately from Nubia or Egypt, and both ascribe great antiquity to their own cultures. If valid, these accounts must refer, as Frank Willett (1960, p. 246) points out, not to the entire population but to the elite groups of leaders. Time and again small groups backed by military power have succeeded in setting themselves up as sovereigns over less tightly organized peoples.[12] Archaeology may some day shed light on this now unknown phase of Nigerian history, though the chances of locating emblems of divine kingship such as the fish-legged figure are rather slight (Thompson 1970; chapter 13 above, note 12). Until that time, we can only conjecture on the infusion of Eastern Empire traits into Nigeria—their significance for the development of leadership, the possible routes by which they came, and the modification effected upon them by local traditions. But if we are to progress toward a better understanding of Africa's rich and variegated past, we must be prepared to undertake such conjectural investigations. For only by being willing to speculate on possibilities will we be able to formulate hypotheses adequate to the complexity of the data; and only by testing and discarding insufficiently supported notions can we move forward on the strength of the more solidly grounded theories of Nigerian art.

12. The best example I know is the case of seventeen shipwrecked Spanish Negroes who established themselves as rulers in a portion of Ecuador in the sixteenth century, from which position the Spanish, despite their technological superiority, were unable to dislodge the ex-slaves for several decades (Estrada and Meggers 1961, pp. 935–936).

REFERENCES

ADHÉMAR, JEAN
1939   *Influences antiques dans l'art du Moyen Age Français.
               Recherches sur les sources et les thèmes d'inspiration.*
               Studies of the Warburg Institute, no. 7. London.
BALTRUŠAITIS, JURGIS
1931   *La stylistique ornementale dans la sculpture romane.*
               Paris.
BERNHEIMER, RICHARD
1931   *Romanische Tierplastik und die Ursprünge ihrer Motive.*
               Munich.
BOUTELL, CHARLES
1907   *English Heraldry.* 9th ed. London.
BRADBURY, R. E.
1957   *The Benin Kingdom and the Edo-speaking Peoples of
               South-Western Nigeria.* Ethnographic Survey of Africa.
               London.
1959   "Chronological Problems in the Study of Benin History."
               Journal of the Historical Society of Nigeria 1, no. 4:
               263–287.
1961   "Ezomo's *Ikegobo* and the Benin Cult of the Hand." *Man*
               61, art. 165: 129–138.
BROOKLYN MUSEUM
1960   *Egyptian Sculpture of the late period 700 B.C. to A.D. 100.*
               New York.
CIRLOT, JUAN-EDUARDO
1958   *Diccionario de símbolos tradicionales.* Barcelona.
COMBAZ, GISBERT
1937   *L'Inde et l'Orient classique.* 2 vols. Paris.
DARK, PHILIP
1957   "Benin: A West African Kingdom." *Discovery* [London].
               n.s., 18: 198–207.
1960   *Benin Art.* (With W. and B. Forman.) London.
1962   *The Art of Benin.* Catalogue. Field Museum of Natural
               History, Chicago.
DEONNA, WALDEMAR
1928   "La sirène, femme-poisson." *Revue Archéologique* 27.
               no. 5: 18–25.
1952   "Ouroboros." *Artibus Asiae* 15, no. 2: 163–170.
DYAKONOVA, H. B., AND SOROKIN, C. C.
1960   *Khotanskie Drevnocti [Khotan Antiquities].* Leningrad.
EGHAREVBA, JACOB
1960   *A Short History of Benin.* 3d ed. Ibadan. First published.
               1934.
ESTRADA, EMILIO, AND MEGGERS, BETTY
1961   "A Complex of Traits of Probable Transpacific Origin on
               the Coast of Ecuador." *American Anthropologist* 63, no.
               5: 913–939.

EYO, EKPO
1971   "Classical Terracottas from Owo." Lecture delivered at the "Symposium on Traditional African Art," Peabody Museum, Harvard University, May 7.

FAGG, WILLIAM B.
1951   "Tribal Sculpture and the Festival of Britain." *Man* 51, art. 124: 72–76.
1963   *Nigerian Images.* New York.

FAGG, WILLIAM, AND PLASS, MARGARET
1964   *African Sculpture, an Anthology.* London.

FORDE, CYRIL DARYLL
1951   *The Yoruba-Speaking Peoples of South-Western Nigeria.* Ethnographic Survey of Africa. London.
1965   "Tropical African Studies." *Africa* 35, no. 1: 30–97.

FRANKFORT, HENRI
1944   "A Note on the Lady of Birth." *Journal of Near Eastern Studies* 3: 198–200.
1954   *The Art and Architecture of the Ancient Orient.* Pelican History of Art. London.

FRASER, DOUGLAS
1962   *Primitive Art.* Garden City, N.Y.
1966   "The Heraldic Woman: A Study in Diffusion." In *The Many Faces of Primitive Art: A Critical Anthology,* edited by D. Fraser, pp. 36–99. Englewood Cliffs, N.J.
1968   *Village Planning in the Primitive World.* New York.

FROBENIUS, LEO
1913   *The Voice of Africa.* 2 vols. London. Translation of *Und Afrika sprach.* 3 vols. Berlin, 1912–13.

GÖBEL, HEINRICH
1923–34 *Wandteppische.* 3 vols. Vol. 2: *Die romanischen Länder.* Leipzig.

GOLDMAN, BERNARD
1960   "A Luristan Water Goddess." *Antike Kunst* 3. no. 2: 53–58.

GRIAULE, MARCEL
1938   *Masques dogons.* Travaux et mémoires de l'Institut d'Ethnologie. Vol. 33. Paris.

HACKIN, JOSEPH
1939   *Recherches archéologiques à Begram.* Paris.
1954   *Nouvelles recherches archéologique à Begram.* Paris.

HALL, H. R.
1928   "A Large Drum from Benin [Yoruba]." *The Museum Journal* 19. no. 2: 130–143.

HEINE-GELDERN, ROBERT
1954   "Die asiatische Herkunft der südamerikanischen Metalltechnik." *Paideuma* 5: 347–423.

HIMMELHEBER, HANS
1965   "Schmuckhaft überladene Negerplastik." *Paideuma* 11: 114–118.

HIND, A. M.
1938–48   *Early Italian Engraving.* 7 vols. London.
LUSCHAN, FELIX VON
1919   *Die Altertümer von Benin.* 3 vols. Berlin.
MORTON-WILLIAMS, PETER
1960a   "Yoruba Responses to the Fear of Death." *Africa* 30, no. 1: 34–40.
1960b   "The Yoruba Ogboni Cult in Oyo." *Africa* 30, no. 4: 362–374.
1964   "An Outline of the Cosmology and Cult Organization of the Oyo Yoruba." *Africa* 34, no. 3: 243–261.
MOULE, THOMAS
1842   *Heraldry of Fish.* London.
NICOLESCU, CORINA
1955/56   "Dekorative Keramik in der alter rümanischen Architektur." *Antiquity and Survival* 1, no. 6: 474–487.
PALAU MARTI, MONTSERRAT
1964   *Le roi-dieu au Bénin.* Paris.
PITT RIVERS, LT.-GEN. [LANE-FOX, A. H.]
1900   *Antique Works of Art from Benin.* London. Reprinted, 1968.
PORTER, A. KINGSLEY
1924   "Spain or Toulouse? and Other Questions." *Art Bulletin* 7: 3–26.
REINACH, SOLOMON
1908   *Répertoire de la statuaire grecque et romaine.* 4 vols. Paris.
ROTH, H. LING
1903   *Great Benin; Its Customs, Art and Horrors.* Halifax, England. Reprinted, New York, 1968.
RUBIN, ARNOLD
1970   Review of Frank Willett, *Ife in the History of West African Sculpture. Art Bulletin* 52, no. 3: 348–354.
RYDER, ALAN F. C.
1965   "A Reconsideration of the Ife-Benin Relationship." *The Journal of African History* 6, no. 1: 25–37.
1969   *Benin and the Europeans, 1485–1897.* New York.
SANTA, ELIZABETH DELLA
1958   "Deux remarquables ivoires nigériens de la collection de LL.AA. le Prince et la Princesse de Ligne au Chateau de Belœil." *Bulletin des Musées Royaux d'Art et d'Histoire* 30: 111–132.
SHAW, THURSTAN
1970   *Igbo-Ukwu: An Account of Archaeological Discoveries in Eastern Nigeria.* 2 vols. Evanston, Ill.
TALBOT, P. AMAURY
1926   *The Peoples of Southern Nigeria.* 4 vols. London.
THOMPSON, ROBERT F.
1969   "Abatan: A Master Potter of the Egbado Yoruba." In

Tradition and Creativity in Tribal Art, edited by Daniel Biebuyck, pp. 120–182. Berkeley.

1970   "The Sign of the Divine King: An Essay on Yoruba Bead-Embroidered Crowns with Veil and Bird Decorations." *African Arts/Arts d'Afrique* 3, no. 3: 8–17, 74–80. (See chapter 13 above.)

TONG, RAYMOND

1958   *Figures in Ebony; Past and Present in a West African City.* London.

TROESCHER, GEORG

1954   "Ein bayerisches Kirchenportal und sein Bilderkreis." *Zeitschrift für Kunstgeschichte*, n.s., 17: 1–60.

VERGER, PIERRE

1957   *Notes sur le culte des Orisa et Vodun.* Institut Français d'Afrique Noire, Mémoires, no. 51. Dakar.

VIENNOT, ODETTE

1958   "Le *makara* dans la décoration des monuments de l'Inde ancienne: positions et fonctions." *Arts Asiatiques* 5, no. 3: 183–206, 272–292.

VOLKMANN, LUDWIG

1923   *Bilderschriften der Renaissance. Hieroglyphik und Emblematik in ihren Beziehungen und Fortwirkungen.* Leipzig.

WAUGH, ARTHUR

1961   *Sea Enchantress: The Tale of the Mermaid and Her Kin.* London.

WILLETT, FRANK

1960   "Ife and Its Archaeology." *The Journal of African History* 1, no. 2: 231–248.

1967   *Ife in the History of West African Sculpture.* London.

1969   "New Light on the Ife-Benin Relationship." *African Forum* 3, no. 4/4, no. 1: 28–34.

1971   *African Art: An Introduction.* London.

WILLIAMS, DENIS

1964   "The Iconology of the Yoruba *edan Ogboni*." *Africa* 34, no. 2: 139–66.

WINGERT, PAUL

1950   *The Sculpture of Negro Africa.* New York.

WITTKOWER, RUDOLF

1938   "Eagle and Serpent: A Study in the Migration of Symbols." *Journal of the Warburg and Courtald Institutes* 2: 293–325.

Art and Leadership

AN OVERVIEW

Douglas Fraser and Herbert M. Cole

In all human societies, no matter how small or egalitarian, there are those who lead and those who follow. This is as true in Africa of small bands of Bushman or Pygmy hunters as it is of the powerful medieval Sudanic states or the more recent kingdom of Benin. Yet the functions performed by African leaders vary greatly. Some leaders may merely determine the auspicious time for planting or harvesting crops, while others may mobilize and direct vast armies for war. The acquisition of these various kinds of authority, although sanctioned by tradition, usually stems in part from individual physical skill, aggressiveness, wisdom, accidents of birth or death, plain good luck, or, more often, from a combination of these. What is common to all leaders is their influence over other people, whether this be in the moral, military, spiritual, economic, social, or political sectors of life.

Another characteristic of leaders is their ability to commission, control, and distribute works of art, and to inform them with meaning. But there is no single pattern of patronage associated with leaders in Africa; art here may be owned outright by the leader, or it may be held in trust by one or more leaders on behalf of special groups or the society at large.

In this overview, leadership is conceived of as operating on a broader, more public scale than is to be seen in mere private life. The nuclear family (parents and children) may be described basically as a nonpublic institution which concentrates on satisfying the immediate physical and emotional needs of its members; the head of such a family is not, in our terms, a leader. But should this family become involved in a jural dispute, say, over land inheritance, then the head of this household becomes a leader, albeit on an elementary level. The same man may of course also be the head of an extended family or lineage or the war chief of his community, and thus in other circumstances might well exercise a different kind of authority of far greater significance.

This mingling of several types of authority in one person is in fact one of the things that gives leadership much of its effectiveness. Thus, the power of leaders in Africa stems not only from their socio-political influence, but also from their religious primacy, economic power, and moral authority as well. A lineage head or chief is spokesman not merely for a social unit but also for its ancestors, of whom he is the living representative. Besides spiritual and judicial powers, moreover, leaders frequently control sizable amounts of wealth in their communities, whether in the form of land, cattle, women, gold, or other valuables. The capacity to bring more than one kind of pressure to bear on their followers is, then, characteristic of almost all African leaders.

However great or numerous an individual's powers may be, the range and effectiveness of his authority is tempered, and in large measure determined, by the nature of the socio-political system of which he is a part. Such systems are enormously varied in Africa and have not yet been satisfactorily classified into discrete types. Two general criteria, useful in comparing different systems, however, are (1) the degree of specialization and the relative distinctness of political roles and structures; and (2) the extent to which these roles, structures, and systems are autonomous from one another or are hieratically ranked (Almond and Powell 1966, p. 42). The differences may be dramatized by an examination of two distinct systems, that of the acephalous Lega people and that of the highly centralized Benin kingdom.

Among the Lega there are no specialized or autonomous political roles or institutions. Spiritual, moral, social, and economic powers are dispersed among all men, although members of the highest grades in the *bwami* society (see Biebuyck, chapter 1 above) play the most significant roles, politically and otherwise. The exercise of authority in Lega groups is intermittent and derives its sanctions from the group. For the Lega, then, it is more appropriate to speak of *influence* rather than of the power to coerce. Compared to the decentralization and lack of specialization in Lega life, the Benin socio-political system is centralized and highly differentiated. The Oba, a sacred king, is at the apex of an elaborate state organization, including a ranked court with specialized hereditary and appointed titles as well as craft and military guilds. Prior to the advent of colonial government, territorial rule and the collection of tribute were administered by titled appointees of the Oba, who had control over the lives of his people in such widely disparate realms as land tenure and spiritual observances. Away from the capital city, however, the complexity of administration decreased; local chiefdoms and villages had less differentiated, but still hieratic structures. Power in these instances was often expressed by means of an art object—especially a sword: "When the Oba delegated to a chief powers of life and death over his own subjects this was marked by the presentation to him of the ceremonial sword, *ada*" (Bradbury 1957, p. 41; see fig. 15.1). Other African societies such as the Akan, Fon, and Kuba have also imbued ceremonial swords with political power, usually by greatly elaborating their forms at the expense of all practical function.

Another way of observing socio-political systems and roles that is especially relevant to our subject is to examine the degree to which the component parts are visible. Undifferentiated or segmentary systems tend to conceal leadership structures so much that anthropologists sometimes have difficulty in ". . . distinguishing the means by which the relations of government . . . are instituted and sanctioned" (Middleton and Tait 1958, p. 2). In such societies, represented here by the Ibo (Cole and Ottenberg, chapters 5 and 6 above) as well as the Lega, there are usually few easily identified leaders, or at least leadership is intermittent and shifts among the spiritual, moral, economic, and social spheres. Nor does any obvious machinery exist for legislation, adjudication, and the implementation of decisions. A community consists of more or less autonomous segments, usually lineages, bound together by certain common interests such as territorial claims, historical traditions, and other values. Symbols of these larger interests may be invoked in time of crisis—war or initiation, for example—as a means of uniting segments to achieve shared goals; but once these ends have been reached, individual segments reassert their normal independence as coordinate socio-political units. Role specialization and division of labor are minimal in these groups, although religious specialists are sometimes quite visible and thus tend to have leadership positions. More frequently, primary influence is vested in the heads of autonomous institutions (such as lineages and local cults) or not in "visible" individuals at all but in whole groups, such as the elders, village councils, or secret societies, or in institutions such as oracles. Art forms identified with these groups are generally "held in trust" for the community and are seldom, if ever, owned outright by individuals. Nevertheless, some degree of influence and prestige usually adheres to those who act as trustees.

FIGURE 15.1. Benin. Decorated ceremonial sword *ada* from Benin City. Swords of this type were given by the Oba to outstanding warrior chiefs. Field Museum of Natural History, Chicago (99492). Ht. 34″ (86.4 cm). (Photograph: Museum.)

Almost all African societies may be placed somewhere on the socio-political continuum that extends from the acephalous systems on the one hand to those such as Benin that show strong differentiation and visibility of structure on the other. Examples of intermediate societies discussed in this book would include the BaKwele and Chokwe, who have chiefs but no elaborate administrative mechanisms, and the Baule, who have fairly strong chiefs, councils of noblemen, and other elaborate socio-political concepts, but whose institutions lack the size, range, and complexity of systems seen among the parent Ghanaian Akan states. On this continuum Cameroons Grasslands kingdoms, with their specialized roles and administrative structures, probably take a place closer to the Ashanti, in fact, than do the Baule.

Just as individual leaders and administrative units are more highly visible in differentiated societies, so too are the elitist functions of their art forms more easily recognized. Paramount leaders often have "paramount" art forms: the Golden Stool, the Kuba commemorative *ndop* figures, and the Oba and Queen Mother heads at Benin. Hierarchically organized socio-political systems usually have a visible hierarchy of art objects (including regalia) which reflect and uphold ranked social positions. A network of roles calls for a network of symbols.

Whether or not a society's degree of political differentiation is reflected precisely in its artistic forms is often difficult to say. Are the nuances and complexities of the leadership sphere sufficiently related to those of the visual domain to link the two in a cause-and-effect manner? The most obvious barrier to such a theory is the uneven distribution of the arts in Africa: one leader may express values or power with a stone or a bundle of magical substances, while his counterpart elsewhere may employ a sculptured form. Another problem is the relative "interchangeability" of the arts in Africa: where one leader may mobilize plastic forms to achieve some end, another, in a comparable situation, may call upon oral arts, music, or the dance.

A METHOD OF STUDY

Since the serious study of African sculpture began some thirty-five years ago, art historians and anthropologists have almost invariably classified this art into "tribal" style areas. This method is still used to clarify local styles and substyles, sometimes down to the level of the individual artist. Valuable as the style-area approach is for certain kinds of geographical classification and description, it is largely irrelevant here since by definition the stylistic nuances that characterize the art of one region will not appear in another area.

Ours must be a comparative study, and to achieve this, we need to be able to juxtapose or contrast art objects—indeed whole classes of forms associated with leaders—without respect for tribal boundaries and style differences. Thus we are less interested in what makes a stool or door specifically Yoruba or Senufo or Igala than we are in the common denominators present in each class and in the ways these classes are associated with leaders in each culture. These ends can perhaps best be reached by isolating three dimensions of African art which exist in all objects, all styles, and all areas. These dimensions—*structure, func-*

tion, and *history*—have the advantage of being separable for analysis, though in African life they are inextricably bound together. A. R. Radcliffe-Brown (1952, pp. 185–186) has demonstrated this in a revealing analogy:

There is not, and cannot be, any conflict between the functional hypothesis and the view that any culture, any social system, is the end-result of a unique series of historical accidents. The process of development of the race-horse from its five-toed ancestor was a unique series of historical accidents. This does not conflict with the view of the physiologist that the horse of today and all its antecedent forms conform or conformed to physiological laws, i.e. to the necessary conditions of organic existence. Paleontology and physiology are not in conflict. One "explanation" of the race-horse is to be found in its history—how it came to be just what it is and where it is. Another and entirely independent "explanation" is to show how the horse is a special exemplification of physiological laws. Similarly one "explanation" of a social system will be its history, where we know it—the detailed account of how it came to be what it is and where it is. Another "explanation" of the same system is obtained by showing that it is a special exemplification of laws of social physiology or social functioning. The other two kinds of explanation do not conflict, but supplement one another.

The usefulness of structure, function, and history for comparative studies of African art may be illustrated by examining a *duen fobara* of the Kalabari Ijaw people of the Niger Delta (fig. 15.2). These large wooden reliefs are screen-like constructions of rectangular shape, the central figure of which represents a deceased head of a "trading house" (now an ancestor), who is flanked by dependents or followers. The screens are, in a sense, semipermanent genealogical records as well as reminders of the special prerogatives (for example, the headpieces, which are also represented) favored by the dead man in life (Horton 1965, p. 34). These objects are sometimes placed in shrines visited by women who wish to have children and are also taken outdoors for use in funerals. In the *duen fobara,* the hieratic scale of the figures, their plaque-like organization, and the use of heraldic flanking all probably indicate influence stemming from the art of Benin, especially the bronze plaques (cf. Baumann 1969, p. 21). At the same time, other structural features of the Ijaw image are clearly not of Benin derivation: the angularity of the figures, the nonorganic rhythmic shaping of forms, the constructivist aesthetic of assembling the object out of many small pieces of wood are structural features not found in Benin but shared by the Ijaw with Ibo and Ibibio-speaking groups in and near the delta. A further historical ramification is the rectangular framing of the screen, which, according to William Fagg (1963, p. 110), probably reflects European

FIGURE 15.2. Kalabari Ijaw. Ancestral screen *duen fobara*. Pitt Rivers Museum, Oxford (65.8.9). Ht. 44.8″ (114 cm). (Photograph: Museum.)

influence. Functionally, too, the *duen fobara* departs from the Benin plaques, which were commemorative castings intended mainly to enhance and ornament the pillars of the Oba's compound. We must therefore consider each dimension—structure, function, and history—separately if we are to gain a better understanding of what is truly characteristic of the arts associated with leadership.

Structure and function differ in one important respect from history. Information on structure and function is almost always available from the art form itself and its context. Historical explanations, on the other hand, are relatively rare in Africa because in most cases we see only the end product of the historical process, earlier solutions having perished. The history of art forms in Africa is, in the main, highly problematical. Historical relationships may be suggested by evidence derived from structure and function as in the *duen fobara,* but there are numerous pitfalls in such an approach. Some masks from the Yaka and Pende people of the Congo will clarify this point.

Both the Yaka and Pende employ numerous masks in "plays" performed at the conclusion of the youths' initiation rites. In both areas, however, there is at least one distinctive mask-type that does not take part in these festivities. The Yaka mask known as *kakunga* is made by a priest and, along with a consort-mask, is kept in a special hut. The high priest of the initiation or one of his aides wears it infrequently to inspire terror in the youths. *Kakunga* masks are large, vertical shapes with features formed by a series of horizontally zoned bulges; they differ markedly in appearance and use from the *tundansi* masks, which are the ones worn or carried by Yaka initiates at the termination of their bush-school training period. The Pende also have a mask known as *giphogo* which differs radically from other types used in the same villages. These *giphogo* are large polychrome (or, more rarely, monochrome) helmet masks which are kept in the chief's hut along with other valuable objects. Like the *kakunga, giphogo* represents high authority, and it promotes fertility, drives away evil, cures illness, appears at the chief's investiture, and accomplishes other things which the smaller and more numerous boys' masks cannot perform. Now in size, shape, and use the Yaka *kakunga* and Pende *giphogo* vaguely recall certain masks from the Chokwe and Luba which are also used in leadership contexts. But historical evidence for such connections is completely lacking. On the other hand, without raising the possibility of historical relationships, which may someday be corroborated (or denied), we cannot even begin to reconstruct a history of African art.

STRUCTURE

The term *structure,* as used here, refers to all the physical properties of art objects—their materials, form, and design—as well as to the various relationships of parts to one another and to the whole. Style and iconography, since they relate to the formal properties of an object, also enter into the structural analysis of art.

A few controlling and pervasive structural principles seem to be characteristic of all the arts associated with leaders, regardless of the type of socio-political system in which they are found. One principle is *contrast,* by which is meant the degree to which leaders' arts stand apart from those of lesser leaders or of the common people. The idea of contrast is perhaps best measured by means of another pervasive structural principle, that of *elaboration.* Invariably, the art objects owned by leaders (or held in trust by them for the common people) are more elaborate than the ordinary, run-of-the-mill objects in the same culture. The numerous ancestor figures of the Baule and Dogon, for instance, are relatively small and uncomplicated standing figures. A few examples, however, are given considerable elaboration, including seated poses, unusual hand positions, stools, jewelry, and complicated hairdressing. These elite figures are characterized by greater size and by more precise attention to detail. Thus, the principles of contrast and elaboration seem to carry in their train such other structural principles as *monumentality* and *particularization* (i.e., largeness and smallness).

The structural properties of leadership objects may also be examined with respect to media and technique of fabrication. African art, of course, is overwhelmingly an art in wood. By contrast, objects in ivory, bronze, brass, or gold, and overlaid beadwork—relatively scarce and often refractory substances requiring specialized techniques of exploitation—are far more limited in distribution, and their appearance generally heralds the presence of leaders. In Owo Yoruba, Benin, and Cameroons, for instance, only the sovereigns (and sometimes their immediate subordinates) are entitled to own or use ivory objects. Among the Lega, Kongo, and Luba, ivory neckrests and pendants also serve elitist purposes. Yet some Congo peoples, such as the Pende, have ivory amulets which are tokens of initiation and reciprocal relations with ancestors and which do not seem to be elitist objects.

African objects in gold, silver, bronze, and brass generally stem from West Guinea Coast societies that have highly visible leadership structures, such as the Baule, the Ghanaian kingdoms, Fon, Yoruba (Ife as well as modern city-states), Benin, and Jukun. The metal objects from these areas are almost always more complex than the corresponding wooden forms. Lost wax (*cire perdue*) castings, which are particularly characteristic of these courtly societies, require highly specialized production techniques. But the demanding nature of this medium has not restricted its exploitation to aristocratic cultures alone. Dan-Kran, Senufo, Bobo, Tiv, and other less centralized peoples also cast objects in brass; yet, in keeping with the character of their socio-political structures, the objects produced in these areas are comparatively simple and unrefined and are not invariably connected with leaders.

Beadwork of various sorts also seems to be an elite medium, particularly in the Cameroons, where it overlies many sorts of objects used by the nobility (see Rudy, chapter 7 above), and in Yorubaland, where beaded crowns are the most significant single emblem of divine kingship (see Thompson, chapter 13 above). Bead appliqués are found also on masks worn by dancers among the highly centralized Kuba peoples. Most (but not all) of these masks function in court-associated roles.

Characteristic of leaders, too, is their desire (and ability) to possess objects in durable materials, objects which when passed down to future generations will reflect the prestige of the line. To some extent this explains the importance of gold and silver, which in Africa are joined by bronze and brass; all four metals may be contrasted with iron, which has been known in Africa for millennia and is used primarily for weapons, implements for agriculture, and other tools—but is rarely artistically elaborated, apart from some areas in Nigeria and the Western Sudan. While there is no clear explanation for this gap, it is worth noting that Robert F. Thompson (1968, pp. 44–45, 63–66) has called attention to the existence among the Yoruba of various aesthetic criteria including smoothness, shininess, and coolness; these aesthetic qualities, lacking in iron work, are especially notable in the four metals and in ivory and beadwork.

Throughout Africa, but especially in the courtly centers, leaders have been responsible for the *proliferation* of art objects and of types and varieties within a single type. Thus the Ashanti and Benin courts and those of the Yoruba and Cameroons kings have seen to it that even items of clothing (sandals, textiles, hats, and jewelry) are so elaborated as to be distinct art objects. The countless swords, staffs, fly whisks, stools, vessels, neckrests, amulets, gold weights, and cosmetic and treasure boxes found in such societies illustrate the multiplication of types or classes of objects.

The tendency toward proliferation may be seen within one of these classes alone. The variety of Benin staffs is paralleled or even exceeded by the proliferation of stools among Akan and related peoples. Both types of objects are status symbols associated with particular ranks or titles; stools among the Akan may even be categorized according to the various activities—traveling, eating, sitting in state, bathing, etc.—in which they are used by their leader/owners. Among somewhat less centralized groups, such as the Pende or Luba, stools and staffs are also associated with chiefs, but here the observable variations appear to reflect regional style differences rather than progressive steps in an administrative hierarchy.

Proliferation of detail (or particularization) in single art objects is also an elite characteristic. It reaches its climax in Africa perhaps in Ashanti containers (*kuduo*) and Benin shrines of the hand (*ikegobo*). One famous *kuduo* (see Fraser, chapter 8, figs. 8.5, 8.6) depicts a ruler smoking a long pipe while being entertained by court musicians; the complexity of this grouping answers exactly to the proliferation of ornamental detail. The chief is the largest figure present, his attendants diminishing in size according to their relative social positions; he is further distinguished from the subordinates by his centrality and frontality —structural principles which also may be observed in Benin ivories and bronzes. This strongly suggests, therefore, that complexity of grouping and proliferation of detail correspond in the aesthetic realm to the elaboration and differentiation of roles and institutions in the socio-political sphere.

Complex compositions with a profusion of detail also frequently show a tendency toward exquisite execution, a structural feature which seems largely confined to the rarified atmospheres of courts. Such exquisiteness is seen in many of the ivory and bronze or brass objects from Nigerian courts, in the tooling of Ashanti silver appliqué—in the fastidious geometric patterns on Kuba cups and cosmetic boxes. The cast-gold pendants and amulets of the Baule, with their delicate surface treatment and occasional filigree work, also illustrate this penchant for fine detail. Miniature masks of metal or ivory worn as pectorals or hip ornaments or attached to clothing are another of the highly detailed art forms associated with many West African courts and some Congolese cultures. The use of intricate detail perhaps conveys a sense of precision, order, and discipline which appeals to leaders.

The art of African elites is almost always more complex iconographically than that of the common people. Specifically courtly themes include the representation of processions, royal animals, buildings, hunting (as a royal sport or ritual), and vegetation; such imagery almost never appears in nonleadership contexts. Another elite genre, seen especially in the Western Sudan and eastern Guinea Coast areas, is the equestrian statue. The rider is often identified as a leading warrior or god in Yoruba and Dogon art, and as a spirit being or important visitor in Senufo and Benin. The horse, like a stool or litter, elevates the leader physically and socially above his people.

Nonrepresentational designs such as the guilloche and "endless knot" also constitute an aspect of aristocratic iconography. Regrettably this subject has received little attention from students of African arts. But it can be no accident that apart from Islamic contributions, which are pronounced in northern Ghana, Nigeria, and the Cameroons and throughout the Western Sudan, Africa's most complex ornamental designs are concentrated in the courtly societies—Akan, Benin, Yoruba, Kongo, and Kuba. The presence of related designs among such central Congo tribes as the Dengese, Biombo, and Lele may be attributed to Kuba influence.

To the best of our knowledge the African artist never attempts *mimesis,* the exact imitation of life forms, as seen in certain Hellenistic, Roman, and Renaissance works. There is *some* correlation, however, between the extent of naturalism favored in a given culture and its degree of socio-political differentiation. Least imitative forms, on the whole, are found among such segmentary or acephalous peoples as the Lega, Ngbaka, or Bobo, whose art is usually quite conventionalized. Such peoples as the Mende, Chokwe, Luba, and Senufo, who have chiefs, produce a more naturalistic sort of art. The brass heads of Ife discussed in chapter 12 by Frank Willett probably represent the climax of this tradition. Yet important exceptions appear, particularly in the case of the extremely naturalistic skin-covered heads of the Ekoi and related Cross River peoples, all of whom are politically fragmented.

Granting that some of Africa's most naturalistic images stem from highly centralized societies such as Ife, Benin, Ashanti, Cameroons Grasslands, and Kuba, the fact remains that in these realistic courtly styles, naturalism is always blended with idealism. Ife heads, perhaps the most sensitive naturalistic "portraits" in Africa, never show any distinguishing blemishes, facial wrinkles indicative of age, or emotional expressions. Nor can such idiosyncrasies be found in the Kuba king "portraits," the gold mask-head of the Ashanti king Kofi Kakari, or in the impersonal Benin images; beside the vast numbers of idealized conventionalized faces of the Oba and his retainers, the acute individualism of two Benin court-dwarf sculptures is exceptional. Historical and functional arguments may be set forward to explain why idealized naturalism is so characteristic of these courtly styles; suffice it to say here that this is another general structural principle of the arts associated with African leaders.

Leaders themselves may be physically affected in a number of ways by the art forms with which they are linked. The bulk of the structural changes so affected can be subsumed under three main headings: elevation, protection, and extension.

The *elevation* of a leader is usually achieved by means of a stool, chair, cushion, sandals, or palanquin. Of these, stools are by far the most widely distributed, suggesting they must have had a long history in Africa; perhaps because of this, stools are not always leaders' prerogatives. Traders' stools, for example, are commonplace in West Africa, although they rarely qualify as works of art. In Ghana, the most "stool-conscious" region in Africa, even small children have their own seats. Nevertheless, the stools owned by Ghanaian leaders are almost invariably larger and more highly embellished than those of common people. Exceptional stools in fact always connote leadership. The Manikongo, ruler of the ancient Kongo Kingdom, was seated on a stool made of ivory when he received the Portuguese explorer Diogo Cão in 1482. Even more extraordinary are the quartz stools found in various sites in Ife and doubtless connected with ancient Onis.

Chairs of "traditional" design, also used as elevating devices, are of relatively limited distribution in Africa, having been introduced by Europeans in the early years of contact. Ghanaian tribes (see figs. 9.5 and 10.1) employ these chairs as leadership symbols, each having its own designs and attributed meanings. The Golden Stool of the Ashanti is even enthroned on a chair of its own (see fig. 8.1). Perhaps of greater aesthetic interest than Ghanaian chairs are those used in the southern Congo by Chokwe, Lunda, Pende, and other chiefs. These chairs do not depart greatly from their Renaissance European models even though the Chokwe in particular decorate every available rung and flat surface of the chair with carvings (see fig. 2.5). As many as eight or ten tiny human or animal figures may be crowded together on one rung, where they engage in scenes based on ritual and everyday life. These chair carvings are among the most complex figural designs produced in the entire Congo.

In addition to stools and chairs, rulers use cushions, sandals, and litters as means of elevation. Geometrically embossed or embroidered leather cushions are found almost exclusively in areas of strong Islamic influence. Decorated sandals are worn in many regions in order to raise the leader above the ground. In the Akan areas of Ghana and the Ivory Coast, the forcible removal of the leader's golden sandals from his feet (bringing him in contact with the polluting earth) signifies his deposition. Palanquins are associated with the nobility in several parts of Africa, though the most elaborate examples are found in Ghana. All these devices serve to give the leader both real and psychological separation whereby he achieves a kind of isolation from the ordinary people, who lack his spatial elevation.

There are two classes of objects that provide *protection* for leaders, shielding or sheltering devices, and architecture. Umbrellas or canopies have shaded the heads of kings in Africa since at least the time of the ancient Mali empire (ca. A.D. 1050–1400), when the Muslim chroniclers Al Omari (ca. 1336) and Ibn Battuta (1352) described these symbols of state. Both authors record that Mali umbrellas were topped with gold birds, precisely the type of finial that now crowns certain Ghanaian canopies (see fig. 8.4). Fon, Yoruba, Benin, and Cameroons rulers also sit under state umbrellas, while other sheltering art forms such as caps, crowns, ceremonial robes, shields, and armor are even more widespread.

The protection provided by architecture is, of course, of a more stationary and permanent sort than that of umbrellas or items of clothing. Important leaders in Africa invariably seem to have the most elaborate compounds (with heavier and taller walls than those of commoners) and often added decorative features, such as houseposts, lintels, reliefs (in mud, wood, or brass), and doors. Court centers in Ashanti, Dahomey, and Benin have had massive and monumental architecture which appears, in its relative permanence, to symbolize the enduring character of divine kingship. Both architecture and umbrellas or canopies tend to create isolating spatial envelopes for leaders that, like elevating devices, separate them conceptually from the mundane, everyday world.

Extension is a more abstract idea than either elevation or protection, and we use it to describe the spatial, physical, and auditory changes wrought when a leader manipulates some kind of implement, either directly or indirectly. Swords and other weapons, it is obvious, can be construed as symbolic (or actual) extensions of the leader's physical power; in Ashanti and Benin ceremonial swords are carried by special retainers, just as is a mace in European parliamentary and academic processions. Other objects which extend the figurative or actual reach of rulers include staffs, bells, gongs, fly whisks, ceremonial adzes, and pipes, which may be used to announce the leader's coming or may be manipulated by him, almost like a European lady's fan, as a theatrical prop to call attention to himself and to communicate nonverbally his relative pleasure or displeasure. Thompson (personal communication) has described instances of this where the leader shakes his decorated fly whisk encouragingly at his followers in a manner almost identical to the leader/chorus responsorial pattern characteristic of so many African musical cultures. Thus, to understand fully the reciprocities between the structure of these art forms and the leaders who use them, we must now begin to look at the objects in the light of their function.

FUNCTION

Like structure, function is an extremely flexible concept. The functional approach to an art object includes an examination not only of its purposes and uses, but also of the reactions people have to it and why they respond as they do. Thus, the simple statement, "The function of this art object is to enhance the power of the chief," fails utterly to convey the complexity of the situation. For the function of an object depends both on its nature and on the particular context in which it is viewed; and since leaders' objects, more than most, frequently operate in several different contexts simultaneously, functional analysis is often a matter of great complexity. To describe an object's function, then, is to articulate the ramified roles it plays in the varying interactions of different persons and groups with it.

A number of the structural principles associated with leadership arts find counterparts in the functional realm. Such structural ideas as elevation, protection, and extension epitomize the notion of *detachment* or isolation which is inherent in the role of leader and therefore an aspect of the functioning of art associated with him.

The concept of *visibility* is applicable equally to structure and function. Personal regalia, elaborate architecture and furnishings, and various objects used by leaders render them more conspicuous and thus enhance their superior status and power to control. The visible contrast between a leader's person and environment and that of his followers provides visual corollary to their socio-political differentiation. A basic function of these arts, then, is to set off in many ways (including aesthetically) the elite from common people.

At the same time, leaders must maintain rapport with those they lead. Art forms further this purpose in a variety of ways. For example, in major Yoruba towns such as Oyo, Abeokuta, Ado Ekiti, and Owo and at Abomey and Benin huge palace precincts act as assembly-points for major rituals involving the king as *rex et sacerdos* of his people. In other instances, such as the great Ashanti Odwira yam festival (see fig. 8.4), art objects are displayed in carefully orchestrated sequences designed in part to maintain aesthetic interest in what is at root a lengthy spiritual observance. This is also true of the masquerading attending the investiture of a minor chief or the funeral of an important man in other societies. Spiritual fealty and political allegiance are renewed and publically recorded, while the dramatic intensity of the ceremony satisfies the emotional and aesthetic need for spectacle, contrast, and significant performance.

But the leader remains the patron. Like a Caesar, he provides both bread and circuses, and in the socio-economic web of gift exchange and redistribution, he keeps the upper hand. Tribute in goods and money from the people usually precedes the ceremony, but the resulting feast emanates from the leader. His control of wealth also enables him to reward the faithful with political privileges which are often expressed in the form of art objects. Compact, permanent, and obtainable only through the chief's patronage, these make treasured documents of service (see Bravmann, chapter 9 above) or emblems of acquired rank or title; as such, they function as ideal reminders of the socio-political hierarchy and of close relations with its source, the paramount leader.

The use of art objects in maintaining rapport extends even into foreign policy. In Iboland (see Cole, chapter 5 above) decorated elephant tusks ensure the safe passage of a titled man in alien communities, while the carrying of certain weapons (swords and *récades*) with emblems by emissaries of the Ashanti and Fon kings conveyed a specific meaning (such as a declaration of war) to the leaders of neighboring states. The high-water mark of Benin City's influence, which probably occurred in the seventeenth and eighteenth centuries, is still evident from the possession of Benin art forms, notably brass pectoral masks, in such remote places as Idah (Igalaland) and Oreri (Iboland, near Igbo-Ukwu). The historical relationship between Ife and Benin, which according to oral tradition predates the sixteenth century, seems to have been expressed largely in terms of art objects. Thus, aesthetic considerations enter into the maintenance of social and political ties with remote and alien peoples.

The basic functions of political leaders in Africa, as elsewhere, are regulation (the controlling of behavior), adjudication (the making and enforcing of legal decisions), distribution (the handing out of material and intangible rewards), and socialization (education and edification by example). Art objects contribute to all of these functions, though, of course, to different degrees.

A great many art objects from African cultures play a major part in the regulation of the societies in question. These objects range from the Lega ivory figures (see Biebuyck, chapter 1 above), with their moralizing lessons, and the satirical masks of southeastern Nigeria (see Ottenberg, chapter 6 above) to certain masks, which have executive roles, used among the Mano, Igala, Bambara, and Idoma peoples, as discussed by George W. Harley (1950) and Roy Sieber (1966). It is important to note here, though, that autocratic or dictatorial power is in fact extremely rare in sub-Saharan African societies. Thus while some masquerades among the Ibo and Ibibio are organized by important elders to extol the beneficence and spiritual power of a tutelary spirit, the same "plays," enacted by younger age-sets, may also ridicule capricious or arbitrary actions taken by important elders or even the elders as a group (see Ottenberg above). Many of the Ashanti objects discussed by Douglas Fraser (chapter 8 above) embody proverbs designed to hold in check the power of the king.

Regulative functions in Africa, particularly in less centralized societies, are often performed by masks. Nowhere is this more dramatically apparent than in the Liberian secret societies, where masked figures serve as judges, executioners, gods, and chiefs, as well as debt collectors, policemen, and other minor officials. Some of these mask-roles are essentially civil and are concerned only with everyday affairs; others represent ultimate spiritual power and could order the taking of human life. Harley (1950, p. 17), speaking of the power held by the custodians of important masks, notes: "Each [custodian] was a big man in ordinary life, but a bigger man because of the secret power conferred on him through the ancestral mask of which he was the keeper. To help him in his work of judging and ruling his people, each had a number of associates who were of some importance in daily life; but they were also of more importance when they functioned as wearers of masks."

Many kinds of art, apart from masks, may contribute to the regulation of behavior. Ghanaian state swords and Lega figurines, for example, sometimes evoke the ideal qualities of a good leader; on one Ashanti state sword is depicted a viper with a bird in its mouth which means, "It is said the viper never attacks without provocation" (Kyerematen 1964, p. 37); in other words, a ruler never acts arbitrarily. Ashanti linguists' staffs, topped by a carving of a hand holding an egg, caution the leader against clutching his power either too tightly or too loosely (Kyerematen 1964, p. 95). Lega figurines wtih multiple heads, as Daniel Biebuyck (chapter 1 above) relates, always signify "The man with many big heads who has seen an elephant on the other side of the large river," a reference to the wisdom and far-sightedness of Lega leaders. These instances of the use of art to encourage good leadership are rather subtle; by contrast, certain Ashanti state swords, when presented to enemies, are nothing less than declarations of war. Similarly, among some Yoruba groups, a particular pair of brass castings (*edan Ogboni*) belonging to the Ogboni society, when given to two adversaries, command them to perform purification rites to obviate sacrilege. Examples could be multiplied; suffice it to say that art forms contribute to the regulating of human conduct in many ways in most parts of Africa.

Adjudication, as a function for art objects, is closely related to regulation. The "Poro" masks identified as "judges" are perhaps the best examples, but the Dan, Ibo, Igala, Senufo, and Bambara, to name a few, also employ masquerades to settle rival claims. Divination and oracles, both of which may involve art forms, also express the judgments of supernatural authorities. In the not-too-distant past ordeals might have been used to decide judicial cases; frequently, this required the presence of a fetish or "power figure." In Africa, therefore, spiritual power and civil power are almost always so intertwined that a decision made in reality by a leader will also seem to have overwhelming sanction from the ancestors or other spirit beings.

Leaders usually have the capacity to *distribute* goods, honors, and statuses to their subjects. The most important function of art in this regard seems to be the differentiation of roles. In the elaborate courtly societies a great many distinct roles must be identified; hence it follows that courtly art forms are more numerous and specialized than is the case in acephalous, loosely organized groups. Yet as the chapters on the Lega (Biebuyck, chapter 1) and Ibo (Cole, chapter 5 and Ottenberg, chapter 6) indicate, segmentary societies are also prone to use art— especially items of personal regalia—as a means of defining roles. By making political rank, occupational specialty, or social status visible, art reflects and reinforces the prevailing socio-political system.

The distributive function of art has particular meaning when leadership status is transferred from one person to another. This occurs when offices and titles are delegated anew and upon the death of an encumbent. The moment the new leader is invested with the material signs and symbols of his rank, his authority is legitimized and validated. Taking on regalia is therefore really tantamount to beginning a new life; should these symbols be destroyed or taken away, however, the experience is equivalent in a ritual sense to death.

If the distributive role of art expresses its capacity to divide, *socialization* emphasizes its unifying and integrating functions. By socialization is meant the education of the people, especially the young, to prevailing values and attitudes so they may be productive members of the society. The fundamental significance of art in the socializing process is its value in helping leaders to communicate with their followers. Hence socialization is involved in the transmission of socio-political messages between people, including the identification and legitimization of rank and the maintenance of contact and rapport. A more specific kind of socialization, however, is the education of the young through initiation rites which may employ a wide variety of art objects, particularly masks. Initiations illuminate the social order, often through mythological "teachings" about cosmogony, the origins of the gods and people, and their division into hierarchies or discrete social units. Masked dances frequently re-enact these cosmic and human beginnings for the edification of the young. In general, the mythology embodies an idealized model of social, political, and religious values which are expressed more concretely in masquerade performances.

The socializing functions of masked dances are found in nearly all cultures which employ masquerades. The well-known *chi-wara* ("working wild animal") dances of the Bambara will serve as an illuminating example. Bringing to mind a mythic creature who taught the people agriculture, these antelope headdresses appear in pairs in the fields during the times when communal farming is done; they represent all the positive values attributed by the Bambara to agriculture and are intended to help the youths become productive members of the group by encouraging them to strive toward the farming ideal, *chi-wara*.

The education or socialization process is, of course, not limited to masquerades. As A. A. Y. Kyerematen (1964, p. 1) has written: "For a people who never themselves developed the art of writing, the regalia of Ghanaian chiefs have been of special significance in that they have not been merely symbols of the kingly office but have served as the chronicles of early history and the evidence of traditional religion, cosmology, and social organization." Just as written documents materialize history in literate communities, so in traditional societies, art forms make the intangible past more real.

Structural factors such as tangibility, durability, the use of rich materials, and iconography also contribute to the symbolic power of visual art forms. The dance, oral recitation, ritual, and music, while of the utmost importance, are fugitive, transitory art forms; they may be performed frequently and greatly valued, but they cannot be consecrated, rubbed, enshrined, worn, delegated, or continuously contemplated. Nor can these art forms specify the appearance of a deity in the way the plastic arts do. Once created, visual forms persist; other arts exist only in performance or memory. Hence, the physical properties of plastic art contribute to its function as an effective, as well as an affective, symbol.

Leaders everywhere reinforce their temporal authority with sanctions drawn from the realm of supernatural forces, whether ancestors, spirits, legendary heroes, or gods. Spiritual hierarchies can be made explicit through art, and so leaders are often at pains to see that supernaturals are properly "brought to life" in images. The very presence of such images, not to mention the sacrifices and other rites surrounding them, serves a socializing role by expressing origins, obligations, values, and the ways of the gods to man. Indeed, such art forms materialize and dramatize what are in many ways the most important leaders in Africa—the otherwise unseen ancestors and deities.

Some thirty years ago, two Africanists wrote: "Members of an African society feel their unity and perceive their common interest in symbols, and it is their attachment to these symbols which more than anything gives their society cohesion and persistence" (Fortes and Evans-Pritchard 1941, p. 17). Now if a symbol may be described as an entity which evokes associations and meanings beyond its own intrinsic existence, clearly artifacts used in rituals, natural objects, music, and mythology convey symbolic associations. Can we doubt that the symbolic force of an Ashanti Odwira ceremony or the appearance of a Benin Oba is not tremendously enhanced by the rich majesty of regalia? Images are receptacles of historical association, spiritual values, and socio-political ideals, the apprehension and understanding of which hinges on the experience and knowledge of the individual viewer. Thus art forms may be described as devices for encrypting in brief space many messages, not all of which are intelligible to any single person. The strength of such symbols lies precisely in the fact that powerful social and psychological bonds are forged between those who hold keys to one or more of the same codes.

Why does an art object become a valued symbol? One factor that apparently contributes to meaningfulness is *uselessness*. The symbolic value of art objects often seems to vary in inverse proportion to their functional utility. Thus in Ghana the most important stool is the one which is *not* sat upon, the most effective weapons, those *not* used in war. The efficacy of a Yoruba or Cameroons chief's housepost carvings is not a consequence of their supporting capacity. But we must look beyond physical inutility to establish the full symbolic force of a leader's object.

Not all symbols, of course, are equally potent. The most important art forms are probably those with the most facets, the greatest variety of symbolic associations. Title insignia and prestige objects in noncourtly societies—for example, a minor Chokwe chief's stool or a Yaka neck-rest—would be examples of rather limited or "small" symbols. Highly differentiated socio-political systems, on the other hand, must create symbols powerful enough to carry over great distances, to the margins of the realm. Relatively few such objects are needed, though, as evidenced by the success of the Ashanti Golden Stool, perhaps because many messages may be encrypted in a single object, allowing differing interpretations in various provincial areas.

The climax of African art—in the functional sense—probably occurs in such symbols of leadership as the Ashanti Golden Stool, the brass Oba heads from Benin, and Kuba king figures, each of which embodies manifold religious, political, ideological, and historical associations. The commemorative statue of the great Kuba king Shyaam (see Vansina, chapter 3 and fig. 3.2 above), for example, makes direct iconographic reference to personal grandeur, political solidarity, prosperity, and the peace of the nation, and symbolic allusions to fertility and economic constraint. This highly charged image also projects Kuba notions of the nature of history, art, and the institution of divine kingship. Such a symbol may be said to be an epitome of the aesthetic, religious, ethical, and social values of an entire society.

HISTORY

History may be broadly defined as changes that occur in structure and function through time. But the study of history is neither the search for regular ordering principles, as in structural analysis, nor the investigation of functional roles and meanings in varying contexts. Rather, the historian tries to offer a plausible accounting for origins and for the changes separating an earlier from a later situation or state. This means, of course, that as well as dealing with regularity, he constantly concerns himself with chance or historical accident. The historian is no more adept at understanding accident than anyone else. But he does try to minimize the invoking of "pure chance" by showing what causal circumstances—structural, functional, and accidental—led up to a particular change and influenced its direction.

The historian of African art faces an extraordinary challenge. For while structural and functional analyses and explanations for most types of objects are readily forthcoming, their history is practically unknown. If the study of African history may be said to be in its youth, that of sub-Saharan art history is still in its infancy. Historical analysis, moreover, differs fundamentally from the structural and functional approaches in that certain problems only arise when seen in time-perspective. For example, a Cameroons Grasslands lintel sculpture showing a chief flanked by two leopards (fig. 15.3) can be explained structurally as an honorific image because of the leader's centrality, or functionally, by reference to the fact that the leopards symbolize the chief's strength. Many observers would be satisfied with one or the other of these explanations, but neither satisfies the historian. Why does the chief raise his hands toward the beasts' throats and why is his position both frontal and symmetrical? Why, if structure and function dictate its form, is the

FIGURE 15.3. Cameroons Grasslands. Bamileke group. Bandjoun area(?). Lintel woodcarving from one of the buildings in a king's compound. The iconography—a chief flanked by and controlling leopards—raises interesting art-historical problems. Paul Chadourne Collection, Musée de l'Homme, Paris (neg. no. C-31-607). (Photograph: Museum.)

leopard-flanked leader-image so rare in Africa, despite the fact that symmetry, frontality, and leopards are equated with leaders throughout the continent? The point is that functional and structural interpretations account for only certain aspects of any form; they do not in themselves fully explain how or why a form evolved. This is especially true in art, where, as a rule, forms are neither based directly on nature nor on a conscious translation of verbal equivalents into plastic images, but rather on previously employed artistic solutions.

Confronting the same Cameroons image, the historically oriented investigator is therefore likely to search for versions of an earlier date, preferably in an area nearby. Since none have survived in Cameroons, his eye will probably fall on leopard-flanked royal images from Benin (fig. 15.4), which can probably be dated to the seventeenth century (Dark 1960, pl. 32). After study, he may decide that some sort of historical connection links the two areas, and he may suggest the direction in which influences flowed. Alternatively, he may argue that the Benin and Cameroons forms share a common heritage or that there is insufficient evidence to support any connection. In the latter event he may explain the resemblance as stemming from structural or functional similarities having nothing to do with historical contact, that is to say, as convergence from unrelated sources. The latter situation—so interesting to the student of structure or function—is for the historian a dead end, since he cannot proceed any further by *historical* methods unless he is willing to grant the possibility of actual links between the two images in question. What interests him—the possibility of historical connection—is precisely what tends to vitiate ideas about structural and functional regu-

FIGURE 15.4. Benin. Brass plaque. Seventeenth century(?). This image is closely related iconographically to the Cameroons carving (fig. 15.3) despite the differences in style and age. British Museum, London (98.1-15.30). 16″ x 12.5″ (40.6 cm x 31.7 cm). (Photograph: Museum.)

larities; conversely, the operation of the latter principles may lead the art historian to mistake a parallel for a historical link. In other words, despite Radcliffe-Browne's views quoted earlier, these approaches do sometimes come into conflict, particularly over the interpretation of ambiguous data. Structuralists and functionalists tend to interpret such uncertain cases ahistorically, while the historian will usually tip the balance in the opposite direction.

In the study of African art, synchronic structural/functional interpretations have sometimes threatened to deny the very idea of an African art history. Most observers trained in the social sciences, particularly in anthropology as it is taught in English-speaking countries, lean toward the structural and functional approaches by the nature of their discipline. And since evidence for a history of African art is relatively scant and connections difficult to prove, some students of this art have opposed attempts at historical studies as fatuous or unscientific. Current interest in African history is helping to dispel this attitude, but the fact remains that until recently, most observers tended to see African art as essentially static, frozen images insusceptible to change and therefore, to historical investigation. Unwittingly such a view perpetuates—to use Melville Herskovits's phrase—a myth of the Negro past. Difficulties apart, we must accept the historicity of African art and try to consider its earlier and later stages and its capacity to evolve.

HISTORY IN AFRICAN ART

Far more is known about the history of art in highly differentiated African societies than in uncentralized groups. This is due partly to the superior record-keeping capacity of the former groups as well as to the durability of many of the materials they tend to use. But the survival of data about art in centralized groups is apparently also a consequence of the role this art plays in marking historical events and in legitimizing power. Early Benin and Kuba kings, for instance, are credited with a considerable number of artistic innovations which in turn are recorded by means of the art objects themselves. The oral data survive in part, it would seem, because they enable a social group to claim the art form as a prerogative or property-right inherited directly from a bygone leader.

Another characteristic of elite groups that enables us to see historical changes in their art is eclecticism. Thus K. A. Busia (1954, p. 191) reports: "Ashanti religion was very hospitable, and the Ashanti took over the beliefs, the gods, and the rites of conquered as well as neighboring tribes." Groups such as the Ashanti maintain extensive trade, ritual, and/or military contacts with other tribes, thus encouraging the spread of art in one direction or the other. René Bravmann (above, chapter 9) explicitly documents the outward dispersion of Ashanti art by such historical mechanisms. Elite groups also seem to have a penchant for alien ideas, many of which have been rapidly assimilated into the African idiom. Thus certain Islamic and European designs were incorporated into Ashanti goldwork, while small European bells were adopted by the Yoruba and Kuba as insignia, and Renaissance chair designs were taken over as chiefs' prerogatives in the southwestern Congo and Ghana. In Benin, Yoruba, and Loango art, the depiction of the aliens themselves provides additional evidence of openness to change. All this indicates that African art, like African culture, has a past.

The difficulties multiply, however, when one attempts historical investigation among peoples with less differentiated socio-political systems. Wood and still more perishable materials predominate here; oral traditions tend to be shallow; and borrowed forms may be harder to recognize in the absence of preservation-minded courtly centers. But the apparent lack of art-historical data in the less differentiated societies should not preclude an attempt to unravel the art history of Africa wherever evidence is found.

ART-HISTORICAL SOURCES

How, then, do we undertake the historical study of African leaders' arts? The sources available to the art historian are several. Most reliable, yet currently underdeveloped, are the data provided by *archaeology,* the reclamation of the past from direct evidence. Leaders' art forms, because they are often more durable or better cared for than the art of commoners, probably enjoy better than ordinary chances of survival. Even so, archaeology is still in its early stages in tropical Africa and is handicapped by poor preservation conditions and the lack of good stratigraphy in most sites. Excavation, moreover, recovers only material objects from which the archaeologist must draw historical inferences. Possibilities of error therefore arise. An instructive example cited by Fagg and Willett (1960, p. 33) is the Fulani conquest of the Yoruba town of Old Oyo in the 1830s, which eventually caused the Fulani of Ilorin to adopt Oyo pottery styles. Examined solely on archaeological grounds, the evidence might well have been interpreted erroneously— that is, as an Old Oyo conquest of the Fulani; because of oral and written records, this we know did not occur. Provided its data are not used uncritically, then, archaeology can help to clarify many art-historical questions.

Archaeologists are currently investigating a number of problems and areas of great interest to the art historian. Digs at Iron-Age sites, for instance, are revealing evidence for the origin and dispersion of metal-working; these discoveries bear upon such historical (and art-historical) subjects as the Bantu expansion, which in turn involve the matter of the relative homogeneity of Gabon-Congo sculpture. Similarly, our earliest data for the history of northern Nigerian sculpture comes from the Nok terracotta finds which are well publicized but still badly in need of scholarly publication and analysis. The evidence suggests that many Nok artifacts were associated with elite groups as early as five centuries before Christ. In southern Nigeria recent radiocarbon tests on material from Igbo-Ukwu and Ife sites have pushed back the dates for the appearance of the highly sophisticated *cire perdue* metal-casting technique in those two areas to the ninth and twelfth centuries A.D. (Willett, chapter 12 above). How these dates will affect the traditional thirteenth-to-fifteenth century origins ascribed in oral tradition to Benin casting is as yet uncertain. Elsewhere, in Ghana, for example, extensive complexes of terracotta art forms, clearly associated with leaders, have been unearthed and await proper analysis and publication. Doubtless, many surprises are still in store for students of African art.

Written records contain nuggets of art-historical data at least as far back as the fourteenth century, when the Muslim chroniclers Al Omari and Ibn Battuta mention seeing gold umbrella-finials in the capital of the ancient Mali empire. In addition to Muslim chronicles, which are useful for several areas of the Western Sudan, there are reports by early travelers, missionaries, and merchants which must be systematically combed for information on the arts. Secondary-source materials and original documents from early periods now housed in Lisbon, the Vatican, and other European archives need also to be carefully scrutinized.

Oral traditions provide a very rich, yet scarcely tapped source for art studies. To be sure, oral evidence must be tested, like any other, for internal and external consistency; but there is no *a priori* reason to dismiss oral tradition as unreliable simply because the method of transmission is other than written. That oral data can shed new light on art-historical relationships is shown in this volume by Sieber's study of Kwahu funerary monuments, Bravmann's discussion of the dispersal of Ashanti regalia, and Jan Vansina's analysis of Kuba royal sculptures.

The chief difficulty in using oral traditions to study African art history is not so much their unreliability as their relative scarcity, particularly in the less differentiated groups. However, Arnold Rubin (1969) has found considerable historical data on the diffusion of mask-types among the Jukun and other peoples in the Benue river valley.

Another possible source of art-historical data is the evidence provided by *linguistics,* including the study of language groupings, names for things, place names (onomastics), and so on. The relevance of language groupings for art history may be illustrated by Fraser's (1962, pp. 46–47) theory linking African figure sculpture to the Niger-Congo language family, one of the four major linguistic groups in Africa. For while wood suitable for carving, sedentary economies, and ancestor veneration occur throughout most of sub-Saharan Africa, figure sculpture is more or less concentrated among Niger-Congo speaking peoples, particularly in West and Central Africa. Figural sculpture, therefore, may well have been one of the traits shared by the Niger-Congo mother cultures well before the time of the Bantu expansion (ca. A.D. 500). More recently, Sieber and Rubin (1968) and Bravmann (1970) have attempted to relate language affiliation to tribal artistic style with an eye to showing historical relationships. Art-historical evidence of a rather localized sort may also be gleaned through linguistic study. R. E. Bradbury (1961, p. 133) has shown that the Benin shrine of the hand (*ikegobo*) is related both linguistically and functionally to Ibo *ikenga* carvings, while Robert G. Armstrong's (1964, pp. 136–139) study of terms used in divination rites may illuminate links among certain western Ibo, Idoma, Igala, Yoruba, Benin, Ewe, and Fon art objects used in divining.

The use of *ethnographic* data is, of course, central in studies of African art. The ethnographies of Africa, for the most part, deal only with the past few decades and frequently from an essentially ahistoric point of view; but even this may be useful since recently produced objects bear the imprint of their origins and of changes due to outside influence. No African peoples lived in complete isolation, and hence it is doubtful if any of the art we see today is entirely "original." What is available to us is perhaps a series of rather late styles that retain traces of their early origins. The difficulty, of course, is in sorting out earlier forms from later influences. Careful analyses of the distribution of distinctive art forms may yield useful data, as two studies of the so-called "three-part" or "horizontal" mask have revealed. Marie Adams (1963) studied the distribution and functional contexts of this mask-type (of which the Senufo "firespitter" may be considered a classic example) throughout West Africa, while Rubin (1969) investigated the same sort of mask among several contiguous groups in the Benue valley. Anthropological materials clearly contain vast amounts of data potentially valuable to art historians.

Nor should we overlook the data provided by the study of other African art forms, particularly *music and the dance*. Plastic art is often inextricably linked with these performing arts, to such an extent that style groupings, distribution patterns, linguistic evidence of diffusion, and so forth discernible in these arts will probably be of considerable value to the art historian. We know, for example, that in many parts of Africa, entire masquerades with their appropriate costumes, music, and dance have been taken over from nearly "alien" peoples. Analysis of one or more of the component art forms may shed some light on the history of the others.

CHANGE

Historical regularities and predictable rates of change are not characteristic of Africa, past or present. Change is volatile, and nowhere more so than in art; for objects, unlike language or social structure, may change without dramatically altering the shape of individual cultures. In addition, style and iconography may evolve along separate lines. Yoruba woodcarvings brought to Germany some three hundred years ago compare closely—stylistically and iconographically—with carvings collected early in this century, yet since 1900, this art—particularly *gelede* masks—has assimilated many new themes without deviating appreciably from the basic canons of Yoruba style. Benin bronze heads, on the other hand, have evolved both stylistically and iconographically over several centuries.

The structural similarities of Kongo "mother-and-child" images and Kuba king statues also raise interesting historical questions. Both figure types are seated on low decorated plinths, both have compact silhouettes, analogous hand positions, carved "jewelry," and other features in common—although the two are markedly different in the fine points of style and in function. Prior to becoming king of the Kuba, Shyaam is said to have traveled to the western part of the Congo, and many of the structural features of his commemorative "portrait" almost certainly derive from Kongo prototypes.

Different stylistic traditions seem to adapt in varying ways to changing circumstances. Thus the art of the Baule, who moved to the Ivory Coast, deviates from the parent Akan model in that new mask types were assimilated; to be sure, much Akan regalia was retained, but terracottas are lacking, and there are other significant differences in motif and style. Nupe figurative art dwindled almost to nothing in the face of conquering Islam, whereas several thoroughly Islamized peoples in western Ghana and the eastern Ivory Coast still retain strong masking traditions which have recently been recorded by Bravmann. Just how conservative or open to change African cultures were before the colonial period is, of course, almost impossible now to ascertain. But it seems clear that these societies must have been much more volatile and dynamic than is customarily supposed.

In spite of the many uncertainties surrounding the evolution of African art, some generalizations may be put forward. Art traditions, it is evident, change at different rates, and the art of leaders probably evolves more rapidly than that of the common people, for the former are exposed more often to alien ideas and values, being, as it were, the cosmopolites of Africa. Some distinction also may be suggested with regard to function, style, and iconography. Of the three, function appears to be the most stable; style tends to be somewhat more variable, with iconography being the most subject to change. Clearly, however, suggestions about rates and types of change in African art must remain tentative until more detailed analyses have been made.

CHARACTERISTIC HISTORICAL PROCESSES

Despite our ignorance of the development of African art, certain characteristic historical processes that result in change can be identified from the available evidence. It must be borne in mind that several kinds of historical process may contribute *simultaneously* to the evolution of an art style.

A widespread but not well documented process that contributes to the distinctiveness of leader's art forms is the *inventiveness* of local artists. Because we have so few records for works of African art made before 1900, it is difficult to assess the importance of independent invention; yet the diversity of forms in the corpus of African art, as well as the variety of expression seen within a single object-type, such as the Yoruba *oshe Shango* (cult staff), speaks clearly for the historical inventiveness of Africa's artists. To be sure, individual patrons also play a major role in the creation of new art forms; the Bamum king Njoya, the Kuba *nyim* Shyaam, and Oba Eresonyen of Benin are credited with being innovative sponsors of the arts, but there must have been hundreds of other leaders of this sort whose names remain unknown to us. In some cultures, notably the Cameroons Grasslands, prominent leaders were also practicing artists, testimony to the high value placed on artistry and creativity by these particular African peoples.

Leaders' arts may also develop by the historical process of *aggrandizement;* this phenomenon occurs when popular art forms are expropriated for the use of leaders. Among the Chokwe (see Crowley, chapter 2 above), for example, mask forms that really belong to the initiation ceremony (*mukanda*) are now depicted on objects belonging to the chief. In the Cameroons Grasslands, secret societies (which probably antedate kingship in that area) employ many masks which are known collectively as *Kwi-fon* (the king's power) and are under his control, being stored in his treasury and only loaned out to the dancers on specific occasions. Some of these masks are portrayed in miniature on brass circlets worn by Cameroons chiefs; it is hard to explain such customs except in terms of the aggrandizement of imagery that originated at a lower, more folk-based level.

Still another process encouraging the development of leaders' arts is *downward dispersion.* Here forms originally restricted to the top echelons of the hierarchy are eventually bestowed on those lower in the system. The best documented instances are from Ashanti, as discussed above by Bravmann in chapter 9, and in Benin, where the Oba is known to have delegated various artistic prerogatives to his court members. The brass bells, *eroro,* worn by warriors and used in Bini ancestor rites, may illustrate this process, as they seem to be related to the pyramidal turret-shapes atop the Oba's palace (Fraser, chapter 14). When objects, styles, or motifs are shared by elite and lesser individuals, aggrandizement or downward dispersion may be suspected, but to determine the direction in which the influence moved is often difficult.

Related to downward dispersion is the phenomenon of *proliferation,* a process carefully documented in purely political terms by Ivor Wilks (1964) in his study of the growth of the Akwapim state in Ghana. While Wilks does not discuss art per se, his demonstration of the proliferation of offices suggests that a dramatic development of regalia must have accompanied these new statuses. Proliferation, like independent invention, aggrandizement, and downward dispersion, would appear to be an internal process affecting the evolution of leadership arts.

The emergence of leaders' arts may also stem from external historical causes. The process of *hiving off* or *migration* has often led to the appearance of an elite art in a new area. The Baga of Guinea and the Baule of the Ivory Coast are excellent examples; Baga art shows strong stylistic evidence of Western Sudanic origins, probably in or near the Bambara area, while the gilded Baule art forms, which Hans Himmelheber (chapter 11 above) analyzes, stem originally from Ghana. Such population shifts naturally result in the wholesale introduction of leadership arts into new areas. Further study of migrations may yield information linking various styles or object-types which have heretofore been considered independent traditions.

Less spectacular than migration, though still arresting, is the process of *outright adoption* of alien leaders' forms; the present cult centering around the magnificent Ife-style seated figure found in the middle Niger Nupe village of Tada is a good case in point. On the whole, though, outright adoption is a much less common art-historical process than *selective borrowing.* For no matter how powerful the influence of the transmitting society may be, as a rule only a small portion of its original ideas can be made available to the recipient culture; hence the only partially understood, adopted form must be assimilated into an already existing, functioning system. This may result in a restructuring of all but the most impervious features of the image and a shift, sometimes drastic, in its function. In certain non-Muslim areas of Ghana, for example, there are found remarkable brass bowls with panels containing what appear to be Arabic inscriptions. On closer examination, however, this "script" proves to be unintelligible, indicating that the local brass-smiths were far more interested in the decorative possibilities of the lettering than in the meaning of the text itself. These bowls apparently function very differently from their Islamic prototypes (Sieber, personal communication).

Apart from selective borrowing and outright adoption, another external process contributing to the emergence of leadership arts is *stimulus diffusion,* the imitation of heard-about traits without direct knowledge of their form or content. This process has probably played a considerable part in the dispersion of forms in the Congo, as, for example, in the Dengese chiefs' portraits described by Jan Vansina (chapter 3 above). These figures vaguely recall the Kuba *ndop* statues, but they do not seem sufficiently close to be the result of direct imitation.

Finally, a historical process worth noting is that stemming from the *dispersion* of various African peoples in the art-producing areas. The extremely broad distribution of masking traditions, for example, suggests that the idea of the mask may predate the early movement of peoples away from a common point of origin. The uneven distribution of "horizontal three-part masks" and the still more sporadic appearance of nonwooden maskettes, on the other hand, suggest later developments which grew out of the fundamental masking concept. But a history of African art which can deal with such remote problems and periods depends to a considerable extent on the solution of many local art-historical questions.

CONCLUSION: THE NEXUS OF ART AND LEADERSHIP

Regardless of political system or stylistic idiom, African leaders have attached enormous significance to their art forms. The strength of this nexus is surely no accident but rather something inhering in the roles that art and leadership play in relation to one another. Art has a unique power to intensify, mobilize, and indeed create public opinion. Leaders for their part have an extraordinary capacity to call art forms into existence, to ramify their meaning, and to cause them to change. In these respects, no one else in African societies—including the artists—approaches their capacities.

The ability of art to endure through time and space permits the formation of an alliance with the personality of the leader through which art and leadership project an image of power. Art contributes the more static element: the tangible, residual symbolic continuity without which neither the office nor the public trust would have meaning. The leader contributes the more dynamic part: the vital energy and flexibility without which authority dissipates for lack of use. Interacting, man and symbol achieve a higher existence than either can reach alone. Together they can transform ordinary time and ordinary space into an extraordinary event—one of those intensified moments in human existence that combine pageantry with mystery, spectacle with order, theater with majesty—moments which are so rightly termed *occasions of state.*

REFERENCES

ADAMS, MARIE
    1963   "The Distribution and Significance of Composite Animal-Headed Masks in African Sculpture." Master's thesis, Fine Arts Library, Columbia University.

ALMOND, GABRIEL A., AND POWELL, G. BINGHAM, JR.
    1966   *Comparative Politics.* Boston.

ARMSTRONG, ROBERT G.
    1964   "The Use of Linguistic and Ethnographic Data in the Study of Idoma and Yoruba History." In *The Historian in Tropical Africa*, edited by J. Vansina, R. Mauny, and L. V. Thomas, pp. 127–144. London.

BAUMANN, HERMANN
    1969   *Afrikanische Plastik und sakrales Königtum. Ein sozialer Aspekt traditioneller afrikanische Kunst.* Bayerische Akademie der Wissenschaften. Philosophische-historische Klasse. Sitzungsberichte, 1968, Part 5.

BOVILL, EDWARD WILLIAM
    1958   *The Golden Trade of the Moors.* London. Revision of *Caravans of the Old Sahara.* London, 1933.

BOWDICH, THOMAS E.
    1819   *Mission from Cape Coast Castle to Ashantee.* London. Reprinted 1966.

BRADBURY, R. E.
    1957   *The Benin Kingdom and the Edo-speaking Peoples of South-Western Nigeria.* Ethnographic Survey of Africa. London.

1961   "Ezomo's *Ikegobo* and the Benin Cult of the Hand." *Man*
                61, art. 165: 129–138.
BRAVMANN, RENÉ A.
1970   *West African Sculpture*. Index of Art in the Pacific North-
                west, no. 1. Seattle.
BUSIA, K. A.
1954   "The Ashanti." In *African Worlds*, edited by D. Forde,
                pp. 190–209. London.
DARK, PHILIP
1960   *Benin Art*. (With W. and B. Forman.) London.
FAGG, WILLIAM, AND WILLETT, FRANK
1960   "Ancient Ife: An Ethnographical Summary." *Odù, A Jour-
                nal of Yoruba, Edo and Related Studies*, no. 8, pp. 21–35.
                Reprinted in *Actes du IVe congrès panafricain de préhis-
                toire* 2 (1962): 357–374. Tervuren.
FORTES, MEYER, AND EVANS-PRITCHARD, E. E., EDS.
1941   *African Political Systems*. London.
FRASER, DOUGLAS
1962   *Primitive Art*. Garden City, N.Y.
1966   *The Many Faces of Primitive Art: A Critical Anthology*,
                edited by Douglas Fraser. Englewood Cliffs, N.J.
GOLDWATER, ROBERT
1960   *Bambara Sculpture from the Western Sudan*. Museum of
                Primitive Art. New York.
GOODY, JOHN R., ED.
1966   *Succession to High Office*. Cambridge, England.
HARLEY, GEORGE W.
1950   *Masks as Agents of Social Control in Northeast Liberia*.
                Papers of the Peabody Museum, vol. 32, no. 2, pp. xiv–
                44. Cambridge, Mass.
HORTON, ROBIN
1965   *Kalabari Sculpture*. Department of Antiquities, Lagos,
                Nigeria.
KYEREMATEN, A. A. Y.
1964   *Panoply of Ghana*. New York.
LLOYD, PETER C.
1960   "Sacred Kingship and Government among the Yoruba."
                Africa 30, no. 3: 221–237.
MAIR, LUCY
1962   *Primitive Government*. Baltimore.
MIDDLETON, JOHN, AND TAIT, DAVID, EDS.
1958   *Tribes without Rulers*. London.
OJO, G. J. AFOLABI
1966   *Yoruba Palaces: A Study of Afins of Yorubaland*. London.
PLANCQUAERT, M.
1930   *Les sociétés secrétes chez les Bayaka*. Bibliothèque Ethno-
                graphic du Congo Belge. Brussels.
RADCLIFFE-BROWN, A. R.
1952   *Structure and Function in Primitive Societies*. London.

RUBIN, ARNOLD
1969   "The Arts of the Jukun-speaking Peoples of Northern
               Nigeria." Ph.D. diss., Indiana University and University
               Microfilms, Ann Arbor, Mich.
SIEBER, ROY
1966   "Masks as Agents of Social Control." In *The Many Faces
               of Primitive Art: A Critical Anthology*, edited by Douglas
               Fraser, pp. 257–263. Englewood Cliffs, N.J.
1967   "African Art and Culture History." In *Reconstructing
               African Culture History*, edited by Creighton Gabel and
               Norman Bennett, pp. 117–137. Boston.
SIEBER, ROY, AND RUBIN, ARNOLD
1968   *Sculpture of Black Africa: The Paul Tishman Collection.*
               Los Angeles County Museum of Art. Los Angeles.
SOUSBERGHE, LÉON DE
1958   *L'art pende.* Académie Royale de Belgique, Mémoires.
               Beaux-Arts, vol. 9, pt. 2. Brussels.
THOMPSON, ROBERT F.
1968   "Esthetics in Traditional Africa." *Art News* 66, no. 9:
               44–45, 63–66.
VANSINA, JAN
1962a   "A Comparison of African Kingdoms." *Africa* 32, no. 4:
               324–335.
1962b   "Long-Distance Trade-Routes in Central Africa." *The
               Journal of African History* 3, no. 3: 375–388.
1966   *Kingdoms of the Savanna.* Madison.
VANSINA, J., MAUNY, R., AND THOMAS, L. V., EDS.
1964   *The Historian in Tropical Africa.* London.
WILKS, IVOR
1964   "The Growth of the Akwapim State: A Study in the Con-
               trol of Evidence." In *The Historian in Tropical Africa*,
               edited by J. Vansina, R. Mauny, and L. V. Thomas, pp.
               390–411. London.
WILLETT, FRANK
1960   "Ife and Its Archaeology." *The Journal of African History*
               1, no. 2: 231–248.
WILLIAMS, DENIS
1964   "The Iconology of the Yoruba *edan Ogboni*." *Africa* 34,
               no. 2: 139–166.

Index

Page numbers in boldface type indicate illustrations.

Abomey, 309
Adae festival, 141, 148, 155
Adansi, 148, 173, 182
Adele, 157
Aderemi, Sir Adesoji, Oni of Ife, 215
Afghanistan, 287
Afikpo Ibo, 5, 99–121, **102, 103, 104, 106, 108**
Agemo cult, 239, 241
Agni, 173n, 175, 182, 185, 190, 191, 205n
Ahinsan, 180
Akan, 137, 142, 143, 155, 162, 175, 185–208, 297, 298, 305, 306, 307, 322
Akang, 90
Ako, 220
Akua'ba, 175
Ancient Near East, 263, 265, 282, 284, 289
Angola, 22, 28, 30, 32, 34, 36, 37, 38
Asen, 249
Ashanti, 4, 5, 137–52, **140, 141, 143, 146–47, 150, 151,** 153–71, 175, 182, 188, 205, 299, 304–24 passim
Asia: central, 266n; Southeast, 266n
Asipim chair, 157, 159

Atutu, 191

Bafut, **130**
Baga, 324
Bahia, Brazil, 249, 252
BaKele, 65
BaKota, 67, 68
Bakowen, 127, **127**, 128
BaKwele, 5, 57–77, **64, 66, 67, 71, 72, 73, 74, 75, 76**, 298
Bambara, 310, 312, 313
Bamileke, 125, **127, 132**
Bamum, 125
Banda, 156–70 passim
Bandjoun, 132
Bangante, **132**
Bangwa, **129**, 133, **134**
Banso (Nsaw), **131**
Bantu, 22, 57, 319
Bari, 266n
Batshioko. *See* Chokwe
Battuta, Ibn, 308, 320
Batufam, 125
Baule, 5, 175, 185–208, **187, 188, 189, 190, 192, 193, 195, 196, 198, 199, 201, 202, 203, 204, 205**, 298, 299, 303, 305, 322

329

Beete, 61–70
Bekom, 128, 129
Benin, 5, 6, 52, 79n, 153, 197, 201, 215–
    21 passim, 236–55 passim, **237, 250,**
    261–90, **264, 265, 266, 268,** 295, 296,
    298, 300-24 passim, **317**
Bini, 218
Biombo, 306
Bom Bosh. *See* Mbomboosh
Bope Kena. *See* Mbop Kyeen
Bope Pelenge. *See* Mbo Pelyeeng aNce
Bornu, 232n
Brazil, 249, 252
Bron, 164
Brong, 156, 159, 164
Brong-Ahafo, 153
Bungu, 21
Bushman, 295
Bushoong, 45, 48, 52
Bwami, 7, 10–11, **12, 13, 14, 16,** 17–20
Bwiti cult, 248

Cameroons, 5, 123–35, **127, 129, 130,**
    131, 132, 134, 303, 304, 306, 308,
    314, 315–16, **316,** 323, 324
Cão, Diogo, 307
Caucasus, 266n
Chiheu, 28, 33
Chihongo, **25,** 27, 32, 38
Chikuza, **26,** 27, 35
Chi-wara, 313
Chizaluke, 28
Chokwe, 5, 21–39, **25, 26, 27, 28, 29,**
    33, 34, 266n, 298, 302, 307, 314, 323
Congo (Kinshasa), 21, 22, 23, 24, 41,
    190, 254, 303, 306, 322, 325
Cuba, 244, 251

Daba, 266n
Dagomba, 156, 158
Dahomey, 185, 227, 249, 252, 254, 255,
    267, 308
Damba, 158
Dan, 312
Dan-Kran, 304
Dengese, 306, 325
Denkyira, 138, 143
Dida, 186
Dje (steer) mask, 200
Dogon, 267, 303, 306

Duen fobara, 300, **301,** 302
Dyula, 156

Ebagoona, 67
Ecuador, 266n
Efik, 90
Egungun cult, 232
Egypt, 263, 267, 289, 290
Ekoi, 91, 306
Ekpe society, 82, 90–92
Eresonyen, Oba, 323
Erinle cult, 272
Eroro, **265,** 265–66, **266,** 324
Eshu, 255
Ewe, 157
Eyinle, 248

Fanti, 163, 182
"Firespitter" mask, 321
Fomena, 181, 182
Fon, 254, 255, 297, 303, 310, 321
Fulani, 319
Fumban, 125, 132

Gabon, 248
Ganguella-Mbwela, 22
Gara image, 233, 236
Gelede masks, 322
Gen (pl., begen), 60, 68–71 passim, **76**
Ghana, 5, 137, 185, 186, 200, 202, 248,
    255, 303–25 passim
Giphogo masks, 302
Glele, Dada Sagbadjou, 254
Golden Stool, 5, **140,** 140-63 passim,
    141, 175, 299, 307, 314, 315
Gon (pl., egon), 57–77, **64, 67, 72, 73,**
    74, 75, 76
Gonja, 156, 158, 159, 163
Guan, 157
Guere, 191
Guinea, 324
Gur, 155n, 156
Guro, 186, 207
Gyaman, 164

Hausa, 242n

Ibibio, 90, 107, 300
Ibo, 5, 79–97, **86, 87, 88, 89, 93,** 99–
    121, **102, 103, 104, 106, 108,** 297,
    300, 310, 312, 321

Ibol, 42, 44, 48, 54n, 55n
Idah, 310
Idoma, 310, 321
Ifa divination, 272
Ife, 5, 209–26, **214**, **215**, **216**, **217**, **218**,
  222, **223**, 232, 233, 237, 243, 244,
  261, 262, 289, 303, 307, 310. 320
Igala, 310, 312, 321
Igbo, 82. *See also* Ibo
Igbo-Ukwu, 85n, 96n, 310, 320
Iginga, 18, 20
Ikegobo, 305, 321
Ikenga, 88, 321
Ikorodo mask, 93, 94
Ile-Ife. *See* Ife
Ivory Coast, 5, 76, 159, 160, 175, 185,
  186, 191, 307, 322, 324

Jebba, 236
Jimini, 160
Jukun, 268, 304, 320

Kakinga, **14**
Kakunga, 302
Kalabari Ijaw, 300, **301**
Kalelwa, 27, **27**
Kanioka, 34
Kaponya (*pl.*, *tuponya*), 34–35
Katanga, 35, 37
Katoyo, **25**, 30
Kente, **141**, 149
Kete, 194
Kindi, 11–20, **12**, **13**, **14**, **16**
Kinsamba, 15–19, **16**
Kofi Kakari, 306
Kongo, 52, 303, 306, 307, 322
Kot aMabiinc, 49, 55n
Kot aMbul, 45, **47**, 48n, 54n
Kot aMbweeky II, 55n
Kot aNce, 51, 52, 55n
Kot aPe, 48, 55n
Krinjabo, 182
Kru, 76, 186, 191
Kuba, 4, 5, 30, 41–55, **42**, **43**, **46**, **47**, **49**,
  190, 194, 197, 224, 297–325 passim
Kuboko Kumozi, **14**
Kuduo, 148, 149, **150**, **151**, 305
Kuk (*pl.*, *ekuk*), 62, 63, 65
Kulango, 155n, 156
Kwa, 219

Kwahu, 5, 173–83, **174**, **176**, **177**, **178**,
  179, **180**, **181**, 320
Kwaka Dua I, 144, 145
Kyerematen, A. A. Y., 137n

Lega, 7–20, **12**, **13**, **14**, **16**, 296, 297,
  310, 311, 312
Lele, 306
Liberia, 76
Ligby (Ligbi), 156
Linya Pwa, 28, **29**
Loango, 319
Lower Congo, 50
Lower Niger Bronze Industry, 267
Lozi (Rotse), 23
Luba, 22, 34, 302, 303, 305
Luba-Kasai, 23
Luchazi, 22
Luena, 22, 36
Lulua, 23, 48
Lunda, 21–24, 36–38, 307
Luvale, 22

Mahi, 254
Makara, 284, 285
Mali empire, 308, 320
Malinke, 186
"Mammy Water," 272
Mamvu, 266n
Mande, 76, 156
Mandefu, 186
Mande-tan, 186
Manikongo, 307
Mano, 310
Mbangala, 22
Mbari, 94
Mbomboosh, 43, **43**, 45, 51
Mboong aLeeng, 44, 46
Mbop aMabiinc, **42**
Mbo Pelyeeng aNce, 45, **46**, 51, 52
Mbop Kyeen, 48, **49**
Mbuun, 52
MeBeeza, 66, 67
Miko miMbul, 48, 49, 54n
Mintadi, 50, 52
Mishaa Pelyeeng aNce, 45, **46**
Mo (Degha), 155n, 156, 160
Mukanda, 25–38 passim, 323
Mwana Pwo, 28, **28**, 32, 37, 38

Nafana, 5, 153, 156, 157, 159–70, **161**, **165**, **167**, **168**, **169**
Ndembu, 38
Ndop, 41–52, **43**, **46**, **47**, **49**, 54–55, 325
Ndyaadal, **71**
New Guinea, 224
New Hebrides, 224
Ngbaka, 266n
Ngondo, 28
Ngulu, 28–29
Ngwyes, 65, 66
Niger-Congo languages, 321
Nigeria, 5, 79, 99, 100, 126, 209–94, 304, 306
Nina, **13**
Njoya, Sultan, 132
Nne Mgbo mask, **102**, 103, **103**
Nok, 224, 288, 320
Noon, 47–48, 50
Nri clan, 85
Ntul aNshedy, 48, 55n
Ntumpani drums, 158
Nubia, 289n, 290
Nuer, 266n
Nupe, 234, **234**, **235**, 322, 324

Odwira festival, 141, **146–47**, 155, 160, 163, 164, 309, 314
Ogboni society, 212, 213, 246, 268, 271, 272, 278, 311
Ofo, 88
Ogun cult, 248, 255
Oguola, Oba, 261, 289
Ohen, Oba, 269, 270
Okomfo Anokye, 139, 140
Okonko society, 90
Okumpka, 101–119 passim, **104**, **106**, **108**
Olokun, 269, 270, 272
Omabe society, 82, 90, 92, 94
Omari, Al, 308, 320
Opoku Ware I, 145
Opoku Ware II, 137
Oramfe, 213
Oreri, 310
Osei Bonsu, 144, 147, 163, 166, 167
Osei Kwadwo, 163
Osei Prempeh I, 144, 152

Osei Prempeh II, 137n, **141**, 144
Osei Tutu, 137–48 passim, 143, 160, 166
Ovonramwen, Oba, 269n
Owo, 219, 220, 268, 270, 272, 274, 285, 303
Oyo, 45, 319
Ozo title system, 82, 83–88 passim, **86**, **87**, 94

Pende, 302, 303, 305, 307
Persia, 242n
Peru, 266n
Philippines, 266n
"Poro" society, 312
Pyaang, 45, 48
Pyaang Mbaanc, 48
Pygmy, 295

Senufo, 160, 186, 200, 201, 306, 312, 321
Shamba Bolongongo. *See* Shyaam aMbul aNgoong
Shango, 213, 268, 270, 272, 323
Sherbro, 276, **277**
Shoowa, 45
Shyaam aMbul aNgoong, **43**, 44, 45, 50, 51, 52, 54n, 315, 322, 323
Sierra Leone, 76, 276, **277**
South Africa, 24
Sudan, Western, 304, 305, 306, 320
Suku, 254
Sumatra, 266n
Syria, 289

Tada, 233, **234**, **235**, 236, 243, 255, 324
Tikar, 125, **130**, **131**
Tiv, 116
Togo, 227
Tsoede, 233n, 234
Tundansi masks, 302
Twi, 158, 162, 167, 173n

Yaka, 302, 314
Yananio, 15
Yoruba, 4, 5, 6, 30, 209–94, **211**, **214**, **215**, **231**, **239**, **240**, **271**, **274**, **275**, **276**, **286**, 303–14 passim, 319, 321, 322, 323; of Cuba, 244, 251

Zambia, 23, 24

DATE DUE